THE MACARTHUR NEW TESTAMENT COMMENTARY
MARK 9-16

John MacArthur

MOODY PUBLISHERS/CHICAGO

Cover Design: Puckett Smartt

Library of Congress Control Number: 2015938541

ISBN 978-0-8024-1031-3

We hope you enjoy this book from Moody Publishers. Our goal is to provide high-quality, thought-provoking books and products that connect truth to your real needs and challenges. For more information on other books and products written and produced from a biblical perspective, go to www.moodypublishers.com or write to:

Moody Publishers
820 N. LaSalle Boulevard
Chicago, IL 60610

7 9 10 8 6

Printed in the United States of America

To Dave Enos,
who has been listening to me preach for more than
three and a half decades. For the past sixteen years he has quietly,
lovingly, faithfully edited my sermons—
with diligent care and great insight—into a form I could use
to shape them into chapters for the commentaries.
His work has been an invaluable ministry to me and every reader.

Contents

Preface

It continues to be a rewarding, divine communion for me to preach expositionally through the New Testament. My goal is always to have deep fellowship with the Lord in the understanding of His Word and out of that experience to explain to His people what a passage means. In the words of Nehemiah 8:8, I strive "to give the sense" of it so they may truly hear God speak and, in so doing, may respond to Him.

Obviously, God's people need to understand Him, which demands knowing His Word of Truth (2 Tim. 2:15) and allowing that Word to dwell in them richly (Col. 3:16). The dominant thrust of my ministry, therefore, is to help make God's living Word alive to His people. It is a refreshing adventure.

This New Testament commentary series reflects this objective of explaining and applying Scripture. Some commentaries are primarily linguistic, others are mostly theological, and some are mainly homiletical. This one is basically explanatory, or expository. It is not linguistically technical but deals with linguistics when that seems helpful to proper interpretation. It is not theologically expansive but focuses on the major doctrines in each text and how they relate to the whole of Scripture. It is not primarily homiletical, although each unit of thought is generally treated as one chapter, with a clear outline and logical flow of thought. Most truths are illustrated and applied with other Scripture. After establishing the context of a passage, I have tried to follow closely the writer's development and reasoning.

My prayer is that each reader will fully understand what the Holy Spirit is saying through this part of His Word, so that His revelation may lodge in the mind of believers and bring greater obedience and faithfulness—to the glory of our great God.

The Unveiled Son
(Mark 9:1–8)

1

And Jesus was saying to them, "Truly I say to you, there are some of those who are standing here who will not taste death until they see the kingdom of God after it has come with power." Six days later, Jesus took with Him Peter and James and John, and brought them up on a high mountain by themselves. And He was transfigured before them; and His garments became radiant and exceedingly white, as no launderer on earth can whiten them. Elijah appeared to them along with Moses; and they were talking with Jesus. Peter said to Jesus, "Rabbi, it is good for us to be here; let us make three tabernacles, one for You, and one for Moses, and one for Elijah." For he did not know what to answer; for they became terrified. Then a cloud formed, overshadowing them, and a voice came out of the cloud, "This is My beloved Son, listen to Him!" All at once they looked around and saw no one with them anymore, except Jesus alone. (9:1–8)

The high point of testimony in Mark's gospel came in the previous section when Peter, in response to Jesus' question, "But who do you say that I am?" declared, "You are the Christ (8:29)." Everything in Mark that came before Peter's declaration leads up to it; everything that followed afterward flows from it. To acknowledge that Jesus is "the Christ [the Messiah], the Son of the living God" (Matt. 16:16), is to make the correct judgment concerning Him. In this section, Peter's confession is confirmed. What he affirmed by faith would be verified by the transfiguration of the Lord so that His divine glory became visible.

No sooner had Peter made his confession than Jesus "began to teach them that the Son of Man must suffer many things and be rejected by the elders and the chief priests and the scribes, and be killed, and after three days rise again" (v. 31). Aghast and dismayed, Peter, in his impudent ignorance, dared to rebuke the Lord (v. 32), and in turn was sharply rebuked by Him. Jesus forcefully told him, "Get behind Me, Satan; for you are not setting your mind on God's interests, but man's" (v. 33).

Like the rest of the Jewish people, the notion of a murdered Messiah was incomprehensible and unacceptable to the Twelve. Later in the ninth chapter, Mark noted that again Jesus "was teaching His disciples and telling them, 'The Son of Man is to be delivered into the hands of men, and they will kill Him; and when He has been killed, He will rise three days later. But they did not understand this statement, and they were afraid to ask Him" (vv. 31–32). In Luke 18:31–34 Jesus again

> took the twelve aside and said to them, "Behold, we are going up to Jerusalem, and all things which are written through the prophets about the Son of Man will be accomplished. For He will be handed over to the Gentiles, and will be mocked and mistreated and spit upon, and after they have scourged Him, they will kill Him; and the third day He will rise again." But the disciples understood none of these things, and the meaning of this statement was hidden from them, and they did not comprehend the things that were said.

Peter and the rest of the apostles eagerly anticipated the glory of the kingdom, but not the scandal of the cross, which Paul described as a stumbling block to the Jewish people (1 Cor. 1:23; cf. Gal. 5:11). After giving the apostles the crushing, disappointing news of His coming death, Jesus encouraged them by telling them that "the Son of Man" will one day come "in the glory of His Father with the holy angels" (Mark 8:38). It was difficult for the disciples to accept that Jesus would die; it would be even more difficult for them when it happened. Thus, **Jesus was saying to them, "Truly I say to you, there are some of those who are standing here who will not taste death** (a Hebrew colloquial expression for dying) **until they see the kingdom of God after it has come with power."** In promising a preview glimpse of the **kingdom** (the Greek word can be translated as "royal splendor"), Jesus was speaking of His transfiguration (cf. Matt. 16:28–17:8; Luke 9:27–36), which would be witnessed by Peter, James, and John, and would move their faith to sight. The Lord's visible manifestation of His divine glory in the transfiguration was the most transcendent miracle recorded in the New Testament prior to the Lord's resurrection. It bolstered the apostles' confidence in His coming revelation of glory.

When God appeared visibly in the Old Testament, He always did so in some form of light, as at the initiation of the priestly service (Lev. 9:23), to Israel (Ex. 16:7, 10), to Moses (Ex. 24:15–18; 33:18–23), at the completion of the tabernacle (Ex. 29:43; 40:34–35), at Israel's rebellion at Kadesh-barnea (Num. 14:10), at the exposure of the sins of Korah, Dathan, and Abiram (Num. 16:19) and the people's subsequent rebellion against Moses and Aaron (v. 42), at Meribah (Num. 20:6), at the dedication of the temple (1 Kings 8:11; 2 Chron. 7:1), and to Ezekiel (Ezek. 1:28; 3:23; 10:4, 18; 11:23). Habakkuk wrote of a future day when "the earth will be filled with the knowledge of the glory of the Lord, as the waters cover the sea" (Hab. 2:14). In each of those instances, the purpose of God's appearance was to strengthen the people's faith.

But the Lord Jesus Christ, the God-Man, was the pure revelation of God's glory. In 1 Corinthians 2:8 Paul referred to Him as the "Lord of glory," while in 2 Corinthians 4:6 the apostle wrote "of the glory of God in the face of Christ." The writer of Hebrews described Jesus as "the radiance of [God's] glory" (1:3), and James referred to Him as "our glorious Lord Jesus Christ" (James 2:1). But with the exception of the transfiguration, that glory was veiled during His life and was revealed in His miraculous signs, not His visible appearance.

This experience, when they "saw His glory, glory as of the only begotten from the Father" (John 1:14), transformed these three men.

Nearing the end of his life, Peter recalled the manifestation of Christ's glory that they witnessed:

> For we did not follow cleverly devised tales when we made known to you the power and coming of our Lord Jesus Christ, but we were eyewitnesses of His majesty. For when He received honor and glory from God the Father, such an utterance as this was made to Him by the Majestic Glory, "This is My beloved Son with whom I am well-pleased"— and we ourselves heard this utterance made from heaven when we were with Him on the holy mountain. (2 Peter 1:16–18)

Mark's account of Jesus' transfiguration may be divided into four sections: the Son's transformation, the saints' association, the sleeper's suggestion, and the sovereign's correction.

THE SON'S TRANSFORMATION

Six days later, Jesus took with Him Peter and James and John, and brought them up on a high mountain by themselves. And He was transfigured before them; and His garments became radiant and exceedingly white, as no launderer on earth can whiten them. (9:2–3)

Mark, along with Matthew (17:1), indicates that the transfiguration took place **six days** after the promise Jesus gave, recorded in verse 1. Luke, however, placed it "some eight days" **later** (9:28). There is no contradiction; Luke included the day the Lord made the promise and the day of the transfiguration, while Matthew and Mark referred to the six days between those two events.

Peter and James and John made up the inner circle of the apostles and were the Lord's most intimate friends. They alone witnessed Jesus' raising of Jairus's daughter (Mark 5:37) and went with Him into Gethsemane (Mark 14:33). Jesus took them with Him in accord with the Law's requirement that truth be confirmed by two or three witnesses (Deut. 17:6; cf. Matt. 18:16; 2 Cor. 13:1; 1 Tim. 5:19; Heb. 10:28).

The Lord **brought them up on a high mountain by themselves** to pray (Luke 9:28). That **mountain** likely was Mt. Hermon (c. 9200 feet in elevation), the highest peak in the vicinity of Caesarea Philippi, where Peter's confession took place (Mark 8:27). Some have suggested Mt. Tabor, but it is too far south of the region of Caesarea Philippi and not a high mountain but rather a hill (it is less than 2000 feet in elevation). Mark, in an understated description of the most striking revelation of God up to that point, notes simply that Jesus **was transfigured before them.** It happened while the disciples were asleep (Luke 9:32), most likely from sorrow at the prospect of the Lord's death, as would later be the case again in Gethsemane (Luke 22:45).

Transfigured translates a form of the verb *metamorphoō*, from which the English word "metamorphosis" derives. It appears four times in the New Testament, always in reference to a radical transformation. Here and in Matthew 17:2 it describes the transfiguration, while in Romans 12:2 and 2 Corinthians 3:18, it refers to the transformation in the lives of believers brought about by salvation. Christ's nature, of course, could not change; only His appearance. The brilliant glory of His divine nature blazed forth through the veil of His humanity, and His face "became different" (Luke 9:29) and "shone like the sun" (Matt. 17:2; cf. Rev. 1:16). In addition to Jesus' face, **His garments became radiant and exceedingly white, as no launderer on earth can whiten them.** Matthew notes that "His garments became as white as light" (17:2), while Luke says that they "became white and gleaming [lit. 'to flash or gleam like lightning']" (9:29). It was that blazing glory that Peter, James, and John saw when they awakened (Luke 9:32).

Jesus had possessed essential glory from all eternity (John 17:5) but veiled it until this moment. His glory will be fully revealed to the whole world in the future when "the sign of the Son of Man will appear in the sky, and … all the tribes of the earth will mourn, and they will see the Son of Man coming on the clouds of the sky with power and great glory" (Matt. 24:30; cf. 25:31 and the description of that event in Rev. 19:11–16).

THE SAINTS' ASSOCIATION

Elijah appeared to them along with Moses; and they were talking with Jesus. (9:4–5)

Elijah and **Moses** existed as glorified spirits in heaven (Heb. 12:23), awaiting the resurrection of their bodies at the end of the future tribulation (Dan. 12:1–2), yet they appeared in visible, glorious (Luke 9:31) bodies. They evidently either received those bodies temporarily for this occasion, or God gave them their permanent resurrection bodies early. The apostles would not, of course, have recognized the two glorified men, so either they introduced themselves, or the Lord did.

As the disciples became fully awake (Luke 9:32), they realized that Elijah and Moses were **talking** with Jesus about His death (Luke 9:31). As noted earlier, Christ's death is the truth for which the transfiguration was intended to prepare the disciples. Jesus was to die, but that could not negate God's plan and the glory that was to come. The testimony of these two very important men confirmed the reality that the Lord Jesus would die.

Moses was the most honored leader in Israel's history, who led the exodus from Egypt when God rescued the nation from captivity. Although he had the authority of a king, he never had a throne. He functioned both as a prophet, proclaiming God's truth to the nation, and as a priest, interceding before God on behalf of His people. He was the human author of the Pentateuch, and the agent through whom God gave His holy Law.

While Moses gave the Law; Elijah was its foremost guardian and fought against every violation of it. He battled Israel's idolatry with courage and powerful warnings of judgment. His preaching was validated by miracles (1 Kings 17–19; 2 Kings 1–2), as Moses had done in Egypt and during Israel's forty years in the wilderness. There was no lawgiver like Moses and no prophet comparable to Elijah. They are the most reliable possible witnesses to Christ's suffering and glory. Nothing could have brought the apostles more assurance and confidence that Jesus' death fulfilled God's purpose than hearing it from Moses and Elijah.

THE SLEEPER'S SUGGESTION

Peter said to Jesus, "Rabbi, it is good for us to be here; let us make three tabernacles, one for You, and one for Moses, and one

for Elijah." For he did not know what to answer; for they became terrified. (9:5–6)

Never at a loss for words despite his recent rebuke (Mark 8:32–33), Peter interrupted the conversation between Jesus, Moses, and Elijah and blurted out, **"Rabbi, it is good for us to be here.** Matthew records that Peter addressed Jesus as "Lord" (17:4); Luke that he addressed Him as "Master" (9:33). Peter's use of all three titles reveals that he repeated his request and how overwhelmed and humbled he and the others were. Holy fear mingled with exhilarating wonder at this glorious and incomprehensible experience. His suggestion, **"let us make three tabernacles, one for You, and one for Moses, and one for Elijah,"** reflects Peter's tenacious desire that the suffering of the cross be avoided. He wanted the three to stay there permanently in their glorious state and establish the kingdom on the spot. According to Luke's account, Peter spoke as Moses and Elijah began to leave. He saw his dream of seeing the kingdom established slipping away and made a last, desperate attempt to stop that from happening. But he **did not know what to answer; for they became terrified.** His fear caused him to express what was uppermost in his mind and, as Luke adds, not realizing what he was saying (Luke 9:33).

Several things prompted Peter's suggestion. He had wanted all along to see the kingdom established, and Jesus' promise in verse 1, "Truly I say to you, there are some of those who are standing here who will not taste death until they see the kingdom of God after it has come with power," had intensified his hope that it soon would be established. That hope reached its peak when he awoke to see Jesus in a transfigured state with Moses and Elijah present in glorified form. Those two prophets could certainly lead the people of Israel into the kingdom, and Elijah was associated with the coming of the kingdom (Mal. 3:1; 4:5–6; see the discussion of 9:9–13 in chapter 2 of this volume). The timing of this event fueled Peter's hopes. The transfiguration took place in the month of Tishri, six months before the Passover. At that time the Feast of Tabernacles (or Booths), which commemorated the exodus from Egypt, was being celebrated. What better time, Peter may have reasoned, for the Messiah to lead His people out of bondage to sin and into His righteous kingdom than during the Feast of Tabernacles (Zech. 14:16–19)?

THE SOVEREIGN'S CORRECTION

Then a cloud formed, overshadowing them, and a voice came out of the cloud, "This is My beloved Son, listen to Him!" All at once they looked around and saw no one with them anymore, except Jesus alone. (9:7–8)

Interrupting Peter's interruption of Jesus, Moses, and Elijah, God arrived. A bright **cloud,** signaling His glorious presence, **formed** and began **overshadowing them.** When **a voice came out of the cloud** and said, **"This is My beloved Son,** "My Chosen One" (Luke 9:35), "with whom I am well-pleased" (Matt. 17:5), **listen to Him!",** the disciples "fell face down to the ground and were terrified" (Matt. 17:6). The Father's command that they listen to the Son was a direct rebuke of Peter. He commanded Peter and the others to be silent and listen to what Jesus had to say about His death.

When the Father had finished speaking, "Jesus came to them and touched them and said, 'Get up, and do not be afraid'" (Matt. 17:7). **All at once they looked around and saw no one with them anymore, except Jesus alone.** The preview of the kingdom was over; it was not to be established at that time. What they had witnessed was not a vision in the mind but an experience of God's actual presence unprecedented since Adam and Eve experienced it in the garden before the fall. Though not without further misgivings and misunderstandings, the disciples would follow Jesus to the cross and then devote the rest of their lives to preaching "Christ crucified, to Jews a stumbling block and to Gentiles foolishness" (1 Cor. 1:23; cf. 2:2; Gal. 3:1).

Like their Lord, Christians will suffer for the sake of the gospel before experiencing the glory of heaven; it is "through many tribulations we must enter the kingdom of God" (Acts 14:22). "We suffer with Him so that we may also be glorified with Him" (Rom. 8:17), because "all who desire to live godly in Christ Jesus will be persecuted" (2 Tim. 3:12). Yet, we understand that "to the degree that [we] share the sufferings of Christ, [we] keep on rejoicing, so that also at the revelation of His glory [we] may rejoice with exultation" (1 Peter 4:13), knowing that "our citizenship is in heaven, from which also we eagerly wait for a Savior, the Lord Jesus

Christ; who will transform the body of our humble state into conformity with the body of His glory, by the exertion of the power that He has even to subject all things to Himself" (Phil. 3:20–21).

When Does Elijah Come?
(Mark 9:9–13)

2

As they were coming down from the mountain, He gave them orders not to relate to anyone what they had seen, until the Son of Man rose from the dead. They seized upon that statement, discussing with one another what rising from the dead meant. They asked Him, saying, "Why is it that the scribes say that Elijah must come first?" And He said to them, "Elijah does first come and restore all things. And yet how is it written of the Son of Man that He will suffer many things and be treated with contempt? But I say to you that Elijah has indeed come, and they did to him whatever they wished, just as it is written of him." (9:9–13)

The distinguishing mark of the true church of Jesus Christ is the proclamation of the cross of Christ and His resurrection. That has been the case from the beginning, as those two themes were the constant subject of the apostolic preachers beginning on the day of Pentecost.

In Acts 3:18 Peter declared to the Jewish people that "the things which God announced beforehand by the mouth of all the prophets, that

His Christ would suffer, He has thus fulfilled." Paul spent three Sabbaths in Thessalonica "explaining and giving evidence that the Christ had to suffer and rise again from the dead, and saying, 'This Jesus whom I am proclaiming to you is the Christ'" (Acts 17:3). To the Corinthians he wrote,

> For the word of the cross is foolishness to those who are perishing, but to us who are being saved it is the power of God.... For indeed Jews ask for signs and Greeks search for wisdom; but we preach Christ crucified, to Jews a stumbling block and to Gentiles foolishness, but to those who are the called, both Jews and Greeks, Christ the power of God and the wisdom of God. (1 Cor. 1:18, 22–24)

The resurrection necessarily followed the cross. In his sermon on the day of Pentecost, Peter boldly declared, "This Jesus God raised up again, to which we are all witnesses" (Acts 2:32). The Jewish religious leaders were "greatly disturbed because [the apostles] were teaching the people and proclaiming in Jesus the resurrection from the dead" (Acts 4:2). In Acts 4:33 Luke notes that "with great power the apostles were giving testimony to the resurrection of the Lord Jesus, and abundant grace was upon them all." Paul "was preaching Jesus and the resurrection" to the pagan philosophers in Athens (Acts 17:18; cf. v. 32). At his hearing before Agrippa, Paul testified of his conviction "that the Christ was to suffer, and that by reason of His resurrection from the dead He would be the first to proclaim light both to the Jewish people and to the Gentiles" (Acts 26:23). Summarizing the vital importance of Christ's resurrection, the apostle wrote,

> Now if Christ is preached, that He has been raised from the dead, how do some among you say that there is no resurrection of the dead? But if there is no resurrection of the dead, not even Christ has been raised; and if Christ has not been raised, then our preaching is vain, your faith also is vain. Moreover we are even found to be false witnesses of God, because we testified against God that He raised Christ, whom He did not raise, if in fact the dead are not raised. For if the dead are not raised, not even Christ has been raised; and if Christ has not been raised, your faith is worthless; you are still in your sins. Then those also who have fallen asleep in Christ have perished. If we have hoped in Christ in this life only, we are of all men most to be pitied. But now Christ has been raised from the dead, the first fruits of those who are asleep. (1 Cor. 15:12–20)

There is no salvation apart from those two central realities, for it is only "if you confess with your mouth Jesus as Lord, and believe in your heart that God raised Him from the dead [that] you will be saved" (Rom. 10:9).

But before the cross, Christ's followers found the notion of His death to be repulsive, objectionable, and unacceptable. When Jesus "began to teach them that the Son of Man must suffer many things and be rejected by the elders and the chief priests and the scribes, and be killed, and after three days rise again.... Peter took Him aside and began to rebuke Him" (Mark 8:31–32). As noted in the previous chapter of this volume, at the transfiguration Peter wanted the Lord to skip the cross and immediately establish the kingdom. Later Jesus "was teaching His disciples and telling them, 'The Son of Man is to be delivered into the hands of men, and they will kill Him; and when He has been killed, He will rise three days later.' But they did not understand this statement, and they were afraid to ask Him" (Mark 9:31–32). As Jesus approached Jerusalem for Passion Week, He said to the disciples,

> "We are going up to Jerusalem, and the Son of Man will be delivered to the chief priests and the scribes; and they will condemn Him to death and will hand Him over to the Gentiles. They will mock Him and spit on Him, and scourge Him and kill Him, and three days later He will rise again." (Mark 10:33–34)

But they ignored that teaching and remained focused on the glory of the kingdom, as the request by James and John for prominent places in the kingdom reveals (vv. 35–40). The transfiguration added to that single-minded focus on the promised kingdom because Peter, James, and John saw Jesus in His *shekinah* glory, alongside Moses and Elijah in glorified bodies.

There was no place in the disciples' thinking for a dying and rising Messiah. What they believed was what the scribes had taught the people and therefore what the people believed. Messiah, in their view, would come to conquer and judge His enemies, bring salvation to the Jewish people, and elevate Israel to world supremacy. After destroying all the enemies of Israel and of God, He would establish His earthly kingdom of righteousness, peace, and knowledge. He would be worshiped, pour out divine blessings on the world, and crush any appearance of evil. Thus, when the disciples heard Jesus repeatedly say that He was going to suffer, be arrested, be mistreated, be killed, and then rise again, they could not accept it. It was a stumbling block for them; a frightening and profoundly disturbing thought.

Still, it was becoming increasingly obvious to Christ's followers that things were not going according to their messianic anticipations and expectations. The Jewish leaders—who were presumably the best qualified to recognize the Messiah—had rejected Jesus (John 7:48; 8:45–46) and were seeking to kill Him (John 5:18; 7:1, 25; 11:53). The people, though curious about Him, were largely unconvinced and unconverted, prompting one of Jesus' followers to ask, "Lord, are there just a few who are being saved?" (Luke 13:23). Many superficial followers were abandoning Him, unwilling to deny themselves, suffer for the sake of His name, and obey Him completely (Luke 9:23; cf. 6:46; Matt. 7:21; John 6:66). The transfiguration helped mitigate the disciples' shock and disappointment at the prospect of the Lord's death by giving three of them a preview of the coming glory.

This passage reveals that in the aftermath of the transfiguration, Jesus was still communicating the importance of His death to the disciples. It contains three features: the prohibition of Christ, the prophecies of Scripture, and the preview of John the Baptist.

THE PROHIBITION OF CHRIST

As they were coming down from the mountain, He gave them orders not to relate to anyone what they had seen, until the Son of Man rose from the dead. They seized upon that statement, discussing with one another what rising from the dead meant. (9:9–10)

As this section opens, Peter, James, and John **were coming down from the mountain** with Jesus. They had just had the experience that filled them with holy terror, causing them to fall to the ground (Matt. 17:6), overwhelmed by the glorious presence of God (cf. Judg. 13:20–22; 1 Chron. 21:16; Ezek. 1:28; 3:23; 43:3; Acts 22:7; Rev. 1:17). After it was over, Jesus compassionately reassured them (Matt. 17:7) and led them down **from the mountain. As they were coming down,** the three disciples were trying to process the meaning of the majestic, yet terrifying scene they had just witnessed. Speechless at first, they were still overcome with wonder and awe—not totally unlike Moses, whose face shone after seeing God's glory (Ex. 34:29–30, 35). Their faith in Jesus had been confirmed by what they had seen and heard and convinced them that He was the Messiah and Son of God. Never again would they be shaken in their confidence as to Jesus' identity. Their faith would be tested by what happened to Him at His arrest, trial, and death, and they would temporarily abandon and deny Him (Mark 14:50, 66–72). But no threat, disappointment, humiliation, dishonor, or suffering on His part or theirs would make them doubt that He was the Messiah and Son of God.

As they descended, Peter, James, and John were probably trying to express their responses when Jesus **gave them orders not to relate to anyone what they had seen, until the Son of Man rose from the dead.** Such commands from the Lord to remain silent were not unusual (cf. Mark 5:43; 7:36; 8:30). Like this one, they were intended to avoid the proclamation of an incomplete gospel. The central truth of the gospel is the death and resurrection of Jesus Christ, not that He healed the sick, raised the dead, or manifested divine glory. Publicizing those things might have diverted the people's attention from His coming suffering and fanned the flames of messianic expectation (cf. John 6:14–15). After **the Son of Man rose from the dead,** it would be obvious that He had come to die and thus conquer sin and death, not the Romans. Unlike others to whom He gave similar instructions (cf. Mark 1:40–45; 7:36), the disciples "kept silent, and reported to no one in those days any of the things which they had seen" (Luke 9:36).

The three immediately **seized upon** the Lord's **statement** and began **discussing with one another what rising from the dead meant.** It was not, of course, that they did not know what a resurrection was. They had seen Jesus raise people from the dead (Matt. 11:5; cf. Matt. 9:24–25; Luke 7:14–15; John 11:43–44) and had even done so themselves (Matt. 10:8). The disciples also understood from the Old Testament that there would be a general resurrection (Job 19:26–27; Dan. 12:1–2). They were not having a discussion about the nature of resurrection in general but about the resurrection of Jesus in particular. They were confused about His death and rising, which did not fit into their view of the Messiah's mission. Trying to understand those events became the subject of their thinking and consequently the topic of their conversation. The disciples believed that they would happen soon, certainly in their lifetime, because they were allowed to speak about them after they took place. They were trying to fit the death and resurrection of Jesus into their belief that the kingdom was imminent, which they continued to believe even after those events took place. At some point during the forty days between Christ's resurrection and ascension, a time He spent "speaking [to them] of the things concerning the kingdom of God" (Acts 1:3), the disciples eagerly asked Him, "Lord, is it at this time You are restoring the kingdom to Israel?" (v. 6). Their question, though misguided, was understandable. As I wrote in my commentary on that verse in an earlier volume in this series,

> After all, here was the resurrected Messiah speaking with them about His kingdom. They knew of no reason the earthly form of the kingdom could not be set up immediately, since the messianic work signaling the end of the age had arrived. It must be remembered that the interval between the two comings of Messiah was not explicitly taught in the Old Testament. The disciples on the road to Emmaus were greatly disappointed that Jesus had not redeemed Israel and set up the kingdom (Luke 24:21). Further, the apostles knew that Ezekiel 36 and Joel 2 connected the coming of the kingdom with the outpouring of the Spirit Jesus had just promised. It is understandable that they hoped the arrival of the kingdom was imminent. Surely it was for this kingdom they had hoped since they first joined Jesus. They had experienced a roller coaster ride of hope and doubt which they now felt might be over. (*Acts 1–12*, The MacArthur New Testament Commentary [Chicago: Moody, 1994], 19–20)

THE PROPHECIES OF SCRIPTURE

They asked Him, saying, "Why is it that the scribes say that Elijah must come first?" And He said to them, "Elijah does first come and restore all things. And yet how is it written of the Son of Man that He will suffer many things and be treated with contempt?" (9:11–12)

The disciples were still not ready to accept the necessity of Christ's suffering and death. They remained confused and hoping for the immediate manifestation of His glory and the establishing of His kingdom, which they assumed would immediately follow His death and resurrection. That led them to ask Jesus, **"Why is it that the scribes** (the experts in the law) **say that Elijah must come first?"**; that is, before the Messiah's arrival.

Their question was a good one, based on an accurate understanding of the Old Testament. Through the prophet Malachi, God said, "'Behold, I am going to send My messenger, and he will clear the way before Me. And the Lord, whom you seek, will suddenly come to His temple; and the messenger of the covenant, in whom you delight, behold, He is coming,' says the Lord of hosts" (Mal. 3:1). In the ancient Near East, kings and rulers were preceded by a herald, or forerunner, who was responsible for making sure that everything was prepared for the monarch's arrival. Isaiah described the work of such a forerunner in Isaiah 40:3–4:

> A voice is calling, "Clear the way for the Lord in the wilderness; make smooth in the desert a highway for our God. Let every valley be lifted up, and every mountain and hill be made low; and let the rough ground become a plain, and the rugged terrain a broad valley."

Before the Messiah's arrival, a messenger would come; "the one referred to by Isaiah the prophet when he said, 'The voice of one crying in the wilderness, "Make ready the way of the Lord, make His paths straight!"'" (Matt. 3:3). That messenger is further identified in Malachi 4:5–6 as "Elijah the prophet" (v. 5).

Before the day of the Lord, the final judgment of the ungodly and the establishment of the kingdom, Elijah will come. He will restore the nation by calling the people to repent, and the remnant will believe and escape the curse. He will bring people together around belief in the true and living God (Mal. 4:6).

The disciples were absolutely convinced that Jesus was the Messiah. But that being the case, where was Elijah? Why was he not present, performing all the duties that, according to tradition, he would do to prepare for Messiah's coming? Should he not have preceded the Lord's

arrival? Jesus replied, **"Elijah does first come and restore all things."**
They were correct; Elijah does come before the Messiah and prepare **all
things** for His coming.

But there was something that they had overlooked. **How is it
written of the Son of Man** (the messianic title taken from Dan. 7:13),
Jesus asked, **that He will suffer many things and be treated with
contempt?** The disciples asked Him how He could be the Messiah if Elijah had not come; He in turn asked them how He could be the Messiah if
He did not suffer as the Old Testament predicted (cf. Pss. 22; 69; Isa. 53;
Zech. 12:10).

Both prophecies will come to pass; Elijah will come, and Messiah
will suffer, since "the Scripture cannot be broken" (John 10:35).

THE PREVIEW OF JOHN THE BAPTIST

**But I say to you that Elijah has indeed come, and they did to him
whatever they wished, just as it is written of him."** (9:13)

Jesus' definitive statement, **"But I say to you that Elijah has
indeed come,"** must have surprised and puzzled the disciples, leaving
them even more confused than they already were. But Elijah had not literally returned; the Lord was referring to the one who came "in the spirit
and power of Elijah" (Luke 1:17)—John the Baptist. There were striking
similarities between the two prophets, including their physical appearance (cf. 2 Kings 1:8 with Mark 1:6) and their powerful, uncompromising
preaching. Yet when the Jewish leaders asked him, "Are you Elijah?" John
replied, "I am not" (John 1:21).

Although the disciples now realized that Jesus was referring to
John the Baptist (Matt. 17:13), Israel had failed to recognize John's significance (Matt. 17:12) and **did to him whatever they wished, just as it
is written of him.** The religious leaders rejected him (Matt. 21:25; Luke
7:33), and Herod imprisoned and killed him (Mark 6:17–29)—the fate
intended for Elijah (1 Kings 19:1–10). No specific Old Testament prophecies predicted the death of Messiah's forerunner, so the phrase **it is written of him** is best understood as having been fulfilled typically by John.

Had Israel realized who John was and accepted his message, he would indeed have been the Elijah who was to come (Matt. 11:14). But since they did not, John was a preview of another who will come in the spirit and power of Elijah before the second coming (possibly one of the two witnesses; cf. Rev. 11:3–12).

The biblical pattern is clear. Elijah was rejected and persecuted; Messiah's forerunner, who came in the spirit and power of Elijah, was rejected and killed, and Messiah Himself was rejected and murdered. In the future, however, the prophesied Elijah will come, the Lord Jesus Christ will return, and the kingdom will be established.

All Things Possible
(Mark 9:14–29)

3

When they came back to the disciples, they saw a large crowd around them, and some scribes arguing with them. Immediately, when the entire crowd saw Him, they were amazed and began running up to greet Him. And He asked them, "What are you discussing with them?" And one of the crowd answered Him, "Teacher, I brought You my son, possessed with a spirit which makes him mute; and whenever it seizes him, it slams him to the ground and he foams at the mouth, and grinds his teeth and stiffens out. I told Your disciples to cast it out, and they could not do it." And He answered them and said, "O unbelieving generation, how long shall I be with you? How long shall I put up with you? Bring him to Me!" They brought the boy to Him. When he saw Him, immediately the spirit threw him into a convulsion, and falling to the ground, he began rolling around and foaming at the mouth. And He asked his father, "How long has this been happening to him?" And he said, "From childhood. It has often thrown him both into the fire and into the water to destroy him. But if

You can do anything, take pity on us and help us!" And Jesus said
to him, "'If You can?' All things are possible to him who
believes." Immediately the boy's father cried out and said, "I do
believe; help my unbelief." When Jesus saw that a crowd was
rapidly gathering, He rebuked the unclean spirit, saying to it,
"You deaf and mute spirit, I command you, come out of him and
do not enter him again." After crying out and throwing him into
terrible convulsions, it came out; and the boy became so much
like a corpse that most of them said, "He is dead!" But Jesus took
him by the hand and raised him; and he got up. When He came
into the house, His disciples began questioning Him privately,
"Why could we not drive it out?" And He said to them, "This kind
cannot come out by anything but prayer." (9:14–29)

The Christian life is a life of faith. Believers, Paul wrote to the
Corinthians, "walk by faith, not by sight" (2 Cor. 5:7). The apostle told the
Galatians, "The life which I now live in the flesh I live by faith in the Son of
God" (Gal. 2:20). Faith "is the assurance of things hoped for, the conviction
of things not seen" (Heb. 11:1), "and without faith it is impossible to please
Him" (v. 6). Jesus said to Thomas, "Because you have seen Me, have you
believed? Blessed are they who did not see, and yet believed" (John
20:29), while Peter reminded his readers, "Though you have not seen Him,
you love Him, and though you do not see Him now, but believe in Him,
you greatly rejoice with joy inexpressible and full of glory" (1 Peter 1:8).
Christians trust in God whom they have not seen, Christ whom
they have not seen, the Holy Spirit whom they have not seen; they
embrace a death and resurrection they have not seen; trust in a justifica-
tion they have not seen; and look forward to eternal life in a heaven they
have not seen. Believers are saved by faith, sanctified by faith, and hold
the hope of glory by faith. That faith is not perfect, but it is sufficient—not
because of human ability but because it is a gift of God (Eph. 2:8–9). It is
not a blind faith but a proven faith anchored in the testimony of the
Word of God, which is "the prophetic word made more sure" (2 Peter 1:19;
cf. Matt. 5:18; 24:35; Luke 16:29–31) and "the word of His grace, which is
able to build [believers] up and to give [them] the inheritance among
all those who are sanctified" (Acts 20:32).

For more than two years, the disciples had walked by sight. They had actually been in the presence of Jesus, the Son of God. They had watched Him react to people and situations, heard His teaching, and witnessed His miracles. They had lived by sight. Soon, however, they would have to live by faith. After His death, they would always have the memory of what they had seen. That memory would be enriched and enhanced by the Spirit of God, allowing them and their associates to record what they had witnessed in the Gospels and be further delineated in the Epistles that they wrote. But no longer would Jesus be physically present with them. He would speak to them through His Word, the Scripture, and empower them in the Holy Spirit

As the Lord moved inexorably toward Jerusalem and His death, resurrection, and ascension, He taught His disciples a series of lessons designed to prepare them to minister in His absence. Those lessons were bracketed by lessons on faith, of which the one recorded in this passage was the first. The Lord also taught them concerning humility, offenses, the seriousness of sin, marriage and divorce, the place of children in the kingdom, earthly riches, true wealth, sacrificial service, and then a final lesson on faith.

Jesus was not present when the incident began, so the disciples were challenged to walk by faith, not by sight—and failed miserably. They were a work in progress, characterized by lack of understanding and shallow faith. In Mark 8:17 Jesus had chided them, "Do you not yet see or understand? Do you have a hardened heart?" and reiterated in verse 21, "Do you not yet understand?"

Matthew (17:14–20) and Luke (9:37–45) also record this incident. Mark's account is more detailed, possibly because Peter, Mark's source for much of the material in his gospel and an eyewitness to this incident, provided many of the dramatic details. The episode took place immediately after the transfiguration, and the contrasts between the two events are striking. The transfiguration happened on a mountain; this happened in the valley below. In the transfiguration, there was glory; here there was suffering. In the transfiguration God dominated the scene; here Satan did. In the transfiguration, the heavenly Father was pleased; in this incident, an earthly father was tormented. In the transfiguration there was a perfect Son; here there was a perverted son. At the transfiguration, fallen men were in holy wonder; in this story, there was a fallen son in unholy horror.

This scene, one of the most striking in the New Testament, may be viewed under five headings: demon possession, disciple perversion, desperate plea, divine power, and decisive prayer.

DEMON POSSESSION

When they came back to the disciples, they saw a large crowd around them, and some scribes arguing with them. Immediately, when the entire crowd saw Him, they were amazed and began running up to greet Him. And He asked them, "What are you discussing with them?" And one of the crowd answered Him, "Teacher, I brought You my son, possessed with a spirit which makes him mute; and whenever it seizes him, it slams him to the ground and he foams at the mouth, and grinds his teeth and stiffens out. (9:14–18*a*)

After the transfiguration, Jesus, Peter, James, and John **came back** down the mountain **to the** nine apostles and other followers and **disciples** of the Lord who had remained in the valley. Just as Moses came down from God's presence on Mt. Sinai to the faithless people of Israel, so also Jesus came down from being in God's presence on the Mount of Transfiguration to find faithless people waiting for Him. When the four arrived, **they saw** that **a large crowd** had gathered **around** the disciples, expecting Jesus to be with them. In addition, there were **some scribes** from the surrounding region present, as always dogging Jesus' steps, seeking something they could use to discredit Him (cf. 3:1–2; Luke 11:53–54; 14:1). Since the Lord was not there, the scribes were **arguing with** His disciples. They were on their own and, as it turns out, things had not gone well.

When Jesus and the three apostles reached the valley, the people spotted Him, and immediately, **when the entire crowd saw Him, they were amazed and began running up to greet Him.** The Greek word translated **amazed** is a strong compound word, leading some to speculate that Jesus was exuding an afterglow from His transfiguration (cf. Ex. 34:29–35). That was not the case, however, since it would have contradicted His command that the disciples tell no one what had happened on the mountain (cf. the discussion of Mark 9:9 in the previous chapter of this volume). In light of that prohibition, Jesus would never have made that supernatural event obvious. The crowd was awestruck as they always were in His presence (cf. Matt. 9:33; 12:23; Mark 2:12), because Jesus was the miracle worker, the one who performed signs, wonders, and healings.

Coming to the defense of His disciples, Jesus asked, **"What are you discussing with them?"** The word translated **discussing** is commonly used to refer to arguments or debates with the Jewish religious leaders (cf. 8:11; 12:28; Acts 6:9; 9:29). Neither the scribes (probably because they were afraid to debate Him) or the disciples (who evidently were not doing well in the debate, and moreover had failed to cast out the demon) answered.

But while they remained silent, **one of the crowd answered Him.** A man came to Jesus and fell on his knees before Him (Matt. 17:14). Shouting to make himself heard above the noise of the crowd (Luke 9:38), he cried out, **"Teacher,** Lord (Matt. 17:15), **I brought You my son** (Luke notes that this was his only son, adding to the pathos of the situation; Luke 9:38), **possessed with a spirit which makes him mute; and whenever it seizes him, it slams him to the ground and he foams at the mouth, and grinds his teeth and stiffens out.** Here was a situation the disciples had failed to handle, which led to their embarrassed silence.

Demons have been actively doing Satan's bidding in the world ever since the fall. They do not usually make their presence known, choosing rather to operate covertly by disguising themselves as angels of light (cf. 2 Cor. 11:14). During Jesus' earthly ministry, however, they launched an all-out assault against Him, manifesting themselves more often openly and to some degree more willingly than is their normal practice. But Jesus unmasked them, forcing them to reveal themselves even when they were unwilling to do so.

This demon would likely have preferred to have remained undiscovered in the boy. Although his father had discerned that his son's condition was the result of demonic activity, others may have diagnosed him as having some kind of a mental disorder. In fact, in Matthew's account of this incident (17:15), his father described his son's symptoms as those of a lunatic (i.e., an epileptic). Those symptoms may have stemmed from the physical battering the demon inflicted on his unfortunate victim. Luke records that the father spoke of the demon mauling his son, using a verb that could be translated "to crush," "to shatter," or "to break in pieces," vividly describing the violence of the demon's assaults on the boy (Luke 9:39).

DISCIPLE PERVERSION

I told Your disciples to cast it out, and they could not do it." And He answered them and said, "O unbelieving generation, how long shall I be with you? How long shall I put up with you? Bring him to Me!" (18*b*–19)

The failure of the **disciples to cast** the demon **out** of the boy was surprising, since Jesus had given them power over demons (Mark 6:7, 13). While the crowd was made up largely of those who did not believe in Jesus and the faith of the boy's father was weak and incomplete, the Lord's rebuke, **"O unbelieving generation,"** was aimed primarily at the disciples. It reveals that the cause of their inability to cast out the demon was their failure to believe. The interjection **O** expresses emotion on Jesus' part (cf. Luke 13:34; 24:25), revealing that the disciples' weak faith was painful to Him.

His rebuke was harsh; Luke 9:41 adds that He also called them a "perverted generation" (cf. Mark 8:38; Deut. 32:5, 20). After all the time they had spent with Him, such lack of trust was inexcusable. Jesus' soliloquy, **"How long shall I be with you? How long shall I put up with you?"** was an expression of holy exasperation, like His rebukes, "You of little faith!" (Matt. 6:30; 14:31) and, "You men of little faith! (Matt. 8:26; 16:8). Acting to do what the disciples had failed to accomplish, Jesus said, **Bring** the boy **to Me!"**

DESPERATE PLEA

They brought the boy to Him. When he saw Him, immediately the spirit threw him into a convulsion, and falling to the ground, he began rolling around and foaming at the mouth. And He asked his father, "How long has this been happening to him?" And he said, "From childhood. It has often thrown him both into the fire and into the water to destroy him. But if You can do anything, take pity on us and help us!" And Jesus said to him, "'If You can?' All things are possible to him who believes." Immediately the boy's father cried out and said, "I do believe; help my unbelief." (9:20–24)

The boy's father was about to get what he so desperately wanted, while the demon would get what he desperately did not want. In response to the Lord's command, **they brought the boy to Him.** While he was still approaching Jesus (Luke 9:42), **when he saw Him, immediately the spirit threw him into a** final, violent **convulsion, and falling to the ground, he began rolling around and foaming at the mouth.**

While this dangerous display of vile demonic power was going on, Jesus calmly **asked his father, "How long has this been happening to him?"** The Lord was not asking, of course, for information that He did not already possess, since He is omniscient. He wanted to bear the father's pain; to have the man tell Him the heartbreaking story of his son's demonic oppression. The father was not coming to an impersonal force but to a person. The healing miracles Christ performed reveal the compassion of God and that He cares about human pain and suffering. Jesus allowed this suffering man to unfold his heart to the sympathetic and merciful Lord.

His reply, **"From childhood,"** indicates that his son had been in this terrible state all his life. It was not due to any sin on the part of either the father or the son but for the glory of God (cf. John 9:1–3). And though the demon had repeatedly tried to kill the boy by throwing **him both into the fire** (commonly used for heating and cooking) **and into the water** (such as wells and pools) **to destroy him,** God preserved him for this moment to bring His Son glory. The father's desperate struggle to keep the demon from killing his son was about to be ended permanently.

Encouraged by the Lord's sympathetic concern for his beleaguered, battered son, the man asked Him pleadingly, **"If You can do anything, take pity on us and help us!"** *Boētheō* (**help**) literally means, "to run to the aid of one who cries for help." His faith was weak and incomplete; he correctly perceived that Jesus was willing to deliver his son, but he was not sure that He had the power to help him. But he was desperate.

Jesus' reply, **"If You can?"** was not a question but an exclamation of surprise. In light of His widespread ministry of healing the sick and casting out demons, how could His ability to cast this one out be in question? His further declaration, **"All things are possible to him who believes,"** is the lesson Jesus intended to teach. This was not the first time He had spoken of the importance of faith (cf. Mark 5:34–36; 6:5–6), nor would it be the last (cf. Mark 10:27; 11:22–24). The lesson that faith is essential to access the power of God applied to all the unbelieving crowd, the father, who was struggling to believe, as well as to the disciples, whose faith was weak and wavering. The disciples especially needed to learn this lesson, since after Christ's death, they would need to access divine power through believing prayer (Matt. 7:7–8; 21:22; Luke 11:9–10; John 14:13–14; 15:7; 16:24; 1 John 3:22; 5:14–15).

Overcome with emotion, **immediately the boy's father cried out and said, "I do believe; help my unbelief."** He was honest enough to admit that though he believed in Jesus' power, he struggled with doubt. Just as he pleaded in desperation for Jesus to deliver his son from the demon, so also did he plead for Jesus to **help** him be delivered from his unbelief. The Lord is not limited by imperfect faith; even the strongest faith is always mixed with a measure of doubt.

DIVINE POWER

When Jesus saw that a crowd was rapidly gathering, He rebuked the unclean spirit, saying to it, "You deaf and mute spirit, I command you, come out of him and do not enter him again." After

crying out and throwing him into terrible convulsions, it came out; and the boy became so much like a corpse that most of them said, "He is dead!" But Jesus took him by the hand and raised him; and he got up. (9:25–27)

While Jesus was talking with the boy's father, the word was spreading that He was there. Seeing **that a crowd was rapidly gathering,** He decided to end the conversation and take action. The compassionate Lord wanted to avoid any further embarrassment for the anguished father and his tormented son. Further, His public ministry was over and He had nothing left to prove, since replete evidence that He was who He claimed to be had already been given. His focus was on instructing His disciples.

Turning to the boy, Jesus **rebuked the unclean spirit** (a description of demons used twenty-two times in the New Testament, half of them in Mark), **saying to it, "You deaf and mute spirit, I command you, come out of him and do not enter him again."** The demon instantly (Matt. 17:18) and permanently left the boy—but not before one last, violent protest (cf. Mark 1:25–26). **After crying out and throwing him into terrible convulsions, it came out.** Exhausted and traumatized by the violent convulsions, **the boy** lay still and **became so much like a corpse that most of** the bystanders **said, "He is dead!" But Jesus** tenderly, compassionately **took him by the hand and raised him** to his feet, **and he got up** and Jesus gave him back to his father (Luke 9:42).

DECISIVE PRAYER

When He came into the house, His disciples began questioning Him privately, "Why could we not drive it out?" And He said to them, "This kind cannot come out by anything but prayer." (9:28–29)

Later, when Jesus and the disciples **came into the house** (probably in Caesarea Philippi), **the disciples began questioning Him privately, "Why could we not drive it out?"** They were puzzled as to their inability to do so on this occasion, since they had successfully cast out demons in the past (Mark 6:13). Jesus replied, **"This kind** (either a reference to a particular kind of demon, or a kind of being, and thus a reference to demons in general) **cannot come out by anything but prayer."** The implication is that emboldened by their earlier successes, the disciples depended on their own power and neglected to pray. The lesson for them was that humble, dependent prayer is the highway that faith takes to the power of God.

Matthew's account adds that Jesus rebuked them for the littleness of their faith (17:20; cf. 6:30; 8:26; 14:31; 16:8; Luke 12:28), revealing that it was that weakness that kept the disciples from praying. But if they had faith the size of a mustard seed, they would have been able to unleash the power of God and overcome any difficulty. The mustard seed, the smallest seed used in agriculture in Israel, does not represent a level of faith to be achieved but rather the minimal faith that believers already have—such as that illustrated by the father.

Jesus healed many without faith, but here the miracle is connected to faith because that is the necessary lesson for the disciples in the future. Their power will come by believing prayer. That man's weak faith was sufficient to bring the power of God to bear on his son's situation. In the same way imperfect but persistent (cf. Luke 11:5–10; 18:1–7) faith is sufficient. It is those who do not ask who do not receive divine power to overcome life's difficulties (James 4:2). The disciples' failure set them up for this invaluable lesson on the necessity of believing, persistent prayer.

The Virtue of Being Last (Mark 9:30–41)

4

From there they went out and began to go through Galilee, and He did not want anyone to know about it. For He was teaching His disciples and telling them, "The Son of Man is to be delivered into the hands of men, and they will kill Him; and when He has been killed, He will rise three days later." But they did not understand this statement, and they were afraid to ask Him. They came to Capernaum; and when He was in the house, He began to question them, "What were you discussing on the way?" But they kept silent, for on the way they had discussed with one another which of them was the greatest. Sitting down, He called the twelve and said to them, "If anyone wants to be first, he shall be last of all and servant of all." Taking a child, He set him before them, and taking him in His arms, He said to them, "Whoever receives one child like this in My name receives Me; and whoever receives Me does not receive Me, but Him who sent Me." John said to Him, "Teacher, we saw someone casting out demons in Your name, and we tried to prevent him because he was not following us." But

Jesus said, "Do not hinder him, for there is no one who will perform a miracle in My name, and be able soon afterward to speak evil of Me. For he who is not against us is for us. For whoever gives you a cup of water to drink because of your name as followers of Christ, truly I say to you, he will not lose his reward." (9:30–41)

As noted in the previous chapter of this volume, chapters 9 and 10 of Mark's gospel record lessons Jesus taught to His disciples. His public ministry in Galilee was over, but He continued to minister privately to the disciples as they journeyed to Jerusalem. The first in that series of lessons was on the importance of faith (see the previous chapter of this volume); this second one was on humility.

Humility is not considered a virtue in our proud, self-centered, egotistical culture, nor was it in the pagan world of Jesus' day. For example Aristotle, one of the most influential philosophers of the ancient world, described pride as the crown of the virtues (*Nicomachean Ethics,* 4.3). Every fallen human heart is a relentless worshiper of itself; fallen human nature is dominated by pride.

But in a bizarre twist, our society diagnoses the cause of people's problems as a lack of pride or self-esteem. Such is not the case, however. No one lacks self-esteem; everyone is consumed with himself or herself to one degree or another. To diagnose the cause of all human ills as a lack of self-esteem leads people to be even more prideful than they already are. Inflating pride under the guise of promoting self-esteem as a psychological benefit exposes people to pride's devastating consequences, including defilement (Mark 7:20–22), dishonor (Prov. 11:2; 29:23), strife (Prov. 28:25), and, most significantly, God's judgment (Pss. 31:23; 94:2; Prov. 16:5, 18; Isa. 2:12, 17; Luke 1:51; James 4:6; 1 Peter 5:5).

Although humility is alien to fallen human nature, it is foundational to the Christian life. The exalted Lord, who declared, "Heaven is My throne and the earth is My footstool. Where then is a house you could build for Me? And where is a place that I may rest?" (Isa. 66:1), went on to say, "But to this one I will look, to him who is humble and contrite of spirit, and who trembles at My word" (v. 2). "He has told you, O man, what is good," wrote the prophet Micah, "and what does the Lord require of you but to do justice, to love kindness, and to walk humbly with your God?"

(Mic. 6:8). In Luke 14:11, Jesus warned, "Everyone who exalts himself will be humbled, and he who humbles himself will be exalted." The apostle Paul implored believers, "Walk in a manner worthy of the calling with which you have been called, with all humility and gentleness, with patience, showing tolerance for one another in love" (Eph. 4:1–2), and further urged them, "Do nothing from selfishness or empty conceit, but with humility of mind regard one another as more important than yourselves" (Phil. 2:3). In Colossians 3:12 he wrote, "So, as those who have been chosen of God, holy and beloved, put on a heart of compassion, kindness, humility, gentleness and patience." Both James (4:6) and Peter (1 Peter 5:5) note that "God is opposed to the proud, but gives grace to the humble," and James added the exhortation, "Humble yourselves in the presence of the Lord, and He will exalt you" (4:10).

Like everyone else, the disciples needed to learn humility because they also battled pride, which was exacerbated by their exalted position as the Messiah's closest followers. The supremely prideful Jewish religious leaders were notoriously poor examples for the people of Israel to follow. The cultural and religious milieu in which they lived made the disciples' struggle with pride all the more difficult.

The Lord's lesson to the disciples on humility was given by both precept and example. He not only modeled humility but also gave the disciples instruction regarding it.

AN EXAMPLE OF HUMILITY

From there they went out and began to go through Galilee, and He did not want anyone to know about it. For He was teaching His disciples and telling them, "The Son of Man is to be delivered into the hands of men, and they will kill Him; and when He has been killed, He will rise three days later." But they did not understand this statement, and they were afraid to ask Him. (9:30–32)

The Lord Jesus Christ described Himself as "gentle and humble in heart" (Matt. 11:29), and demonstrated that humility throughout His life, most notably by washing the disciples' feet (John 13:3–15). Summing up the humility Jesus displayed in His incarnation, Paul wrote,

> Have this attitude in yourselves which was also in Christ Jesus, who, although He existed in the form of God, did not regard equality with God a thing to be grasped, but emptied Himself, taking the form of a bond-servant, and being made in the likeness of men. Being found in appearance as a man, He humbled Himself by becoming obedient to the point of death, even death on a cross. (Phil. 2:5–8)

Christ's "death on a cross" is the ultimate expression of His humility and is the theme of verses 30–32. The setting for the Lord's teaching regarding His death was the journey from the region of Caesarea Philippi, where He was transfigured (probably on Mt. Hermon; see the discussion of 9:2 in chapter 1 of this volume) to Capernaum, the headquarters of His Galilean ministry.

As they traveled **through Galilee,** Jesus **did not want anyone to know about it.** His public ministry in that region was over (see the discussion of 9:25 in the previous chapter of this volume), and His focus was on the private instruction of His disciples. Later, there would be some brief public ministry in Judea and Perea (Luke 9:51–19:27; John 7–11) and even a couple of brief return visits to Galilee (e.g., Luke 17:11–37). But Galilee would no longer be His base of operations.

As was frequently the case, the Lord **was teaching His disciples** that **"the Son of Man** (a messianic title taken from Dan. 7:13) **is to be delivered into the hands of men, and they will kill Him; and when He has been killed, He will rise three days later"** (cf. 8:31; 9:12; 10:33–34). That was the primary truth that they needed to understand—and that they were unable to comprehend or accept. As it was for their fellow Jews (1 Cor. 1:23), a crucified Messiah was a stumbling block for the disciples; a dying Messiah was utterly incomprehensible and unacceptable to them. For that reason Jesus exhorted them, "Let these words sink into your ears; for the Son of Man is going to be delivered into the hands of men" (Luke 9:44). They needed to listen carefully and understand what He was saying to them about His death.

Delivered translates a form of the Greek verb *paradidōmi,* which literally means "to hand over." It was used repeatedly in a legal sense to describe Jesus' being handed over for judgment and punishment (10:33;

15:1, 10, 15; Matt. 17:22; 20:18–19; 26:2; 27:2, 18, 26; Luke 9:44; 18:32; 20:20; 23:25; 24:7, 20; John 18:30, 35, 36; 19:16; Acts 3:13). In human terms, the elders, chief priests, scribes, and people (cf. 8:31; Matt. 27:1–2; Acts 3:13), Judas (Matt. 26:24), and Pilate (Matt. 27:26) all were guilty of delivering Jesus to judgment and death. But ultimately, Jesus "was delivered over by the predetermined plan and foreknowledge of God" (Acts 2:23).

Not only did the disciples struggle with the reality that the Jews and Romans would **kill Him** but also that **when He** had **been killed, He** would **rise three days later.** They understood Jesus' power over death, having seen Him raise dead people. But the question that must have troubled them was that if He died, who would raise Him? Thus, they **did not understand this statement.**

The uncertainty in their minds about Christ's death and resurrection, coupled with their grief (cf. Matt. 17:23), also caused the disciples to be **afraid to ask Him** for more information. Jesus compassionately chose not to reveal information to them that He knew would devastate their faith; instead, He "concealed [it] from them so that they would not perceive it" (Luke 9:45).

Instruction on Humility

They came to Capernaum; and when He was in the house, He began to question them, "What were you discussing on the way?" But they kept silent, for on the way they had discussed with one another which of them was the greatest. Sitting down, He called the twelve and said to them, "If anyone wants to be first, he shall be last of all and servant of all." Taking a child, He set him before them, and taking him in His arms, He said to them, "Whoever receives one child like this in My name receives Me; and whoever receives Me does not receive Me, but Him who sent Me." John said to Him, "Teacher, we saw someone casting out demons in Your name, and we tried to prevent him because he was not following us." But Jesus said, "Do not hinder him, for there is no one who will perform a miracle in My name, and be able soon afterward to speak evil of Me. For he who is not against us is for

**us. For whoever gives you a cup of water to drink because of your
name as followers of Christ, truly I say to you, he will not lose his
reward."** (9:33–41)

Capernaum, located on the northwest shore of the Sea of
Galilee, was Jesus' adopted hometown (Matt. 4:13). Several of the apos-
tles also were associated with Capernaum, including Peter and Andrew
(Mark 1:21,29), who moved there from Bethsaida (John 1:44), James and
John (Mark 1:19–21), and Matthew, whose tax collector's booth was in or
near the city (Matt. 9:1,9).

When He was in the house (possibly Peter's; see the discussion
of Peter's house in *Mark 1–8*, The MacArthur New Testament Commentary [Chicago: Moody, 2015], chap. 5), **He began to question** the disciples, asking them, **"What were you discussing on the way?"** Jesus'
instruction to the disciples highlighted four negative effects of pride, and
concluded by noting one positive effect of humility.

PRIDE DESTROYS UNITY

**But they kept silent, for on the way they had discussed with one
another which of them was the greatest.** (9:34)

During the long walk from Caesarea Philippi to Capernaum, the
disciples had been having a prolonged and heated discussion. Not wanting to admit what they had been talking about, **they kept silent** in embarrassment. The discussion had been another episode in their long-running
debate over **which of them was the greatest** (cf. 10:35–45), which,
incredibly, was still going on at the Last Supper on the night before the
Lord's death (Luke 22:24). The Lord had just spoken to them about His
humiliation (vv. 30–32), but all they could think about was their exaltation.

There can be no real unity among proud people, because only
humble people love. The disciples' constant focus on their own personal
glory had far-reaching consequences, as I wrote in a previous volume in
this series:

This was a disturbing and potentially disastrous development. These men were the first generation of gospel preachers, and would be the leaders of the soon to be founded church. With so much riding on them and so much opposition from the hostile world, they needed to be unified and supportive of each other. The danger revealed here is that pride ruins unity by destroying relationships. Relationships are based on loving sacrifice and service; on selfless deferring to and giving to others. Pride, being self-focused, is indifferent to others. Beyond that, it is ultimately judgmental and critical, and therefore divisive. Because of that pride is the most common destroyer both of relationships and churches. It plagued the Corinthian church, causing Paul to ask, "For since there is jealousy and strife among you, are you not fleshly, and are you not walking like mere men?" (1 Cor. 3:3; cf. 2 Cor. 12:20). Knowing that pride is the wedge Satan uses to split churches and splinter relationships, the Lord stressed to the disciples the crucial necessity of humility. (*Luke 6–10*, The MacArthur New Testament Commentary [Chicago: Moody, 2011], 301)

As Paul wrote to the church at Philippi, believers are to be constantly "standing firm in one spirit, with one mind striving together for the faith of the gospel" (Phil. 1:27).

PRIDE FORFEITS HONOR

Sitting down, He called the twelve and said to them, "If anyone wants to be first, he shall be last of all and servant of all." (9:35)

Ironically, pride keeps people from obtaining the very honor that they seek. Proud people—even those in ministry—battle for position and seek to promote themselves, but end up forfeiting true honor and often end in humiliation. Honor is reserved for the humble. Like many in our day, the disciples viewed spiritual pride as normal, desirable, and legitimate. After all, pride characterized the most revered men in Israel, the religious leaders, who "[did] all their deeds to be noticed by men.... they broaden[ed] their phylacteries and lengthen[ed] the tassels of their garments. They love[d] the place of honor at banquets and the chief seats in the synagogues, and respectful greetings in the market places, and being called Rabbi by men" (Matt. 23:5–7; cf. 6:1–5).

Jesus knew what the disciples were thinking (Luke 9:47), even if they refused to express it. **Sitting down,** as rabbis commonly did when they taught, **He called the twelve and said to them, "If anyone wants to be first, he shall be last of all and servant of all."** Pursuing accolades, affirmation, and exaltation from men forfeits the true reward (Matt. 6:1–5) that comes to those who are willing to be last, not to those who have to be first.

PRIDE REJECTS DEITY

Taking a child, He set him before them, and taking him in His arms, He said to them, "Whoever receives one child like this in My name receives Me; and whoever receives Me does not receive Me, but Him who sent Me." (9:36–37)

The **child** (perhaps, as some have suggested, one of Peter's children) served as an object lesson for Christ's instruction. Jesus used young children several times as illustrations of humility. They have not yet accomplished or achieved anything; they have no power or honor but are weak, dependent, and ignored (rabbis considered it a waste of time to teach the Torah to a child under the age of twelve).

Little children are analogous to believers; therefore Jesus said, **"Whoever receives one child like this in My name receives Me; and whoever receives Me does not receive Me, but Him who sent Me."** The profound reality is that how Christians treat fellow believers is how they treat Christ. Conversely, those who reject other believers reject Him.

Matthew's account of this incident in chapter 18 elaborates on that theme. No doubt hoping Jesus would settle once and for all their dispute over which of them was the greatest, the disciples asked Him, "Who then is greatest in the kingdom of heaven?" (v. 1). The Lord's reply was startling: "Truly I say to you, unless you are converted and become like children, you will not enter the kingdom of heaven" (v. 3). Nothing could have been further removed from their cultural and religious perspective. The proud religious overachievers, who expected to receive the highest places of honor in the kingdom, will not even enter it. On the other hand, those with humble, childlike faith will be the greatest in the kingdom of heaven (v. 4).

But what Jesus said next was even more sobering and shocking: "Whoever causes one of these little ones who believe in Me to stumble, it would be better for him to have a heavy millstone hung around his neck, and to be drowned in the depth of the sea" (v. 6). It would be better to suffer a horrible death than offend a believer; one in whom Christ lives (Gal. 2:20) and who is spiritually joined to Him (1 Cor. 6:17). Reinforcing God's care for His children, the Lord warned His hearers, "See that you do not despise one of these little ones, for I say to you that their angels in heaven continually see the face of My Father who is in heaven" (v. 10). All heaven is watching how God's children are treated.

PRIDE CREATES EXCLUSIVITY

John said to Him, "Teacher, we saw someone casting out demons in Your name, and we tried to prevent him because he was not following us." But Jesus said, "Do not hinder him, for there is no one who will perform a miracle in My name, and be able soon afterward to speak evil of Me. For he who is not against us is for us. (9:38–40)

His conscience troubled by the Lord's rebuke of their pride, **John said to Him, "Teacher, we saw someone casting out demons in Your name, and we tried to prevent him because he was not following us."** The incident he referred to is not recorded in Scripture, but the exorcist was actually casting out demons, in contrast to the sons of Sceva (Acts 19:13–16; cf. Matt. 7:21–23). Although this man was a true follower of Christ, John and the others **tried to prevent him because he was not following** them; in other words, he was not one of their group. **"Do not hinder him,"** Jesus admonished him, **"for there is no one who will perform a miracle in My name, and be able soon afterward to speak evil of Me."** Since he was a legitimate follower of Jesus, this man would proclaim the truth about Him.

The principle is clear: **he who is not against** Christ and His followers **is for** them. Paul's response concerning those who sought to build a reputation for themselves by denigrating the apostle and his ministry illustrates that truth:

> Some, to be sure, are preaching Christ even from envy and strife, but some also from good will; the latter do it out of love, knowing that I am appointed for the defense of the gospel; the former proclaim Christ out of selfish ambition rather than from pure motives, thinking to cause me distress in my imprisonment. What then? Only that in every way, whether in pretense or in truth, Christ is proclaimed; and in this I rejoice. (Phil. 1:15–18)

HUMILITY GAINS REWARD

For whoever gives you a cup of water to drink because of your name as followers of Christ, truly I say to you, he will not lose his reward." (9:41)

In contrast to the devastating negative consequences of pride, the Lord's concluding point stresses the positive aspect of humility. It is such humility, expressed even in a small act of kindness, such as giving **a cup of water to drink** to those who are **followers of Christ,** that results in true and eternal **reward.**

The words of Solomon in Proverbs 22:4 provide a fitting summary of our Lord's teaching in this passage: "The reward of humility and the fear of the Lord are riches, honor and life."

Radical Discipleship (Mark 9:42–50)

5

"Whoever causes one of these little ones who believe to stumble, it would be better for him if, with a heavy millstone hung around his neck, he had been cast into the sea. If your hand causes you to stumble, cut it off; it is better for you to enter life crippled, than, having your two hands, to go into hell, into the unquenchable fire, where their worm does not die, and the fire is not quenched. If your foot causes you to stumble, cut it off; it is better for you to enter life lame, than, having your two feet, to be cast into hell, where their worm does not die, and the fire is not quenched. If your eye causes you to stumble, throw it out; it is better for you to enter the kingdom of God with one eye, than, having two eyes, to be cast into hell, where their worm does not die, and the fire is not quenched. For everyone will be salted with fire. Salt is good; but if the salt becomes unsalty, with what will you make it salty again? Have salt in yourselves, and be at peace with one another." (9:42–50)

In this unique portion of Scripture, replete with graphic terminology, dramatic acts, severe warnings, and shocking threats, the Lord Jesus Christ reveals the radical nature of true discipleship. The word "radical" may be understood in two ways. First, it can mean "basic,""fundamental," or "foundational," describing something primary, intrinsic, or essential. Paradoxically, the second and more common meaning of "radical" is something that deviates by its extreme; something "fanatical,""severe," or "revolutionary."

The Lord's message is essential for the time in which we live, when much of so-called Christianity, even evangelical Christianity, is marked by superficiality. The language here is severe, extreme, and forceful, in keeping with the nature of our Lord's repeated calls to true discipleship. He charged people to repent (Matt. 4:17; Luke 13:3, 5), to deny themselves (Matt. 16:24)—even to the point of suffering or dying for His sake (Matt. 10:38; Luke 9:23), to be willing to forsake all family ties (Luke 14:26–27), to hate their own lives (Luke 14:26) in the sense of being willing to lose them (John 12:25), and to forsake everything (Matt. 19:27; Luke 5:11, 27–28) and unconditionally follow Him (John 12:26).

This passage displays four aspects of radical discipleship: radical love, radical purity, radical sacrifice, and radical obedience.

RADICAL LOVE

"Whoever causes one of these little ones who believe to stumble, it would be better for him if, with a heavy millstone hung around his neck, he had been cast into the sea. (9:42)

Because He is zealous for the corporate righteousness of His church, Jesus called for love for other believers that prevents leading them into sin. God has always been protective of His people. When He made a covenant with Abraham, He told him, "I will bless those who bless you, and the one who curses you I will curse" (Gen. 12:3). "Do not touch My anointed ones," He cautioned, "and do My prophets no harm" (Ps. 105:15). Speaking to Israel in Zechariah 2:8, God likened assaulting His people to poking Him in the eye: "He who touches you, touches the apple [pupil] of His eye."

The truth about how believers are to treat one another is based on the principle the Lord expressed in Mark 9:37, "Whoever receives one child like this in My name receives Me; and whoever receives Me does not receive Me, but Him who sent Me." As noted in the exposition of that verse in chapter 4 of this volume, since Christ lives in every believer, how one treats a believer is how one treats Christ, and how one treats Christ is how one treats God. In the upper room on the eve of the crucifixion, Jesus said to the disciples, "Truly, truly, I say to you, he who receives whomever I send receives Me; and he who receives Me receives Him who sent Me" (John 13:20). Paul reminded the Corinthians that "the one who joins himself to the Lord is one spirit with Him" (1 Cor. 6:17) and declared in Galatians 2:20, "I have been crucified with Christ; and it is no longer I who live, but Christ lives in me; and the life which I now live in the flesh I live by faith in the Son of God, who loved me and gave Himself up for me." On his way to Damascus to persecute Christians, Paul encountered the risen, glorified Jesus Christ, who demanded of him, "Saul, Saul, why are you persecuting Me?" (Acts 9:4; cf. 22:7–8; 26:14–15). In the judgment, how people treat Christians will be considered how they treated Christ:

> Then the King will say to those on His right, "Come, you who are blessed of My Father, inherit the kingdom prepared for you from the foundation of the world. For I was hungry, and you gave Me something to eat; I was thirsty, and you gave Me something to drink; I was a stranger, and you invited Me in; naked, and you clothed Me; I was sick, and you visited Me; I was in prison, and you came to Me." Then the righteous will answer Him, "Lord, when did we see You hungry, and feed You, or thirsty, and give You something to drink? And when did we see You a stranger, and invite You in, or naked, and clothe You? When did we see You sick, or in prison, and come to You?" The King will answer and say to them, "Truly I say to you, to the extent that you did it to one of these brothers of Mine, even the least of them, you did it to Me." Then He will also say to those on His left, "Depart from Me, accursed ones, into the eternal fire which has been prepared for the devil and his angels; for I was hungry, and you gave Me nothing to eat; I was thirsty, and you gave Me nothing to drink; I was a stranger, and you did not invite Me in; naked, and you did not clothe Me; sick, and in prison, and you did not visit Me." Then they themselves also will answer, "Lord, when did we see You hungry, or thirsty, or a stranger, or naked, or sick, or in prison, and did not take care of You?" Then He will answer them, "Truly I say to you, to the extent that you did not do it to one of the least of these, you did not do it to Me."

These will go away into eternal punishment, but the righteous into eternal life. (Matt. 25:34–46)

The truth that how one treats a believer is how one treats Christ prompted the Lord's warning against causing **one of these little ones who believe to stumble.** Clearly, this does not refer to physical children, as the phrase **who believe** shows. *Skandalizō* (**stumble**) refers to causing someone to be tripped by temptation and fall, or to be led into sin (cf. its similar use in 2 Cor. 11:29). Verses 43, 45, and 47 of Mark 9, along with Matthew 5:29–30 and 1 Corinthians 8:13, call for drastic action to avoid being led into sinful behaviors that lead unregenerate sinners to eternal punishment in hell.

Jesus' statement that **it would be better for** one who leads a believer into sin than **if, with a heavy millstone hung around his neck, he had been cast into the sea**—in other words, that it is better to die a horrible death by drowning than to cause another Christian to sin—must have shocked His hearers. But according to 1 Corinthians 13, love takes no pleasure in seeing someone fall into sin; it "does not rejoice in unrighteousness, but rejoices with the truth" (v. 6). Peter wrote that Christians are to "keep fervent in [their] love for one another" (1 Peter 4:8). That kind of all-encompassing love does not solicit sin; it covers it. Fervent love stimulates others to holiness. It thinks more highly of others than of oneself, elevates them, and encourages them to righteousness (Phil. 2:3–4). Jesus called for radical love, the kind of righteous love that would never be a cause of sinful solicitation to another person.

Such sinful solicitation may happen in one of four ways.

First, by direct temptation; that is, by overtly enticing someone to sin against the law of God. That may involve specific sins, such as lying, gossiping, cheating, stealing, or committing sexual sins, or in more general terms inducing people to love the world, or drawing them into ungodly enterprises and activities. Potiphar's wife "looked with desire at Joseph, and she said, 'Lie with me'" (Gen. 39:7). "If sinners entice you," Solomon warned, "do not consent" (Prov. 1:10). Proverbs 7:6–23 relates the story of a brazenly immoral woman who seduced a foolish young man:

For at the window of my house I looked out through my lattice, and I saw among the naive, and discerned among the youths a young man lacking sense, passing through the street near her corner; and he takes the way to her house, in the twilight, in the evening, in the middle of the night and in the darkness. And behold, a woman comes to meet him, dressed as a harlot and cunning of heart. She is boisterous and rebellious, her feet do not remain at home; She is now in the streets, now in the squares, and lurks by every corner. So she seizes him and kisses him and with a brazen face she says to him: "I was due to offer peace offerings; today I have paid my vows. Therefore I have come out to meet you, to seek your presence earnestly, and I have found you. I have spread my couch with coverings, with colored linens of Egypt. I have sprinkled my bed with myrrh, aloes and cinnamon. Come, let us drink our fill of love until morning; let us delight ourselves with caresses. For my husband is not at home, he has gone on a long journey; he has taken a bag of money with him, at the full moon he will come home." With her many persuasions she entices him; with her flattering lips she seduces him. Suddenly he follows her as an ox goes to the slaughter, or as one in fetters to the discipline of a fool, until an arrow pierces through his liver; as a bird hastens to the snare, so he does not know that it will cost him his life.

Second, by indirect temptation. In Ephesians 6:4 Paul cautioned parents, "Do not provoke your children to anger" by such things as inattention, lack of affection, lack of forgiveness, lack of kindness, or overbearing expectations.

Third, by setting an example that will cause others to sin. Paul warned against doing so in Romans 14:13, when he wrote, "Therefore let us not judge one another anymore, but rather determine this—not to put an obstacle or a stumbling block in a brother's way." In verse 21 he elaborated on that principle: "It is good not to eat meat or to drink wine, or to do anything by which your brother stumbles." Instead,

We who are strong ought to bear the weaknesses of those without strength and not just please ourselves. Each of us is to please his neighbor for his good, to his edification. For even Christ did not please Himself; but as it is written, "The reproaches of those who reproached You fell on Me." (15:1–3)

Finally, by failing to stimulate others to righteousness, ignoring the exhortation of Hebrews 10:24: "Let us consider how to stimulate one another to love and good deeds."

RADICAL PURITY

If your hand causes you to stumble, cut it off; it is better for you to enter life crippled, than, having your two hands, to go into hell, into the unquenchable fire . . . If your foot causes you to stumble, cut it off; it is better for you to enter life lame, than, having your two feet, to be cast into hell . . . If your eye causes you to stumble, throw it out; it is better for you to enter the kingdom of God with one eye, than, having two eyes, to be cast into hell, where their worm does not die, and the fire is not quenched. (9:43, 45, 47–48)

This point is closely connected to the previous one. Christians cannot lead others into righteousness unless they are righteous themselves; if one's own heart is impure, he will lead others into sin. Therefore Jesus called for radical, severe dealing with sin. The consequences of not doing so are devastating, as the seventeenth-century English Puritan John Owen notes:

> Where sin, through the neglect of mortification, gets a considerable victory, it breaks the bones of the soul (Ps. 31:10; 51:8), and makes a man weak, sick, and ready to die (Ps. 38:3–5), so that he cannot look up (Ps. 40:12; Isa. 33:24); and when poor creatures will take blow after blow, wound after wound, foil after foil, and never rouse up themselves to a vigorous opposition, can they expect anything but to be hardened through the deceitfulness of sin, and that their souls should bleed to death (2 John 8)? (Kelly M. Kapic and Justin Taylor, eds., *Overcoming Sin and Temptation* [Wheaton: Crossway, 2006], 54)

The Old Testament account of Samuel hacking Agag to pieces (1 Sam. 15:33) is a good analogy for the need for Christians to take drastic steps to defeat the sin that remains in their lives. That is explicitly commanded in the New Testament. "For if you are living according to the flesh," Paul wrote, "you must die; but if by the Spirit you are putting to death the deeds of the body, you will live" (Rom. 8:13). In Colossians 3:5 he added, "Therefore consider the members of your earthly body as dead to immorality, impurity, passion, evil desire, and greed, which amounts to idolatry." Christians are to "deny ungodliness and worldly desires and to live sensibly, righteously and godly in the present age" (Titus 2:12). Peter exhorted his readers to "abstain from fleshly lusts which wage war against the soul" (1 Peter 2:11).

The mention of body parts—**hand, foot,** and **eye**—emphasizes that the battle against sin includes all aspects of believers' lives; what they do, where they go, and what they see. The references to **hell** as the disastrous alternative indicate that these statements are calls to the initial repentance and faith in Jesus Christ that accompanies salvation (cf. James 4:8). They prompt people to remove anything in their lives that would be a barrier to entering into eternal **life** in the **kingdom of God.** But the present tense of the verb translated **causes** in these verses indicates that the struggle against temptation and sin is continual. There is no salvation apart from a heart that seeks after righteousness (Matt. 5:6). But that initial commitment then becomes the believer's lifelong pattern (Rom. 13:14; 1 Cor. 9:24–27; 2 Cor. 7:1). Jesus called for radical, severe action against anything that hinders the pursuit of holiness, righteousness, and purity throughout the Christian life.

The action He had in mind both here and in the similar metaphoric language in Matthew 5:29–30 was not, of course, physical mutilation. Misguided ascetics over the centuries have foolishly assumed that the way to defeat sin was through emasculating or otherwise mutilating themselves. But a person with one hand, foot, or eye is no less capable of sinning, because no matter what body parts are lost, sin remains in the heart:

> And He was saying, "That which proceeds out of the man, that is what defiles the man. For from within, out of the heart of men, proceed the evil thoughts, fornications, thefts, murders, adulteries, deeds of coveting and wickedness, as well as deceit, sensuality, envy, slander, pride and foolishness. All these evil things proceed from within and defile the man." (Mark 7:20–23; cf. v. 15)

James added, "Each one is tempted when he is carried away and enticed by his own lust. Then when lust has conceived, it gives birth to sin; and when sin is accomplished, it brings forth death" (James 1:14–15; cf. Prov. 4:23).

Gehenna (**hell**) appears twelve times in the New Testament, all but one of those uses by Christ (vv. 43, 45, 47; Matt. 5:22, 29, 30; 10:28; 18:9; 23:15, 33; Luke 12:5; cf. James 3:6). As the reference to **unquenchable fire** indicates, *gehenna* always refers to the eternal hell, the lake of fire, never to the place of the dead in general, which is identified by a different word, *hades.* The name *gehenna* derives from the Old Testament valley of Hinnom, located just south of Jerusalem (Josh. 15:8; 18:16; 2 Kings 23:10; 2 Chron. 28:3; 33:6; Neh. 11:30; Jer. 7:31–32; 19:2, 6; 32:35). There the apostate Jewish people sacrificed infants to Molech, the abominable false god of the Ammonites (1 Kings 11:7), by burning them to death (2 Kings 17:17; 21:6; Jer. 32:35)—an appalling practice that God strictly prohibited (Lev. 18:21; 20:2–5) and strongly condemned (Jer. 7:31–32; 32:35). Both the wicked kings Ahaz (2 Chron. 28:3) and Manasseh (before he repented, 2 Chron. 33:6) sacrificed their children in the valley of Hinnom. Because of those sacrifices, the place became known as Topheth, which derives from a Hebrew word meaning drum. Evidently drums were beaten loudly to drown out the screams of the babies being burned alive. As part of his reforms, the godly king Josiah destroyed that place of sacrifice. The valley of Hinnom was turned into Jerusalem's garbage dump, where a fire burned continually in the midst of the rubbish. It thus became a graphic illustration of eternal hell, a place **where their worm does not die, and the fire is not quenched** (cf. Isa. 66:24).

These words compose the strongest call to discipleship our Lord ever gave. He challenges everyone to either deal radically with sin, or be cast into the eternal garbage pit of hell, "the outer darkness" (Matt. 8:12), "the furnace of fire" (Matt. 13:42), where "there will be weeping and gnashing of teeth" (Matt. 22:13).

RADICAL SACRIFICE

For everyone will be salted with fire. (9:49)

The meaning of this cryptic and difficult saying can best be understood by examining Scripture passages in which salt and fire are mentioned together. Ezra 6:9 and Ezekiel 43:23–24 connect both salt and fire with the Old Testament sacrifices. Salt, a preservative, was added to the sacrifices when they were burned as a symbol of God's enduring covenant. Specifically, the grain offering seems to be in view here. In Leviticus 2:13, God commanded the people of Israel, "Every grain offering of yours, moreover, you shall season with salt, so that the salt of the covenant of your God shall not be lacking from your grain offering; with all your offerings you shall offer salt."

The grain offering, one of the five Old Testament offerings along with the burnt, peace, sin, and guilt offerings, was an offering of consecration, symbolizing total devotion to the Lord. Just as salt symbolized God's enduring faithfulness, so **everyone,** that is all believers, should make a long-term, enduring, permanent sacrifice of their lives to God; "to present [their] bodies a living and holy sacrifice, acceptable to God, which is [their] spiritual service of worship" (Rom. 12:1).

Radical Obedience

Salt is good; but if the salt becomes unsalty, with what will you make it salty again? Have salt in yourselves, and be at peace with one another." (9:50)

In the days before refrigeration, **salt** was **good** because it was the most widely used preservative for food. Chemically, salt (sodium chloride) is very stable and does not easily degrade. But sometimes salt gathered from the vicinity of the Dead Sea was contaminated with gypsum. If not properly processed, it could lose its effectiveness as a preservative and become **unsalty** and tasteless (Luke 14:34). Since it could not be made **salty again,** such salt was "useless either for the soil or for the manure pile; [and was] thrown out" (Luke 14:35).

Thus, Jesus' command, **Have salt in yourselves,** is a call to radical obedience; to a holy life preserved by righteousness. He then gave the disciple a direct practical application, commanding them to **"be at peace with one another"**—a fitting challenge to those proud, self-serving, hypercompetitive men who were constantly bickering over which of them was the greatest (cf. 9:34; Matt. 18:1–4; 20:20–24; Luke 22:24).

When believers engage in radically loving, pure, sacrificial, obedient discipleship, they will be radical witnesses. Christians are the only true "salt of the earth" (Matt. 5:13). There are no other spiritual influences for modeling the truth other than the lives of true disciples of Jesus Christ, who are known by the radical nature of their discipleship.

The Truth about Divorce (Mark 10:1–12)

6

Getting up, He went from there to the region of Judea and beyond the Jordan; crowds gathered around Him again, and, according to His custom, He once more began to teach them. Some Pharisees came up to Jesus, testing Him, and began to question Him whether it was lawful for a man to divorce a wife. And He answered and said to them, "What did Moses command you?" They said, "Moses permitted a man to write a certificate of divorce and send her away." But Jesus said to them, "Because of your hardness of heart he wrote you this commandment. But from the beginning of creation, God made them male and female. For this reason a man shall leave his father and mother, and the two shall become one flesh; so they are no longer two, but one flesh. What therefore God has joined together, let no man separate." In the house the disciples began questioning Him about this again. And He said to them, "Whoever divorces his wife and marries another woman commits adultery against her; and if she herself divorces her husband and marries another man, she is committing adultery." (10:1–12)

Divorce has lost all its negative stigma and has become a widely accepted, extremely popular option in society. As the church is shaped by the culture, it has also become increasingly accepted and common there. Still, views regarding divorce run the gamut among Christians from allowing it for any reason, to forbidding it for any reason. But those who tolerate it are becoming the majority.

The church's view of divorce, however, must not be based on the shifting sands of societal norms but on the bedrock of biblical truth. And the Bible is not unclear on the subject, nor are the correct interpretations elusive, in spite of the claims of some. The most important question is not what anyone says about divorce but what God thinks of it. The biblical answer to that question is straightforward and unambiguous. In His own words God declared the bottom line: "'I hate divorce,' says the Lord, the God of Israel" (Mal. 2:16).

Israel's history provides the backdrop for that divine attitude. After centuries of rebellion and idolatry, God's devastating judgment fell on Israel so that the nation suffered seventy years of captivity in Babylon. When the exiles returned from exile, they rebuilt Jerusalem and the temple, though their religion had degenerated into mere external ritualism. Their attitudes toward God were demeaning, unrighteous, and hardhearted. Despite their outward show of religion, their hearts were full of sin and disobedience. Malachi's prophecy, written after the return from exile, indicted the people for their sins in very specific terms and called them to repentance.

Writing at about the same time, Nehemiah identified the same sins that Malachi saw and denounced. One of those sins characterizing postexilic Israel was intermarriage with pagan women:

> In those days I [Nehemiah] also saw that the Jews had married women from Ashdod, Ammon and Moab. As for their children, half spoke in the language of Ashdod, and none of them was able to speak the language of Judah, but the language of his own people. So I contended with them and cursed them and struck some of them and pulled out their hair, and made them swear by God, "You shall not give your daughters to their sons, nor take of their daughters for your sons or for yourselves. Did not Solomon king of Israel sin regarding these things? Yet among the many nations there was no king like him, and he was loved by his God, and God made him king over all Israel; nevertheless the foreign

women caused even him to sin. Do we then hear about you that you have committed all this great evil by acting unfaithfully against our God by marrying foreign women?" Even one of the sons of Joiada, the son of Eliashib the high priest, was a son-in-law of Sanballat the Horonite, so I drove him away from me. Remember them, O my God, because they have defiled the priesthood and the covenant of the priesthood and the Levites. (Neh. 13:23–29)

It was the divorcing of their Jewish wives to marry pagan Gentile women that the Lord condemned through Malachi. The priests were taking the lead in this violation of God's law (Mal. 2:1), setting a corruptive example that the rest of the people readily followed (v. 8). The Lord warned them that judgment would follow unless they repented and turned from their sinful ways (vv. 2–13). They had profaned the temple by their marriages to pagan idolaters, and dealt treacherously with their Jewish wives by violating the marriage covenant (v. 14). That history led to God's declaration, "I hate divorce" (v. 16).

As this section opened, Jesus and the Twelve left the house in Capernaum where He had taught them regarding humility and radical discipleship (9:28–50). With the Lord's ministry in Galilee at an end, they headed for **Judea,** where Jesus ministered for about six months. Mark (along with Matthew) does not record His ministry in Judea (though Luke and John do) but goes directly to the Lord's subsequent ministry in the **region . . . beyond the Jordan** to the east, known as Perea. His ultimate destination, of course, was Jerusalem and His death on the cross. Large **crowds,** consisting of both Jews who lived in that region and Galileans traveling through Perea to avoid Samaria **gathered around Him again, and, according to His custom, He once more began to teach** and heal (Matt. 19:2) **them.** Dogging His steps as usual, seeking an opportunity to discredit Him before the people, were His bitter and relentless enemies, the Pharisees.

The Lord's teaching on the subject of divorce, given in the context of a discussion with the Pharisees, may be examined under four headings: the confrontation, the clarification, the contention, and the accommodation.

THE CONFRONTATION

Some Pharisees came up to Jesus, testing Him, and began to question Him whether it was lawful for a man to divorce a wife. (10:2)

The **Pharisees** who approached **Jesus** and **began to question Him whether it was lawful for a man to divorce a wife** were not seeking truth. They were well aware of His teaching on the subject, since He had stated it publicly (cf. Matt. 5:31–32). Instead, they were testing Him, hoping to discredit Him in the eyes of the people. Like their post-exilic ancestors, the leaders and people of Jesus' day also viewed divorce and remarriage as acceptable. The Old Testament standard had long since been abandoned. In its place an accommodating view, championed by the prominent rabbi Hillel (110 B.C.–A.D. 10), had made divorce easy. According to that view, a man was permitted to divorce his wife for anything she did that displeased him, even such trivial matters as burning his dinner, allowing someone to see her ankles, letting her hair down, making a negative comment about her mother-in-law, or if all else failed, because he found someone else that he preferred to her.

The Pharisees planned to portray Jesus as an intolerant hard-liner, who identified both the people and their leaders as adulterers and adulteresses. That, they hoped, would turn the populace against Him. In addition, Perea was ruled by Herod Antipas, who had imprisoned and, at the behest of his wife, Herodias, executed John the Baptist for disapproving of his own immoral divorce and remarriage (Mark 6:17–18). Perhaps, they reasoned, Herod and Herodias might do the same to Jesus if He publicly opposed divorce.

THE CLARIFICATION

But from the beginning of creation, God made them male and female. For this reason a man shall leave his father and mother, and the two shall become one flesh; so they are no longer two, but one flesh. What therefore God has joined together, let no man separate. (10:6–9)

As will be discussed later in this chapter, Jesus ignored the rabbinic teachings and traditions and went straight to the Old Testament. From it, He gave four reasons why God hates divorce and it is unlawful.

First, because marriage is an indissoluble union between one man and one woman. According to Matthew 19:4, Jesus prefaced His reply with a pointed rebuke of the Pharisees' spiritual pride. "Have you not read?" Despite their vaunted expertise in the law of Moses, Jesus indicted them for their ignorance of it. Adam and Eve form the pattern for marriage, since at **the beginning of creation, God made** one **male and** one **female.** Divorce then was impossible, since there were no other people to remarry.

Second, because of the strength of the union. The Hebrew word translated "joined" in Genesis 2:24 denotes the strongest possible bond and can be translated "cling," "fasten its grip," "follow closely," "hold fast," "stay close," "stick together," or "stuck." Marriage involves two people unbreakably connected together, glued and pursuing hard after each other to be united in mind, will, spirit, body, and emotion.

Third, because of the unbreakable unity of the marriage bond. So strong is the union between husband and wife that the **two . . . become one flesh; so they are no longer two, but one flesh.** That indivisible oneness is seen most clearly in the product of the **two**—their children. Breaking the marriage bond also breaks the family bond, inflicting further damage.

Finally, because marriage is God's work. Every marriage is an act of God by which He bestows upon a man and a woman the common grace of a fulfilling union producing children. Since it is God who creates the partnership, breaking a marriage destroys something divinely made. Therefore, Jesus commanded, **"What therefore God has joined together, let no man separate."**

Divine revelation on marriage and divorce was clear and unambiguous. It offered no support for the contemporary Jewish view that divorce was permissible for any reason. Several related principles may be noted. First, adultery was forbidden (Ex. 20:14) and punishable by death (Lev. 20:10). Second, premarital sex was also punished (Lev. 19:20). Third, coveting another person's spouse was forbidden (Ex. 20:17; cf. Matt. 5:28).

It is the unavoidable conflict in marriage that may lead to divorce, hostility that stems from the fall and the resulting curse on Adam (Gen. 3:17–19) and Eve (v. 16) and their descendants. The man is cursed in relation to his work and the woman is cursed in connection with bearing children and submitting to her husband.

The curse on the woman in particular provides helpful insight on why there is conflict in marriage: "Your desire will be for your husband, and he will rule over you." That is not a reference to a woman's normal romantic, psychological, or emotional attraction to her husband, since it is part of the curse. The Hebrew word translated "desire" is only used one other time in the Pentateuch, in Genesis 4:7. There God warned Cain, "Sin is crouching at the door; and its desire is for you, but you must master it." The same language is used in the curse on the woman in 3:16—she will desire to control her husband, and he will have to master her. Commenting on this verse, John H. Sailhamer writes,

> [The Hebrew word translated "desire"] is "unusual and striking" (BDB, p. 1003). Apart from 3:16, it occurs only in Gen. 4:7 and S of Songs 7:10. Its use in S of Songs shows that the "longing" can refer to physical attraction, but in Gen. 4:7 the "longing" carries the sense of a desire to overcome or defeat another. . . . The way that the whole of this section of the curse . . . foreshadows the Lord's words to Cain in 4:7 . . . "it desires to have you but you must master it" suggests that the author intended the two passages to be read together. If so, the sense of "desiring" in 3:16 should be understood as the wife's desire to overcome or gain the upper hand over her husband. In the same way, the sense of [the Hebrew word] is as in the NIV: "he will rule over you." Within the context of the Creation account in chapters 2 and 3, this last statement stands in sharp contrast to the picture of the man and the woman as "one flesh" . . . and the picture of the woman as a "helper suitable for him." The Fall has had its effect on the relationship of the husband and wife. ("Genesis," in Frank E. Gaebelein, ed. *The Expositor's Bible Commentary* [Grand Rapids: Baker, 1990], 2:58)

Before the fall Adam and Eve were free from disagreement, working jointly to "be fruitful and multiply, and fill the earth, and subdue it; and rule over the fish of the sea and over the birds of the sky and over every living thing that moves on the earth" (Gen. 1:28). They complemented each other perfectly and lived together in harmony as co-regents over creation.

But after the temptation by Satan and their fall, that perfect harmony was shattered for them and every other married couple coming from them. Wives, by the curse, seek to be independent of their husband's authority, to dominate the relationship and impose their will on their husbands. Husbands, on the other hand, by the same curse, seek to suppress their wives' revolt against their authority, often in a harsh, ungracious, autocratic manner. This regular conflict between two sinners, living intimately together, can produce animosity that leads to divorce.

THE CONTENTION

And He answered and said to them, "What did Moses command you?" They said, "Moses permitted a man to write a certificate of divorce and send her away." (10:3–4)

Not only did the Lord clarify the biblical teaching on divorce, He also challenged the Pharisees' unbiblical view. Cutting through the rabbinic accretions, He pointed them back to the Old Testament's teaching by asking, **"What did Moses command you?"** They had a ready answer, since they believed they had found a passage in the Law that supported their view that divorce was permissible for any reason. Confidently **they said** to Jesus, **"Moses permitted a man to write a certificate of divorce and send her away."** The passage in question is Deuteronomy 24:1–4:

> When a man takes a wife and marries her, and it happens that she finds no favor in his eyes because he has found some indecency in her, and he writes her a certificate of divorce and puts it in her hand and sends her out from his house, and she leaves his house and goes and becomes another man's wife, and if the latter husband turns against her and writes her a certificate of divorce and puts it in her hand and sends her out of his house, or if the latter husband dies who took her to be his wife, then her former husband who sent her away is not allowed to take her again to be his wife, since she has been defiled; for that is an abomination before the Lord, and you shall not bring sin on the land which the Lord your God gives you as an inheritance.

They camped on the word "indecency" and, as noted earlier in this chapter, expanded it to mean virtually anything they desired.

There is, however, no command or explicit permission given to divorce anywhere in this passage; it merely describes a situation in which a man gets married, decides he does not like his wife, divorces her, and she marries someone else. The sole command is in verse 4: In such cases "her former husband who sent her away is not allowed to take her again to be his wife." Far from commanding or even permitting divorce, this injunction merely forbids a man to remarry a woman that he has divorced who has then been married to someone else. The passage recognizes and regulates the reality of divorce without condoning or condemning it.

The Hebrew word translated "indecency" literally means "nakedness," not in a physical sense but in the sense of something shameful. The same word is used in Deuteronomy 23:14 to describe things in the camp of Israel that the holy God must not see. The term does not refer to adultery, the only biblical grounds for divorce, but to sinful behavior short of adultery. It describes things that violate normal social responsibility and behavior in a civilized culture and hence are disrespectful of others. The word certainly cannot be extrapolated to mean anything that a man disliked about his wife, as the Pharisees were doing.

THE ACCOMMODATION

But Jesus said to them, "Because of your hardness of heart he wrote you this commandment." . . . In the house the disciples began questioning Him about this again. And He said to them, "Whoever divorces his wife and marries another woman commits adultery against her; and if she herself divorces her husband and marries another man, she is committing adultery." (10:5, 10–12)

Although the Law decreed that adulterers were to be executed, God was merciful in the application of that law. After his extramarital affair with Bathsheba, "David said to Nathan, 'I have sinned against the

Lord.' And Nathan said to David, 'The Lord also has taken away your sin; you shall not die'" (2 Sam. 12:13). By the time of Christ, few people were being executed for adultery. Not only were people not being executed for adultery, they also were divorcing their wives at will, all the while deluding themselves into thinking the Old Testament permitted them to do so. The Old Testament recognized divorce on the grounds of adultery and God mercifully suspended the death sentence for adulterers **because of** the people's **hardness of heart,** which is why Moses **wrote** them **this commandment.** But the Pharisees and others in Christ's day were so far from God's standard for marriage that they were divorcing their wives on the slightest whim.

Back **in the house** in Perea where they were staying, **the disciples began questioning Him about this again,** seeking further clarification. In reply, Jesus succinctly summarized the divine position: **"Whoever divorces his wife and marries another woman commits adultery against her; and if she herself divorces her husband and marries another man, she is committing adultery."** Yet God did permit divorce in some unusual circumstances. In Deuteronomy 7:1–3 God strictly prohibited the Israelites from intermarrying with the pagan people of Canaan:

> When the Lord your God brings you into the land where you are entering to possess it, and clears away many nations before you, the Hittites and the Girgashites and the Amorites and the Canaanites and the Perizzites and the Hivites and the Jebusites, seven nations greater and stronger than you, and when the Lord your God delivers them before you and you defeat them, then you shall utterly destroy them. You shall make no covenant with them and show no favor to them. Furthermore, you shall not intermarry with them; you shall not give your daughters to their sons, nor shall you take their daughters for your sons.

Yet that is exactly what the people did after the exile (Ezra 9:1–2). After being rebuked by Ezra

> Shecaniah the son of Jehiel, one of the sons of Elam, said to Ezra, "We have been unfaithful to our God and have married foreign women from the peoples of the land; yet now there is hope for Israel in spite of this. So now let us make a covenant with our God to put away all the wives and their children, according to the counsel of my lord and of

> those who tremble at the commandment of our God; and let it be done
> according to the law." (10:2–3)

The result was mass divorce (vv. 5–44). While God hates divorce, He hates idolatry even more; divorce was a lesser evil than having Israel relapse into the idolatrous false religion that had led to the Babylonian exile.

Israel committed spiritual adultery in her relationship with God. Yet He was faithful to His covenant with David and did not divorce Judah (Isa. 50:1), though there would be a time of separation. The apostate northern kingdom (Israel), however, was not ruled by kings from the Davidic line, and after patiently waiting despite centuries of idolatry, He did divorce Israel for her spiritual infidelity (Jer. 3:8). Joseph, a righteous man, could legally have divorced Mary for her supposed infidelity (a Jewish betrothal, far more binding than a modern engagement, could only be ended by a divorce, Matt. 1:19). Those two illustrations demonstrate that, as noted above, adultery was the only grounds for divorce in the Old Testament.

The New Testament also affirms that adultery is grounds for divorce. Although Mark does not mention the so-called exception clause, Matthew does (19:9; cf. 5:32). Adultery does not have to end a marriage (cf. the story of Hosea and his adulterous wife, Gomer, in the book of Hosea). But God's sparing the life of an unrepentant adulterer is not meant to penalize that person's innocent spouse. The New Testament also reveals that if an unbeliever divorces a believer, the latter is free to remarry (1 Cor. 7:15).

As they realized the seriousness of the marriage relationship, "the disciples said to [Jesus], 'If the relationship of the man with his wife is like this, it is better not to marry'" (Matt. 19:10). That may be true in theory, but in practice, "Not all men can accept this statement, but only those to whom it has been given" (v. 11). Not everyone can be fulfilled in a single state (1 Cor. 7:9).

What makes a strong marriage; one that will stand firm against the pressures to divorce? In the inspired words of the apostle Paul,

> Husbands ought also to love their own wives as their own bodies. He
> who loves his own wife loves himself; for no one ever hated his own

flesh, but nourishes and cherishes it, just as Christ also does the church, because we are members of His body. For this reason a man shall leave his father and mother and shall be joined to his wife, and the two shall become one flesh. This mystery is great; but I am speaking with reference to Christ and the church. Nevertheless, each individual among you also is to love his own wife even as himself, and the wife must see to it that she respects her husband. (Eph. 5:28–33)

Why Jesus Blessed the Little Children (Mark 10:13–16)

7

And they were bringing children to Him so that He might touch them; but the disciples rebuked them. But when Jesus saw this, He was indignant and said to them, "Permit the children to come to Me; do not hinder them; for the kingdom of God belongs to such as these. Truly I say to you, whoever does not receive the kingdom of God like a child will not enter it at all." And He took them in His arms and began blessing them, laying His hands on them. (10:13–16)

This incident is recorded in all three Synoptic Gospels (cf. Matt. 19:13–15; Luke 18:15–17). Although brief, it is of great significance, because it answers the important question of what happens eternally to infants or young children when they die.

The answer Jesus gave, that they are part of God's kingdom, ran counter to the prevailing view of the apostate Judaism of His day. According to the Pharisees' works-righteousness system, such children were incapable of understanding and keeping the law, or of performing any good works that would earn salvation. Hence, the idea that they could enter the kingdom was absurd.

By identifying young children as part of His kingdom despite their inability to do anything to earn salvation, Jesus did more than merely violate the conventional wisdom of the day. The salvation of such children is as a powerful an illustration of the biblical truth that salvation is by grace alone as any reality. Thus, this incident stands in sharp contrast to the one that immediately follows it in all three Synoptic Gospels, namely, the Lord's encounter with a rich, young ruler (see chapter 8 of this volume). That man seemed to have the inside track to the kingdom. He was extremely wealthy (Luke 18:23), fastidiously self-righteous (Mark 10:20), and deeply religious (Luke calls him a "ruler" [Luke 18:18], probably of a local synagogue). Yet he remained outside of the kingdom (Matt. 19:23), while these children were in it.

The crucial incident may be viewed under four headings: the sought for blessing, the sharp rebuke, the special care, and the salvation analogy.

THE STORY'S SETTING

And they were bringing children to Him so that He might touch them; (10:13*a*)

Jewish parents commonly brought their **children** to the elders of the local synagogue or to prominent rabbis so that they might pronounce blessing on them. In a similar vein, the Old Testament records the paternal blessings of their children by Noah (Gen. 9:26–27), Isaac (Gen. 27:1–41), and Jacob (Gen. 49:28). Because of His great affection for children, parents often brought theirs to Jesus (cf. 9:36–37; Matt. 21:15–16). His affection for children, however, did not make Him naively sentimental about them. Jesus understood that children were sinners, and used a story about peevish and obstinate children to rebuke the Pharisees for their rejection of Him and John the Baptist (Matt. 11:16–19).

Paidia (**children**) is a general term for children. In his account of this incident, however, Luke used a form of the word *brephos*, which refers specifically to unborn babies, newborns, or young infants (Luke 18:15; cf. 1:41, 44; 2:12, 16; Acts 7:19; 1 Peter 2:2). Many parents in the huge crowd (Matt. 19:2), who saw His love, power, and majesty, and heard His preaching and teaching about the kingdom, salvation, and eternal life, were bringing their babies to Jesus **so that He might touch them.** These were parents who wanted their children to know God, to be a part of His kingdom, and to have eternal life, as any sensible parents would. They wanted Jesus to pray for their children's spiritual well-being; that God would show favor to them.

THE SHARP REBUKE

but the disciples rebuked them. (10:13*b*)

The **disciples,** still influenced by the works-righteousness system in which they had been raised, were not on board with the parents' enthusiastic desire to have Jesus bless their children. They saw the children as little more than unnecessary interruptions to the Lord's ministry, and sharply **rebuked** the parents for disturbing Him. **Rebuked** translates a form of the verb *epitimaō*, an intensified form of the verb *timaō*. *Epitimaō* means "to censure," or "to reprimand"; the related noun is translated "punishment" in 2 Corinthians 2:6. Mark used the word to describe Jesus' rebuke of demons (Mark 1:25; 3:12; 9:25), and a storm (4:39), His warning to the disciples not to reveal that He was the Messiah (8:30), Peter's rebuke of Jesus (8:32) and the Lord's subsequent rebuke of Peter (8:33), and the crowd's rebuke of a blind man who kept calling out to Jesus (10:48).

THE SPECIAL BLESSING

But when Jesus saw this, He was indignant and said to them, "Permit the children to come to Me; do not hinder them; for the kingdom of God belongs to such as these. (10:14)

The disciples' overzealous rebuke of the parents prompted an **indignant** response from Jesus. The verb translated **indignant** is also a strong word, meaning "angry," "irate," or "outraged." It describes the reaction of the scribes and Pharisees to the children in the temple who were hailing Jesus as the Messiah (Matt. 21:15), the reaction of the other ten disciples to the request by James and John for the chief seats in the kingdom (Mark 10:41), the reaction of some present when a woman anointed Jesus with expensive perfume (Mark 14:4), and the reaction of a synagogue official when Jesus healed on the Sabbath (Luke 13:14). The term indicates that Jesus was seriously agitated at the disciples for the way they treated the children. Nor did Jesus rebuke the parents who brought their children to Him. The disciples were the sole target of His rebuke, because of their wrong assumptions and misunderstanding of Scripture.

Nothing was said about the spiritual condition of the parents, or whether they were believers or unbelievers. The children's faith was also a nonissue. Such children are not by conscious choice unbelievers or believers; they can neither receive divine salvation truth, nor reject it.

The Lord's response to the disciples was emphatic. **"Permit the children to come to Me,"** He commanded; **"do not hinder them."** The present tense of the verb translated **hinder** indicates that the disciples were to continue to allow the parents and their children to have access to Christ. It was essential that the children be allowed to come to Him because, as He told the disciples, **"the kingdom of God** (the sphere of salvation) **belongs to such as these."** The Lord's statement is unqualified; there are no caveats, conditions, or restrictions attached to it. He did not apply it only to the children of faithful Jews, circumcised (or baptized) children, elect children, or only to those infants present on that particular occasion. Luke's use of the Greek word *toioutōn* ("such as these") instead of *toutois* ("these") indicates that Jesus was referring to all those who are unable to believe savingly because they have not reached the point of personal accountability (Luke 18:16).

It is obvious that Jesus did not pronounce blessing on people outside His kingdom. All such people belong to Satan's kingdom (John 8:44; Col. 1:13; 1 John 3:8) and are cursed. Babies, before they reach the age when they understand good and evil (which varies from child to child), are under God's gracious, special care. If they die before that time, their souls will go to heaven; once past that point, God will hold them responsible if they fail to repent and believe the gospel.

The comforting truth that young children who die will go to heaven does not, of course, mean that they are not sinners, even though they have not consciously chosen to sin. The Bible is clear that every human since the fall has been born a sinner, inheriting Adam's sinful nature, which he passed on to all his descendants (Rom. 5:12–21; cf. the tragic refrain "and he died" in the genealogy recorded in Gen. 5). That corrupt nature is present from conception. David wrote, "Behold, I was brought forth in iniquity, and in sin my mother conceived me" (Ps. 51:5). Psalm 58:3 confirms the reality that "the wicked are estranged from the womb; these who speak lies go astray from birth." In Genesis 8:21 God said, "The intent of man's heart is evil from his youth" (cf. Isa. 48:8). Proverbs 22:15 notes that "foolishness is bound up in the heart of a child." The very fact that babies can die demonstrates the reality that they are not morally neutral (the historic position of Pelagianism, Semi-Pelagianism, and Arminianism) but sinners, since death results from sin; it is the wages sin pays everyone (Rom. 6:23).

That all infants without exception grow up to be sinful adults offers further proof that they are sinners. In 1 Kings 8:46 Solomon noted that "there is no man who does not sin." David pleaded to God, "Do not enter into judgment with Your servant, for in Your sight no man living is righteous" (Ps. 143:2). Solomon asked rhetorically, "Who can say, 'I have cleansed my heart, I am pure from my sin'?" (Prov. 20:9). In Ecclesiastes 7:20 he added, "Indeed, there is not a righteous man on earth who continually does good and who never sins." God said through Jeremiah, "The heart is more deceitful than all else and is desperately sick; who can understand it?" (Jer. 17:9). Paul affirmed the universality of sin in the human race when he wrote, "There is none righteous, not even one; there is none who understands, there is none who seeks for God; all have turned aside, together they have become useless; there is none who does good, there is not even one" (Rom. 3:10–12). Sinfulness is not a condition that people enter when they sin but one they are born into that causes them to do evil. In other words, people are not sinners because they sin; they sin because they are sinners. So babies and young children are in

God's kingdom solely by an act of His grace.

It is not true, however, that such children have eternal life and then lose it once they reach the condition of accountability,since eternal life,by definition,cannot be less than eternal (John 3:15–16;5:24;6:40,54; 10:28–29). Instead, God holds them in a condition of grace until they reach the age where they become accountable before Him.That temporary, conditional grace will become eternal for those who die before becoming accountable.The Bible teaches that they are viewed as innocent in God's sight. God referred to the young children in Israel as those "who this day have no knowledge of good or evil" (Deut. 1:39). God withheld His judgment on Nineveh in part because of the children in the city "who [did] not know the difference between their right and left hand" (Jonah 4:11). Since they are not old enough to know the difference between right and wrong, young children are not culpable for breaking God's law and are innocent before Him (cf. Jer. 19:4–5, where God referred to children sacrificed to Baal as innocent and Ezek. 16:21, where He called them "My children"). Explaining why God graciously spares such children R. A. Webb wrote,

> If a dead infant were sent to hell on no other account than that of original sin, there would be a good reason to the Divine Mind for the judgment, because sin is a reality. But the child's mind would be a perfect blank as to the reason of its suffering. Under such circumstances, it would know suffering but it would have no understanding of the reason for its suffering.It could not tell itself why it was so awfully smitten, and consequently, the whole meaning and significance of its sufferings, being to it a conscious enigma, the very essence of the penalty would be absent and justice would be disappointed, cheated of its validation. (*The Theology of Infant Salvation* [Richmond, Va.: Presbyterian Committee of Publications, 1907], 42)

In the midst of his suffering, Job lamented,

> Why did I not die at birth,
> Come forth from the womb and expire?
> Why did the knees receive me,
> And why the breasts, that I should suck?
> For now I would have lain down and been quiet;
> I would have slept then, I would have been at rest,

With kings and with counselors of the earth,
Who rebuilt ruins for themselves;
Or with princes who had gold,
Who were filling their houses with silver.
Or like a miscarriage which is discarded, I would not be,
As infants that never saw light.
There the wicked cease from raging,
And there the weary are at rest. (Job 3:11–17)

So intense was his suffering that Job wished he had been a miscarriage or a stillborn child and entered directly into heavenly rest.

As I noted in an earlier volume in this commentary series,

Perhaps the most helpful illustration in the Old Testament of the salvation of infants who die is found in 2 Samuel 12. After David's horrific sins of committing adultery with Bathsheba and then murdering her husband in a botched attempt to cover it up, he was rebuked by Nathan the prophet. After David confessed his sin (v. 13), Nathan assured him of God's forgiveness, but informed him that one of the consequences of his sin was that his son with Bathsheba would die (v. 14). For seven days, the distraught king fasted and prayed for the life of his son. When he perceived that the child was dead, David "arose from the ground, washed, anointed himself, and changed his clothes; and he came into the house of the Lord and worshiped. Then he came to his own house, and when he requested, they set food before him and he ate" (v. 20). His astonished "servants said to him, 'What is this thing that you have done? While the child was alive, you fasted and wept; but when the child died, you arose and ate food'" (v. 21). David explained that while the child was still alive, there was hope that God would relent and spare his life (v. 22). But after the child died, there was no further point in fasting (v. 23).

Then David confidently said at the end of verse 23, "I will go to him, but he will not return to me." He knew that after his own death, he would be in God's presence (cf. Ps. 17:15), and the certainty that he would be reunited with his son in heaven secured for him comfort and hope.

In contrast, when his rebellious adult son Absalom died, David was inconsolable (2 Sam. 18:33–19:4). He knew that after he died, he would be reunited with his son by Bathsheba. But David knew there was no such hope of a reunion after death with Absalom, the murderer (2 Sam. 13:22–33) and rebel. (*Luke 18–24*, The MacArthur New Testament Commentary [Chicago: Moody, 2014], 29)

The salvation of infants who die has been the church's teaching for centuries. The great reformer John Calvin wrote,

Those little children have not yet any understanding to desire his blessing; but when they are presented to him, he gently and kindly receives
them, and dedicates them to the Father by a solemn act of blessing.…
To exclude from the grace of redemption those who are of that age
would be too cruel … it is presumption and sacrilege to drive far from
the fold of Christ those whom he cherishes in his bosom, and to shut
the door, and exclude as strangers those whom he does not wish to be
forbidden to come to him. (*Commentary on a Harmony of Matthew,
Mark, and Luke* [Edinburgh: Calvin Translation Society, 1845), 2:389,
390–91)

The eminent nineteenth-century theologian Charles Hodge wrote, "Of
such [children] He tells us is the kingdom of heaven, as though heaven
was, in great measure, composed of the souls of redeemed infants" (*Systematic Theology* [repr., Grand Rapids: Eerdmans, 1979], 1:27). B. B.
Warfield, the respected nineteenth-century Princeton theologian, also
argued that Scripture teaches the salvation of infants:

Their destiny is determined irrespective of their choice, by an unconditional decree of God, suspended for its execution on no act of their
own; and their salvation is wrought by an unconditional application of
the grace of Christ to their souls, through the immediate and irresistible
operation of the Holy Spirit prior to and apart from any action of their
own proper wills … And if death in infancy does depend on God's
providence, it is assuredly God in His providence who selects this vast
multitude to be made participants of His unconditional salvation …
This is but to say that they are unconditionally predestined to salvation
from the foundation of the world. If only a single infant dying in infancy
be saved, the whole Arminian principle is traversed. If all infants dying
such are saved, not only the majority of the saved, but doubtless the
majority of the human race hitherto, have entered into life by a non-
Arminian pathway. (Cited in Loraine Boettner, *The Reformed Doctrine of
Predestination* [Phillipsburg, N.J.: Presbyterian and Reformed, 1980],
143–44; for a further discussion of the salvation of infants, see John
MacArthur, *Safe in the Arms of God* [Nashville: Thomas Nelson, 2003].)

THE SALVATION ANALOGY

**Truly I say to you, whoever does not receive the kingdom of God
like a child will not enter it at all."** (10:15)

The salvation of young children is an apt analogy that demonstrates that salvation is entirely by grace. It is a deathblow to any form of legalism, since such children obviously can do nothing to merit salvation. The Lord's solemn declaration, **"Truly I say to you, whoever does not receive the kingdom of God like a child will not enter it at all,"** was a severe rebuke of the legalistic works-righteousness system of the Pharisees and their followers and, by extension, of all who trust in their good works to save them.

Drawing the passage to a close, verse 16 notes that Jesus **took** the children **in His arms and began blessing them,** laying His hands on them. In a wonderful gesture, recorded only by Mark, the Lord emphasized the special place these children have in the kingdom. The verb translated took **them in His arms** is a compound verb that means, "to enfold in one's arms," just as one would do with a baby. He embraced them and began blessing them one by one. The sense of the verb translated **blessing** is that Jesus blessed them fervently, praying for each one of them with His hands on them, a very familiar blessing posture. The Lord's acceptance pictures the reality that that salvation is by grace alone. The salvation of a child who dies without having performed any meritorious works is the greatest illustration of that foundational biblical truth. Upon the death of a child or one with a child's mind, God applies the sacrifice of the Savior to them and they are declared and made righteous in the same moment.

The greatest blessing parents can confer on their children is to lovingly evangelize them. That is their highest priority as stewards of their children's lives once they are old enough to understand and believe the gospel. Their children's salvation is a sovereign work of God, but parents are the agents by which that divine work is accomplished. They are the primary missionaries in the lives of their children.

The Tragedy of a Selfish Seeker
(Mark 10:17–31)

8

As He was setting out on a journey, a man ran up to Him and knelt before Him, and asked Him, "Good Teacher, what shall I do to inherit eternal life?" And Jesus said to him, "Why do you call Me good? No one is good except God alone. You know the commandments, 'Do not murder, do not commit adultery, do not steal, do not bear false witness, do not defraud, honor your father and mother.'" And he said to Him, "Teacher, I have kept all these things from my youth up." Looking at him, Jesus felt a love for him and said to him, "One thing you lack: go and sell all you possess and give to the poor, and you will have treasure in heaven; and come, follow Me." But at these words he was saddened, and he went away grieving, for he was one who owned much property. And Jesus, looking around, said to His disciples, "How hard it will be for those who are wealthy to enter the kingdom of God!" The disciples were amazed at His words. But Jesus answered again and said to them, "Children, how hard it is to enter the kingdom of God! It is easier for a camel to go through the eye of a

**needle than for a rich man to enter the kingdom of God." They
were even more astonished and said to Him, "Then who can be
saved?" Looking at them, Jesus said, "With people it is impossible, but not with God; for all things are possible with God." Peter
began to say to Him, "Behold, we have left everything and followed You." Jesus said, "Truly I say to you, there is no one who
has left house or brothers or sisters or mother or father or children or farms, for My sake and for the gospel's sake, but that he
will receive a hundred times as much now in the present age,
houses and brothers and sisters and mothers and children and
farms, along with persecutions; and in the age to come, eternal life.
But many who are first will be last, and the last, first."** (10:17–31)

The Bible teaches that sinners do not seek God on their own (Ps.
14:2–3). The Lord Jesus Christ affirmed that reality when He declared, "No
one can come to Me unless the Father who sent Me draws him ... For this
reason I have said to you, that no one can come to Me unless it has been
granted him from the Father" (John 6:44, 65). The apostle Paul, reflecting
Old Testament Scripture, wrote, "There is none righteous, not even one;
there is none who understands, there is none who seeks for God; all have
turned aside, together they have become useless; there is none who does
good, there is not even one" (Rom. 3:10–12). Clever marketing techniques
and strategies will not enable superficial, self-centered sinners—who are
"dead in [their] trespasses and sins," walking "according to the course of
this world, according to the prince of the power of the air, of the spirit that
is now working in the sons of disobedience," living lives controlled by
"the lusts of [the] flesh, indulging the desires of the flesh and of the
mind, and [who are] by nature children of wrath" (Eph. 2:1–3)—to desire
salvation by hearing the gospel. That is the work of God. Only God, by the
miracle of regeneration, empowers the sinner to seek Him by repentance
and faith in the gospel (cf. John 3:1–8).

Still, the Bible commands sinners to seek God, not pursue the fulfillment of their own selfish desires. Isaiah declared, "Seek the Lord while
He may be found; call upon Him while He is near" (Isa. 55:6), and God
said to wayward Israel, "Thus says the Lord to the house of Israel, 'Seek Me
that you may live'" (Amos 5:4, 6). Those who truly seek God must do so on

His terms, not theirs. That involves seeking Him with all one's heart and soul. "You will seek the Lord your God," Moses told the children of Israel, "and you will find Him if you search for Him with all your heart and all your soul" (Deut. 4:29). In Jeremiah 29:13 God Himself declared, "You will seek Me and find Me when you search for Me with all your heart" (cf. 1 Chron. 28:9; Ps. 119:2, 10).

On the other hand, those who pursue their own self-centered agenda instead of seeking God are like King Rehoboam of Judah, who "did evil because he did not set his heart to seek the Lord" (2 Chron. 12:14; cf. Ps. 10:4).

This passage introduces one such selfish seeker. The incident it describes was an actual encounter between a wealthy, influential young man and Jesus; it is not a parable or story. Christ's response to him demonstrates that superficial interest in eternal life must be confronted, not accommodated. The man was confronted with the choice between himself and God; between fulfillment in this life and fulfillment in the life to come. He never questioned the truthfulness of what Jesus said. He did not equivocate or argue; he just walked away. When it became clear that what Jesus was offering was going to cost him his pride and his possessions, he decided that the price was too high, even for eternal life.

This young man seemed at first to be the ideal seeker. Some people have to be persuaded of the basic truths of Scripture's teaching concerning God, heaven, hell, and eternal life. Apparently, no such pre-evangelism was necessary in his case; in fact, the first thing he did when he came to Jesus was ask Him how to obtain eternal life. He seemed to be ready; according to contemporary evangelistic methodology, Jesus should have used appropriate language and offered acceptable terms to lead this hot prospect to a salvation prayer. But Jesus never called for a prayer or the popular "decision." Instead, He put a massive stumbling block in his way, forcing him to decide what was more valuable to him: God and the life to come, or his own will and the riches of this present life. Sadly, he chose to follow his own will and not God's. He wanted eternal life, but not enough to forsake his pride and possessions. Instead, he wanted to add eternal life to what he already possessed on his own terms.

This tragic story of an outwardly devout man who failed the most important test of his life unfolds in two parts: the story of his encounter with Jesus, and the education the Lord gave His disciples from that encounter.

THE ENCOUNTER

As He was setting out on a journey, a man ran up to Him and knelt before Him, and asked Him, "Good Teacher, what shall I do to inherit eternal life?" And Jesus said to him, "Why do you call Me good? No one is good except God alone. You know the commandments, 'Do not murder, do not commit adultery, do not steal, do not bear false witness, do not defraud, honor your father and mother.'" And he said to Him, "Teacher, I have kept all these things from my youth up." Looking at him, Jesus felt a love for him and said to him, "One thing you lack: go and sell all you possess and give to the poor, and you will have treasure in heaven; and come, follow Me." But at these words he was saddened, and he went away grieving, for he was one who owned much property.
(10:17–22)

The encounter plays out in the dialogue between Jesus and this young man.

THE SEEKER'S QUESTION

As He was setting out on a journey, a man ran up to Him and knelt before Him, and asked Him, "Good Teacher, what shall I do to inherit eternal life?" (10:17)

This incident took place in the southern part of the region known as Perea, located east of the Jordan River. Jesus was on His way to Jerusalem (Mark 10:32) for the final time, where He would die and rise again. One day, **as He was setting out on a journey** in that region, something unexpected happened (Matt. 19:16 introduces this account with the Greek phrase *kai idou* ["and behold"])—**a man ran up to Him and knelt before Him.** What made that surprising, even shocking, is the identity of the man. Matthew notes that he was young (Matt. 19:16), Luke that he was a ruler (probably of a synagogue [Luke 18:18]), and all three report that he was extremely wealthy (Matt. 19:22; Mark 10:22; Luke 18:23).

Several things about this rich, influential man who had achieved much according to the religious system of his day would have shocked the bystanders. First, he **ran up to** Jesus. Middle Eastern men of status did not run. Running necessitated gathering up the long robes worn by both men and women, thus exposing the legs, and was considered undignified and even shameful. He also **knelt before** Christ, assuming a humble, worshipful posture in the presence of the one whom the religious establishment hated as a false prophet and sought to kill. Further, he addressed Jesus respectfully as **Good Teacher.**

As noted earlier in this chapter, this rich, young ruler seemed to be a sure-fire prospect. He recognized his need, in contrast to the Pharisee depicted in Luke 18:9–14. Despite all of his religious achievements, he knew that he did not have eternal life and, therefore, lacked a confident hope of heaven.

Further, he urgently sought the eternal life that he knew he did not possess. Disregarding his reputation and his dignity, he humbly came to Jesus publicly, unlike Nicodemus (John 3:2).

He also came to the right person. Unlike many who futilely pursue spiritual truth from the wrong teacher, the wrong church, or the wrong religion, he came to the Lord Jesus Christ, who alone is the "the way, and the truth, and the life" (John 14:6; cf. 1 John 5:20).

Finally, he asked the right question: **"What shall I do to inherit eternal life?"** Consistent with the legalistic system of self-righteousness that he was part of, he was looking for knowledge of the ultimate good work that would finally permit him to obtain eternal life. Despite all of his religious achievements, there was a nagging fear in his mind that salvation was still missing. There was an unsatisfied guilt; an unfulfilled longing; a painful doubt about his relationship to God. **Eternal life** refers to a quality of life, not a quantity; not merely to living forever but rather to possessing the very life of God, which He graciously grants to believers.

This man's fundamental problem lay in his misunderstanding and misuse of the word **good,** which he used loosely in relation to Christ. He meant no more by it than to commend Him as a good **teacher,** in other words, one sent from God (cf. John 3:2). By the same token, he considered himself and his fellow religionists equally good. In light of that, the purpose of Jesus' counterquestion becomes clear. He did not reply as He did to the similar question, "What shall we do, so that we may work the works of God?" (John 6:28) by saying, "This is the work of God, that you believe in Him whom He has sent" (v. 29; cf. Acts 16:31). The omniscient Lord, who knew what was in the hearts of men (John 2:25), did not challenge this man to believe, because He knew that he first needed to come to grips with the looming judgment of sin over his head, and the need for repentance and forgiveness by divine mercy—to escape eternal wrath.

THE SAVIOR'S CHALLENGE

And Jesus said to him, "Why do you call Me good? No one is good except God alone. You know the commandments, 'Do not murder, do not commit adultery, do not steal, do not bear false witness, do not defraud, honor your father and mother.'" (10:18–19)

The Lord's reply, **"Why do you call Me good? No one is good except God alone,"** was not, of course, a disavowal of His deity. That would have contradicted His explicit claims elsewhere (e.g., John 5:17–18; 8:24, 58; 10:30–33). Its purpose was to rebuke this man's inadequate understanding of the word **good** and redefine it in relation to God. **Good,** unlike "bad," is absolute, not relative. People may be more or less good or bad, but only God is absolutely, perfectly, eternally good. Before the gospel can be presented to them, people must understand that they are not good in God's sight, and that no amount of human effort or religious observance can make them so (Rom. 3:20, 28; Gal. 2:16; Eph. 2:8–9; Phil. 3:9; 2 Tim. 1:9; Titus 3:5).

The law is "holy, and the commandment is holy and righteous and good" (Rom. 7:12). Divine revelation in the law demonstrates and defines God's perfect righteousness, holiness, and absolute goodness, and is the standard to which all who would achieve salvation by their own righteousness cannot attain (Matt. 5:48; cf. Lev. 11:45; 19:2; 1 Peter 1:16). The law shows sinners how perfectly good God is and how utterly evil they are, producing guilt, fear, dread, remorse, and the inevitable reality of divine judgment. It is "our tutor to lead us to Christ, so that we may be justified by faith" (Gal. 3:24). But like the Jewish people of Jesus' day, this man had twisted the law into a means of establishing his own goodness and righteousness (Rom. 9:30–32).

Before his conversion, the apostle Paul had been much like this religious sinner. He was "circumcised the eighth day, of the nation of Israel, of the tribe of Benjamin, a Hebrew of Hebrews; as to the Law, a Pharisee; as to zeal, a persecutor of the church; as to the righteousness which is in the Law, found blameless" (Phil. 3:5–6). As he wrote in Galatians 1:13–14, he was a rising star in first-century Judaism: "For you have heard of my former manner of life in Judaism, how I used to persecute the church of God beyond measure and tried to destroy it; and I was advancing in Judaism beyond many of my contemporaries among my countrymen, being more extremely zealous for my ancestral traditions." But as he was enabled by the Spirit of God to truly understand the law, he saw himself for what he was:

> What shall we say then? Is the Law sin? May it never be! On the contrary, I would not have come to know sin except through the Law; for I would not have known about coveting if the Law had not said, "You shall not covet." But sin, taking opportunity through the commandment, produced in me coveting of every kind; for apart from the Law sin is dead. I was once alive apart from the Law; but when the commandment came, sin became alive and I died; and this commandment, which was to result in life, proved to result in death for me; for sin, taking an opportunity through the commandment, deceived me and through it killed me. So then, the Law is holy, and the commandment is holy and righteous and good. Therefore did that which is good become a cause of death for me? May it never be! Rather it was sin, in order that it might be shown to be sin by effecting my death through that which is good, so that through the commandment sin would become utterly sinful. (Rom. 7:7–13)

The goodness of God's nature is revealed in the law, and when Paul measured himself against the law, he realized that he was not at all righteous, but a wretched sinner. He likened his best morality and religiosity to "dung" (Phil. 3:4–8 KJV).

The Lord then challenged this man to, like Paul would later do, judge himself by the law and realize that he was not good. Jesus reminded him that he knew **the commandments** and was responsible to keep them (Matt. 19:17). He then gave him a sample list: **"Do not murder, do not commit adultery, do not steal, do not bear false witness, do not defraud, honor your father and mother."** All but one of those examples were taken from the second half of the Ten Commandments, which deals with human relationships, as opposed to the first five commandments, which deal with a person's relationship to God.

THE SEEKER'S DELUSION

And he said to Him, "Teacher, I have kept all these things from my youth up." (10:20)

Far from being convicted by his inability to attain to the perfection of the law, this young ruler, like his fellow religionists, was convinced that his law-keeping vindicated his righteousness. His claim to have **kept all these things from** his **youth up** to that moment revealed his utter failure to truly understand his sinfulness. His self-righteousness had blinded him to the law's revelation of his sin (cf. Jer. 17:9). To him, as to the Pharisees and rabbis, the law was concerned merely with external behavior. It was that mistaken notion that Jesus corrected in the Sermon on the Mount (Matt. 5:20–48). If he had truly understood the law, he would have realized, as Paul came to understand, that it condemned the hatred, lustful thoughts, covetousness, lies, and dishonoring of his parents that were part of the fabric of his wretched heart. Instead of keeping the law as he imagined, he violated it daily in his mind, which is as wicked as lawless behavior.

THE SAVIOR'S COMMAND

Looking at him, Jesus felt a love for him and said to him, "One thing you lack: go and sell all you possess and give to the poor,

and you will have treasure in heaven; and come, follow Me." But at these words he was saddened, and he went away grieving, for he was one who owned much property. (10:21–22)

Motivated by **a love for him,** Jesus said, **"One thing you lack: go and sell all you possess and give to the poor, and you will have treasure in heaven; and come, follow Me."** The Lord's command and the man's response, **but at these words he was saddened, and he went away grieving, for he was one who owned much property,** further exposed his failure to keep the law. Not only was he a violator of the second five of the Ten Commandments but also a criminal transgressor of the first five. He was guilty of blaspheming God, by worshiping another god—his wealth and possessions—and God tolerates no rivals. "No one can serve two masters;" Jesus said, "for either he will hate the one and love the other, or he will be devoted to one and despise the other. You cannot serve God and wealth" (Matt. 6:24). Earthly wealth and temporal satisfaction was this man's god.

Jesus preached the law to him, but not the gospel. Sinners are not ready for the good news of the gospel until they accept the bad news that the law condemns them as guilty sinners. As a highly respected, revered, and honored religious leader, he viewed his prosperity and his exalted position in the synagogue as evidence that he was good and God was pleased with him. He was unwilling to acknowledge that he was a sinner, affirm that his good works could not save him, and cast himself on God's grace and mercy, and submit to Christ's lordship. Tragically, at the crossroads of his eternal destiny, face-to-face with the Savior, he took the broad way that leads to destruction and rejected the narrow way that alone leads to eternal life.

THE EDUCATION

And Jesus, looking around, said to His disciples, "How hard it will be for those who are wealthy to enter the kingdom of God!" The disciples were amazed at His words. But Jesus answered again and said to them, "Children, how hard it is to enter the kingdom

of God! It is easier for a camel to go through the eye of a needle than for a rich man to enter the kingdom of God." They were even more astonished and said to Him, "Then who can be saved?" Looking at them, Jesus said, "With people it is impossible, but not with God; for all things are possible with God." Peter began to say to Him, "Behold, we have left everything and followed You." Jesus said, "Truly I say to you, there is no one who has left house or brothers or sisters or mother or father or children or farms, for My sake and for the gospel's sake, but that he will receive a hundred times as much now in the present age, houses and brothers and sisters and mothers and children and farms, along with persecutions; and in the age to come, eternal life. But many who are first will be last, and the last, first." (10:23–31)

The lesson Jesus drew from the tragic story of the rich young ruler elaborates on His statement in Mark 8:35, "For whoever wishes to save his life will lose it, but whoever loses his life for My sake and the gospel's will save it." That man, who had seemed to be sincerely seeking eternal life, ended up forfeiting his eternal soul forever for love of self and earthly riches. The Lord's instruction unfolds in two parts: the poverty of riches, and the riches of poverty.

THE POVERTY OF RICHES

And Jesus, looking around, said to His disciples, "How hard it will be for those who are wealthy to enter the kingdom of God!" The disciples were amazed at His words. But Jesus answered again and said to them, "Children, how hard it is to enter the kingdom of God! It is easier for a camel to go through the eye of a needle than for a rich man to enter the kingdom of God." They were even more astonished and said to Him, "Then who can be saved?" Looking at them, Jesus said, "With people it is impossible, but not with God; for all things are possible with God." (10:23–27)

After watching sadly as the rich young ruler walked away **Jesus, looking around, said to His** astonished **disciples, "How hard it will be for those who are wealthy to enter the kingdom of God!"** They had been surprised when the seemingly hopeful prospect rejected Jesus' terms and abruptly turned and left. **The disciples were** even more **amazed at His words** concerning the difficulty the rich find in entering the kingdom. In their culture, as previously noted, it was assumed that wealth and power were signs of God's blessing.

On the contrary, entering the kingdom is difficult for the rich for at least three reasons. First, their wealth gives them a false sense of security. Paul commanded Timothy, "Instruct those who are rich in this present world not to be conceited or to fix their hope on the uncertainty of riches, but on God, who richly supplies us with all things to enjoy" (1 Tim. 6:17).

Second, they are also consumed with the things of the world, and where their treasure is, their hearts will be also (Matt. 6:21). In 1 Timothy 6:10 Paul warned, "For the love of money is a root of all sorts of evil, and some by longing for it have wandered away from the faith and pierced themselves with many griefs." The apostle John issued a similar warning:

> Do not love the world nor the things in the world. If anyone loves the world, the love of the Father is not in him. For all that is in the world, the lust of the flesh and the lust of the eyes and the boastful pride of life, is not from the Father, but is from the world. (1 John 2:15–16)

Those who grasp wealth are like the rich fool in the Lord's parable:

> And He told them a parable, saying, "The land of a rich man was very productive. And he began reasoning to himself, saying, 'What shall I do, since I have no place to store my crops?' Then he said, 'This is what I will do: I will tear down my barns and build larger ones, and there I will store all my grain and my goods. And I will say to my soul, "Soul, you have many goods laid up for many years to come; take your ease, eat, drink and be merry." But God said to him, 'You fool! This very night your soul is required of you; and now who will own what you have prepared?' So is the man who stores up treasure for himself, and is not rich toward God." (Luke 12:16–21)

Finally, the rich tend to be selfish, pursuing self-fulfillment and self-gratification, like the wealthy man in the Lord's story, who ignored the needy beggar at his gate (Luke 16:19–31).

Those psychological reasons, however, are not the Lord's point here, since the rich man of whom He spoke was an outwardly religious person. According to the simplistic (and wrong) theology of first-century Judaism, wealth was a sign of God's blessing. Conversely, they saw the poor as cursed by God. Further, those who were wealthy had the means to pay for more sacrifices than did the poor. They also could afford to give more alms and buy more offerings than other people, and the Jews believed that almsgiving was key to entering the kingdom. The apocryphal book of Tobit said, "It is better to give alms than to lay up gold: for alms doth deliver from death, and shall purge away all sin. Those that exercise alms and righteousness shall be filled with life" (Tobit 12:8–9; cf. Sirach 3:30). Thus, in the Jewish religious system, it should be easy for the rich to enter the kingdom of God, not impossible.

Not surprisingly, the **disciples were** shocked and **amazed at** Jesus' **words,** which seemed counterintuitive to them. Their reaction indicates that they had not yet completely broken free from the legalistic system in which they had been raised. **But Jesus answered again and said to them, "Children, how hard it is to enter the kingdom of God!"** Far from toning down His statement, the Lord repeated it and broadened it to include everyone, not just the rich. He then gave an illustration of how difficult it is to enter God's kingdom:

> In reality, it is impossible for the rich to buy their way into the kingdom, as the proverbial statement, "It is easier for a camel to go through the eye of a needle than for a rich man to enter the kingdom of God" indicates. The Persians expressed impossibility with a familiar proverb stating that it would be easier for an elephant to go through the eye of a needle. The Jews picked up the proverb, substituting a camel for an elephant, since camels were the largest animals in Palestine.
>
> Some, unwilling to face the stark reality that the saying implies, have attempted to soften it. Noting the similarity between the Greek words *kamelos* (camel) and *kamilos* (a large rope or cable), some suggest that a copyist erred by substituting the former for the latter. It is unlikely, however, that all three Synoptic Gospels would have been changed in the same way. Nor would a scribe make the statement harder rather

than easier. He might change the wording from "camel" to "cord," but not from "cord" to "camel." But even a rope could no more go through the eye of a needle than a camel could. Others imagine that the reference is to a small gate [in] Jerusalem's wall that camels could only enter with great difficulty. But there is no evidence that such a gate ever existed. Nor would any person with common sense have attempted to force a camel through such a small gate even if one had existed; they would simply have brought their camel into the city through a larger gate. The obvious point of that picturesque expression of hyperbole is not that salvation is difficult, but rather that it is humanly impossible for everyone by any means, including the wealthy (cf. Mark 10:23–24). Sinners are aware of their guilt and fear, and may even desire a relationship with God that would bring forgiveness and peace. But they cannot hold on to their sinful priorities and personal control and think to come to God on their own terms. The young man illustrates that reality. (John MacArthur, *Luke 18–24,* The MacArthur New Testament Commentary [Chicago: Moody, 2014], 41–42)

Even more astonished, the disciples **said to Him, "Then who can be saved?" Looking at them, Jesus** told them plainly, **"With people it is impossible, but not with God; for all things are possible with God"** (cf. the similar phrase used in Luke 1:37 to refer to the virgin birth). Sinners, by their own power, will, and efforts, cannot save themselves (Jer. 13:23); only a sovereign act of God can change the heart (John 1:11–13; 3:3–8; 6:44, 65).

When sinners, by the work of the Spirit, reach the point where they desire to repent and be saved, having acknowledged their guilt, they can only cry out to God and ask Him graciously to forgive their sins and save them from judgment through Jesus Christ. Their only plea, like the repentant tax collector, is "God, be merciful to me, the sinner!" (Luke 18:13).

THE RICHES OF POVERTY

Peter began to say to Him, "Behold, we have left everything and followed You." Jesus said, "Truly I say to you, there is no one who has left house or brothers or sisters or mother or father or children or farms, for My sake and for the gospel's sake, but that he will receive a hundred times as much now in the present age, houses and brothers and sisters and mothers and children and farms,

along with persecutions; and in the age to come, eternal life. But many who are first will be last, and the last, first." (10:28–31)

As **Peter** pointed out, unlike the rich young ruler and many other would-be followers (cf. John 6:66; Luke 9:59–62), the disciples had **left everything and followed** Christ. Matthew records that Peter followed that statement with the question, "What then will there be for us?" (Matt. 19:27). In reply **Jesus said, "Truly I say to you, there is no one who has left house or brothers or sisters or mother or father or children or farms, for My sake and for the gospel's sake, but that he will receive a hundred times as much now in the present age, houses and brothers and sisters and mothers and children and farms, along with** the inevitable **persecutions** they will face (Acts 14:22). All believers become part of the church, the body of Christ. While many lose their earthly families when they become Christians, they find that they have gained the heavenly family and are given many fathers, mothers, sisters, and brothers in Christ.

That mutual caring has marked the true church of Jesus Christ since its inception on the day of Pentecost. When the church was born, it consisted in part of pilgrims who had come from Jewish settlements outside of Israel. After their conversion, the new believers did not want to go home because there were no churches except for the one in Jerusalem. They stayed, some of them permanently, in the homes of the believers who were already there. Those believers fed them, housed them, and loved and cared for them. Years later, the apostle Paul would travel all over the Mediterranean region, collecting an offering to take back to the Jerusalem church so it could continue to care for the needy believers there (2 Cor. 8–9).

But it is not only in this present life that those who have left everything behind to follow Christ will be rewarded; **in the age to come,** they will be blessed with **eternal life** in heaven. In response to Peter's question regarding him and his fellow apostles, Jesus replied, "Truly I say to you, that you who have followed Me, in the regeneration [the millennial kingdom] when the Son of Man will sit on His glorious throne, you also shall sit upon twelve thrones, judging the twelve tribes of Israel" (Matt. 19:28).

The Lord's concluding statement, **"But many who are first will be last, and the last, first,"** means simply that all will wind up equal possessors of heaven's treasures (cf. Matt. 19:30–20:16).

The rich who reject Christ will be spiritually poor forever. On the other hand, those who forsake all to follow Him will receive eternal riches. Those who store up their treasure in heaven understand the truth expressed by the missionary and martyr Jim Elliot: "He is no fool who gives what he cannot keep to gain what he cannot lose" (Elisabeth Elliot, *Shadow of the Almighty* [New York: Harper & Row, 1979], 247).

A Preview of Messianic Suffering (Mark 10:32–34)

9

They were on the road going up to Jerusalem, and Jesus was walking on ahead of them; and they were amazed, and those who followed were fearful. And again He took the twelve aside and began to tell them what was going to happen to Him, saying, "Behold, we are going up to Jerusalem, and the Son of Man will be delivered to the chief priests and the scribes; and they will condemn Him to death and will hand Him over to the Gentiles. They will mock Him and spit on Him, and scourge Him and kill Him, and three days later He will rise again." (10:32–34)

One of the false claims critics and skeptics make in an attempt to discredit the Lord Jesus Christ is that His death was an unplanned, unexpected misfortune. Some maintain that Jesus, though His intentions were good, badly miscalculated the people's willingness to tolerate His teaching and went too far. Others see Him as a misguided nationalist, whose attempts to ignite a revolution against Rome ended in disaster. To others, He was merely another religious fanatic who, swept away by His own

89

popularity, entertained delusions of grandeur. In any case, they charge the way things turned out was certainly not the way He had intended.

Nothing could be further from the truth. Opposite from being caught by surprise, Jesus knew from the beginning what would happen to Him. Every aspect of His death was prophesied seven centuries before His birth:

> Behold, My servant will prosper, He will be high and lifted up and greatly exalted. Just as many were astonished at you, My people, so His appearance was marred more than any man and His form more than the sons of men. Thus He will sprinkle many nations, kings will shut their mouths on account of Him; for what had not been told them they will see, and what they had not heard they will understand. Who has believed our message? And to whom has the arm of the Lord been revealed? For He grew up before Him like a tender shoot, and like a root out of parched ground; He has no stately form or majesty that we should look upon Him, nor appearance that we should be attracted to Him. He was despised and forsaken of men, a man of sorrows and acquainted with grief; and like one from whom men hide their face He was despised, and we did not esteem Him. Surely our griefs He Himself bore, and our sorrows He carried; yet we ourselves esteemed Him stricken, smitten of God, and afflicted. But He was pierced through for our transgressions, He was crushed for our iniquities; the chastening for our well-being fell upon Him, and by His scourging we are healed. All of us like sheep have gone astray, each of us has turned to his own way; but the Lord has caused the iniquity of us all to fall on Him. He was oppressed and He was afflicted, yet He did not open His mouth; like a lamb that is led to slaughter, and like a sheep that is silent before its shearers, so He did not open His mouth. By oppression and judgment He was taken away; and as for His generation, who considered that He was cut off out of the land of the living for the transgression of my people, to whom the stroke was due? His grave was assigned with wicked men, yet He was with a rich man in His death, because He had done no violence, nor was there any deceit in His mouth. But the Lord was pleased to crush Him, putting Him to grief; if He would render Himself as a guilt offering, He will see His offspring, He will prolong His days, and the good pleasure of the Lord will prosper in His hand. As a result of the anguish of His soul, He will see it and be satisfied; by His knowledge the Righteous One, My Servant, will justify the many, as He will bear their iniquities. Therefore, I will allot Him a portion with the great, and He will divide the booty with the strong; because He poured out Himself to death, and was numbered with the transgressors; yet He Himself bore the sin of many, and interceded for the transgressors. (Isa. 52:13–53:12)

Before Jesus was born an angel told His father, Joseph, that Mary "will bear a Son; and you shall call His name Jesus, for He will save His people from their sins" (Matt. 1:21). Anticipating the cross, Jesus said, "Now My soul has become troubled; and what shall I say, 'Father, save Me from this hour? But for this purpose I came to this hour'" (John 12:27). Jesus alluded to His death throughout His ministry:

> And Jesus said to them, "While the bridegroom is with them, the attendants of the bridegroom cannot fast, can they? So long as they have the bridegroom with them, they cannot fast. But the days will come when the bridegroom is taken away from them, and then they will fast in that day." (Mark 2:19–20)

> But I have a baptism to undergo, and how distressed I am until it is accomplished! (Luke 12:50)

> And He said to them, "Go and tell that fox [Herod Antipas], 'Behold, I cast out demons and perform cures today and tomorrow, and the third day I reach My goal.' Nevertheless I must journey on today and tomorrow and the next day; for it cannot be that a prophet would perish outside of Jerusalem." (Luke 13:32–33; cf. vv. 34–35)

> But first He must suffer many things and be rejected by this generation. (Luke 17:25)

On three occasions in the Synoptic Gospels, Jesus provided specific details of His death to His disciples (Mark 8:31; cf. Matt. 16:21; Luke 9:22; Mark 9:31; cf. Matt. 17:22–23; Luke 9:44). The present passage and the parallel accounts in Matthew and Luke (Matt. 20:17–19; Luke 18:31–34), relate the last of those three predictions.

The reason Jesus was able to make specific and accurate predictions concerning His death is twofold: First, because He knew the Old Testament perfectly, and second, because He possessed perfect divine knowledge. Jesus' teaching on this occasion may therefore be examined under two headings: prophetic Scripture, and personal omniscience.

PROPHETIC SCRIPTURE

They were on the road going up to Jerusalem, and Jesus was walking on ahead of them; and they were amazed, and those who

followed were fearful. And again He took the twelve aside and began to tell them what was going to happen to Him. (10:32)

This lesson took place while Jesus, accompanied by a large crowd (cf. Matt. 20:29), was **on the road going up to Jerusalem** via Jericho. They had left the Jordan River, where they had crossed back into Israel after traveling south from Galilee through Perea (the region east of the Jordan) to avoid passing through Samaria (cf. John 4:9). **Jesus was walking on ahead of them,** going willingly to His death. With resolute conviction, He walked ahead of everyone, pulling His anxious, confused, hopeless followers along with Him by the sheer force of His presence. The Twelve in particular **were amazed,** fearful, even fatalistic (cf. John 11:15), since they had, as noted above, already received instruction from the Lord about what was to take place. But even the rest of **those who followed were fearful.** They were confused as to why the one they fervently hoped was the Messiah was walking into the deadly danger that faced Him in Jerusalem.

To help prepare them for what lay ahead, Jesus **took the twelve aside and began to tell them** once again **what was going to happen to Him.** As it happened, they had a difficult enough time coping with His betrayal, arrest, trials, crucifixion, and death. Had they not been forewarned, the level of doubt and fear they would have experienced would have been far greater. But when those events took place, the knowledge that things were unfolding just as Jesus had predicted reassured them that God was in complete control.

The Twelve were familiar with the Old Testament, because it was read and taught in the synagogues all their lives. But under the influence of the bizarre, mystical teaching propounded by the Pharisees and scribes, they lacked a true understanding of the revelation. Throughout His ministry Jesus had challenged the rabbinic misinterpretation of the Old Testament (e.g., Matt. 5:21–48; 15:2–6; Mark 7:8–9; cf. Titus 1:14; Mark 7:7). Now, with His death imminent, the Lord intensified His instruction of the disciples.

Luke records that He spoke to them about "all things which are written through the prophets about the Son of Man [that would] be accomplished" (Luke 18:31). His death was promised in the Old Testament, not in vague, general terms but very specifically.

For example, the sacrificial system, which was initiated (Gen. 3:21) and mandated (Leviticus) by God, of necessity pointed to one final sacrifice, as the writer of Hebrews makes clear:

> Both gifts and sacrifices are offered which cannot make the worshiper perfect in conscience. (Heb. 9:9)

> For the Law, since it has only a shadow of the good things to come and not the very form of things, can never, by the same sacrifices which they offer continually year by year, make perfect those who draw near. Otherwise, would they not have ceased to be offered, because the worshipers, having once been cleansed, would no longer have had consciousness of sins? But in those sacrifices there is a reminder of sins year by year. (Heb. 10:1–3)

> By this will we have been sanctified through the offering of the body of Jesus Christ once for all. Every priest stands daily ministering and offering time after time the same sacrifices, which can never take away sins; but He, having offered one sacrifice for sins for all time, sat down at the right hand of God. (Heb. 10:10–12)

Jesus would surely also have pointed out that Psalm 22 graphically described the details of His death on the cross—even though crucifixion was unknown in Israel at the time that psalm was written. The psalm opens with the words our Lord spoke on the cross, "My God, my God, why have You forsaken me?" (v. 1; cf. Matt. 27:46). Verses 6–8 predict the scorn and mockery heaped on Jesus by His enemies:

> But I am a worm and not a man, a reproach of men and despised by the people. All who see me sneer at me; they separate with the lip, they wag the head, saying, "Commit yourself to the Lord; let Him deliver him; let Him rescue him, because He delights in him." (cf. Luke 23:35–39)

Verse 16 says of His tormentors, "They pierced my hands and my feet"—an obvious reference to crucifixion.

Verses 14–17 describe the physical suffering the Lord endured on the cross:

> I am poured out like water, and all my bones are out of joint; my heart is like wax; it is melted within me. My strength is dried up like

a potsherd, and my tongue cleaves to my jaws; and You lay me in the dust of death. For dogs have surrounded me; a band of evildoers has encompassed me; they pierced my hands and my feet. I can count all my bones. They look, they stare at me.

This remarkably accurate prediction even records the detail that His executioners would divide up Jesus' garments: "They divide my garments among them, and for my clothing they cast lots" (v. 18; cf. Luke 23:34).

Surely He spoke of that greatest prophecy of His birth, life, death, resurrection, and glory—Isaiah 53. The Old Testament also predicted numerous other details of Jesus' life and ministry, including

His triumphal entry (Zech. 9:9; Matt. 21:4–5)

His enemies' rage against Him (Ps. 2:1–3; Acts 4:25–28)

His desertion by His friends (Zech. 13:7; Matt. 26:31)

His betrayal for thirty pieces of silver (Zech. 11:12; Matt. 26:15)

His being lifted up (a reference to His death by crucifixion [Num. 21:8–9; John 3:14])

That none of His bones would be broken (Ex. 12:46; Ps. 34:20; John 19:31–37)

That He would be given vinegar to drink (Ps. 69:21; Matt. 27:34)

That His side would be pierced (Zech. 12:10; John 19:34,37)

That though His grave would be assigned to be with wicked men (as was common with crucified criminals), He would actually be buried in a rich man's tomb (Isa. 53:9; Matt. 27:57–60)

That He would rise victorious over death (Ps. 16:10; Acts 2:25–31)

That He would ascend to the place of honor at the Father's right hand (Ps. 110:1; Acts 2:34–35)

Jesus "was determined to go to Jerusalem" (Luke 9:51) to fulfill all that the Old Testament predicted concerning His death, burial, resurrection, and ascension. After His resurrection, He would go back through all the Old Testament prophecies to explain again the predictions with their fulfillment (Luke 24:26–27, 32, 44–47). It was then that His disciples really understood because they had experienced the truth and because "He opened their minds to understand the Scriptures" (Luke 24:45).

PERSONAL OMNISCIENCE

saying, "Behold, we are going up to Jerusalem, and the Son of Man will be delivered to the chief priests and the scribes; and they will condemn Him to death and will hand Him over to the Gentiles. They will mock Him and spit on Him, and scourge Him and kill Him, and three days later He will rise again." (10:33–34)

In addition to the Old Testament teaching noted above, Jesus had knowledge of the events surrounding His death that only one who knew the future could possess. That is yet another display of His divine omniscience (cf. His knowledge of people's hearts [John 2:24–25; cf. Luke 6:8; 11:17]; the precise location of where Peter would find a fish with a coin in its mouth [Matt. 17:27; cf. John 21:5–6]; that a woman whom He had met for the first time had had five husbands [John 4:18]; where the colt He would ride in the triumphal entry would be located and what its owners would say when the disciples took it [Luke 19:30–34]; that the disciples would meet a man carrying a pitcher who would show them the place where they would eat the Last Supper [Luke 22:10]; and that Jerusalem would be destroyed four decades later [Luke 21:20]).

This prediction of His death provides added perspective on the magnitude and intensity of our Lord's suffering. The Twelve knew, of course, that they were **going up to Jerusalem** to celebrate the Passover. What they did not yet fully grasp was that Jesus would be the Passover Lamb, the ultimate and acceptable sacrifice that alone would satisfy God and bring to an end the symbolic sacrificial system. One reason that Jesus needed to explain those truths to them in advance is that the concept of a dying Messiah was completely foreign to what they had been taught all their lives (cf. Luke 9:44–45). The nineteenth-century historian Emil Schürer summarized the Jewish people's expectations regarding the coming of Messiah and the establishing of His kingdom as follows: First, the coming of Messiah would be preceded by a time of tribulation. Second, in the midst of the turmoil an Elijah-like prophet would appear heralding Messiah's coming. Third, Messiah would establish His glorious kingdom and vindicate His people. Fourth, the nations would ally themselves together to fight Messiah. Fifth, Messiah would destroy all those opposing nations. Sixth, Jerusalem would be restored and made new and glorious. Seventh, the dispersed Jews scattered all over the world would return to Israel. Eighth, Israel would become the center of the world and all the nations would be subjugated to the Messiah. Finally, the Messiah would establish His kingdom, which would be a time of eternal peace, righteous, and glory (*A History of the Jewish People in the Time of Jesus Christ* [New York: Scribners, 1896], 2:154–78). Such a perspective on Messiah's coming left no room for a dead, or even a risen Messiah.

The messianic title **Son of Man** (Dan. 7:13–14), emphasizing His incarnation, is Jesus' favorite designation of Himself, used by Him eighty-one times in the Gospels. The nature of His suffering as a man may be examined under five headings.

First, the Son of Man suffered disloyalty. He was betrayed and **delivered** to the Jewish religious leaders by one of the twelve men who were closest to Him. While Psalm 41:9 predicted that the Messiah would be betrayed by a friend, only Jesus knew that Judas Iscariot would be the betrayer (John 6:70–71). Judas betrayed Christ to the Jewish authorities for a mere thirty pieces of silver, just as the Scriptures predicted (Zech. 11:12). Cynically, with feigned respect, he pointed out Jesus to His captors with a kiss (Luke 22:47–48).

Second, Jesus suffered rejection by Israel (John 1:1; cf. Isa. 53:3) from first of all the **chief priests and the scribes.** The **chief priests** included the high priest and all living former high priests, the captain of the temple, who served as an assistant to the high priest, and various other high-ranking priests who oversaw the work of the rank-and-file priests. The **scribes** were the experts in the rabbinic and Old Testament law. Most were Pharisees, although some were Sadducees. Together, they made up Israel's religious aristocracy. The people also rejected Christ before Pilate, screaming "Crucify Him!" (Matt. 27:22). Even the men closest to Him temporarily abandoned Him when after His arrest, "all the disciples left Him and fled" (Matt. 26:56). But most profoundly, Jesus was rejected by the Father, causing Him to cry out on the cross, "My God, My God, why have You forsaken Me?" (Matt. 27:46; cf. Ps. 22:1).

Third, Jesus suffered injustice. After a series of illegal, unjust, mock trials, Israel's leaders would **condemn Him to death and** would **hand Him over to the Gentiles.** After another series of trials before the Gentile rulers Pilate and Herod, Jesus, despite being repeatedly declared not guilty by them (cf. Luke 23:4, 14–15, 22; John 18:38; 19:4, 6), would be sentenced to death (Mark 15:15). The holy, just, and righteous second person of the Trinity was falsely accused of sin (John 9:24), sedition, insurrection (Luke 23:13–14), and blasphemy (Matt. 9:3; 26:65; John 10:33). And His trials were monumental demonstrations of injustice at every point.

Fourth, Jesus suffered ridicule. The sinless Son of God, in whom "all the fullness of Deity dwells in bodily form" (Col. 2:9), was mocked and mistreated and spat upon by those holding Him in custody during His Jewish trials (Luke 22:63), members of the Sanhedrin (Matt. 26:67–68), Herod and his soldiers (Luke 23:11), and Pilate's soldiers (Matt. 27:27–31). The ridicule continued even while He was on the cross; "the rulers were sneering at Him, saying, 'He saved others; let Him save Himself if this is the Christ of God, His Chosen One'" (Luke 23:35). The soldiers also mocked Him, coming up to Him, offering Him sour wine, and saying, 'If You are the King of the Jews, save Yourself!'" (vv. 36–37). Even one of those crucified alongside Him "was hurling abuse at Him, saying, 'Are You not the Christ? Save Yourself and us!'" (v. 39). The reviling and abuse that He had faced throughout His ministry (cf. John 9:28; 1 Peter 2:23) intensified at His death.

Fifth, Jesus suffered bodily injury. He was beaten multiple times while in custody. Then, shortly before His crucifixion, the Romans would brutally **scourge Him** with a whip with multiple thongs, at the end of which were tied pieces of glass, bone, rock, or metal. So severe was the damage from scourging that many died from it.

Finally, Jesus' enemies would kill Him. He would be executed, in the most horribly cruel manner imaginable—crucifixion. Frederic Farrar wrote,

> For indeed a death by crucifixion seems to include all that pain and death can have of horrible and ghastly—dizziness, cramp, thirst, starvation, sleeplessness, traumatic fever, tetanus, publicity of shame, long continuance of torment, horror of anticipation, mortification of untended wounds—all intensified just up to the point at which they can be endured at all, but all stopping just short of the point which would give to the sufferer the relief of unconsciousness. The unnatural position made every movement painful; the lacerated veins and crushed tendons throbbed with incessant anguish; the wounds, inflamed by exposure,

gradually gangrened; the arteries—especially of the head and stomach—became swollen and oppressed with surcharged blood; and while each variety of misery went on gradually increasing, there was added to them the intolerable pang of a burning and raging thirst; and all these physical complications caused an internal excitement and anxiety which made the prospect of death itself—of death, the awful unknown enemy, at whose approach man usually shudders most—bear the aspect of a delicious and exquisite release. ("The Crucifixion A.D. 30," in Rossiter Johnson, Charles F. Horne, and John Rudd, eds. *The Great Events by Famous Historians* [Project Gutenberg EBook, 2008], 3:47–48)

So intense was the Lord's suffering that the New Testament frequently refers to them in the plural (e.g., 2 Cor. 1:5; Phil. 3:10; Heb. 2:10; 1 Peter 1:11; 4:13; 5:1). And centuries before they happened, Isaiah 53 described them in detail, as noted earlier in this chapter. The sinless Son of God suffered and died so that His people might have eternal life. In the words of the apostle Peter,

You have been called for this purpose, since Christ also suffered for you, leaving you an example for you to follow in His steps, who committed no sin, nor was any deceit found in His mouth; and while being reviled, He did not revile in return; while suffering, He uttered no threats, but kept entrusting Himself to Him who judges righteously; and He Himself bore our sins in His body on the cross, so that we might die to sin and live to righteousness; for by His wounds you were healed. For you were continually straying like sheep, but now you have returned to the Shepherd and Guardian of your souls. (1 Peter 2:21–25; cf. 1:18–19; 3:18; Matt. 20:28; John 10:15; Rom. 5:8–10; Eph. 5:2, 25; Titus 2:13; 1 John 3:16; Rev. 1:5; 5:9)

The Greatness of Humility (Mark 10:35–45)

10

James and John, the two sons of Zebedee, came up to Jesus, saying, "Teacher, we want You to do for us whatever we ask of You." And He said to them, "What do you want Me to do for you?" They said to Him, "Grant that we may sit, one on Your right and one on Your left, in Your glory." But Jesus said to them, "You do not know what you are asking. Are you able to drink the cup that I drink, or to be baptized with the baptism with which I am baptized?" They said to Him, "We are able." And Jesus said to them, "The cup that I drink you shall drink; and you shall be baptized with the baptism with which I am baptized. But to sit on My right or on My left, this is not Mine to give; but it is for those for whom it has been prepared." Hearing this, the ten began to feel indignant with James and John. Calling them to Himself, Jesus said to them, "You know that those who are recognized as rulers of the Gentiles lord it over them; and their great men exercise authority over them. But it is not this way among you, but whoever wishes to become great among you shall be your servant; and whoever

wishes to be first among you shall be slave of all. For even the Son of Man did not come to be served, but to serve, and to give His life a ransom for many." (10:35–45)

Pride is the seminal sin that rules all fallen hearts. The Bible repeatedly emphasizes that God hates pride and honors humility. Proverbs 8:13 declares, "The fear of the Lord is to hate evil," and then names pride as the first example of evil. Heading a list of seven things God hates are "haughty [proud] eyes" (Prov. 6:16–17). Isaiah wrote

> The proud look of man will be abased and the loftiness of man will be humbled, and the Lord alone will be exalted in that day. For the Lord of hosts will have a day of reckoning against everyone who is proud and lofty and against everyone who is lifted up, that he may be abased. . . . the pride of man will be humbled and the loftiness of men will be abased. (Isa. 2:11–12, 17)

Psalm 31:23 adds that "The Lord . . . fully recompenses the proud doer," and Proverbs 16:5 that "everyone who is proud in heart is an abomination to the Lord; assuredly, he will not be unpunished." The apostle John cautions that "all that is in the world, the lust of the flesh and the lust of the eyes and the boastful pride of life, is not from the Father, but is from the world" (1 John 2:16).

Because of the danger of pride, the Bible commands that it be avoided. In Romans 12:16 Paul wrote, "Do not be haughty in mind." In Psalm 75:5 God commanded, "Do not speak with insolent pride."

Scripture also records the devastating consequences of pride. The proud forfeit any relationship with God, who "regards the lowly, but the haughty He knows from afar" (Ps. 138:6). Proverbs 11:2 notes, "When pride comes, then comes dishonor." The proud "cry out, but [God] does not answer because of the pride of evil men" (Job 35:12). According to Proverbs 16:18, "Pride goes before destruction, and a haughty spirit before stumbling" (cf. 15:25; 18:12). In a similar vein, Proverbs 29:23 notes that "A man's pride will bring him low." Moses warned Israel,

> Beware that you do not forget the Lord your God by not keeping His commandments and His ordinances and His statutes which I am com-

> manding you today; otherwise, when you have eaten and are satisfied, and have built good houses and lived in them, and when your herds and your flocks multiply, and your silver and gold multiply, and all that you have multiplies, then your heart will become proud and you will forget the Lord your God who brought you out from the land of Egypt, out of the house of slavery. (Deut. 8:11–14)

But Israel failed to heed Moses' warning. "As they had their pasture, they became satisfied, and being satisfied, their heart became proud; therefore they forgot Me" (Hos. 13:6). In her Magnificat, Mary said that God "has scattered those who were proud in the thoughts of their heart" (Luke 1:51). Both James (James 4:6) and Peter (1 Peter 5:5) declare that "God is opposed to the proud, but gives grace to the humble" (cf. Prov. 3:34).

Illustrations of pride include the wicked in general (Rom. 1:30) and false teachers in particular (1 Tim. 6:3–4), Hezekiah (2 Chron. 32:25), Pharaoh (Neh. 9:10), Israel (Hos. 5:5), Babylon (Jer. 50:29), Nebuchadnezzar (Dan. 4:30; 5:20), Belshazzar (Dan. 5:22–23), Edom (Obad. 3), and above all, Satan (Isa. 14:12–14; Ezek. 28:17; 1 Tim. 3:6).

Summarizing the biblical teaching regarding pride, Proverbs 21:4 states, "Haughty eyes and a proud heart, the lamp of the wicked, is sin.

On the other hand, humility is a virtue that God honors and blesses and the Bible commands. "What does the Lord require of you," asks Micah 6:8 rhetorically, "but to do justice, to love kindness, and to walk humbly with your God?" In Ephesians 4:1–2 Paul commanded that believers "walk in a manner worthy of the calling with which [they] have been called, with all humility." To the Philippians he wrote, "Do nothing from selfishness or empty conceit, but with humility of mind regard one another as more important than yourselves" (Phil. 2:3), and gave similar instructions in Colossians 3:12: "So, as those who have been chosen of God, holy and beloved, put on a heart of compassion, kindness, humility, gentleness and patience."

Peter also stressed the importance of humility. In 1 Peter 3:8 he wrote, "All of you be harmonious, sympathetic, brotherly, kindhearted, and humble in spirit," while in 5:5–6 he added, "All of you, clothe yourselves with humility toward one another, for God is opposed to the proud, but gives grace to the humble. Therefore humble yourselves under the mighty hand of God, that He may exalt you at the proper time."

Among the many blessings bestowed on the humble are honor (Prov. 15:33; 18:12; 22:4; 29:23; Luke 1:52; James 4:10), strength (Ps. 10:17), instruction (Ps. 25:9), prosperity (Ps. 37:11), deliverance (Ps. 76:9), wisdom (Prov. 11:2), and fellowship with God (Isa. 66:2).

Humility always marks the godly. Abraham described himself as "but dust and ashes" (Gen. 18:27); Isaac was willing to allow himself to be offered as a sacrifice to God (Gen. 22:1–18); Jacob declared himself to be "unworthy of all the lovingkindness and of all the faithfulness," which God had shown to him (Gen. 32:10). "Moses was very humble, more than any man who was on the face of the earth" (Num. 12:3). Gideon said to God, "O Lord, how shall I deliver Israel? Behold, my family is the least in Manasseh, and I am the youngest in my father's house" (Judg. 6:15). David's prayer of praise to God displayed his humility:

> So David blessed the Lord in the sight of all the assembly; and David said, "Blessed are You, O Lord God of Israel our father, forever and ever. Yours, O Lord, is the greatness and the power and the glory and the victory and the majesty, indeed everything that is in the heavens and the earth; Yours is the dominion, O Lord, and You exalt Yourself as head over all. Both riches and honor come from You, and You rule over all, and in Your hand is power and might; and it lies in Your hand to make great and to strengthen everyone. Now therefore, our God, we thank You, and praise Your glorious name. But who am I and who are my people that we should be able to offer as generously as this? For all things come from You, and from Your hand we have given You. For we are sojourners before You, and tenants, as all our fathers were; our days on the earth are like a shadow, and there is no hope. O Lord our God, all this abundance that we have provided to build You a house for Your holy name, it is from Your hand, and all is Yours." (1 Chron. 29:10–16)

John the Baptist "was preaching, and saying, 'After me One is coming who is mightier than I, and I am not fit to stoop down and untie the thong of His sandals'" (Mark 1:7). Hezekiah (2 Chron. 32:26), Manasseh (2 Chron. 33:12), Josiah (2 Chron. 34:27), Job (Job 40:4; 42:6), Isaiah (Isa. 6:5), a centurion (Matt. 8:8), a Syrophoenician woman (Matt. 15:27), Peter (Luke 5:8), and Paul (Acts 20:19) are other notable examples of humility.

Paradoxically, the supreme example of humility is the one most worthy to be exalted—the Lord Jesus Christ. In Matthew 11:29 He described Himself as "gentle and humble in heart." He modeled humility by washing the disciples' feet (John 13:14–15). But the most profound illustration of Christ's humility is His incarnation and sacrificial death:

> Have this attitude in yourselves which was also in Christ Jesus, who, although He existed in the form of God, did not regard equality with God a thing to be grasped, but emptied Himself, taking the form of a bond-servant, and being made in the likeness of men. Being found in appearance as a man, He humbled Himself by becoming obedient to the point of death, even death on a cross. (Phil. 2:5–8)

Pride is the defining sin of humanity and the source of all other sins. All temptations are based upon self-gratification, which is an expression of pride and self-love. The disciples, although they were redeemed and the Holy Spirit was with them so that they loved Jesus and believed in His kingdom, still struggled with pride. They were, after all, common men of humble origins. The thought of being elevated to a position of honor far beyond anything they or anyone else in their nation had achieved was very intoxicating to them.

Unfortunately, their privileged understanding of spiritual truth (Matt. 13:11) did not result in humility. Instead, it stirred up their pride. The principle the Lord had given them in verse 31, "Many who are first will be last, and the last first," meant that they were all equal. Yet the disciples still perceived themselves as superior to each other, as this incident reveals. Peter's statement, "Behold, we have left everything and followed You" (10:28; cf. Matt. 19:27), further exposed the collective pride of the Twelve. They had denied themselves, left all behind, and followed Jesus into the unknown. Now they wanted to know what was in it for them. Consequently, they found the Lord's teaching regarding His death (e.g., 8:31; 9:31; 10:32–34) troubling and did not want to discuss it (cf. 9:32).

This incident, manifesting apostolic pride, is similar to the earlier one in Mark 9:33–37 and the later one in Luke 22:24–27. In the other two incidents, the disciples argued over who was the greatest among them; here James and John assumed that that they were the great ones and acted accordingly. The incident and the lesson Jesus subsequently taught the Twelve reveals two disparate paths to greatness: self-promotion, and self-denial. One is godly, the other sinful. One characterizes the kingdom of God, the other the kingdom of the world.

SELF-PROMOTION

James and John, the two sons of Zebedee, came up to Jesus, saying, "Teacher, we want You to do for us whatever we ask of You." And He said to them, "What do you want Me to do for you?" They said to Him, "Grant that we may sit, one on Your right and one on Your left, in Your glory." But Jesus said to them, "You do not know what you are asking. Are you able to drink the cup that I drink, or to be baptized with the baptism with which I am baptized?" They said to Him, "We are able." And Jesus said to them, "The cup that I drink you shall drink; and you shall be baptized with the baptism with which I am baptized. But to sit on My right or on My left, this is not Mine to give; but it is for those for whom it has been prepared." Hearing this, the ten began to feel indignant with James and John. Calling them to Himself, Jesus said to them, "You know that those who are recognized as rulers of the Gentiles lord it over them; and their great men exercise authority over them. (10:35–42)

This section reveals three characteristics of self-promotion: it is motivated by selfish ambition, unveiled in arrogant overconfidence, and makes for ugly competitiveness.

SELF-PROMOTION IS MOTIVATED BY SELFISH AMBITION

James and John, the two sons of Zebedee, came up to Jesus, saying, "Teacher, we want You to do for us whatever we ask of You." And He said to them, "What do you want Me to do for you?" They said to Him, "Grant that we may sit, one on Your right and one on Your left, in Your glory." (10:35–37)

As befits the nickname "Sons of Thunder" given them by Jesus (Mark 3:17), **James and John, the two sons of Zebedee,** were brash, bold men. Luke 9:51–56 records an incident that reveals their passionate, fiery personalities:

> When the days were approaching for His ascension, He was deter-
> mined to go to Jerusalem; and He sent messengers on ahead of Him,
> and they went and entered a village of the Samaritans to make arrange-
> ments for Him. But they did not receive Him, because He was traveling
> toward Jerusalem. When His disciples James and John saw this, they
> said,"Lord, do You want us to command fire to come down from heaven
> and consume them?" But He turned and rebuked them, [and said,"You
> do not know what kind of spirit you are of; for the Son of Man did not
> come to destroy men's lives, but to save them."] And they went on to
> another village.

Along with another set of brothers, Peter and Andrew, James and John
made up the innermost circle of the Twelve, those closest to Jesus. Peter,
James, and John alone had the privilege of being with Jesus at some of
the key events of His ministry, including the transfiguration (Matt. 17:1),
the raising of Jairus's daughter (Luke 8:51), and His agonizing time of
prayer inside the garden of Gethsemane (Mark 14:33). Their privileged
position caused James and John to view themselves as superior to the
eight disciples in the other two groups, if not Peter and Andrew as well.

They also believed they had a personal advantage over the rest
of the apostles in their quest for honor and glory. According to Matthew's
account of this incident, James and John were accompanied by their
mother when they approached Jesus. A comparison of Matthew's, Mark's,
and John's accounts of the crucifixion reveals four women who were
specifically mentioned: Jesus' mother, Mary, Mary the wife of Clopas (and
mother of James the son of Alphaeus and his brother Joseph; cf. Matt.
27:56; Mark 15:40), Mary Magdalene, and a fourth described only as "His
mother's sister" (John 19:25). By process of elimination, she must have
been Salome (Mark 15:40), the mother of the sons of Zebedee (Matt.
27:56) and the sister of Mary the mother of Jesus, and hence His aunt.
James and John boldly played the family card by bringing her along
(Matt. 20:20), thinking to leverage the request they were about to make to
Jesus. She did not ask anything for herself; she would find fulfillment
through her sons and the honor they would bring to the family.

So James and John, with their mother, brashly **came up to Jesus**
and before making their request said to Him (Matt. 20:21), **"Teacher, we
want You to do for us whatever we ask of You."** Like a child trying to
manipulate a parent, they asked the Lord to grant their request before

telling Him what it was. He, of course, refused to grant them the carte blanche approval they sought. Instead, **He said to them, "What do you want Me to do for you?"** Echoing their mother's initial request, **they said to Him, "Grant that we may sit, one on Your right and one on Your left, in Your glory."** Their request reflects the common practice of ancient rulers to elevate their highest ranking, most intimate family members and associates to the places of honor on either side of them.

This shockingly prideful request showed that, for all the time they had been with Him, the two had not learned humility, even after observing Jesus, the flawless model of it. James and John also deliberately depreciated the other apostles as being beneath them and unworthy of the honor they deserved. They were manipulative, consumed by a strong, self-promoting ambition, the expression of which revealed the ugly condition of their hearts (cf. Mark 7:21–22).

SELF-PROMOTION IS MANIFESTED IN ARROGANT OVERCONFIDENCE

But Jesus said to them, "You do not know what you are asking. Are you able to drink the cup that I drink, or to be baptized with the baptism with which I am baptized?" They said to Him, "We are able." And Jesus said to them, "The cup that I drink you shall drink; and you shall be baptized with the baptism with which I am baptized. But to sit on My right or on My left, this is not Mine to give; but it is for those for whom it has been prepared." (Mark 10:38–40)

Warning the ignorant brothers of the magnitude and folly of their request, **Jesus said to them, "You do not know what you are asking. Are you able to drink the cup that I drink, or to be baptized with the baptism with which I am baptized?"** The cup (cf. Matt. 26:39; John 18:11) and **baptism** (cf. Luke 12:50) are references to the Lord's suffering. To **drink the cup** is an Old Testament idiom meaning to fully experience something, in this case God's wrath (cf. Pss. 11:6; 75:8; Isa. 51:17, 22; Jer. 25:15–17; 49:12). Christ's point is that reward and honor in the kingdom are relative to the degree of earthly suffering endured.

Displaying the same overconfidence that Peter would when he adamantly insisted that he would not deny Jesus (both in the upper room [Luke 22:33; John 13:37], and in Gethsemane [Matt. 26:33; Mark 14:31]), James and John insisted, **"We are able."** Their answer revealed that they did not understand the ramifications of what they were asking. When the moment of crisis came, their overconfidence was exposed, and they fled along with the rest of the apostles (Matt. 26:56). Jesus went on to tell them, **"The cup that I drink you shall drink; and you shall be baptized with the baptism with which I am baptized. But to sit on My right or on My left, this is not Mine to give; but it is for those for whom it has been prepared."** James would be the first of the Twelve to be martyred, executed by Herod Agrippa I (Acts 12:2); John would be the last, near the end of the first century during the reign of Emperor Trajan. They would suffer, but the Father (Matt. 20:23) will sovereignly decide the places of honor in the kingdom. Jesus' acknowledgment, it **"is not Mine to give,"** affirms His submission to the Father during the incarnation.

SELF-PROMOTION MAKES FOR UGLY COMPETIVENESS

Hearing this, the ten began to feel indignant with James and John. Calling them to Himself, Jesus said to them, "You know that those who are recognized as rulers of the Gentiles lord it over them; and their great men exercise authority over them. (10:41–42)

After they made their pitch, **the ten began to feel indignant with James and John.** The rest of the apostles were furious, not because James's and John's blatant manifestation of pride offended their spiritual sensibilities but because the two approached Jesus first. The Twelve's selfish competitiveness survived until the very end; even on the solemn occasion of the Last Supper, "there arose also a dispute among them as to which one of them was regarded to be greatest" (Luke 22:24).

Seizing on this sinful attitude, Jesus called the Twelve together and told them, **"You know that those who are recognized as rulers of the Gentiles lord it over them; and their great men exercise**

authority over them. The apostles were influenced by the prevailing leadership style of the world, which saw the **rulers of the Gentiles lord** their exalted position **over** their subjects. Rulers were and still are ambitious, autocratic, self-promoting, confident, arrogant, prideful, dictatorial, and domineering.

The world has always been filled with ambitious, overconfident, competitive self-promoters, who know no limits to their ambition. Many reach the heights of power. Driven by corrupt, proud hearts, they seek power at the expense of others. Ambition, overconfidence, and competitiveness mark the worldly pursuit of greatness by self-promotion.

SELF-DENIAL

But it is not this way among you, but whoever wishes to become great among you shall be your servant; and whoever wishes to be first among you shall be slave of all. For even the Son of Man did not come to be served, but to serve, and to give His life a ransom for many." (10:43–45)

Continuing His lesson, Jesus contrasted the worldly, self-promoting path to greatness with true greatness in God's kingdom. He told the apostles, **"But it is not this way among you, but whoever wishes to become great among you shall be your servant; and whoever wishes to be first among you shall be slave of all."** Paradoxically, the path to greatness in the kingdom lies in humble self-denial; in being a **servant** and a **slave of all.**

The desire to be honored in the kingdom is a noble desire. Paul wrote, "Therefore we also have as our ambition, whether at home or absent, to be pleasing to Him" (2 Cor. 5:9). To that end he "discipline[d his] body and [made] it [his] slave, so that, after [he had] preached to others, [he would] not be disqualified" (1 Cor. 9:27). Nearing the end of his life, he penned,

> I have fought the good fight, I have finished the course, I have kept the faith; in the future there is laid up for me the crown of righteousness,

which the Lord, the righteous Judge, will award to me on that day; and not only to me, but also to all who have loved His appearing. (2 Tim. 4:7)

The apostle John cautioned believers, "Watch yourselves, that you do not lose what we have accomplished, but that you may receive a full reward" (2 John 8). "Behold, I am coming quickly," Jesus declared, "and My reward is with Me, to render to every man according to what he has done" (Rev. 22:12).

But the road to that greatness in the kingdom lies in selfless service. *Diakonos* (**servant**) literally refers to those who waited on tables (it is so used in John 2:5, 9). *Doulos,* though frequently translated "servant" in English Bibles, actually means **slave** (cf. John MacArthur, *Slave* [Nashville: Thomas Nelson, 2010]). The Lord's point is that believers are to consider everyone their master, and themselves slaves to serve all.

The perfect example of such humble service is the Lord Jesus Christ, **the Son of Man.** Unlike the world's leaders, He **did not come to be served, but to serve;** not merely to be Lord and Master but also to be a slave of His Father and do His will (John 4:34; 17:4), and to serve sinners by the sacrifice of Himself. As noted earlier, the most profound illustration of Christ's humble service and obedience to the Father is His death (Phil. 2:5–8), when He gave **His life a ransom** (*lutron;* the price paid for the release of a slave) **for many.** Having made the greatest sacrifice, Jesus received the greatest honor:

> For this reason also, God highly exalted Him, and bestowed on Him the name which is above every name, so that at the name of Jesus every knee will bow, of those who are in heaven and on earth and under the earth, and that every tongue will confess that Jesus Christ is Lord, to the glory of God the Father. (Phil. 2:9–11)

In His vicarious, substitutionary death on behalf of sinners, He gave His life to pay to God in full the price of sin for all the people who would ever be saved throughout history. Christ's death propitiated God's wrath and fulfilled the demands of His justice for the elect, the redeemed. The one sacrifice of the Son of Man paid the ransom for the **many** who believe (Rom. 5:12–21; 1 Tim. 2:6; 1 Peter 2:24).

The Final
Miracle of Mercy
(Mark 10:46–52)

11

Then they came to Jericho. And as He was leaving Jericho with His disciples and a large crowd, a blind beggar named Bartimaeus, the son of Timaeus, was sitting by the road. When he heard that it was Jesus the Nazarene, he began to cry out and say, "Jesus, Son of David, have mercy on me!" Many were sternly telling him to be quiet, but he kept crying out all the more, "Son of David, have mercy on me!" And Jesus stopped and said, "Call him here." So they called the blind man, saying to him, "Take courage, stand up! He is calling for you." Throwing aside his cloak, he jumped up and came to Jesus. And answering him, Jesus said, "What do you want Me to do for you?" And the blind man said to Him, "Rabboni, I want to regain my sight!" And Jesus said to him, "Go; your faith has made you well." Immediately he regained his sight and began following Him on the road. (10:46–52)

This passage marks a milestone in our Lord's ministry. It is the last of His healings recorded in Mark's gospel, and one of the last before His death (He also healed the ear of the high priest's slave in Gethsemane [John 18:10], and performed healings in the temple after He drove out the merchants [Matt. 21:14]). It is also the next to last miracle recorded by Mark (the last was the withering of the fig tree in Mark 11:12–14, 20–21). Jesus' first miracle had taken place in Cana, a village in Galilee not far from Nazareth, where He turned water into wine (John 2:1–11); this one took place in the vicinity of Jericho. From Nazareth in the north of Galilee to Jericho in the south of Judea, Jesus bracketed Israel with countless miracles, which conclusively exhibited His absolute power over nature, disease, and the demonic realm. Those miracles demonstrated both His deity and His compassion. The ultimate miracle, His resurrection from the dead, was still to come. But before that final and greatest miracle, the Servant of the Lord would become the suffering servant; the anointed one would become the rejected one, and the sovereign Lord would become the sacrificial Lamb of God.

In keeping with the divine timetable, Jesus was on His way to Jerusalem for one final time (Mark 10:32–34). The hour of darkness had come to face the hatred and animosity of the religious leaders of Israel, be rejected by the nation, and be crucified by the godless Romans at the behest of the Jews and fulfill the will of His Father. The fickle crowd that hailed Him at the triumphal entry would a few days later scream for His execution. Israel would descend into the spiritual darkness of the greatest period of apostasy in its history—one that would see the nation execute its Lord and Messiah and continue down to the present. Although Christ's death was according to God's predetermined plan, that did not lesson the guilt of those involved (Acts 2:23).

After the healing and salvation of the two blind men and the conversion of Zaccheus (Luke 19:1–10) in the vicinity of Jericho, there are no conversions recorded during the final days of the Lord's earthly ministry, until a thief and a centurion were redeemed at the cross. Fittingly, all four men were despised outcasts—two blind men assumed to be under God's judgment for their sins, a criminal, and a soldier in the hated Roman occupation force. Thus, the salvation of Zaccheus and the two blind men (only one of whom is mentioned by Mark) are the last flickers of light before the darkness of Christ's suffering begins. Mark's account of the healing of one of the blind men may be simply divided into two parts: the blind man's faith, and the Savior's power.

THE BLIND MAN'S FAITH

Then they came to Jericho. And as He was leaving Jericho with His disciples and a large crowd, a blind beggar named Bartimaeus, the son of Timaeus, was sitting by the road. When he heard that it was Jesus the Nazarene, he began to cry out and say, "Jesus, Son of David, have mercy on me!" Many were sternly telling him to be quiet, but he kept crying out all the more, "Son of David, have mercy on me!" (10:46–48)

After crossing the Jordan River from Perea back into Israel, Jesus and those traveling with Him **came to Jericho.** Moving south from Galilee, they had detoured through Perea, located east of the Jordan, as was customary for Galileans seeking to avoid traveling through Samaria (cf. John 4:9). From Jericho, they would make the arduous six-hour ascent of the steep path leading up to Jerusalem.

Jericho was located approximately fifteen miles northeast from Jerusalem and about five miles west from the Jordan River. The flourishing New Testament city of Jericho was not far from the ruins of the Old Testament city (destroyed during Israel's original conquest of the land). That there were these two cities of Jericho in Jesus' day may explain why Matthew and Mark state that the healing took place while Jesus was leaving Jericho (i.e., the ruins of the Old Testament city), while Luke states that it occurred while He was approaching Jericho (i.e., the New Testament city). Those statements could also mean simply that the blind men were healed somewhere in the general vicinity of Jericho.

The noted nineteenth-century historian Alfred Edersheim gave a vivid description of **Jericho** as it was in Jesus' day:

> The ancient City occupied not the site of the present wretched hamlet, but lay about half an hour to the north-west of it, by the so-called Elisha-Spring. A second spring rose an hour further to the north-north-west. The water of these springs, distributed by aqueducts, gave, under a tropical

sky, unsurpassed fertility to the rich soil along the "plain" of Jericho, which is about twelve or fourteen miles wide.... *Josephus* describes it as the richest part of the country, and calls it a little Paradise. Antony had bestowed the revenues of its balsam-plantations as an Imperial gift upon Cleopatra, who in turn sold them to Herod. Here grew palm-trees of various kinds, sycamores, the cypress-flower, the myro-balsamum, which yielded precious oil, but especially the balsam-plant. If to these advantages of climate, soil, and productions we add, that it was, so to speak, the key of Judæa towards the east, that it lay on the caravan-road from Damascus and Arabia, that it was a great commercial and military centre, and lastly, its nearness to Jerusalem, to which it formed the last "station" on the road of the festive pilgrims from Galilee and Peræa—it will not be difficult to understand either its importance or its prosperity.

We can picture to ourselves the scene, as our Lord on that afternoon in early spring beheld it. There it was, indeed, already summer, for, as *Josephus* tells us, even in winter the inhabitants could only bear the lightest clothing of linen. We are approaching it from the Jordan. It is protected by walls, flanked by four forts. These walls, the theatre, and the Amphitheatre, have been built by Herod; the new palace and its splendid gardens are the work of Archelaus. All around wave groves of feathery palms, rising in stately beauty; stretch gardens of roses, and especially sweet-scented balsam-plantations—the largest behind the royal gardens, of which the perfume is carried by the wind almost out to sea, and which may have given to the city its name (Jericho, "the perfumed"). It is the Eden of Palestine, the very fairyland of the old world. And how strangely is this gem set! Deep down in that hollowed valley, through which tortuous Jordan winds, to lose his waters in the slimy mass of the Sea of Judgment. The river and the Dead Sea are nearly equidistant from the town—about six miles. Far across the river rise the mountains of Moab, on which lies the purple and violet colouring. Towards Jerusalem and northwards stretch those bare limestone hills, the hiding-place of robbers along the desolate road towards the City. There, and in the neighbouring wilderness of Judæa, are also the lonely dwellings of anchorites [hermits]—while over all this strangely varied scene has been flung the many-coloured mantle of a perpetual summer. And in the streets of Jericho a motley throng meets: pilgrims from Galilee and Peræa, priests who have a "station" here, traders from all lands, who have come to purchase or to sell, or are on the great caravan-road from Arabia and Damascus—robbers and anchorites, wild fanatics, soldiers, courtiers, and busy publicans—for Jericho was the central station for the collection of tax and custom, both on native produce and on that brought from across Jordan. (*The Life and Times of Jesus the Messiah* [repr., Grand Rapids: Eerdmans, 1971], 2:349–51. Italics in original)

Not far from Jericho was a massive rock formation casting its shadow over the city as the sun set each evening. Some believe that it was in this severe, rugged, barren land of steep cliffs and deep canyons that the Lord was tempted by Satan.

The **large crowd** accompanying **Jesus** and **His disciples** would have drawn the interest of many of Jericho's inhabitants. Jesus, as always, was the focus of intense interest, all the more so since word of His raising of dead Lazarus to life had filtered down the hill from Bethany.

In the crowd lining the road along which Jesus was walking was **a blind beggar named Bartimaeus** who, as his name indicates, was **the son of Timaeus,** along with his unnamed blind companion. That only Bartimaeus is named suggests that by the time Mark wrote his gospel, he may have become a well-known figure in the early church. The two blind beggars were **sitting by the road,** necessarily for being seen by the people.

Blindness, common in the ancient world (cf. Matt. 11:5; 15:30; 21:14), as always was caused by birth defects, injury, or disease. The malady was so familiar to His hearers that Jesus used it to illustrate spiritual ignorance (e.g., Matt. 15:14; Luke 4:18; 14:13). Beggars also were numerous in Israel (cf. Luke 16:3; Acts 3:2, 10). The blind, like all those with disabilities, were despised and reduced to begging (cf. John 9:8), since they were considered to be sinners under God's judgment (John 9:1–2). Jesus' reference to the Pharisees as blind leaders of the blind (Matt. 15:14; 23:16–24) was thus an extremely severe rebuke of those who despised the blind as cursed.

In response to Bartimaeus's question about what was happening, the bystanders told him that Jesus and those accompanying Him were passing by (Luke 18:36). **When** Bartimaeus **heard that it was Jesus the Nazarene, he began to cry out** (Gk. *kradzō*; "to shout with a loud voice," or "to scream" [cf. Matt. 21:9, 15; 27:23, 50; Mark 3:11; 5:5; John 1:15; 7:28], sometimes, as here, for help [e.g., Matt. 14:30; 15:22; Mark 9:24]) **and say, "Jesus, Son of David, have mercy on me!"** Instead of referring to Jesus as **the Nazarene,** thereby associating Him with His hometown of Nazareth (cf. Luke 18:37), Bartimaeus addressed Him by the familiar messianic title **Son of David** (Matt. 1:1; 9:27; 12:23; 15:22; 21:9, 15; 22:42; cf. Rev. 22:16). According to 2 Samuel 7, the Messiah would be David's greater son, the heir to his throne (cf. Mark 11:10; Luke 1:32). He would be the king who would bring the fulfillment of all the promises to Abraham and David. Jesus was a descendant of David, as were His earthly father, Joseph, and His mother, Mary (Matt. 1:6,16,20; Luke 1:27; 2:4; 3:23–38).

Bartimaeus's repeated request to the one he acknowledged as Israel's Messiah was, **"Have mercy on me!"** That was the typical plea of the afflicted, but it was more than mere words for this man; it was the cry of his heart. He knew he did not deserve anything, because according to Jewish theology, his blindness was God's curse on him due to his sin. In asking for mercy, undeserved kindness, he acknowledged that he was a sinner. His mind saw the light before his eyes did.

Bartimaeus's sad plight and repeated cries for mercy elicited no sympathy from the crowd. **Many** of them, including "those who led the way" (i.e., were in charge of crowd control; Luke 18:39), **were sternly telling him to be quiet.** But their disdain for this outcast beggar who was making a nuisance of himself placed no restraint on him. Ignoring the crowd's attempts to silence him and being drawn to Jesus surely by the Holy Spirit, Bartimaeus **kept crying out all the more, "Son of David, have mercy on me!"**

THE SAVIOR'S POWER

And Jesus stopped and said, "Call him here." So they called the blind man, saying to him, "Take courage, stand up! He is calling for you." Throwing aside his cloak, he jumped up and came to Jesus. And answering him, Jesus said, "What do you want Me to do for you?" And the blind man said to Him, "Rabboni, I want to regain my sight!" And Jesus said to him, "Go; your faith has made you well." Immediately he regained his sight and began following Him on the road. (10:49–52)

The focus of the story now shifts from the blind, desperate beggar to the creator Lord who had the supernatural power to heal him. Demonstrating the sympathy that marked His dealings with those in need (cf. Matt. 9:36; 14:14; 15:32; Mark 1:41; Luke 7:13), **Jesus stopped and said, "Call him here."** The Lord's response changed the crowd's attitude toward Bartimaeus, at least for the moment. Curious, hoping to see Jesus perform another miracle, **they called the blind man, saying to him, "Take courage, stand up! He is calling for you."**

Acting in eager faith, without doubt or hesitation, Bartimaeus reacted immediately to the Lord's summons. **Throwing aside his cloak, he jumped up and,** no doubt led by someone from the crowd, **came to Jesus.** When Bartimaeus came to Him, Jesus said, **"What do you want Me to do for you?"** The Lord's question reveals a very different attitude than that of James and John (see the exposition of 10:35–45 in the previous chapter of this volume). The high King of heaven, the Son of God, the second person of the Trinity incarnate, offered to serve a debased, lowly, outcast, and unworthy sinner.

Bartimaeus responded, **"Rabboni, I want to regain my sight!"** By using the terms **Rabboni** ("my master") and "Lord" as Matthew records (Matt. 20:33), he placed himself in submission to Jesus as his sovereign. Unlike James and John, who thought they deserved elevation, he knew he deserved nothing. He sought only mercy, to receive what he did not deserve. That he asked that he might **regain** his sight suggests that he had not been born blind.

After touching his eyes (Matt. 20:34) and saying to him, "Receive your sight" (Luke 18:42) **Jesus said to him, "Go; your faith has made you well."** The use of the Greek verb *sōzō* (**well**), which is used frequently in the New Testament to refer to salvation (e.g., Matt. 1:21; 19:25; Luke 8:12; 9:24; 13:23; 19:10; John 10:9; Acts 2:21; 4:12; 16:30, 31; Rom. 5:9, 10; 10:9, 13; 1 Cor. 1:18; Eph. 2:8; 1 Tim. 1:15; 2 Tim. 1:9; Titus 3:5), instead of *iaomai* ("to heal"), along with their messianic recognition of Jesus, indicates that Bartimaeus and the other blind man (Matt. 20:34) received not merely physical healing but also eternal salvation. **Immediately** the two men **regained** their **sight and began following Him on the road—** another sign that in addition to physical sight, their spiritual eyes were opened.

At this point it is helpful to note that six features characterized Christ's healing ministry.

First, Jesus healed with a word, a touch, or some other gesture.

Second, Jesus healed instantly. There were no progressive healings, in which the people He cured gradually got better. Peter's mother-in-law's symptoms vanished at once and she was fully restored to health

(Luke 4:38–39). Similarly, the centurion's servant "was healed that very moment" (Matt. 8:13); a woman with a hemorrhage was healed "immediately" (Mark 5:29); the ten lepers were cleansed of their disease as soon as they left to show themselves to the priests (Luke 17:14); after Jesus "stretched out His hand and touched [another leper] ... immediately the leprosy left him" (Luke 5:13); when Jesus commanded the crippled man at the pool of Bethesda, "Get up, pick up your pallet and walk. Immediately the man became well, and picked up his pallet and began to walk" (John 5:8–9). Some argue that the Lord's healing of the blind man in Bethsaida (Mark 8:22–25) was an example of a progressive healing. But the man's statement, "I see men, for I see them like trees, walking around" (v. 24), merely defined his preexisting condition of blindness. The actual healing was instantaneous (v. 25). Had Jesus' healings not been instantaneous, His critics could have claimed that the people became better as a result of natural processes.

Third, Jesus healed totally. Peter's mother-in-law was cured of all her symptoms and went at once from being bedridden to serving a meal. When Jesus healed a man "covered with leprosy" (Luke 5:12), "the leprosy left him" (v. 13). It was the same with all of Jesus' healings; "the blind receive[d] sight and the lame walke[d], the lepers [were] cleansed and the deaf hear[d]" (Matt. 11:5).

Fourth, Jesus healed everyone. Unlike modern false healers, He did not leave behind long lines of disappointed, distraught people who were not healed. Matthew 4:24 says that "the news about Him spread throughout all Syria; and they brought to Him all who were ill, those suffering with various diseases and pains, demoniacs, epileptics, paralytics; and He healed them." According to Matthew 12:15, "Many followed Him, and He healed them all," while Luke 6:19 notes that "all the people were trying to touch Him, for power was coming from Him and healing them all." So widespread was Jesus' healing that He, in effect, banished disease from Israel during the three years of His ministry.

Fifth, Jesus healed organic disease, not vague, ambiguous, invisible ailments such as lower back pain, heart palpitations, or headaches. On the contrary, with creative power, He restored full mobility to paralyzed limbs, full sight to blind eyes, full hearing to deaf ears, and fully cleansed leprous skin. Jesus healed "every kind of disease and every kind of sickness among the people" (Matt. 4:23; cf. 9:35). All of Jesus' healings were undeniable, miraculous signs, as even His most bitter enemies admitted (John 11:47).

Finally, Jesus raised the dead—not those who were in a temporary coma, or whose vital signs fluctuated during surgery, but a young man in his casket on his way to the graveyard (Luke 7:11–15), a young girl whose death was apparent to all (Mark 5:22–24, 35–43), and a man who had been dead for four days (John 11:14–44)

Not all of those who witnessed this amazing miracle believed in Jesus, as the two blind men did. Nevertheless, they could not deny that they had witnessed a miracle. As a result, "when all the people saw it, they gave praise to God" (Luke 18:43; cf. John 3:1–2).

This passage is significant for several reasons. First, it is a model of salvation before the cross. Bartimaeus understood that he was a sinner, under God's judgment, and in need of mercy. He acknowledged Jesus as the Messiah, who came to save His people from their sins (Isa. 53:5–6; Matt. 1:21), and as his sovereign Lord.

Second, Jesus' response shows that He does not ignore those who cry out to Him for mercy (Matt. 11:28; John 6:37).

Third, Jesus is deeply compassionate over the plight of hurting, lost sinners.

Finally, although the Lord Jesus has absolute power over disease, He did not come merely to heal the sick but "to seek and to save that which was lost" (Luke 19:10).

The False Coronation of the True King (Mark 11:1–11)

12

As they approached Jerusalem, at Bethphage and Bethany, near the Mount of Olives, He sent two of His disciples, and said to them, "Go into the village opposite you, and immediately as you enter it, you will find a colt tied there, on which no one yet has ever sat; untie it and bring it here. If anyone says to you, 'Why are you doing this?' you say, 'The Lord has need of it'; and immediately he will send it back here." They went away and found a colt tied at the door, outside in the street; and they untied it. Some of the bystanders were saying to them, "What are you doing, untying the colt?" They spoke to them just as Jesus had told them, and they gave them permission. They brought the colt to Jesus and put their coats on it; and He sat on it. And many spread their coats in the road, and others spread leafy branches which they had cut from the fields. Those who went in front and those who followed were shouting: "Hosanna! Blessed is He who comes in the name of the Lord; Blessed is the coming kingdom of our father David; Hosanna in the highest!" Jesus entered Jerusalem

**and came into the temple; and after looking around at every-
thing, He left for Bethany with the twelve, since it was already
late.** (11:1–11)

This passage introduces the final week of our Lord's life and public ministry. The week began with His arrival at Jerusalem on the tenth
day of the first month in the Jewish calendar, the month Nisan, in the year
A.D. 30. That was Passover Week; the triumphal entry was on Monday the
tenth, and Passover followed on Friday the fourteenth of the month.

The traditional title for the event described in this passage, the triumphal entry, does not capture what was happening. This was not in any
sense—earthly, Jewish, or heavenly—the coronation of Jesus Christ. The
crowd's delirious reaction was not a genuine expression of faith in or
praise for Israel's true King. There were no formalities associated with the
event; no dignitaries, no regalia, no fanfare. Nor was this event God's coronation of His Son. Despite its outward appearance, it was an event unlike
any other coronation. Coronations are not humble, unexpected, sponta-
neous, unofficial, or superficial. This event was all of those. Nor are true
coronations reversed a few days afterward, with the one who had been
exalted and praised being rejected and executed. Although Jesus was
heaven's true King, deserving of all exaltation, honor, worship, and praise,
this was not a real coronation; it was, in fact, the false coronation of the
true King.

The official investiture of the Lord Jesus Christ takes place in two
stages. The first, His heavenly coronation, took place at His ascension
when "He sat down at the right hand of the Majesty on high" (Heb. 1:3; cf.
1:13; 8:1; 10:12; 12:2), and "God highly exalted Him, and bestowed on Him
the name which is above every name" (Phil. 2:9). The second, earthly
phase of His coronation will take place in the future. The Lord Jesus will
return to earth, not riding on a donkey's colt but coming out of heaven
on a white horse followed by the armies of heaven (holy angels and
redeemed people), also riding on white horses (Rev. 19:11–15). When He
arrives, He will judge and destroy the ungodly, and establish His throne in
Jerusalem. Jesus will reign there for a thousand years in the millennial
kingdom (Rev. 20:4) and beyond that throughout all eternity in the new
heaven and the new earth (Luke 1:33; cf. Isa. 9:7; Dan. 2:44).

Mark's account of this event began as Jesus and those accompanying Him **approached Jerusalem,** ascending the steep path leading up the hill from Jericho. The Lord's public ministry in Galilee, Judea, and Perea was ended, and His death was little more than a week away. The entourage of people with Jesus had grown after two startling events took place in the vicinity of Jericho: the healing and salvation of two blind beggars (see the exposition of 10:46–52 in the previous chapter of this volume) and the conversion of the hated and reviled tax collector Zaccheus (Luke 19:2–9). Those events, coupled with the Lord's recent raising of Lazarus from the dead, heightened the crowd's excitement and enthusiasm as they headed for Jerusalem to celebrate Passover, the high point of the Jewish year.

Not only was this supposed coronation bogus, it was also premature. Before Jesus comes to reign, He had to die (cf. the discussion of 10:32–34 in chapter 9 of this volume). Up to this point Jesus had not permitted an open, public declaration that He was the Messiah. After Peter's affirmation that He was the "the Christ, the Son of the living God" (Matt. 16:16), Jesus "warned the disciples that they should tell no one that He was the Christ" (v. 20). Following the spectacular miracle of the feeding of the five thousand plus in Galilee, the people exclaimed, "This is truly the Prophet who is to come into the world." So Jesus, perceiving that they were intending to come and take Him by force to make Him king, withdrew again to the mountain by Himself alone" (John 6:14–15), thwarting their attempt. The Lord knew that any significant public escalation of His popularity would increase the threat He posed to the Jewish leaders. That might have provoked them to bring about His death prematurely.

Now, however, the time had come in the divinely determined plan for Jesus to die. He therefore permitted such a massive display of popular acclaim (some suggest there may have been as many as one hundred thousand people involved in the triumphal entry procession) that the religious leaders had no choice. The threat of a revolt by the estimated two million people who flooded Jerusalem for Passover could not be ignored. As the religious leaders well knew, that would provoke a massive response from the Romans, resulting in the destruction of the nation and the loss of their own privileged position (John 11:47–50).

THE FAITHFUL ARRIVAL

at Bethphage and Bethany, near the Mount of Olives, He sent two of His disciples, and said to them, "Go into the village opposite you, and immediately as you enter it, you will find a colt tied there, on which no one yet has ever sat; untie it and bring it here. If anyone says to you, 'Why are you doing this?' you say, 'The Lord has need of it'; and immediately he will send it back here." They went away and found a colt tied at the door, outside in the street; and they untied it. Some of the bystanders were saying to them, "What are you doing, untying the colt?" They spoke to them just as Jesus had told them, and they gave them permission. They brought the colt to Jesus and put their coats on it; and He sat on it. (11:1b–7)

On Saturday six days before the Passover (John 12:1), Jesus arrived **at** the small villages of **Bethphage** (possibly "house of figs") **and Bethany** (possibly "house of dates"), **near the Mount of Olives.** On the next day, Sunday, He attended a dinner in His honor at the home of Simon the leper in Bethany (Matt. 26:6–13). On that same day a "large crowd of the Jews then learned that He was there; and they came, not for Jesus' sake only, but that they might also see Lazarus, whom He raised from the dead" (John 12:9).

Christ's entry into Jerusalem took place the following day (John 12:12), Monday of Passion Week, not on Sunday as Christians have traditionally believed. This chronology eliminates the problem of the Gospels having no record of Jesus' activities on Wednesday, which would be the case if the triumphal entry were on Sunday. It is difficult to explain how there could be a day omitted in the account of the most momentous week of Christ's life, especially since the events of all the other days are carefully accounted for.

Further evidence that the triumphal entry was on Monday comes from the Law's requirement that the Passover lambs be selected on the tenth day of the first month (Nisan) and sacrificed on the fourteenth day (Ex. 12:2–6). In the year our Lord was crucified, the tenth of Nisan fell on Monday of Passover Week. When He entered Jerusalem on that day, Jesus came to fulfill the role of the Father's chosen Lamb (John 1:29,36) in much the same way and on the same day as the Jewish people chose their Passover lambs. Completing the parallel, Christ, the one true sacrifice that took away sin, was killed on Friday, the fourteenth day of Nisan, with thousands of other lambs, whose blood could never take away sin (cf. Heb. 10:4).

According to this chronology of Passion Week, Jesus returned to Bethany Monday night after the triumphal entry, and came back into Jerusalem on Tuesday, when He cursed the fig tree and cleansed the temple. On Wednesday He was involved in controversy with the leaders of Israel, gave a sermon on His second coming, and Judas planned his betrayal of Him. On Thursday His disciples prepared for the Passover meal, which they celebrated in the upper room. From there the Lord and the disciples went to Gethsemane, where He was betrayed and arrested. After several trials before the Sanhedrin and the secular rulers Pilate and Herod Thursday night into early Friday morning, the Lord was crucified on Friday. Saturday He was in the grave and Sunday He came back to life.

On Monday, the Lord **sent two of His disciples** (perhaps Peter and John; cf. Luke 22:8), **and said to them, "Go into the village opposite you** (probably Bethphage, since Jesus was likely staying with Mary, Martha, and Lazarus in Bethany), **and immediately as you enter it, you will find a colt tied there, on which no one yet has ever sat; untie it and bring it here.** The details of what the disciples found there clearly demonstrate Christ's omniscience (cf. John 1:47–48; 2:25). He told them that they would **find a** donkey (John 12:14; cf. Zech. 9:9) **colt** (and its mother; Matt. 21:22) **tied.** Jesus had not been to Bethphage, nor had He sent anyone to arrange for the colt to be available. The detail that the colt was one **on which no one yet** had **ever sat** provides further evidence of His omniscience, as does His knowledge that the disciples would be asked as they untied the colt, "Why are you untying it?" (Luke 19:31). The Lord also knew that when they replied, **"The Lord has need of it,"** the colt's owner (evidently a believer in Jesus) and the **bystanders** would permit them to take it.

Events unfolded just as the omniscient Lord had said they would. The two disciples **went away and found a colt tied at the door, outside in the street; and they untied it.** As Jesus had predicted, **some of**

the bystanders were saying to them, "What are you doing, untying the colt?" But the disciples spoke to them just as Jesus had told
them, and they gave them permission. The two men brought the
colt to Jesus (most likely back in Bethany) and put their coats on it,
forming a makeshift saddle so that the Lord would not have to ride bare-
back, and He sat on it.

It is true that David rode a mule (1 Kings 1:33, 38, 44), which
Solomon also rode to his coronation (1 Kings 1:32–40). But by riding the
donkey colt, Jesus was not merely identifying with Davidic tradition.
Instead, "This took place to fulfill what was spoken through the prophet:
'Say to the daughter of Zion, "Behold your king is coming to you, gentle,
and mounted on a donkey, even on a colt, the foal of a beast of burden"'"
(Matt. 21:4–5). Matthew was referring to a prophecy made centuries earlier
by Zechariah, who wrote, "Rejoice greatly, O daughter of Zion! Shout in triumph, O daughter of Jerusalem! Behold, your king is coming to you; He is
just and endowed with salvation, humble, and mounted on a donkey,
even on a colt, the foal of a donkey" (Zech. 9:9). That Jesus meekly rode a
donkey's colt signifies the reality that in His first coming He came not to
reign but to die.

Jesus fulfilled another Old Testament prophecy that day, Daniel's
prophecy of the seventy weeks. As various scholars (most notably Sir
Robert Anderson [*The Coming Prince*] and Harold Hoehner [*Chronological Aspects of the Life of Christ*]) have demonstrated, the day that He
entered Jerusalem was the precise date predicted by Daniel centuries
earlier. The significance of what was happening largely escaped the disciples. Looking back on this event decades later, John wrote, "These things
His disciples did not understand at the first; but when Jesus was glorified
[after the ascension], then they remembered that these things were written of Him, and that they had done these things to Him" (John 12:16).

THE FAITHLESS APPROVAL

And many spread their coats in the road, and others spread leafy
branches which they had cut from the fields. Those who went in
front and those who followed were shouting: "Hosanna! Blessed

**is He who comes in the name of the Lord; Blessed is the coming
kingdom of our father David; Hosanna in the highest!"** (11:8–10)

As Jesus approached Jerusalem, the crowd's excitement intensified. **Many** of the people **spread their coats in the road, and others
spread leafy branches which they had cut from the fields.** Spreading **their coats in the road** in front of Jesus was a customary way of
expressing submission to a monarch. It acknowledged that the king was
elevated above the common people, and symbolically affirmed that they
were under his feet. Superficially and momentarily at least, the crowd
was acknowledging Jesus as the messianic king. The **leafy branches** of
palm trees (John 12:13), **which** others in the crowd **had cut from the
fields,** symbolized joy and victory. According to the apocryphal book of
First Maccabees, when the Jews during the intertestamental period
recaptured Jerusalem from the Syrians, they "entered it with praise and
palm branches" (1 Macc. 13:51; cf. 2 Macc. 10:7).

The crowd's enthusiasm stemmed in large part from "all the miracles which they had seen" (Luke 19:37). Those miracles included the
recent bringing Lazarus back from being dead for four days, and the
healing of the two blind men at Jericho. Expressing their excitement and
hope, the people **were shouting: "Hosanna! Blessed is He who comes
in the name of the Lord; Blessed is the coming kingdom of our
father David; Hosanna in the highest!"** The exclamation **Hosanna**
("Save now") was a messianic accolade, which Matthew links to the messianic title Son of David (Matt. 21:9, 15; cf. Mark 12:35). The expressions
Blessed is He who comes in the name of the Lord (cf. Ps. 118:26)
and **Blessed is the coming kingdom of our father David** also express messianic praise and hope. The crowd's exclamation, **"Hosanna in
the highest!"** was the supreme expression of praise.

The people, however, were not pleading for salvation from sin but
for blessing, prosperity, and deliverance from Roman rule and oppression. They sought the fulfillment of all the promises connected with Messiah's reign. And when Jesus did not deliver those promises, which will be
fulfilled in connection with His second coming, their faithless approval
would turn to hostile rejection. As noted earlier, Jesus came the first time
to die (10:32–34, 45). Tragically, many who on Monday exuberantly hailed

Him as the Messiah and shouted praises to God would on Friday scream for His execution. Thus, they would share in the responsibility for the death of their Messiah, as Peter declared in his sermon on the day of Pentecost:

> Men of Israel, listen to these words: Jesus the Nazarene, a man attested to you by God with miracles and wonders and signs which God performed through Him in your midst, just as you yourselves know—this Man, delivered over by the predetermined plan and foreknowledge of God, you nailed to a cross by the hands of godless men and put Him to death. (Acts 2:22–23)

While for the moment their hopes were sky-high, their faithless praise did not fool Jesus:

> When He approached Jerusalem, He saw the city and wept over it, saying, "If you had known in this day, even you, the things which make for peace! But now they have been hidden from your eyes. For the days will come upon you when your enemies will throw up a barricade against you, and surround you and hem you in on every side, and they will level you to the ground and your children within you, and they will not leave in you one stone upon another, because you did not recognize the time of your visitation." (Luke 19:41–44)

They would reject Him, and in response God would bring down on themselves devastating judgment at the hands of the Romans, resulting in the destruction of the nation.

THE FATEFUL APPRAISAL

Jesus entered Jerusalem and came into the temple; and after looking around at everything, He left for Bethany with the twelve, since it was already late. (11:11)

Mark's anticlimactic statement reinforces the reality that this was no true coronation. At the same time, it foreshadows the Lord's assault on the temple, which would take place the following day (Tuesday). Having come **into the temple,** Jesus, **after looking around at** all the corruption there, **left for Bethany with the twelve, since it was already late** in the day.

Like the fickle crowd, sinners will turn on Jesus when He does not satisfy their selfish whims. False coronations like the one described in this passage take place every day. Unscrupulous false teachers promise their deluded followers that Jesus will make them rich, heal them, fulfill all their dreams, and grant all their desires. When such unbiblical, selfish, man-centered promises fail to come to pass, and trouble comes into their lives instead, many grow disillusioned and turn against Jesus. (I examine the danger posed by the prosperity gospel in my books _Strange Fire_ [Nashville: Thomas Nelson, 2013], and _Charismatic Chaos_ [Grand Rapids: Zondervan, 1992].)

The redeemed, on the other hand, acknowledge Jesus as their sovereign King (Acts 17:7; cf. Rev. 17:14; 19:16), worthy of their complete submission (1 Peter 3:15; cf. 2 Cor. 4:5) and reverent worship (Matt. 14:33; 28:9, 17; Luke 24:52; John 9:38; cf. Heb. 1:6). Theirs is a true coronation of Jesus; as the writer of the familiar hymn "Lead Me to Calvary" expressed it,

> King of my life, I crown Thee now,
> Thine shall the glory be.

Nothing but Leaves
(Mark 11:12–21)

13

On the next day, when they had left Bethany, He became hungry. Seeing at a distance a fig tree in leaf, He went to see if perhaps He would find anything on it; and when He came to it, He found nothing but leaves, for it was not the season for figs. He said to it, "May no one ever eat fruit from you again!" And His disciples were listening. Then they came to Jerusalem. And He entered the temple and began to drive out those who were buying and selling in the temple, and overturned the tables of the money changers and the seats of those who were selling doves; and He would not permit anyone to carry merchandise through the temple. And He began to teach and say to them, "Is it not written, 'My house shall be called a house of prayer for all the nations'? But you have made it a robbers' den." The chief priests and the scribes heard this, and began seeking how to destroy Him; for they were afraid of Him, for the whole crowd was astonished at His teaching. When evening came, they would go out of the city. As they were passing by in the morning, they saw the fig tree withered from

the roots up. Being reminded, Peter said to Him, "Rabbi, look, the fig tree which You cursed has withered." (11:12–21)

This passage introduces a monumental day in redemptive history. On Tuesday of Passion Week, the Lord Jesus Christ, in a complete reversal of the Jewish people's messianic hopes and expectations, in essence pronounced a curse on the temple. That curse, consigning it to God's judgment, by extension included the corrupt religious leaders and the entire nation. In a shocking turn of events, Israel, the covenant nation, chosen (Deut. 7:6; 14:2; 1 Kings 3:8; Pss. 105:6; 135:4; Isa. 44:1; Amos 3:2) and blessed (Gen. 12:2–3; Num. 22:12; Deut. 1:11; Ps. 33:12) by God, was cursed by God's Messiah, because of its rejection of Him. That rejection would culminate on Friday when the crowd, urged on by the religious leaders, called for the execution of the Son of God.

Jesus' cursing of the fig tree, the only destructive miracle recorded in the Gospels, serves as a symbol previewing the coming destruction of the temple. The Lord's assault on the temple and the merchants polluting it is a prediction by action of the temple's destruction. His cursing of the fig tree, and thus symbolically the temple, manifests God's displeasure with the place, its leaders, and the people who worshiped there.

Throughout the nation's history, the temple had been the heart of Israel's religious life. For centuries before the first temple was built, Israel's worship occurred around the tabernacle, which was in effect a mobile temple (cf. Ex. 25–30; 35:30–40:38; Lev. 10:1–7). The first fixed temple was planned by David (2 Sam. 7:1–11; 1 Chron. 22:1–19), who purchased the site of the temple (Mt. Moriah [2 Chron. 3:1], where centuries earlier Abraham had been told by God to offer Isaac [Gen. 22:2]), and built by Solomon (1 Kings 8:1–66). After centuries of apostasy and rebellion, God withdrew His presence from the temple (Ezek. 9:3; 10:4, 18–19; 11:22–23), and it was destroyed in 586 B.C. by the forces of the Babylonian king Nebuchadnezzar (2 Kings 25:9; 2 Chron. 36:19; Isa. 64:11).

After the seventy-year Babylonian captivity, the returned exiles under the leadership of Zerubbabel rebuilt the temple. That second temple did not at all approach the splendor of Solomon's temple. Smaller and less ornate, the sight of it caused those old enough to remember the first temple to weep (Ezra 3:12). This second temple was desecrated during the intertestamental period by the diabolical Seleucid ruler Antiochus IV (Epiphanes), as predicted in Daniel's prophecy (Dan. 11:31).

In 20 B.C. Herod the Great began the restoration and expansion of Zerubbabel's temple, a long process (cf. John 2:20) that continued until A.D. 64—a mere six years before the Romans destroyed the temple in A.D. 70. It is this rebuilt and enlarged temple that is in view in this passage.

The story of the temple reflects Israel's history of apostasy, which culminated in the rejection and murder of the Messiah. Since the Romans destroyed Herod's temple in A.D. 70, no new temple has been built. In the future, however, there will be two more temples. A temple will be built during the tribulation, which Antichrist will desecrate (Matt. 24:15; 2 Thess. 2:4), and a final temple will be built during the millennial kingdom (Ezek. 40–43). In the eternal state, there will be no need for a temple, "for the Lord God the Almighty and the Lamb are its temple" (Rev. 21:22).

This passage, which previews the demolition of Herod's temple, may be examined under two headings: the curse previewed and portrayed in analogy, and the curse previewed and portrayed in action.

THE CURSE PREVIEWED AND PORTRAYED IN ANALOGY

On the next day, when they had left Bethany, He became hungry. Seeing at a distance a fig tree in leaf, He went to see if perhaps He would find anything on it; and when He came to it, He found nothing but leaves, for it was not the season for figs. He said to it, "May no one ever eat fruit from you again!" And His disciples were listening. (11:12–14)

On Tuesday, **the next day** after the triumphal entry on Monday (see the discussion of 11:1–11 in the previous chapter of this volume), Jesus and the disciples **left** the home of Mary, Martha, and Lazarus in **Bethany** for Jerusalem. On the way, Jesus **became hungry.** Though He was God incarnate, Jesus was also fully man and thus subject to the limitations of being human (cf. Heb. 2:14). He not only regularly experienced hunger, as on this occasion and at His temptation (Matt. 4:2), but also thirst (John 4:7) and weariness (Mark 4:38; John 4:6). Perhaps the Lord had not eaten breakfast before they left, possibly because He chose to spend time in prayer. Jesus knew that He faced a formidable task that day that would require strength and energy, and thus He needed food.

In the **distance** Jesus saw **a fig tree in leaf,** and **He went to see if perhaps He would find anything on it.** Fig trees were ubiquitous in Israel and are mentioned about fifty times in Scripture. It was reasonable for the Lord to expect to find immature fruit on this fig tree, even though **it was not the season for figs.** Although the main fig harvest was in late summer and fall, small but edible unripe figs (cf. Isa. 28:4; Hos. 9:10; Mic. 7:1) appeared in spring, about the time of Passover, before the leaves did. Since the tree in question had leaves, it would be expected to have figs.

But despite its promising appearance, the tree was barren. There were no figs on it, **nothing but leaves.** Seeing that, the Lord cursed the fig tree and **said to it, "May no one ever eat fruit from you again!"** According to Matthew's account, He declared, "No longer shall there ever be any fruit from you" (Matt. 21:19); hence, no one would be able to eat any from it. Jesus pronounced a curse (see the discussion of v. 21 below) on the fig tree that killed it.

The barren fig tree graphically illustrates the empty pretense of worship in the temple. Through the prophet Isaiah, God, using another agricultural metaphor, pronounced a similar judgment on Israel:

> Let me sing now for my well-beloved a song of my beloved concerning His vineyard. My well-beloved had a vineyard on a fertile hill. He dug it all around, removed its stones, and planted it with the choicest vine. And He built a tower in the middle of it and also hewed out a wine vat in it; then He expected it to produce good grapes, but it produced only worthless ones. "And now, O inhabitants of Jerusalem and men of Judah, judge between Me and My vineyard. What more was there to do for My vineyard that I have not done in it? Why, when I expected it to produce good grapes did it produce worthless ones? So now let Me tell you what I am going to do to My vineyard: I will remove its hedge and it will be consumed; I will break down its wall and it will become trampled ground. I will lay it waste; it will not be pruned or hoed, but briars and thorns will come up. I will also charge the clouds to rain no rain on it." For the vineyard of the Lord of hosts is the house of Israel and the men of Judah His delightful plant. Thus He looked for justice, but

behold, bloodshed; for righteousness, but behold, a cry of distress. (Isa. 5:1–7)

Quoting Isaiah 29:13, Jesus condemned the hypocrisy of the scribes and Pharisees: "You hypocrites, rightly did Isaiah prophesy of you: 'This people honors Me with their lips, but their heart is far away from Me. But in vain do they worship Me, teaching as doctrines the precepts of men'" (Matt. 15:7–9; cf. 23:13–36).

The destruction of the temple would not take place immediately. But as another parable in which a fig tree symbolized Israel (Luke 13:6–9) teaches, God's patient withholding of judgment was temporary. It would not be until four decades later, in A.D. 70, that Roman forces under the command of Titus would sack Jerusalem and burn and level the temple.

While **His disciples were listening** to Jesus talk about the fig tree, they no doubt remembered what the Lord said in Matthew 7:16–20, where He declared that false teachers are known by their fruits. They might also have remembered Deuteronomy 28:15–68, where Moses warned of the curses that would befall Israel should the people disobey God. Ultimately, the temple and the fruitless religious system it represented would be destroyed because Israel's leaders and people "not knowing about God's righteousness and seeking to establish their own ... did not subject themselves to the righteousness of God" (Rom. 10:3).

THE CURSE PREVIEWED AND PORTRAYED IN ACTION

Then they came to Jerusalem. And He entered the temple and began to drive out those who were buying and selling in the temple, and overturned the tables of the money changers and the seats of those who were selling doves; and He would not permit anyone to carry merchandise through the temple. And He began to teach and say to them, "Is it not written, 'My house shall be called a house of prayer for all the nations'? But you have made it a robbers' den." The chief priests and the scribes heard this, and began seeking how to destroy Him; for they were afraid of Him, for the whole crowd was astonished at His teaching. When

evening came, they would go out of the city. As they were passing by in the morning, they saw the fig tree withered from the roots up. Being reminded, Peter said to Him, "Rabbi, look, the fig tree which You cursed has withered." (11:15–21)

To the surprise and dismay of the people, Jesus, contrary to their messianic hopes and expectations, did not assault the Roman oppressors but attacked the temple, leaders, and worshipers instead. When **they came to Jerusalem** Tuesday morning, Jesus **entered the temple.** He did not, however, come to worship. As He had done at the beginning of His ministry (John 2:13–16), Christ came to declare the divine intolerance for the religious activities going on there, and for a day, at least, purge the courts of corruption by evicting the merchants polluting it. In between those two assaults, Jesus regularly confronted the apostasy and iniquity of Israel's religion and called the nation back to true worship of God through faith in Him (cf. John 4:23–24). The people of God are those "who worship in the Spirit of God and glory in Christ Jesus and put no confidence in the flesh" (Phil. 3:3).

Jesus, of course, was fully aware of the disturbing realities, inequities, and injustices that marred Jewish culture—the tax collectors who extorted money from the people, the abuse of the poor and the sick, whose conditions were deemed to be God's judgment on their sins, as well as many other evils that called for social reform and political action. But though disturbed by them, Jesus did not address any of those issues. He never deviated from the issue of worship, which dominated His life and ministry. A person's repentance and saving knowledge of God dominated His purpose and ultimately nothing else could be addressed or corrected until that was made right.

Judgment on the nation began with the temple. *Hieros* (**temple**) is the general term for the temple grounds as a whole, the vast complex that was able to accommodate thousands of worshipers. Within this area were several inner courts nested one inside of another. The innermost were the Holy of Holies and the Holy Place, which were designated by a different word for temple (*naos*). The outer court was the Court of the Gentiles, beyond which Gentiles were forbidden to go on pain of death.

What was happening in the Court of the Gentiles was gross corruption in the name of God. Such an outrage was blasphemy that filled Jesus with holy wrath. The Father's house had been turned into a commerce center, where hundreds of thousands of animals and the other items needed for the sacrifices were bought and sold. Money changers had also set up shop there. They provided a needed service. The temple tax could only be paid using Jewish or Tyrian coins, so foreigners had to exchange their money for acceptable coinage. But because they had a monopoly, granted by Annas and Caiaphas, the money changers charged exorbitant fees for their services.

The operations in the Court of the Gentiles had become known as the Bazaar of Annas, so named after the greedy high priest before whom Jesus would first be tried after His arrest in Gethsemane (John 18:13–23). Though Annas had been deposed by the Romans, he still retained the title of high priest and wielded tremendous power and influence behind the scenes. Along with his equally wicked son-in-law Caiaphas, the current high priest Annas ran the temple's business, acquiring extreme wealth in the process. They sold franchises to the merchants for exorbitant prices and then skimmed off a huge percentage of the profits that the vendors made.

All of this had combined to turn the temple of God into a place of abuse and extortion. The sound of praise and prayers had been replaced by the bawling of oxen, the bleating of sheep, the cooing of doves, and the loud haggling of merchants and their customers. Filled with holy anger at the crass desecration of His Father's house, Jesus made His way through the temple complex to the Court of the Gentiles and **began to drive out those who were buying and selling in the temple, and overturned the tables of the money changers and the seats of those who were selling doves.**

Instantly, the Lord Jesus turned the Bazaar of Annas into complete chaos. He so threatened the merchants that they fled as He overturned the money changers' tables and sent their coins rolling on the ground with the money changers, no doubt, desperately scrambling after them. He also yanked the seats out from under the dove sellers (Matt. 21:12) and frightened them out of the temple. The Lord displayed the same zeal that He had the first time He cleared the temple, which had reminded His disciples of Psalm 69:9: "Zeal for Your house has consumed me" (cf. John 2:17).

In addition to evicting the merchants, Jesus also stopped people from using the temple grounds as a shortcut to carry goods into the city, as **He would not permit anyone to carry merchandise through the temple.** This was an amazing display of singular authority and strength on the part of the Lord, who would have encountered significant resistance from the merchants. It forcefully demonstrates that the Lord hates those who pervert worship, especially for their own greed.

Mark relates a brief excerpt from what was undoubtedly a lengthy Old Testament exposition, noting that Jesus, subsequent to all this furious chaos, **began to teach and say to them, "Is it not written, 'My house shall be called a house of prayer for all the nations'? But you have made it a robbers' den."** The first quote, **My house shall be a house of prayer,** is from Isaiah 56:7, where God declares, "My house will be called a house of prayer for all the peoples." Prayer is the essence of worship, and the temple was where people came to commune with God (Ps. 65:4) and meditate on His majesty and glory (Ps. 27:4). The temple was not only for the Jews but also **for all the nations.**

There was no place for a Gentile proselyte to go to worship God except for the temple, as there were no temples outside of Israel. For example, Philip encountered "an Ethiopian eunuch, a court official of Candace, queen of the Ethiopians, who was in charge of all her treasure; and he had come to Jerusalem to worship" at the temple (Acts 8:27). Solomon, in his prayer of dedication for the temple, asked God "that [His] eyes may be open toward this house night and day, toward the place of which [He had] said, 'My name shall be there,' to listen to the prayer which Your servant shall pray toward this place" (1 Kings 8:29). Later in his prayer, Solomon extended that request to include Gentiles:

> Also concerning the foreigner who is not of Your people Israel, when he comes from a far country for Your name's sake (for they will hear of Your great name and Your mighty hand, and of Your outstretched arm); when he comes and prays toward this house, hear in heaven Your dwelling place, and do according to all for which the foreigner calls to You, in order that all the peoples of the earth may know Your name, to fear You, as do Your people Israel, and that they may know that this house which I have built is called by Your name. (vv. 41–43)

But the noisy, smelly, busy **robbers' den** that the temple had become was the antithesis of a place where quiet, thoughtful, instructional, prayerful worship of God could take place. Jesus' likening the temple to a robbers' den is a reference to Jeremiah 7:11: "'Has this house, which is called by My name, become a den of robbers in your sight? Behold, I, even I, have seen it,' declares the Lord." Robbers frequently hid in caves, from which they would issue forth to rob and plunder. That is what the temple had become; instead of the highest place of teaching, prayer, and worship, it was the lowest—a domain of plunder run by thieves.

Not surprisingly, the religious leaders were shocked and outraged by Jesus' solo devastation of their temple marketplace. Therefore when **the chief priests and the scribes heard** of what had happened, they **began seeking how to destroy** Jesus; **for they were afraid of Him, for the whole crowd was astonished at His teaching.** Their hatred was escalated by Jesus' growing popularity and continued healings (Matt. 21:14) and teaching (Luke 19:47). Fearful of the threat He posed to them economically and to their prestige among the people (John 11:48), they intensified their efforts to destroy Him.

Mark noted that **when evening came,** Jesus and the Twelve **would go out of the city** and return to Bethany (cf. Mark 14:3). **As they were passing by** it on Wednesday **morning** on their way back to Jerusalem, **they saw the fig tree withered from the roots up.** Peter's remark, **"Rabbi, look, the fig tree which You cursed has withered,"** affirms that what the Lord curses will be destroyed. The destruction of the corrupted religious system centered on the temple began that Tuesday. It would accelerate dramatically on Friday when God tore the veil separating the Holy Place from the Holy of Holies from top to bottom, and be completed four decades later by the Romans.

But that is not the end of Israel's story. As Paul asked rhetorically in Romans 11:1–2, "I say then, God has not rejected His people, has He? May it never be! For I too am an Israelite, a descendant of Abraham, of the tribe of Benjamin. God has not rejected His people whom He foreknew." It is true that "a partial hardening has happened to Israel until the fullness of the Gentiles has come in" (v. 25). But in the future the redeemed remnant of Israel will "look on Me whom they have pierced; and they will mourn for Him, as one mourns for an only son, and they will weep bitterly over Him like the bitter weeping over a firstborn" (Zech. 12:10), "and so all Israel will be saved" (Rom. 11:26). Until then, Jews are fellow members of the body of Christ with Gentiles (1 Cor. 12:13; Gal. 3:28; Eph. 2:11–16; Col. 3:11).

The Necessities for Effective Prayer (Mark 11:22–25)

14

And Jesus answered saying to them, "Have faith in God. Truly I say to you, whoever says to this mountain, 'Be taken up and cast into the sea,' and does not doubt in his heart, but believes that what he says is going to happen, it will be granted him. Therefore I say to you, all things for which you pray and ask, believe that you have received them, and they will be granted you. Whenever you stand praying, forgive, if you have anything against anyone, so that your Father who is in heaven will also forgive you your transgressions." (11:22–25)

In this brief passage our Lord reminded the disciples of the goodness God displays by granting access to heaven's power through prayer. The lesson took place on Wednesday morning of Passion Week as the Lord and the disciples were walking from Bethany to Jerusalem. As noted in the previous chapter of this volume, on their way to Jerusalem from Bethany the previous day (Tuesday), Jesus had previewed the future destruction of the temple by cursing a barren fig tree (11:12–14).

The question arises as to why the Lord would insert a lesson on prayer at this point. There was, however, a critical need for that instruction. In just a few days Jesus, God in human flesh, would no longer be physically present with the disciples. And though Jesus repeatedly stressed the importance of prayer and taught them specifically the elements of prayer (Matt. 6:9–13), His presence with them had restrained the urgency of their prayer lives. There was little reason for them to pray to God for what they could ask for and receive directly from Jesus. He provided provision, direction, protection, correction, and the patient instruction they needed.

But the familiar experience of His presence was about to change dramatically for the disciples. They were going to go from having Christ present all the time to not having Him present at all. They would become like believers of succeeding generations, who depend solely on prayer to access God's power and provision for their needs. Like them, the disciples would become totally dependent on one whom they could not see (cf. John 20:29; 1 Peter 1:8). That would be a monumental alteration of their lives, and they needed to know that their Lord Jesus would sustain them through the means of prayer (John 14:13–14; 15:16; 16:23–24, 26).

This important lesson reveals five components of effective prayer: its historical, theological, spiritual, practical, and moral components.

THE HISTORICAL COMPONENT OF PRAYER

On their way back to Bethany Tuesday evening in the darkness, the disciples had not noticed that the cursed fig tree had died. But "as they were passing by ... the [next] morning, they saw the fig tree withered from the roots up" (11:20). Noticing that Peter commented, "Rabbi, look, the fig tree which You cursed has withered" (v. 21). The transition from that comment to the Lord's teaching on prayer seems somewhat abrupt. The connection, however, is that the cursing of the fig tree demonstrated the power of divine judgment. Peter, along with the rest of the disciples, was "amazed and asked, 'How did the fig tree wither all at once?'" (Matt. 21:20). They wanted to know how that display of divine judgmental power occurred. The Lord's reply was that the power came from God (see the discussion of v. 22 below), and they could access it through prayer.

The disciples' reference to the miraculous withering of the fig tree illustrates the historical foundation of effective prayer. God, who can miraculously affect a tree, will powerfully provide for His people. Confidence in prayer starts with remembering how God has displayed His power in the past. There would be little motive to call on the Lord for help in the present or future if He had not demonstrated His power in the past. More than a dozen times in Deuteronomy, Moses charged Israel, poised to enter Canaan, to remember what God had done for them in the past (4:10; 5:15; 7:18; 8:2, 18; 9:7, 27; 15:15; 16:3, 12; 24:9, 18, 22). In Isaiah 46:8–10 God challenged Israel,

> Remember this, and be assured; recall it to mind, you transgressors. Remember the former things long past, For I am God, and there is no other; I am God, and there is no one like Me, declaring the end from the beginning, and from ancient times things which have not been done, Saying, "My purpose will be established, and I will accomplish all My good pleasure."

In Psalm 77:1–10 Asaph expressed his despair over God's apparent forsaking of him. But in the second half of the psalm, he encouraged himself by recalling God's past acts of power:

> I shall remember the deeds of the Lord; surely I will remember Your wonders of old. I will meditate on all Your work and muse on Your deeds. Your way, O God, is holy; What god is great like our God? You are the God who works wonders; You have made known Your strength among the peoples. You have by Your power redeemed Your people, the sons of Jacob and Joseph. The waters saw You, O God; the waters saw You, they were in anguish; the deeps also trembled. The clouds poured out water; the skies gave forth a sound; Your arrows flashed here and there. The sound of Your thunder was in the whirlwind; the lightnings lit up the world; the earth trembled and shook. Your way was in the sea and Your paths in the mighty waters, and Your footprints may not be known. You led Your people like a flock by the hand of Moses and Aaron. (vv. 11–20)

In Psalm 105:5 the psalmist called on God's people to "remember His wonders which He has done, His marvels and the judgments uttered by His mouth." Overwhelmed with despair because of persecution by his enemy, David said, "I remember the days of old; I meditate on all Your doings; I muse on the work of Your hands" (Ps. 143:5). The Old Testament, New Testament, and the record of the history of the redeemed church provide a strong foundation of confidence that God hears and answers the prayers of His people (cf. Rom. 15:4).

THE THEOLOGICAL COMPONENT OF PRAYER

And Jesus answered saying to them, "Have faith in God. (11:22)

The Lord's response to Peter's comment, **"Have faith in God,"** is a call to trust in God and not doubt Him (Matt. 21:20). The theological component of prayer is not concerned with the nature of personal **faith** but the character of the living **God.** To have an effective prayer life requires trusting God's power, purpose, promise, plans, and will. Prayer focuses on honoring God's name, advancing His kingdom, and accomplishing His will (Matt. 6:9–10). In contrast, selfish prayer will not be answered. "You ask and do not receive," James warned, "because you ask with wrong motives, so that you may spend it on your pleasures" (James 4:3; cf. v. 15). In his first epistle the apostle John stressed that prayer must be consistent with God's will: "This is the confidence which we have before Him, that, if we ask anything according to His will, He hears us" (1 John 5:14; cf. John 14:13–14).

In his letter to the Philippians, the apostle Paul provided an example of trusting God because of what He has done:

> Now I want you to know, brethren, that my circumstances have turned out for the greater progress of the gospel, so that my imprisonment in the cause of Christ has become well known throughout the whole praetorian guard and to everyone else, and that most of the brethren, trusting in the Lord because of my imprisonment, have far more courage to speak the word of God without fear. (Phil. 1:12–14; cf. 1 Peter 4:19)

God's faithfulness in allowing Paul's powerful witness to the Word of God despite his circumstances encouraged other Christians in Rome to trust in God and boldly preach the gospel.

The Spiritual Component of Prayer

Truly I say to you, whoever says to this mountain, 'Be taken up and cast into the sea,' and does not doubt in his heart, but believes that what he says is going to happen, it will be granted him. (11:23)

Trusting God is not merely an abstract, theoretical exercise in systematic theology; it is personal and practical. The Lord's promise in this verse is startlingly broad and generous. It is introduced by the word **truly** (*amēn*), which, as it is here, is used more than one hundred times in the New Testament for emphasis. The term **whoever** applies the principle related here to all believers.

The particular **mountain** to which Jesus referred is not identified. It may have been the Mount of Olives (from which the Dead Sea is visible) or the temple mount (Mt. Moriah). Most likely, however, the reference was to a hypothetical, not literal mountain. Jesus was not referring to physically casting an actual mountain into the sea as if that would occur commonly. No one has ever seen such happen by prayer. His statement, **"Whoever says to this mountain, 'Be taken up and cast into the sea,' and does not doubt in his heart, but believes that what he says is going to happen, it will be granted him,"** was hyperbole, an analogy or figure of speech intended to teach a spiritual principle. In extrabiblical Jewish literature, rabbis who demonstrated unusual ability to solve very difficult problems were sometimes referred to as removers or rooters up of mountains.

The Lord's point is that when confronted by an overwhelming issue without an apparent human solution, if a believer **does not doubt in his heart, but believes that what he says is going to happen,** his prayer request **will be granted him.** The **doubt** to which Jesus referred is not, as many false teachers assert, doubting one's faith. Faith in itself has no power; it merely accesses God's power. The caution here is against doubting God's nature and power. James writes that those who pray "must ask in faith without any doubting, for the one who doubts is like the surf of the sea, driven and tossed by the wind. For that man ought not to expect that he will receive anything from the Lord, being a double-minded man, unstable in all his ways" (James 1:6–8).

The faith required to activate God's power need not be great faith. Peter's faith was strong enough to enable him to climb out of a boat in the midst of a raging storm on the Sea of Galilee (Matt. 14:29). Yet his faith failed before he reached Jesus (v. 30), causing the Lord to label it "little faith" (v. 31). The father of a demon-possessed boy expressed doubt as to whether Jesus could deliver his son (Mark 9:22). After Jesus said to him, "All things are possible to him who believes," thus rebuking his weak faith (v. 23), "immediately the boy's father cried out and said, 'I do believe; help my unbelief'" (v. 24). That weak, imperfect faith was enough; Jesus cast the demon out of the boy (vv. 25–27). The Lord also rebuked the disciples for having little faith in God's provision (Matt. 6:30; 16:8–10; Luke 12:28), protection (Matt. 8:26), and power (Matt. 17:20), as well as in their own ability to humbly forgive others (Luke 17:5–6).

No one's faith is perfect, unmixed with doubt. But even weak but confidently prayerful faith in the person and power of God is enough to draw down heaven's power.

THE PRACTICAL COMPONENT OF PRAYER

Therefore I say to you, all things for which you pray and ask, believe that you have received them, and they will be granted you. (11:24)

The practical component of prayer is obvious, yet necessary. In order to receive **all** the **things** that God promises through prayer, one must first **ask** for them. James put it simply: "You do not have because you do not ask" (James 4:2). In the Sermon on the Mount, Jesus said,

> Ask, and it will be given to you; seek, and you will find; knock, and it will be opened to you. For everyone who asks receives, and he who seeks finds, and to him who knocks it will be opened. Or what man is there among you who, when his son asks for a loaf, will give him a stone? Or if he asks for a fish, he will not give him a snake, will he? If you then, being evil, know how to give good gifts to your children, how much more will your Father who is in heaven give what is good to those who ask Him! (Matt. 7:7–11)

But Jesus' promise, **"All things for which you pray and ask, believe that you have received them, and they will be granted you,"** is not a carte blanche guarantee to grant all greedy, selfish requests. It is true that "no good thing does [God] withhold from those who walk uprightly" (Ps. 84:11). But those and similar promises are qualified; all prayer requests must be consistent with God's will. After chiding believers for not asking God for what they need, James cautioned, "You ask and do not receive, because you ask with wrong motives, so that you may spend it on your pleasures" (4:3). Jesus cried out to the Father in Gethsemane, "Abba! Father! All things are possible for You; remove this cup from Me;" but then added, "Yet not what I will, but what You will" (Mark 14:36).

Jesus repeatedly stressed that truth to the apostles in the upper room:

> Whatever you ask in My name [i.e., consistent with His person and purpose], that will I do, so that the Father may be glorified in the Son. If you ask Me anything in My name, I will do it. (John 14:13–14)

> If you abide in Me, and My words abide in you, ask whatever you wish, and it will be done for you. (John 15:7)

> You did not choose Me but I chose you, and appointed you that you would go and bear fruit, and that your fruit would remain, so that whatever you ask of the Father in My name He may give to you. (John 15:16)

> Truly, truly, I say to you, if you ask the Father for anything in My name, He will give it to you. Until now you have asked for nothing in My name; ask and you will receive, so that your joy may be made full.... In that day you will ask in My name, and I do not say to you that I will request of the Father on your behalf. (John 16:23–24, 26)

Believers are called to pour out their hearts before God in persistent, passionate prayer (Ps. 62:8), but their prayers must always be qualified by the desire that His will, not theirs, be done. Such prayers acknowledge that His will is greater, purer, wiser, more generous, more gracious, and more merciful than anything they could ever imagine.

THE MORAL COMPONENT OF PRAYER

Whenever you stand praying, forgive, if you have anything against anyone, so that your Father who is in heaven will also forgive you your transgressions." (11:25)

This truth repeats Christ's teaching in the Sermon on the Mount (Matt. 6:14; Mark 11:26 does not appear here in the earliest and most reliable Greek manuscripts of the New Testament, so was borrowed from Matt. 6:15 and inserted later by an unknown scribe). Standing was a common posture for prayer (cf. Matt. 6:5; Luke 18:11, 13), along with kneeling (2 Chron. 6:13; Ps. 95:6; Luke 22:41; Acts 20:36), lying prostrate (Num. 16:22; Josh. 5:14; 1 Chron. 21:16–17; Matt. 26:39), and spreading or lifting up hands (Isa. 1:15; Ps. 28:2; Lam. 2:19; 1 Tim. 2:8).

The Lord's command, **"Forgive, if you have anything against anyone,"** expresses the moral component of prayer. Forgiveness of others is required of believers **so that** their **Father who is in heaven will also forgive their transgressions.** The forgiveness in view here is not the eternal forgiveness that accompanies salvation, which is not based on works (Acts 10:43; Eph. 1:7; cf. Rom. 3:23–24, 28; 5:1; Gal. 2:16; 3:11, 24; Titus 3:7) and cannot be lost. As was the case in the Sermon on the Mount (Matt. 6:14–15), Christ referred here to relational forgiveness—the sins that are part of believers' daily lives and disrupt their enjoyment of fellowship with the Lord. Jesus' washing of the apostles' feet in the upper room illustrates the difference:

> So He came to Simon Peter. He said to Him, "Lord, do You wash my feet?" Jesus answered and said to him, "What I do you do not realize now, but you will understand hereafter." Peter said to Him, "Never shall You wash my feet!" Jesus answered him, "If I do not wash you, you have no part with Me." Simon Peter said to Him, "Lord, then wash not only my feet, but also my hands and my head." Jesus said to him, "He who has bathed needs only to wash his feet, but is completely clean; and you are clean, but not all of you." (John 13:6–10)

Appalled at the thought of the Lord Jesus, God in human flesh, performing the task of the lowest of slaves by washing his feet, Peter protested. But when Jesus told him it was necessary if he were to have any part with

Him, Peter, in his typically impetuous fashion, leaped to the other extreme. He asked the Lord to wash his entire body, not merely his feet. But Jesus replied that those who had been bathed, that is, washed clean of sin through eternal salvation (cf. 1 Cor. 6:11; Eph. 5:26; Titus 3:5), need only to have their feet washed. The complete cleansing of the redeemed at salvation does not ever need to be repeated. But they still need the daily cleansing of sanctification from the defilement of the indwelling sin that remains in them and attracts iniquities.

To attempt to pray while harboring an unforgiving attitude against another person is self-defeating. Since the Bible commands believers, "Be kind to one another, tender-hearted, forgiving each other, just as God in Christ also has forgiven you" (Eph. 4:32); to fail to do so is a sin. And since the psalmist wrote, "If I regard (i.e., look upon with favor and refuse to confess and forsake) wickedness in my heart, the Lord will not hear" (Ps. 66:18), such a person's prayers will not be heard. The choice believers face is clear: hold a grudge or have their prayers heard. To put it another way, one cannot accept the full, gracious forgiveness of God and then be unforgiving of someone else (cf. Matt. 18:23–35).

The disciples got the message on the importance of prayer. After Jesus ascended to heaven forty days after His resurrection

> They returned to Jerusalem from the mount called Olivet, which is near Jerusalem, a Sabbath day's journey away. When they had entered the city, they went up to the upper room where they were staying; that is, Peter and John and James and Andrew, Philip and Thomas, Bartholomew and Matthew, James the son of Alphaeus, and Simon the Zealot, and Judas the son of James. These all with one mind were continually devoting themselves to prayer, along with the women, and Mary the mother of Jesus, and with His brothers. (Acts 1:12–14)

Those prayers would be answered on the day of Pentecost, when the Holy Spirit descended on the apostles. Thus empowered, the apostles proclaimed the gospel, thousands were saved, and the church was born. If the church is to see God's power unleashed in the lives of its members and in its corporate ministry, it too must "pray without ceasing" (1 Thess. 5:17).

The Confrontation over Authority (Mark 11:27–33)

15

They came again to Jerusalem. And as He was walking in the temple, the chief priests and the scribes and the elders came to Him, and began saying to Him, "By what authority are You doing these things, or who gave You this authority to do these things?" And Jesus said to them, "I will ask you one question, and you answer Me, and then I will tell you by what authority I do these things. Was the baptism of John from heaven, or from men? Answer Me." They began reasoning among themselves, saying, "If we say, 'From heaven,' He will say, 'Then why did you not believe him?' But shall we say, 'From men'?"—they were afraid of the people, for everyone considered John to have been a real prophet. Answering Jesus, they said, "We do not know." And Jesus said to them, "Nor will I tell you by what authority I do these things." (11:27–33)

This passage initiates the final confrontation between the Lord Jesus Christ and the apostate heads of Israel's religious system. It began on Wednesday of Passion Week and culminated in His crucifixion on Friday. The initial phase of that confrontation runs through the end of Mark 12.

As the Gospels make clear, the Jewish leaders hated Jesus for what He said, both against their hypocrisy and their legalistic works righteousness (e.g., Matt. 23:1–36; Mark 12:1–12). But their challenge recorded in this passage was not sparked by what Jesus said but by His outrageous behavior. On Tuesday the Lord had assaulted the temple, which, with its crass commercialization by the high priests Annas and Caiaphas, symbolized the corrupt Jewish religion. That incident ignited this confrontation on Wednesday of Passion Week.

As they had when Jesus drove the corrupters out of it at the outset of His ministry (John 2:13–18), the leaders challenged His authority to launch this assault on the temple. Two Greek words translated "authority" in the New Testament reveal the scope of the Lord's legitimate dominion. *Dunamis* refers to the power or ability; *exousia* to the right or privilege. Because Jesus possesses authority infinitely, never in His earthly ministry did He ask any humans for permission to enact His and the Father's will.

Jesus repeatedly affirmed His absolute authority. In Matthew 28:18 He declared, "All authority has been given to Me in heaven and on earth." Earlier in Mathew's gospel He said, "All things have been handed over to Me by My Father" (Matt. 11:27). In John 3:35 He added, "The Father loves the Son and has given all things into His hand" (cf. John 13:3); in other words, He granted Him "authority over all flesh" (John 17:2). The writers of the New Testament epistles also affirmed Jesus' absolute authority over all things (1 Cor. 15:27; Eph. 1:21–22; Phil. 2:9–11; Heb. 1:2; 1 Peter 3:22). Christ's sovereign authority over all things offers clear proof of His deity.

Jesus not only taught with authority (Matt. 7:29; Mark 1:22, 27) but also acted with divine authority. He claimed the right to forgive sin (Mark 2:10), and the implications were not lost on His opponents. After Jesus forgave the sin of a paralyzed man whom He had miraculously healed, "The scribes and the Pharisees began to reason, saying, 'Who is this man who speaks blasphemies? Who can forgive sins, but God alone?'" (Luke 5:21).

Jesus also demonstrated His complete authority over the forces of hell. On one occasion when He cast a demon out of a man, those who witnessed the miracle "debated among themselves, saying, 'What is this? A new teaching with authority! He commands even the unclean spirits, and they obey Him'" (Mark 1:27).

Another aspect of Christ's sovereign dominion is His right to grant eternal salvation. In the prologue to his gospel, the apostle John wrote, "But as many as received Him, to them He gave the right to become children of God, even to those who believe in His name" (John 1:12). Later in John's gospel Jesus declared, "All that the Father gives Me will come to Me, and the one who comes to Me I will certainly not cast out" (6:37), and in 7:37–38 "Jesus stood and cried out, saying, 'If anyone is thirsty, let him come to Me and drink. He who believes in Me, as the Scripture said, "From his innermost being will flow rivers of living water."'" In Matthew 11:28–30 He invited people to come to Him for salvation: "Come to Me, all who are weary and heavy-laden, and I will give you rest. Take My yoke upon you and learn from Me, for I am gentle and humble in heart, and you will find rest for your souls. For My yoke is easy and My burden is light."

The extent of the Lord Jesus' authority is also revealed by the Father's granting Him the right to be the ultimate judge. "For not even the Father judges anyone," Jesus declared, "but He has given all judgment to the Son ... and He gave Him authority to execute judgment, because He is the Son of Man" (John 5:22, 27).

Finally, Christ has full authority over life and death. In John 10:18 He said, "No one has taken [My life] away from Me, but I lay it down on My own initiative. I have authority to lay it down, and I have authority to take it up again. This commandment I received from My Father," and in Revelation 1:18 He added, "[I am] the living One; and I was dead, and behold, I am alive forevermore, and I have the keys of death and of Hades."

Although Jesus' authority is infinite and absolute, it is always exercised in perfect agreement with the will of the Father. That truth is a particular emphasis of John's gospel.

Therefore Jesus answered and was saying to them, "Truly, truly, I say to you, the Son can do nothing of Himself, unless it is something He sees the Father doing; for whatever the Father does, these things the Son also does in like manner." (5:19)

I can do nothing on My own initiative. As I hear, I judge; and My judgment is just, because I do not seek My own will, but the will of Him who sent Me. (5:30)

For I have come down from heaven, not to do My own will, but the will of Him who sent Me. (6:38)

So Jesus said, "When you lift up the Son of Man, then you will know that I am He, and I do nothing on My own initiative, but I speak these things as the Father taught Me." (8:28)

For I did not speak on My own initiative, but the Father Himself who sent Me has given Me a commandment as to what to say and what to speak. (12:49)

Do you not believe that I am in the Father, and the Father is in Me? The words that I say to you I do not speak on My own initiative, but the Father abiding in Me does His works. (14:10)

Jesus spoke these things; and lifting up His eyes to heaven, He said, "Father, the hour has come; glorify Your Son, that the Son may glorify You, even as You gave Him authority over all flesh, that to all whom You have given Him, He may give eternal life." (17:2)

That Jesus never sought permission from the Jewish authorities for His teaching and actions—thus treating them and their religious positions with disdain—infuriated them. It led to their bringing about His execution at the hands of the Romans (Acts 2:23). Their hearts were hardened; they were children of Satan (John 8:44) and apostate enemies of God.

This clash between them and Jesus, the climax of three years of animosity on their part (cf. Mark 2:6–7, 16, 18, 24; 3:2–6, 22; 7:5–8; 8:11–12; 10:2), unfolds in three scenes: the confrontation, counter, and condemnation.

THE CONFRONTATION

They came again to Jerusalem. And as He was walking in the temple, the chief priests and the scribes and the elders came to

Him, and began saying to Him, "By what authority are You doing these things, or who gave You this authority to do these things?" (11:27–28)

When the Lord and His disciples **came again to Jerusalem** from Bethany on Wednesday morning, He began **walking in the temple** grounds. As noted in the exposition of 11:15 in chapter 13 of this volume, the temple encompassed a vast complex of courtyards and buildings. As He had throughout His ministry, Jesus, in a typically rabbinic method of teaching, was walking among the thousands milling around the temple grounds (cf. John 10:23) "teaching the people ... and preaching the gospel" (Luke 20:1; cf. 4:18; 8:1; 19:47; Matt. 4:17; 11:1; Mark 1:38–39; John 18:20). The Lord occupied center stage in the temple courtyard. It was His classroom, His pulpit; it was God's temple for one final day, where the truth would dominate in the place of lies.

Christ's message on this occasion was likely a summary of what He had taught throughout His ministry. He surely talked about the wretchedness of sin, and the folly of hypocritical, legalistic false religion that could not restrain it, the hopelessness of trying to achieve righteousness by one's own efforts, and the folly of pretentious prayers and superficial religious deeds, performed to be seen by men rather than God (cf. Matt. 6:1–5; 23:5–7). His teaching must have included warnings about the inevitability of divine judgment and eternal hell, about the need for humility, bankruptcy of spirit, and a broken and contrite heart, the hope for reconciliation for all transgressions, peace, and reconciliation with God, based on the compassionate love of God for sinners, the promise of forgiveness, entrance to the kingdom of salvation, eternal life, and the hope of heaven. He probably talked about false humility and the danger of spiritual pride, and surely reminded His hearers about the cost of following Him through self-denial (Luke 9:23–24). His teaching likely also included such subjects as the persecution and suffering those who identified with Him would face, the importance of the Word of God, honesty, true riches, repentance, faith, grace, and mercy. In short, the Lord's teaching would have encompassed everything pertaining to the good news of salvation.

Christ's powerful teaching both enraged and alarmed **the chief**

priests (the current and former high priests and other high-ranking priests) **and the scribes** (mostly Pharisees) **and the elders.** These three disparate groups are often mentioned together (cf. Matt. 27:41; Mark 14:43; 15:1; Luke 9:22; 22:66). Although on many matters they disagreed with each other, they were in full agreement that Jesus had to be eliminated.

Desperately attempting to silence Him before He further discredited them in the eyes of the people, they **came to Him, and began saying to Him, "By what authority are You doing these things, or who gave You this authority to do these things?"** This question was not prompted by curiosity; it was an attack (the Greek word translated "confronted" in Luke 20:1 can be translated "attacked" [Acts 17:5]). The Jewish leaders faced a dilemma. On the one hand, "the chief priests and the scribes and the leading men among the people were trying to destroy [Jesus]" (Luke 19:47). But "they could not find anything that they might do, for all the people were hanging on to every word He said" (v. 48). They were furious in their hatred, but paralyzed as to any action against Jesus because His teaching had captivated the people.

Still they refused to give up on their plan to trap the Lord into discrediting Himself publicly with the hope that trap could lead to support for their murderous intent. Knowing that in the past He had claimed that His authority had come directly from God, they assumed He would do so again. They would then accuse Him of blasphemy and call for His execution. In reality, however, they were the blasphemers (Luke 22:65).

The Counter

And Jesus said to them, "I will ask you one question, and you answer Me, and then I will tell you by what authority I do these things. Was the baptism of John from heaven, or from men? Answer Me." They began reasoning among themselves, saying, "If we say, 'From heaven,' He will say, 'Then why did you not believe him?' But shall we say, 'From men'?"—they were afraid of the people, for everyone considered John to have been a real prophet. Answering Jesus, they said, "We do not know." (11:29–33*a*)

The Lord's devastating response evaded their clumsy attempt to trap Him and in turn trapped them in an inescapable dilemma. He prefaced it by saying **to them, "I will ask you one question, and you answer Me, and then I will tell you by what authority I do these things."** By answering a question with a question, Jesus was being neither rude nor evasive. To interact in this fashion was accepted rabbinic practice, designed to force the questioner to consider the issue at a deeper level. In this case, the Lord's counterquestion unmasked their hypocrisy. As noted above, they already knew that He claimed that His authority came from God. They were not pursuing knowledge but rather trying to get Him to repeat that claim publicly, so they could accuse Him of blasphemy.

The Lord's counterquestion, **"Was the baptism of John from heaven, or from men? Answer Me,"** put the religious chiefs squarely between the proverbial rock and hard place. John the Baptist was the extremely popular forerunner of the Messiah, the greatest prophet who had ever lived up until his time. He was chosen by God and ministered in the wilderness, preaching repentance in preparation for the Messiah. The phrase **baptism of John** extends to encompass his entire ministry; his preaching, his teaching, his calling of the people to preparedness and repentance, and most importantly, his declaration that Jesus was the Messiah. Christ challenged them to declare whether they believed John's ministry was of divine or human origin.

That challenge turned the tables on the Lord's attackers and put them in an impossible quandary. They withdrew temporarily and **began reasoning** (dialoging, debating) **among themselves,** futilely seeking a way out of their dilemma. On the one hand, if they said **"From heaven,"** they would have no answer for Christ's inevitable follow-up question, **"Then why did you not believe him?"** Nor were they comfortable putting their official seal of approval on one whom they did not believe was a true prophet (Luke 7:28–30), and who had publicly denounced them:

> But when [John] saw many of the Pharisees and Sadducees coming for baptism, he said to them, "You brood of vipers, who warned you to flee from the wrath to come? Therefore bear fruit in keeping with repentance; and do not suppose that you can say to yourselves, 'We have Abraham for our father'; for I say to you that from these stones

God is able to raise up children to Abraham. The axe is already laid at the root of the trees; therefore every tree that does not bear good fruit is cut down and thrown into the fire." (Matt. 3:7–10)

But on the other hand, they did not dare reply, **"From men,"** because **they were afraid of the people, for everyone considered John to have been a real prophet.** Denying the popular view that John was a true prophet would have had severe—possibly even fatal—consequences. Luke records that they said to one another, "But if we say, 'From men,' all the people will stone us to death, for they are convinced that John was a prophet" (Luke 20:6). To reject God's true prophet was tantamount to rejecting and blaspheming God Himself.

Since the only two alternatives were unacceptable to them, the religious leaders could only reply, **"We do not know."** To thus plead ignorance was a bitter pill for these proud, egotistical men to swallow, since they viewed themselves as the unrivaled experts in theological matters and wisdom in debate.

THE CONDEMNATION

And Jesus said to them, "Nor will I tell you by what authority I do these things." (11:33*b*)

Having reduced His opponents to silence, Jesus ended the discussion with a condemnation of them. He was through communicating with them. After three years of teaching, and performing miracles to verify His claims (John 5:36), the Lord had provided ample proof that He was the Messiah. No further information would be granted. They had rejected the light, and the light had gone out (cf. John 12:35). Jesus would not cast pearls before swine (Matt. 7:6). Their house was left to them desolate (Matt. 23:37–38).

There is a limit to God's patience, as I noted in an earlier volume in this series:

Those who hard-heartedly reject the light will eventually be abandoned to judicial darkness. God said of the pre-flood world, "My Spirit shall not strive with man forever, because he also is flesh; nevertheless his days shall be one hundred and twenty years" (Gen. 6:3). In a prayer of repentance, the returned exiles from the Babylonian captivity confessed regarding their ancestors, "You bore with them for many years, and admonished them by Your Spirit through Your prophets, yet they would not give ear. Therefore You gave them into the hand of the peoples of the lands" (Neh. 9:30). Isaiah adds, "But they rebelled and grieved His Holy Spirit; therefore He turned Himself to become their enemy, He fought against them" (Isa. 63:10). Through the prophet Jeremiah God reminded wayward Israel, "I solemnly warned your fathers in the day that I brought them up from the land of Egypt, even to this day, warning persistently, saying, 'Listen to My voice.' . . . Therefore thus says the Lord, 'Behold I am bringing disaster on them which they will not be able to escape; though they will cry to Me, yet I will not listen to them'" (Jer. 11:7, 11). Luke 19:41 says that "when [Jesus] approached Jerusalem, He saw the city and wept over it, saying, 'If you had known in this day, even you, the things which make for peace! But now they have been hidden from your eyes.'"

The merciful, saving message of the gospel would still be extended to the people, and thousands would be saved on the Day of Pentecost and beyond. But for the hard-hearted leaders, the door of opportunity was shut. (*Luke 18–24,* The MacArthur New Testament Commentary [Chicago: Moody, 2014], 117–18)

The unique authority that Jesus possessed to say and do what He wanted to was, amazingly, delegated to the apostles. In Luke 9:1 He "called the twelve together, and gave them power and authority over all the demons and to heal diseases." Having that delegated authority, they spoke the same truth and wielded the same power that Jesus did.

There were unique elements of that authority given only to the apostles: signs and wonders and miracles. But the authority to proclaim the truth has been passed down to all Christians in the Scripture. Paul wrote to Titus, "These things speak and exhort and reprove with all authority. Let no one disregard you" (Titus 2:15). Though Titus was not an apostle, he was still commanded to proclaim sound doctrine with authority. Believers also may confidently proclaim God's revealed truth with authority.

The most important reality in this lost, fallen, sinful world is divine truth. The only way people can hear is through believers, who are the instruments in whom God has deposited His Spirit and to whom He has entrusted His Word. "How then will they call on Him in whom they have not believed?" Paul asked in Romans 10:14,"How will they believe in Him whom they have not heard? And how will they hear without a preacher?"

Jesus also promised eternal authority to those in His future, glorious kingdom:"He who overcomes, and he who keeps My deeds until the end, to him I will give authority over the nations" (Rev. 2:26). The glorious reality is that the Father has all authority, He gives it to the Son, and the Son will delegate it to believers in the future.

The Rejected Cornerstone (Mark 12:1–12)

16

And He began to speak to them in parables: "A man planted a vineyard and put a wall around it, and dug a vat under the wine press and built a tower, and rented it out to vine-growers and went on a journey. At the harvest time he sent a slave to the vine-growers, in order to receive some of the produce of the vineyard from the vine-growers. They took him, and beat him and sent him away empty-handed. Again he sent them another slave, and they wounded him in the head, and treated him shamefully. And he sent another, and that one they killed; and so with many others, beating some and killing others. He had one more to send, a beloved son; he sent him last of all to them, saying, 'They will respect my son.' But those vine-growers said to one another, 'This is the heir; come, let us kill him, and the inheritance will be ours!' They took him, and killed him and threw him out of the vineyard. What will the owner of the vineyard do? He will come and destroy the vine-growers, and will give the vineyard to others. Have you not even read this Scripture: 'The stone which the

builders rejected, this became the chief corner stone; this came about from the Lord, and it is marvelous in our eyes'?" And they were seeking to seize Him, and yet they feared the people, for they understood that He spoke the parable against them. And so they left Him and went away. (12:1–12)

Throughout history, skeptical unbelievers have claimed that Jesus was surprised by His unexpected rejection and death; that He was an unwitting, unwilling victim. Some who advocate that pernicious and false view imagine that Jesus was merely a sage; a philosopher who taught morality and ethics. To others Jesus was a revolutionary, a crusader for social and political justice whose attempt to incite a revolution against Rome went horribly wrong. Managing to antagonize both the Jewish and Roman authorities, Jesus quite unintentionally got Himself executed.

But that blasphemous caricature of the Lord Jesus Christ as a well-intentioned but misguided martyr exists only in the minds of "those who are perishing" (1 Cor. 1:18). Jesus was no victim. Neither the Romans nor the Jews had the power to take His life. "I lay down My life so that I may take it again," Jesus declared. "No one has taken it away from Me, but I lay it down on My own initiative. I have authority to lay it down, and I have authority to take it up again. This commandment I received from My Father" (John 10:17–18). Far from being a surprise, His death was the very reason that Christ came into the world.

Fully anticipating His death, Jesus said, "Now My soul has become troubled; and what shall I say, 'Father, save Me from this hour'? But for this purpose I came to this hour" (John 12:27; cf. Luke 22:22). In Mark 8:31 Mark notes that "He began to teach [His followers] that the Son of Man must suffer many things and be rejected by the elders and the chief priests and the scribes, and be killed, and after three days rise again."

After the transfiguration, as Jesus, Peter, James, and John "were coming down from the mountain, He gave them orders not to relate to anyone what they had seen, until the Son of Man rose from the dead" (Mark 9:9), thus affirming that He knew He would die and rise again. In verse 31 of that same chapter, He "was teaching His disciples and telling them, 'The Son of Man is to be delivered into the hands of men, and they will kill Him; and when He has been killed, He will rise three days later'" (cf. Matt. 26:2). As Jesus and those accompanying Him on His final journey to Jerusalem "were on the road going up to Jerusalem … He took the twelve aside and began to tell them what was going to happen to Him, saying, 'Behold, we are going up to Jerusalem, and the Son of Man will be delivered to the chief priests and the scribes; and they will condemn Him to death and will hand Him over to the Gentiles'" (Mark 10:32–33). In verse 45 He added, "For even the Son of Man did not come to be served, but to serve, and to give His life a ransom for many" (cf. Heb. 2:14–15; 1 John 3:5, 8). He declared to Nicodemus, "As Moses lifted up the serpent in the wilderness, even so must the Son of Man be lifted up" (John 3:14; cf. 8:28; 18:31–32).

At the Last Supper Jesus said of His betrayer, Judas Iscariot, "The Son of Man is to go, just as it is written of Him; but woe to that man by whom the Son of Man is betrayed! It would have been good for that man if he had not been born" (Matt. 26:24). After the resurrection, Jesus chided the two disciples on the road to Emmaus for not knowing His teaching concerning His death: "O foolish men and slow of heart to believe in all that the prophets have spoken! Was it not necessary for the Christ to suffer these things and to enter into His glory?" (Luke 24:25–26). Not long afterward, He reminded the eleven remaining apostles, "Thus it is written, that the Christ would suffer and rise again from the dead the third day" (v. 46).

The apostolic preachers also taught that Jesus' death was precisely God's plan. In the first Christian sermon ever preached, Peter boldly declared, "This Man [Jesus], delivered over by the predetermined plan and foreknowledge of God, you nailed to a cross by the hands of godless men and put Him to death" (Acts 2:23). Later Peter added, "The things which God announced beforehand by the mouth of all the prophets, that His Christ would suffer, He has thus fulfilled" (Acts 3:18). The apostles and the early believers prayed, "For truly in this city there were gathered together against Your holy servant Jesus, whom You anointed, both Herod and Pontius Pilate, along with the Gentiles and the peoples of Israel, to do whatever Your hand and Your purpose predestined to occur" (Acts 4:27–28). The apostle Paul told those gathered in the synagogue in Pisidian Antioch,

Those who live in Jerusalem, and their rulers, recognizing neither [Jesus] nor the utterances of the prophets which are read every Sabbath, fulfilled these by condemning Him. And though they found no ground for putting Him to death, they asked Pilate that He be executed. When they had carried out all that was written concerning Him, they took Him down from the cross and laid Him in a tomb. (Acts 13:27–29)

Jesus told the parable recorded here by Mark on Wednesday of Passion Week, after the triumphal entry on Monday displayed His popularity and His assault on the temple on Tuesday displayed His power. Despite the crowds' public show of enthusiasm for Him, the Lord knew that in two days it was the Father's will that they would turn on Him and He would be crucified. The supernatural evil force behind His death would be the devil (Luke 22:53; John 13:2). The human driving force behind His execution would be the intense hatred of the Jewish religious leaders. They resented His popularity, seeing in it a grave threat to their own popularity, and consequently their influence, power, and prestige. They also hated Him for disrupting their lucrative business operations in the temple.

The leaders' desire to murder Jesus and His understanding of His coming death come together in this parable. The Lord masterfully drew them in to this dramatic, unforgettable story graphically depicting their perverse, murderous craving, until they indicted themselves. Matthew (21:28–22:14) records three parables Jesus told on this occasion; Mark mentions only this one. This story traps the murderous leaders because it is designed to incite the listeners' hostility against the tenant farmers and their outrageous, lethal behavior. As the hypocritical religious leaders became outraged at such wicked behavior, they indicted themselves.

Mark's account of this incident divides logically into two sections: the parable and the interpretation.

THE PARABLE

And He began to speak to them in parables: "A man planted a vineyard and put a wall around it, and dug a vat under the wine press and built a tower, and rented it out to vine-growers and

went on a journey. At the harvest time he sent a slave to the vine-growers, in order to receive some of the produce of the vineyard from the vine-growers. They took him, and beat him and sent him away empty-handed. Again he sent them another slave, and they wounded him in the head, and treated him shamefully. And he sent another, and that one they killed; and so with many others, beating some and killing others. He had one more to send, a beloved son; he sent him last of all to them, saying, 'They will respect my son.' But those vine-growers said to one another, 'This is the heir; come, let us kill him, and the inheritance will be ours!' They took him, and killed him and threw him out of the vineyard. What will the owner of the vineyard do? He will come and destroy the vine-growers, and will give the vineyard to others. (12:1–9)

As was the case with all of Jesus' **parables,** this one used familiar imagery from everyday life to illustrate a spiritual principle. It draws on the familiar illustration of Israel as a vineyard depicted in Isaiah 5, from which the statement **planted a vineyard and put a wall around it, and dug a vat under the wine press and built a tower** is directly quoted (vv. 1–2). This **man** did everything possible to ensure the success of his **vineyard.** He removed the stones from it, no doubt using them to build **a wall around it, dug a vat under the wine press** to collect the juice from the crushed grapes, **and built a tower** to serve as a lookout post, offer shelter for the workers, and provide storage for seed and tools.

Having fully prepared his vineyard, the owner rented it out to **vine-growers and went on a journey.** Such an arrangement was common; an absentee landlord rented his land to tenant farmers for an agreed upon share of the harvest proceeds, which he would receive after the crop was gathered. When the initial **harvest time** (which may have been as long as five years after the vineyard was planted) came, **he sent a slave to the vine-growers,** in order to receive some of the produce of the vineyard from the vine-growers. This was normal, expected behavior; the authorized representative came from the vineyard owner to receive the amount due the owner under the terms of the contract.

But in an unexpected response, the criminal vine-growers refused to pay the vineyard owner his agreed upon share. Instead, in violence

they took his slave **and beat** (a form of the verb *derō*; lit., "to remove the skin," vividly depicting the severity of the beating) **him and sent him away empty-handed.** This action would have shocked the sensibilities of Christ's hearers. Such wicked behavior was outrageous cruelty, flagrant ingratitude, as well as open defiance of the terms of the contract to which they had agreed.

Undeterred by their defiant refusal to pay, the vineyard owner **sent them another slave** to collect. He, however, was treated no better than the first. The vine-growers **wounded him in the head** (lit., "struck him in the head"; cf. the contemporary slang phrase "bashed his head in") **and treated him shamefully** (from a verb that could also be translated "insult," or "dishonor").

The violence escalated dramatically when the vineyard owner sent a third slave—**they killed** him, evidently by stoning him to death (cf. Matt. 21:35). In an amazing display of patience with the hostile, recalcitrant vine-growers, the vineyard owner sent **many others** of his servants, but the vine-growers responded by **beating some and killing others.** Finally, in a remarkably generous display of patience and mercy toward those murderous tenants, the vineyard owner made one more appeal to them to honor what was right. **He had one more** representative **to send, a beloved son; he sent him last of all to them, saying, "They will respect my son."** The Lord often introduced surprising elements into His stories, and this decision would certainly have been one of them. His hearers would have expected the owner of the vineyard to muster an armed force and, with the backing of the legal authorities, to exact justice by executing those who had slaughtered his servants (cf. Gen. 9:6). That he would instead send his son would have seemed shocking, inexplicable, unacceptable, even foolish to them.

Though the vineyard owner hoped the vine-growers would respect his own son, such was not to be the case; they had other plans. Realizing the opportunity that had been afforded them, **those** wicked **vine-growers said to one another, "This is the heir; come, let us kill him, and the inheritance will be ours!"** According to traditional law, land that remained unclaimed for three years would become the property of those working it. If they killed the heir, they reasoned, the land could be theirs.

Having chosen their vicious course, they took immediate action. **They took** the son **and killed him and,** disdaining even the common decency of a burial, **threw him out of the vineyard,** leaving his body to be consumed like roadkill. This vile act of killing was the final shock. Thus, when Jesus asked His audience, **What will the owner of the vineyard do?** with noble outrage they immediately responded, "He will bring those wretches to a wretched end, and will rent out the vineyard to other vine-growers who will pay him the proceeds at the proper seasons" (Matt. 21:41). Jesus agreed that the owner of the vineyard would **come and destroy the vine-growers, and** would **give the vineyard to others,** thus affirming their reaction.

At this point the full implications of the Lord's story settled into clarity in the minds of the leaders and the people. They realized that Jesus had just led them to condemn themselves. By taking the side of the vineyard owner and condemning the tenants, they had passed sentence on themselves (see the discussion of v. 12 below). Backpedaling away from their self-declared sentence, they cried out, "May it never be!" (*mē genoito*; the strongest term of negation in the Greek language) (Luke 20:16).

THE INTERPRETATION

Have you not even read this Scripture: 'The stone which the builders rejected, this became the chief corner stone; this came about from the Lord, and it is marvelous in our eyes'?" (12:10–11)

What caused the leaders and the people to recoil in horror from their condemnation of the vine-growers was their realization of what the elements in Christ's story represented. The man who planted and owned the vineyard represents God (cf. Isa. 5:1–2); the vineyard represents Israel (cf. Isa. 5:7). The vine-growers represent the Jewish leaders, who were responsible as stewards of God's possession to care for Israel. The journey taken by the owner represents Old Testament history, beginning with Abraham. During that time, God gave His people the law and ordained priests and scribes to teach it to them, so they could obey Him and properly worship Him. The harvest represents the time when God expected to see the spiritual fruit that should have resulted from Israel's understanding of and obedience to the law. Instead of the fruit of obedient worship and love for God, Israel produced only the worthless grapes (Isa. 5:4) of rebellion and unrighteousness.

The slaves dispatched by the owner represent the Old Testament prophets from Moses to John the Baptist. They were sent by God to denounce Israel's sin and call the nation to repentance, and so produce a fruitful harvest for God's honor and glory.

But Israel mistreated and rejected those God-sent preachers. Commentator Alfred Plummer wrote,

> "The uniform hostility" of kings, priests, and people to the Prophets is one of the most remarkable features in history of the Jews. The amount of hostility varied, and it expressed itself in different ways, on the whole increasing in intensity; but it was always there. Deeply as the Jews lamented the cessation of Prophets after the death of Malachi, they generally opposed them, as long as they were granted to them. Till the gift was withdrawn, they seemed to have had little pride in this exceptional grace shown to the nation, and little appreciation of it or thankfulness for it. (*An Exegetical Commentary on the Gospel According to S. Matthew* [New York: Scribner's, 1910], 297)

The second-century Christian apologist Justin Martyr reports that Isaiah was sawn in half with a wooden saw (*Dialogue of Justin with Trypho, a Jew,* chap. 120; cf. Heb. 11:37). Jeremiah was constantly mistreated, falsely accused of treason (Jer. 37:13–16), thrown into a pit (Jer. 38:9), and, according to tradition, stoned to death by the Jews. Ezekiel faced similar hatred and hostility (cf. Ezek. 2:6); Amos was forced to flee for his life (Amos 7:10–13); Zechariah was rejected (Zech. 11:12), and Micaiah was struck in the face (1 Kings 22:24). Both the Old Testament (e.g., Jer. 7:23–26; 25:4–6) and the New Testament (e.g., Matt. 23:29–39; Luke 6:22–23; 11:49; 13:34; Acts 7:51–52) rebuked Israel for rejecting and persecuting the prophets.

By creating this riveting parable, Jesus made it clear to those who sought to murder Him that He knew exactly what they were planning to do to Him. He, God's beloved Son and final messenger (Heb. 1:1–2), was represented by the owner's son in the parable. Just as the owner's son was not a slave but his son, so also Jesus was not merely another prophet but the Son of God. The leaders wanted control over the inheritance (Israel in the story). Therefore just as the tenants killed the owner's son and threw him out of the vineyard, so also would the religious leaders reject and throw Jesus out of the nation, by turning Him over to the Romans, who would kill Him outside of Jerusalem. The Jewish leaders would prove themselves to be "sons of those who murdered the prophets" (Matt. 23:31). They would "fill up ... the measure of the guilt of [their] fathers" (v. 32) by killing both the Son of God and the Christian preachers who would proclaim the truth about Him after His death. As a result, "upon [them would] fall the guilt of all the righteous blood shed on earth, from the blood of righteous Abel to the blood of Zechariah, the son of Berechiah, whom [they] murdered between the temple and the altar" (v. 35).

The vineyard owner's destruction of the rebellious tenants depicts God's judgment on Israel in A.D. 70. God was remarkably patient with His disobedient, rebellious people. The prior judgments on the nation had been centuries earlier, at the hands of the Assyrians on the northern kingdom (Israel) in 722 B.C., and the Babylonians on the southern kingdom (Judah) in 586 B.C. The coming destruction of Israel and especially Jerusalem was devastating. Tens of thousands of Jews were slaughtered, and thousands more sold into slavery. The temple was destroyed, bringing to an end the entire religious system of sacrifices, priests, rituals, and ceremonies that depended on it. The religious leaders of the nation had utterly failed in their stewardship, which was taken from them in a devastating judgment, as had happened centuries earlier when the Babylonians sacked Jerusalem and destroyed the temple.

Not only was the apostate leaders' stewardship over God's people taken away from them, it was also granted to the unlikeliest group imaginable—the apostles. Those twelve ordinary despised Galileans, not trained in the rabbinic schools and outside the religious establishment, would become the recipients and stewards of the divine revelation, which they would be enabled to disseminate to the world. Jesus had already given them authority over demons and disease, and to proclaim the gospel (Mark 6:7, 12–13). The next night, in the upper room, He would promise them the divine revelation through the Holy Spirit that would inspire them and their close associates to write the New Testament (John

14:26; 15:26–27; 16:13–14). For that reason, when the early church met, they studied the doctrine taught by the apostles (Acts 2:42; cf. 1 Cor. 4:1; Eph. 2:19–20; 3:1–5; 2 Peter 3:2). All who would subsequently hold to and proclaim the apostles' doctrine follow in their line.

Although the parable had ended, the death of the Son could not be the end of the story. For the conclusion, Jesus transitioned from the metaphor of a vineyard to that of a building. His question, **"Have you not even read this Scripture?"** indicted the Jewish leaders for their ignorance of Scripture, for failing to understand the teaching of Psalm 118:22 that **the stone which the builders rejected, this became the chief corner stone; this came about from the Lord, and it is marvelous in our eyes.** The one whom they rejected would become the **chief corner stone,** a reference to the most important part of a stone building that set the foundation and the correct angles for all aspects of its construction. Jesus, the chief cornerstone in the eternal kingdom of God, supports the entire structure and symmetry of God's glorious kingdom of salvation. As Peter boldly declared to the Sanhedrin, "He is the stone which was rejected by you, the builders, but which became the chief corner stone" (Acts 4:11; cf. Eph. 2:20; 1 Peter 2:6–7).

To Israel's leaders in their ignorance, the stone did not measure up. It was a rejected stone, inadequate, imperfect, unacceptable, not to be the head of the corner, unable to support the whole structure and symmetry of God's glorious kingdom. But they were dead wrong. Jesus is God's cornerstone, the very one of whom was said two days earlier during the triumphal entry, "Blessed is He who comes in the name of the Lord" (Mark 11:9). Matthew adds to the account a final word from the Lord: "Therefore I say to you, the kingdom of God will be taken away from you and given to a people, producing the fruit of it. And he who falls on this stone will be broken to pieces; but on whomever it falls, it will scatter him like dust" (Matt. 21:43–44). This was a terrible reiteration of crushing judgment. It was also a prophecy of the church, God's new people composed of Jews and Gentiles born at Pentecost. Did not the psalmist have this in mind when he wrote, "This is the Lord's doing; it is marvelous in our eyes. This is the day which the Lord has made; let us rejoice and be glad in it"? (Ps. 118:23–24).

THE RESPONSE

And they were seeking to seize Him, and yet they feared the people, for they understood that He spoke the parable against them. And so they left Him and went away. (12:12)

Enraged, the leaders **were seeking to seize** Jesus, **for they understood** at last **that He spoke the parable against them.** But the time in God's plan for Him to die was still two days away, so they were not able to arrest Him, because **they feared the people.** Unlike most of Jesus' parables, which hid truth from unbelievers (Matt. 13:10–13, 34–35), this audience understood the point of Jesus' parable. They knew that their ancestors had persecuted and killed the prophets, and that their leaders sought to kill Jesus, but they were not yet ready to stop listening to Him (cf. Luke 21:37–38). Yet even they would soon turn against Him and cry out to the Roman governor Pilate, "Crucify Him!" (Matt. 27:22, 23) and, "His blood shall be on us and on our children!" (v. 25).

Though the religious leaders **left** Jesus **and went away,** they would soon be back in His presence physically (Mark 12:13). But having scorned the indicting judgment parable and rejected the chief cornerstone Himself, they were permanently damned. As was the case with them, Jesus is for all people, either the judgment stone for those who reject Him (Luke 20:18; Rom. 9:32–33a; 1 Peter 2:7–8), or the chief cornerstone of God's salvation kingdom for those who believe in Him (1 Peter 2:6; Rom. 9:33b).

The Pathology of a Religious Hypocrite (Mark 12:13–17)

17

Then they sent some of the Pharisees and Herodians to Him in order to trap Him in a statement. They came and said to Him, "Teacher, we know that You are truthful and defer to no one; for You are not partial to any, but teach the way of God in truth. Is it lawful to pay a poll-tax to Caesar, or not? Shall we pay or shall we not pay?" But He, knowing their hypocrisy, said to them, "Why are you testing Me? Bring Me a denarius to look at." They brought one. And He said to them, "Whose likeness and inscription is this?" And they said to Him, "Caesar's." And Jesus said to them, "Render to Caesar the things that are Caesar's, and to God the things that are God's." And they were amazed at Him. (12:13–17)

The miraculous life and works of the Lord Jesus Christ clearly and convincingly demonstrated His deity. His virgin birth led to a sinless life, which perfectly displayed God's mercy, compassion, and love. Christ's power over the demonic realm, disease, death, and the natural world, and fulfillment of Old Testament prophecy was undeniable. Even

His opponents never denied His supernatural power, miracles, and unequaled wisdom (Matt. 7:28; John 7:46). Nor did they deny His sinless life; His challenge, "Which one of you convicts Me of sin?" (John 8:46) went unanswered.

But though they could not deny the supernatural nature of Jesus' life and deeds, the Jewish religious leaders hated and rejected Him. For three years, beginning with His first assault on the temple (John 2:13–20), they had dogged His steps. They were the gatekeepers, the ones who were supposed to shepherd God's people, to preserve and teach the divine truth revealed in the Old Testament. Yet when Jesus, the promised Messiah, came, rather than honor and accept Him, they sought to destroy Him and succeeded. Instead of their Lord and King, they viewed Him as the enemy of the religion they taught and believed, and of the traditions by which they lived their lives. Faced with the choice of repenting and believing in Him, or eliminating Him, the religious leaders, chose the latter.

Jesus, of course, was well aware of their hatred and intention to kill Him. He spoke of it often to His disciples. Earlier on that Wednesday of Passion Week, He crafted a parable that reflected on Israel's past leaders for persecuting and murdering the prophets, and indicted the present leadership for plotting to kill the Son of God (see the exposition of that parable in the previous chapter).

The entry of Jesus into Jerusalem on Monday demonstrated His unparalleled popularity, so before they could kill Jesus, they first had the task of turning the people against Him. In an amazing display of wicked cunning, they managed in a few days to manipulate a complete reversal of the people's attitude toward Him. The same Passover crowd that had enthusiastically embraced Jesus as the Messiah on Monday would on Friday cry out, "Crucify Him!" (Mark 15:13–14).

To bring about the death of the Lord Jesus, the Jewish leaders not only had to turn the people against Him, they needed also to persuade the Romans to execute Him. To accomplish both, the Sanhedrin decided to set three traps for Jesus; this passage records the first of the three. By so doing, Israel's rulers revealed the dark sins of deception that dominated them, including hatred, pride, flattery, deception, and above all, their consummate hypocrisy. Three aspects of that hypocrisy stand out in this passage. Religious hypocrites make awkward alliances against the truth, will say anything to gain their ground, and falsely pretend to pursue the truth.

RELIGIOUS HYPOCRITES MAKE
AWKWARD ALLIANCES AGAINST THE TRUTH

Then they sent some of the Pharisees and Herodians to Him in order to trap Him in a statement. (12:13)

Satan can orchestrate all the various forms of false religion under his control to attack the truth, and history records some of those unholy alliances. Truth, on the other hand, cannot make alliances with error. After scheming to eliminate Jesus (Matt. 22:15) and sending "spies who pretended to be righteous, in order that they might catch Him in some statement" (Luke 20:20), the Sanhedrin sprang its first machination: **they sent some of the Pharisees and Herodians to Him in order to trap Him in a statement.** The Greek word translated **trap** appears only here in the New Testament, and refers to a hunter capturing an animal or a fisherman catching a fish. These men masqueraded as emissaries and agents of the true and living God, stewards of divine truth, and faithful shepherds of Israel—all the while seeking to have His Son the Messiah put to death.

Their plan was to force the action of their hated enemies, the Romans. Rome was very sensitive to the potential of insurrection, especially during the Passover season with its high enthusiasm and massive crowds, and could be counted on to move with force against any rebels. If they could trap Jesus into making an anti-Roman statement, they could report Him to the governor as a political revolutionary. By "deliver[ing] Him to the rule and the authority of the governor" (Luke 20:20), they would discredit Him in the eyes of the people. Jesus' arrest would prove that He had no power over the Romans, and hence could not deliver Israel from Rome's iron grip, as they expected Messiah to do.

The nineteenth-century American author Charles Dudley Warner once wrote, "Politics makes strange bedfellows." So also does false religion. The **Pharisees and Herodians** were ideological antagonists who could not have been more opposite in their political and religious views. The Pharisees were the most extreme advocates of religious law and conduct; the Herodians the least religious and violators of all that was sacred to Jews. The Pharisees were most concerned with the law of God; the Herodians were most concerned with the law of Rome. The Pharisees were most devoted to Israel; the Herodians were most devoted to Rome. The Pharisees were intensely religious; the Herodians were intensely political. Essentially, the Herodians were sycophants to Caesar and loyal to the Herodian family, in this case, Herod Antipas, the governor of Galilee and Perea. Antipas was not Jewish; he was half Idumaean and half Samaritan. After his father Herod the Great died, Antipas had been made ruler (under the ultimate authority and allowance of Rome) of a portion of his father's kingdom.

Though the Pharisees despised the Herodians, they knew they could be useful in their plot to eliminate Jesus. Wanting to get rid of Jesus because of His withering critiques of their aberrant theology and their hypocritical personal lives, they knew that the Romans would not execute Jesus because of a theological dispute with His fellow Jews. Gallio, the Roman proconsul of Achaia, would later illustrate that Roman reticence to intervene in Jewish theological matters. When the Jews at Corinth accused the apostle Paul before him of "persuad[ing] men to worship God contrary to the law" (Acts 18:13), he refused to get involved:

> But when Paul was about to open his mouth [in his own defense] Gallio said to the Jews, "If it were a matter of wrong or of vicious crime, O Jews, it would be reasonable for me to put up with you; but if there are questions about words and names and your own law, look after it yourselves; I am unwilling to be a judge of these matters." And he drove them away from the judgment seat. (vv. 14–16; cf. 23:29; 25:18–20)

The Pharisees therefore intended to trap Jesus into making an inflammatory political statement in front of the Herodians, who would then report that to Rome's agents, Herod and Pilate. If they handled their plot well, the Romans, ever on the alert for any sign of rebellion, could be baited into arresting and executing Jesus as a threat to their power. Already aware that He had entered Jerusalem on Monday at the head of tens of thousands of fervently enthusiastic followers, they also knew that

He had single-handedly thrown the merchants out of the temple on Tuesday, and thus were no doubt already alerted to Him as a potential troublemaker.

RELIGIOUS HYPOCRITES WILL
SAY ANYTHING TO GAIN THEIR GROUND

They came and said to Him, "Teacher, we know that You are truthful and defer to no one; for You are not partial to any, but teach the way of God in truth. (12:14*a*)

False religionists often resort to flattery as a ploy to advance their agenda. Cults that deny the truth about the Lord Jesus claim to love and honor Him. This delegation, sent by the Sanhedrin, **came** to Jesus and flatteringly addressed Him as **teacher,** a term of honor reserved for rabbis. It must have been hard for them to bring themselves to address the one whom they hated and whose doctrine they despised by that honorable title.

But what they said next must have been an even more painful lie if they had any functioning conscience. **"We know that You are truthful,** they said to Him. Luke records that they even added, "You speak and teach correctly" (*orthōs*, from which the English word "orthodoxy" derives, Luke 20:21). Of course they did not believe that He taught correctly and spoke the truth, or else they would not have so viciously opposed Him. The reality is that they viewed Him as a deceiver, liar, and fraud, who had to be silenced by death. Their flattery, however, had at least two devious purposes. First, they were pretending to identify with the people who, for the most part, did believe that Jesus taught the truth. The religious leaders wanted to convince the people that they, too, were legitimate truth seekers. Second, and more important, they wanted to inflate the Lord's pride, hoping that would keep Him from dodging the question they were about to ask Him.

But they were not yet finished flattering Jesus. Not only did they declare Him to be truthful but also said that He would **defer to no one.** Their point was that Christ was so committed to the truth that He did not

equivocate and change His message based on human opinion or negative consequences. He was **not partial to any.** Boldly they reinforced
their earlier flattery that He was truthful by affirming that Jesus taught
the way of God in truth. All that they said about Him was true, but they
did not believe any of their own words. Such is the extreme deception of
their false praise. Ironically, Jesus would soon demonstrate His impartial
refusal to defer to anyone by issuing a scathing denunciation and judgment of these very men and those who sent them (Matt. 23:1–36).

RELIGIOUS HYPOCRITES FALSELY PURSUE THE TRUTH

**Is it lawful to pay a poll-tax to Caesar, or not? Shall we pay or
shall we not pay?" But He, knowing their hypocrisy, said to them,
"Why are you testing Me? Bring Me a denarius to look at." They
brought one. And He said to them, "Whose likeness and inscription is this?" And they said to Him, "Caesar's." And Jesus said to
them, "Render to Caesar the things that are Caesar's, and to
God the things that are God's." And they were amazed at Him.**
(12:14b–17)

Thinking that they had the people and Jesus drawn in to their
deception, the Pharisees and Herodians sprang their trap. With feigned
sincerity and respect for His answer as a truth teller, they asked Him, **"Is
it lawful** (according to divine law) **to pay a poll-tax to Caesar, or
not? Shall we pay or shall we not pay?"** In reality they were only
attempting to discredit Him publicly by forcing Him into an inescapable
dilemma. Their expectation was that Jesus would have to answer that
Jews should not have to pay the tax, because doing so would be a violation of God's law. The people paid taxes to idolatrous Rome not by
choice but because they were forced into doing so. They loathed Rome
and its occupying presence in their land. Because they believed that the
land of Israel and everything in it belonged to God, they hated giving
anything to pagan idol worshipers whose presence desecrated God's
land.

Among the numerous taxes imposed on them by Rome (e.g., on

imports, transportation, land, crops, etc.; Luke used a general term for such taxes in Luke 20:22), the universally abhorred payment by the Jewish people was the **poll-tax.** This was a tax not on their land or their goods but on their persons. It consisted of one denarius (a day's wages for a common laborer) per person per year. What made this tax more hateful than the rest was its implication that Caesar owned them, while they were truly God's possession (cf. John 8:33). They had been made subjects to another god, a violation of the first commandment (Ex. 20:3).

The issue of taxation had always been an explosive one, and occasionally the Jews' smoldering resentment flared up into open revolt. In A.D. 6, a Galilean named Judas, the founder of the Zealots (to which Jesus' disciple Simon had belonged; Mark 3:18), led a revolt in Galilee in response to a Roman census connected with collecting the poll-tax (see the reference to this revolt in Acts 5:37). Though the revolt was crushed and Judas and his followers killed, Jewish resentment against paying taxes to Rome lingered. Eventually, it would help trigger the Jewish revolt against Rome in A.D. 66–70 that led to the devastation of Israel and the destruction of the temple and Jerusalem.

Given that background, if Jesus answered that they should not pay the tax, the Herodians would view Him as another Judas of Galilee and report Him to the Romans. On the other hand, if He answered that they should pay taxes, the people would turn on Him and His popularity would plummet.

At this point the focus of the story turns from the devious manipulations of the Sanhedrin to the infinite knowledge and wisdom of the Lord Jesus Christ. Since "He Himself knew what was in man" (John 2:25), He understood **their hypocrisy,** "detected their trickery" (Luke 20:23), and "perceived their malice" (Matt. 22:18). Therefore Jesus **said to them, "Why are you testing Me?"** Matthew notes that He added, "you hypocrites" (Matt. 22:18). As noted above, the delegation did not approach Jesus looking for an answer to an honest question. They were not pursuing the truth but rather seeking to snare Him in a manner that would lead to His execution.

The Lord's response was simple and profound. He called for them to **bring** Him **a denarius to look at.** It may have taken them some time to find one, since most Jews refused to carry them. A **denarius** was a silver coin minted under the authority of the emperor and equal to a day's wages for a Roman soldier or a common Jewish laborer (cf. Matt. 20:2). A denarius in Jesus' day probably bore the image of Tiberius Caesar who, since he was the adopted son of the deified emperor Augustus, was the son of a god. The Jews therefore considered the coins to be miniature idols, and carrying them to be a violation of the second commandment's prohibition of idolatry (Ex. 20:4).

Eventually, **they** located one and **brought** it to Jesus, no doubt expecting Him to denounce the coin, and by extension the false god Caesar, and declare that the law of the true Lord forbids paying tribute to him. When He responded with that expected reply, the Herodians would immediately report Him to Pilate. The governor would have no choice but to have Jesus arrested, discrediting Him in the eyes of the Jewish populace. As noted above, the people expected Messiah to overthrow the Romans, not be captured by them.

The Lord's unexpected retort, however, shattered their evil expectation. **"Render to Caesar the things that are Caesar's,"** He told them, **"and to God the things that are God's."** The profundity of that far-reaching statement should not be overshadowed by its simplicity. Jesus clearly taught that paying taxes to a secular government is an obligation; the Greek verb translated **render** refers to repaying something that is owed.

Scripture teaches that government is an institution of God. In Romans 13:1–7 Paul wrote,

> Every person is to be in subjection to the governing authorities. For there is no authority except from God, and those which exist are established by God. Therefore whoever resists authority has opposed the ordinance of God; and they who have opposed will receive condemnation upon themselves. For rulers are not a cause of fear for good behavior, but for evil. Do you want to have no fear of authority? Do what is good and you will have praise from the same; for it is a minister of God to you for good. But if you do what is evil, be afraid; for it does not bear the sword for nothing; for it is a minister of God, an avenger who brings wrath on the one who practices evil. Therefore it is necessary to be in subjection, not only because of wrath, but also for conscience' sake. For because of this you also pay taxes, for rulers are servants of God, devoting themselves to this very thing. Render to all what is due them: tax to whom tax is due; custom to whom custom; fear to whom fear; honor to whom honor.

Peter wrote of that same truth in his first epistle:

> Submit yourselves for the Lord's sake to every human institution, whether to a king as the one in authority, or to governors as sent by him for the punishment of evildoers and the praise of those who do right. For such is the will of God that by doing right you may silence the ignorance of foolish men. (1 Peter 2:13–15)

Submitting to the government also involves praying for those in positions of authority, as Paul wrote to Timothy: "First of all, then, I urge that entreaties and prayers, petitions and thanksgivings, be made on behalf of all men, for kings and all who are in authority, so that we may lead a tranquil and quiet life in all godliness and dignity" (1 Tim. 2:1–2).

Civil authority is an expression of common grace. There has been no legitimate sacral society since the end of Israel's theocracy, and there will be none until the reign of the Lord Jesus Christ on earth in His millennial kingdom. In between there is no such thing as a Christian government, or a Christian nation. But even secular governments provide many benefits for their citizens. The Romans' military might provided peace, security, and protection. The roads they built and the shipping networks they maintained expedited the flow of goods that added to their subjects' prosperity. It was just and fair for them to expect the services they provided to be paid for by those who benefited from them. Caesar had his sphere, and not to pay him his due was to rob him. Jesus affirmed the role of government to collect taxes for its support because it is God's ordained means for man's protection and well-being. The only time government may be legitimately disobeyed is when it commands something contrary to the law of God, or forbids something commanded by it.

Of far greater importance than giving Caesar his due is to render **to God the things that are God's.** The Jewish leaders balked at giving Caesar what was due him, but far worse they disregarded giving to God what was due to Him. The most immediate and blatant example of that was their refusal to honor His Son, the Lord Jesus Christ, to whom all honor is due, since to honor Him is to honor God (John 5:23; cf. Matt. 17:5). All people owe God obedience to the greatest commandment in His law: "You shall love the Lord your God with all your heart, and with all your soul, and with all your mind, and with all your strength" (Mark 12:30;

see the exposition of that verse in chapter 19).

The denarius belonged to Caesar and bore his image; people belong to God and bear His image. The coin can be rendered to Caesar in obedience to temporal law, but obedience and honor is to be rendered to God in light of divine law.

The Sanhedrin's initial attempt to lure Jesus onto their hook had failed dismally. But though **they were amazed at Him** because of the profound wisdom in the simplicity of His reply, they had no intention of reexamining their obligation to God. Instead, they became morosely silent (Luke 20:26) and left, defeated again (Matt. 22:22).

In the end, since their attempt to suck Jesus into incriminating Himself through flattery failed, they were left only to resort to an outright lie. He would not say anything to indict Himself, so they took Him before Pilate and "they began to accuse Him, saying, 'We found this man misleading our nation and forbidding to pay taxes to Caesar, and saying that He Himself is Christ, a King'" (Luke 23:1–2). Such sinful stubbornness revealed that like all who persist in religious hypocrisy, they were in a hopeless, irremediable, and unredeemable spiritual condition.

Biblical Ignorance in High Places (Mark 12:18–27)

18

Some Sadducees (who say that there is no resurrection) came to Jesus, and began questioning Him, saying, "Teacher, Moses wrote for us that if a man's brother dies and leaves behind a wife and leaves no child, his brother should marry the wife and raise up children to his brother. There were seven brothers; and the first took a wife, and died leaving no children. The second one married her, and died leaving behind no children; and the third likewise; and so all seven left no children. Last of all the woman died also. In the resurrection, when they rise again, which one's wife will she be? For all seven had married her." Jesus said to them, "Is this not the reason you are mistaken, that you do not understand the Scriptures or the power of God? For when they rise from the dead, they neither marry nor are given in marriage, but are like angels in heaven. But regarding the fact that the dead rise again, have you not read in the book of Moses, in the passage about the burning bush, how God spoke to him, saying, 'I am the God of Abraham, and the God of Isaac, and the God of Jacob'? He

is not the God of the dead, but of the living; you are greatly mistaken." (12:18–27)

Throughout their history, the Jewish people had always believed in the resurrection, which they saw unfolding in two dimensions. They believed there would be a national restoration of Israel, as prophesied in Ezekiel's vision of the valley of dry bones (Ezek. 37:1–14; cf. Isa 26:19). Israel would be raised to political prominence and political domination. All the promises to Abraham and David, along with the rest of the kingdom promises, would be fulfilled. Concurrent with that national resurrection would be the rise of the Messiah, the Son of David, whom they viewed as a military conqueror and king like David. The national resurrection under the Messiah would raise Israel from death to life and glory.

The Jewish people drew their view of a national resurrection from their confidence in a personal resurrection. The Old Testament apocryphal writings express that confident hope, as does the Talmud. An apocryphal writing known variously as the Apocalypse of Baruch, or 2 Baruch, describes the traditional Jewish belief in life after death:

> For the earth shall then assuredly restore the dead, [[Which it now receives, in order to preserve them]]. It shall make no change in their form, but as it has received, so shall it restore them, and as I delivered them unto it, so also shall it raise them. For then it will be necessary to show to the living that the dead have come to life again, and that those who had departed have returned (again). And it shall come to pass, when they have severally recognized those whom they now know, then judgment shall grow strong, and those things which before were spoken of shall come. And it shall come to pass, when that appointed day has gone by, that then shall the aspect of those who are condemned be afterwards changed, and the glory of those who are justified. For the aspect of those who now act wickedly shall become worse than it is, as they shall suffer torment. Also (as for) the glory of those who have now been justified in My law, who have had understanding in their life, and who have planted in their heart the root of wisdom, then their splendour shall be glorified in changes, and the form of their face shall be turned into the light of their beauty, that they may be able to acquire and receive the world which does not die, which is then promised to them. For over this above all shall those who come then lament, that they rejected My law, and stopped their ears that they might not hear wisdom or receive understanding. When therefore they see those, over whom they are now exalted, (but) who shall then be exalted and

glorified more than they, they shall respectively be transformed, the latter into the splendour of angels, and the former shall yet more waste away in wonder at the visions and in the beholding of the forms. For they shall first behold and afterwards depart to be tormented. But those who have been saved by their works, and to whom the law has been now a hope, and understanding an expectation, and wisdom a confidence, shall wonders appear in their time. For they shall behold the world which is now invisible to them, and they shall behold the time which is now hidden from them: and time shall no longer age them. For in the heights of that world shall they dwell, and they shall be made like unto the angels, and be made equal to the stars, and they shall be changed into every form they desire, from beauty into loveliness, and from light into the splendour of glory. (50:2–51:10)

More importantly, the Old Testament teaches that there will be a future, bodily resurrection:

As for me, I know that my Redeemer lives, and at the last He will take His stand on the earth. Even after my skin is destroyed, yet from my flesh I shall see God; whom I myself shall behold, and whom my eyes will see and not another. (Job 19:25–27)

Therefore my heart is glad and my glory rejoices; my flesh also will dwell securely. For You will not abandon my soul to Sheol; nor will You allow Your Holy One to undergo decay. You will make known to me the path of life; in Your presence is fullness of joy; in Your right hand there are pleasures forever. (Ps. 16:9–11)

But God will redeem my soul from the power of Sheol, for He will receive me. (Ps. 49:15)

With Your counsel You will guide me, and afterward receive me to glory. (Ps. 73:24)

If I ascend to heaven, You are there; if I make my bed in Sheol, behold, You are there. (Ps. 139:8)

Many of those who sleep in the dust of the ground will awake, these to everlasting life, but the others to disgrace and everlasting contempt. (Dan. 12:2)

But while most of the Israelites believed in both a national and a personal resurrection, there was one significant exception to the majority position—the Sadducees. They were one of the four major sects in first-century Israel, along with the Pharisees, Essenes (ascetic monastics), and Zealots (political revolutionaries dedicated to the overthrow of Roman rule). Of the four, the Sadducees and the Pharisees were the most influential.

As noted above, the **Sadducees** directly opposed the common Jewish belief by claiming **that there is no resurrection.** That led to theological controversy with the Pharisees, since "the Sadducees [said] that there is no resurrection, nor an angel, nor a spirit, but the Pharisees acknowledged them all" (Acts 23:8). The Sadducees rightly rejected the Pharisees' absurdly literal view of the next life, which was based not on the Pentateuch's teaching but on the other books, tradition, and speculation. For example, the consensus among the Pharisees was that people would be raised with the same infirmities, defects, characteristics, and relationships they had when they died. Many also believed that all Jews would be raised in Israel; some even arguing that there were tunnels all over the earth through which the bodies of Jews buried elsewhere would roll to Israel.

Although few in number, the Sadducees had considerable influence. They included many of the aristocratic, wealthy, and influential leaders in Israel, including the high priests, the chief priests (cf. Luke 19:47; 20:1, 19), and most of the Sanhedrin. Holding all the positions of authority over the temple made up for the Sadducees' lack of numbers.

Politically, the Sadducees' highest agenda was cooperation with Rome. Since they believed that life in this world is all there is, the Sadducees pursued power, wealth, position, and control. If obtaining those things required them to cooperate with their Roman overlords, they were more than willing to oblige them. Their accommodations to Rome caused them to be hated by the people in general. The Sadducees also ran the profitable business operations located on the temple grounds and were obviously furious with Jesus for twice disrupting their lucrative enterprise. They also feared that He might incite a rebellion that could cost them their privileged positions—or even lead to the destruction of their nation (cf. John 11:47–50).

Theologically, the Sadducees, while in one sense liberal in their denial of the resurrection, angels, and the age to come, were in another sense conservative. They rejected the oral traditions and rabbinic prescriptions that the Pharisees accepted and acknowledged only Scripture as authoritative. Further, the Sadducees were very narrow and strict and interpreted the Mosaic law more literally than others did. They also were more fastidious in the matters of ritual purity prescribed in the law.

The Sadducees held to the primacy of the Mosaic law, set forth in the five books of Moses, Genesis, Exodus, Leviticus, Numbers, and Deuteronomy. They were convinced that the rest of the Old Testament was subordinate to the writings of Moses and merely a commentary on it. They argued that nowhere in those five books is the resurrection taught and therefore any writing—even the rest of the Old Testament—that appeared to teach the resurrection must be understood in a different way. They constantly opposed those who taught the resurrection, not only the Pharisees but also the apostolic preachers (Acts 4:1–3; 5:17, 28).

Consistent with their denial of any future life, the Sadducees lived the present one as if there were no tomorrow (cf. Isa. 22:13; 1 Cor. 15:32). Further, since they were annihilationists and believed the soul did not survive death, they believed there were ultimately no penalties for bad behavior or rewards for good behavior, which rendered them religious, theistic humanists. Therefore they had no interest in personal salvation through the Messiah. Though they fastidiously observed the Mosaic law, they, even more so than the Pharisees, cruelly oppressed the common people. They took advantage of their positions of power and influence to indulge themselves at the expense of the populace, who became their victims.

Jesus' assault on the theology of the Pharisees and the economics of the Sadducees caused those two groups, who were separated by their beliefs, to unite in their hatred of Him. The Pharisees attempted to destroy Jesus by trapping Him into making an inflammatory anti-Roman statement (cf. Luke 20:19–26), expecting that He would then be seized by the Romans and executed. The Sadducees, on the other hand, sought to discredit Him in the eyes of the people as ignorant by asking Him a question He could not answer. They decided to set up an impossible dilemma concerning the issue of marriage relationships after the supposed resurrection—a question designed to make belief in the resurrection appear absurd and Jesus appear foolish.

The confrontation between the Sadducees and the Son of God consists of two points: the absurd scenario proposed by the Sadducees, and the astute solution given by Him in reply. The Sadducees sought to trick Jesus with a logical absurdity that would make Him appear ridiculous to the people. Instead, they were revealed to be the fools, woefully ignorant both of the teaching of Scripture and the power of God.

THE ABSURD SCENARIO

"Teacher, Moses wrote for us that if a man's brother dies and leaves behind a wife and leaves no child, his brother should marry the wife and raise up children to his brother. There were seven brothers; and the first took a wife, and died leaving no children. The second one married her, and died leaving behind no children; and the third likewise; and so all seven left no children. Last of all the woman died also. In the resurrection, when they rise again, which one's wife will she be? For all seven had married her." (12:19–23)

Like the Pharisees and Herodians (Mark 12:13), the Sadducees addressed Jesus respectfully before the people as **Teacher,** attempting to continue the flattery. They also raised the expectation among the people that He should be able to answer their question. His inability to do so would then reveal Him to be an incompetent teacher who, the Sadducees expected, the people would abandon as unwise, and so clearly not the Messiah.

As their introductory statement, **Moses wrote for us that if a man's brother dies and leaves behind a wife and leaves no child, his brother should marry the wife and raise up children to his brother,** indicates, their question concerned the instruction regarding levirate marriage in Deuteronomy 25:5–6:

> When brothers live together and one of them dies and has no son, the wife of the deceased shall not be married outside the family to a strange man. Her husband's brother shall go in to her and take her to himself as wife and perform the duty of a husband's brother to her. It shall be that the firstborn whom she bears shall assume the name of his dead brother, so that his name will not be blotted out from Israel.

The purpose of levirate marriage was to keep inheritances within the tribe. It only applied when the surviving brother was single; he was not to divorce his existing wife, nor marry his deceased brother's wife in addition to his own. The principle predates the Mosaic law, as the story of Onan (Gen. 38:6–10) indicates. Perhaps the most notable example of levirate marriage in the Old Testament is Boaz's marriage to his relative Elimelech's widowed daughter-in-law, Ruth (Ruth 2:1; 4:1–13). The story reveals that when there was no surviving unmarried brother to marry the widow, another close relative would assume the responsibility.

The Sadducees confronted Jesus with a hypothetical situation, designed to make the Pharisees' and Jesus' excessively literal view of the life after death seem absurd:

> **There were seven brothers; and the first took a wife, and died leaving no children. The second one married her, and died leaving behind no children; and the third likewise; and so all seven left no children. Last of all the woman died also. In the resurrection, when they rise again, which one's wife will she be? For all seven had married her.**

They were confident that His inability to answer their carefully crafted, yet absurd question would destroy any thought of Him as Messiah in the eyes of the people.

THE ASTUTE SOLUTION

Jesus said to them, "Is this not the reason you are mistaken, that you do not understand the Scriptures or the power of God? For when they rise from the dead, they neither marry nor are given in marriage, but are like angels in heaven. But regarding the fact that the dead rise again, have you not read in the book of Moses, in the passage about the burning bush, how God spoke to him, saying, 'I am the God of Abraham, and the God of Isaac, and the God of Jacob'? He is not the God of the dead, but of the living; you are greatly mistaken." (12:24–27)

Instead of fumbling over how to reply and then failing to come up with a coherent answer as the Sadducees expected, Jesus asked them a counterquestion that served to indict them for their ignorance. **"Is this not the reason you are mistaken,** He asked, **that you do not understand the Scriptures or the power of God?"** The Lord's reply flipped the tables on them, metaphorically speaking. They had asked the question hoping to reveal His supposed ignorance and incompetence. Yet His question not only exposed them as fools but also unqualified to be teachers themselves, since they demonstrated lack of understanding of both the **Scriptures** and **the power of God.**

Mistaken translates a form of the verb *planaō*, which means "to wander," or "to go astray" (the noun form of this verb is the source of the English word "planet"). Due to their ignorance of **Scripture,** the Sadducees had wandered from the truth into error. Further, the grammatical structure of the phrase, **Is this not the reason you are mistaken,** suggests that they were not only negatively ignorant but also positively unwilling. They had neither the ability nor the willingness to understand the Scriptures—a charge that could be leveled against all false teachers.

The Sadducees failed to comprehend that the Scriptures teach the reality of the resurrection (even in the Pentateuch, as Jesus soon demonstrated). Thus it follows logically that they also failed to comprehend **the** resurrection, life-giving **power of God,** which is declared in Scripture. Surely the God who spoke the universe and all its inhabitants into existence has the power to raise the dead in the life to come. Like all proponents of false religion, they were spiritually dead and blinded to the truth.

The Sadducees' failure to understand God's power would later be paralleled by some who were troubling the church at Corinth. They denied the physical resurrection of the body and argued for a purely spiritual one, a teaching consistent with the Greek philosophy of the day. In 1 Corinthians 15:35–53, the apostle Paul rebuked their folly:

> But someone will say, "How are the dead raised? And with what kind of body do they come?" You fool! That which you sow does not come to life unless it dies; and that which you sow, you do not sow the body which is to be, but a bare grain, perhaps of wheat or of something else. But God gives it a body just as He wished, and to each of the seeds a

body of its own. All flesh is not the same flesh, but there is one flesh of men, and another flesh of beasts, and another flesh of birds, and another of fish. There are also heavenly bodies and earthly bodies, but the glory of the heavenly is one, and the glory of the earthly is another. There is one glory of the sun, and another glory of the moon, and another glory of the stars; for star differs from star in glory. So also is the resurrection of the dead. It is sown a perishable body, it is raised an imperishable body; it is sown in dishonor, it is raised in glory; it is sown in weakness, it is raised in power; it is sown a natural body, it is raised a spiritual body. If there is a natural body, there is also a spiritual body. So also it is written, "The first man, Adam, became a living soul." The last Adam became a life-giving spirit. However, the spiritual is not first, but the natural; then the spiritual. The first man is from the earth, earthy; the second man is from heaven. As is the earthy, so also are those who are earthy; and as is the heavenly, so also are those who are heavenly. Just as we have borne the image of the earthy, we will also bear the image of the heavenly. Now I say this, brethren, that flesh and blood cannot inherit the kingdom of God; nor does the perishable inherit the imperishable. Behold, I tell you a mystery; we will not all sleep, but we will all be changed, in a moment, in the twinkling of an eye, at the last trumpet; for the trumpet will sound, and the dead will be raised imperishable, and we will be changed. For this perishable must put on the imperishable, and this mortal must put on immortality.

Actually, it was not the reality of the resurrection that was absurd, it was the Sadducees' contrived question. The answer to their question is simple and straightforward: there is no marriage in heaven. **When** people **rise from the dead, they neither marry nor are given in marriage, but are like angels in heaven.** The pronoun **they** refers to those living in the present age, whom Luke, in the parallel account, described using the Hebraism "sons of this age" (Luke 20:34; cf. 16:8). Like other human relationships, marriage is for this present life only. There will be no need in heaven for sex, reproduction, and families to maintain the population. There will be only one relationship between the glorified saints —perfect love and joy. Since they will be **like** the **angels in heaven,** who are glorious, eternal beings and do not reproduce or die, those eternally living in God's presence "cannot even die anymore" (Luke 20:36) and hence do not need to be replaced. Nor will there be any need for marriage and family relationships to pass truth and righteousness from generation to generation, since everyone will be in perfect holy union with the triune God and each other. Because of the eternal perfection of every person, there will be no need for marriage partners to complement and complete each other, as husbands and wives do in this life.

The Sadducees' misguided objection to the resurrection was irrelevant and indicative of their ignorance regarding life in the age to come. Having disposed of it quickly, Jesus then refuted their claim that the Pentateuch did not teach the resurrection, once again exposing their inexcusable ignorance of Scripture. **"But regarding the fact that the dead rise again,"** He said to these men who prided themselves on their knowledge of the writings of Moses, **"have you not read in the book of Moses, in the passage about the burning bush** (Ex. 3:6) **how God spoke to him, saying, 'I am the God of Abraham, and the God of Isaac, and the God of Jacob'? He is not the God of the dead, but of the living; you are greatly mistaken."** In that passage (Ex. 3:6) God used the present tense, saying to Moses, "I am the God of your father, the God of Abraham, the God of Isaac, and the God of Jacob." He did not say, in the past tense, "I was," even though all three men had already died. The past tense would have been appropriate to use if those three no longer existed (cf. the similar use of the present tense in relation to those who had died in Gen. 26:24; Ex. 3:15–16; 4:5). The God who declared Himself to be the God of Abraham, Isaac, and Jacob does not receive worship from people who no longer exist; **He is not the God of the dead, but of the living.** Once again, the Sadducees' **mistaken** misunderstanding of Scripture had caused them to wander and go astray from the truth (see the discussion of v. 24 above). It should be noted that the Lord Himself affirms the inerrancy and accuracy of Scripture by making His entire point based on the tense of one verb. In John 10 He made His case based on one word (vv. 34–36), and declared that "Scripture cannot be broken" (v. 35) anywhere, not even one word can be removed or altered (cf. Matt. 5:17–18; 2 Tim. 3:15–17; 2 Peter 1:20–21).

For believers, the truth of the resurrection is a comforting reality. The sorrow, suffering, and sin that marks this present life will end. We will one day receive a glorified body, perfect in every way, when God "transform[s] the body of our humble state into conformity with the body of [Christ's] glory, by the exertion of the power that He has even to subject all things to Himself" (Phil. 3:21). We will perfectly love God and each other, and be able to worship God in holy perfection. We will have perfect knowledge: "Now we see in a mirror dimly, but then face to face; now I know in part, but then I will know fully just as I also have been fully known" (1 Cor. 13:12). We will be perfectly motivated to do perfect service, rendering perfect obedience. The redeemed will never be weary, tired, bored, discouraged, or disappointed but will experience eternally undiminished joy, unmarred by any sadness or sorrow, because God "will wipe away every tear from their eyes; and there will no longer be any death; there will no longer be any mourning, or crying, or pain; the first things have passed away" (Rev. 21:4; cf. Isa. 25:8).

Loving God
(Mark 12:28–34)

19

One of the scribes came and heard them arguing, and recognizing that He had answered them well, asked Him, "What commandment is the foremost of all?" Jesus answered, "The foremost is, 'Hear, O Israel! The Lord our God is one Lord; and you shall love the Lord your God with all your heart, and with all your soul, and with all your mind, and with all your strength.' "The second is this, 'You shall love your neighbor as yourself.' There is no other commandment greater than these." The scribe said to Him, "Right, Teacher; You have truly stated that He is one, and there is no one else besides Him; and to love Him with all the heart and with all the understanding and with all the strength, and to love one's neighbor as himself, is much more than all burnt offerings and sacrifices." When Jesus saw that he had answered intelligently, He said to him, "You are not far from the kingdom of God." After that, no one would venture to ask Him any more questions. (12:28–34)

Love for God is the foundation of the Christian life, it is the defining characteristic identifying a true believer. Christians are those who love the one true and living God; the God of the patriarchs; "the God and Father of our Lord Jesus Christ" (Rom. 15:6; 2 Cor. 1:3; 11:31; Eph. 1:3; 1 Peter 1:3). True spiritual and eternal life begins with loving Him imperfectly in this life, and culminates in loving Him perfectly in heaven. Love for God is is also a universal command, disobedience to which brings divine judgment and everlasting punishment. Hell will be forever populated by those who refused to love God.

The confrontation in these verses, like the two that preceded it (see chapters 17 and 18), took place on Wednesday of Passion Week. All that day the Lord's presence and teaching had dominated the temple courts, where on Tuesday He had chased out the corrupt merchants who had turned it into a den of thieves.

The religious leaders of Israel, particularly the Sadducees, were outraged by the Lord's assault on their temple. The Sanhedrin was also infuriated with His assaults on their aberrant theology and corrupt religious system, and jealous of His popularity with the people. That adulation had reached its zenith two days earlier on Monday when He entered Jerusalem, hailed as the Messiah by thousands of people.

Desperate to kill Jesus and end the threat He posed to their influence and power, the Sanhedrin kept up the effort to discredit Him publicly in the eyes of the people. But "when they sought to seize Him, they feared the people, because they considered Him to be a prophet" (Matt. 21:46; cf. Luke 22:2, 6). Therefore they needed to find a way to reverse the people's approval. In addition, since they did not have the authority under Roman occupation to execute anyone (John 18:31), they needed to persuade the Romans that Jesus was a threat to Caesar so they would have reason to execute Him.

To accomplish those twin goals, the Sanhedrin attempted to entrap Jesus with a series of three questions. The first two attempts, by the Pharisees and Herodians (Mark 12:13–17), and by the Sadducees (vv. 18–27), had ignominiously failed. This passage describes the third and final attempt. It may be examined under four headings: the approach, the question, the response, and the reaction.

THE APPROACH

One of the scribes came and heard them arguing, and recognizing that He had answered them well, (12:28*a*)

The appearance of **one of the scribes** initiated the third wave of the Sanhedrin's foray on Jesus. They had evidently paused to regroup after the failure of their first two attempts (cf. Matt. 22:34) but were now ready to take the offensive again. That the members of the Sanhedrin, as Matthew noted, "gathered themselves together" against Jesus fulfilled the prophecy of Psalm 2:2: "The kings of the earth take their stand and the rulers take counsel together against the Lord and against His Anointed," as Acts 4:25–28 reveals:

> [Lord, You] by the Holy Spirit, through the mouth of our father David Your servant, said, "Why did the Gentiles rage, and the peoples devise futile things? The kings of the earth took their stand, and the rulers were gathered together against the Lord and against His Christ." For truly in this city there were gathered together against Your holy servant Jesus, whom You anointed, both Herod and Pontius Pilate, along with the Gentiles and the peoples of Israel, to do whatever Your hand and Your purpose predestined to occur.

This particular scribe, like most of his fellow scribes, was a Pharisee (Matt. 22:35; "lawyer" is an alternate title for "scribe," and Luke referred to scribes as "teachers of the law" in Luke 5:17). **Scribes** were professional scholars specializing in the interpretation and application of the law of Moses, the Old Testament, and rabbinic regulations. They were given the respectful title of Rabbi ("great one"), which they eagerly prized (Matt. 23:6–7), though others who taught the Word of God might also receive that title (cf. John 1:38, 49; 3:2; 6:25, where it is given to Jesus). It was the lawyers who were the theologians of the religious system the Pharisees practiced.

Though sent by the Sanhedrin in an attempt to discredit Jesus, this man seems to have been more honest in his inquiry than those in the two first two delegations. He evidently overheard at least part of Jesus' devastating refutation of the Sadducees' argument concerning the resurrection, since Mark notes that after he **heard them arguing,** he recognized **that** Jesus **had answered them well.** Mark also records that after their discussion, Jesus said that this scribe was "not far from the kingdom of God" (v. 34).

"What commandment is the foremost of all?" (12:28*b*)

At first glance, the question crafted by the Sanhedrin seems innocuous; unlike their first two attempts to ensnare the Lord, the potential trap is not readily apparent. Their intention, however, was simple. The Pharisees believed that the message that Jesus preached was contrary to the teaching of the law of Moses. While the Pharisees and Sadducees disagreed over whether the rest of the Old Testament was inspired Scripture, both groups agreed that the five books of Moses were. The question decided upon was one they could all agree on.

The Sanhedrin hoped that Jesus would answer by giving a commandment not found in the law of Moses, thereby elevating Himself above it. The people revered Moses as the greatest figure in the Old Testament. He led Israel out of captivity in Egypt and through the forty years of wandering in the wilderness to the border of the Promised Land. It was Moses who received the law and brought it to the people. He experienced God's visible and glorious presence (Ex. 24:1–2) and "the Lord used to speak to Moses face to face, just as a man speaks to his friend" (Ex. 33:11; cf. Num. 12:6–8; Deut. 34:10).

In the eyes of both the people and the leaders, Moses was the supreme figure in their history. No one, they believed, could be closer to God than he was, and therefore no reflection of the Word of God could be purer and truer than that which came through Moses. If Jesus answered the scribe's question by elevating Himself and His teaching above Moses and the law given by God to him, the Sanhedrin could denounce Him as a heretic and discredit Him. If they had heard the Sermon on the Mount, they would have known that He explicitly denied any intent to alter or to do away with any of the Old Testament Scripture:

> Do not think that I came to abolish the Law or the Prophets; I did not come to abolish but to fulfill. For truly I say to you, until heaven and earth pass away, not the smallest letter or stroke shall pass from the Law until all is accomplished. (Matt. 5:17–18)

The scribe's question, **"What commandment is the foremost of all?"** is one that had been much discussed and debated among the rabbis, as chronicled in the rabbinical writings. They eventually decided that there were 613 laws in the Pentateuch (the five books of Moses— Genesis, Exodus, Leviticus, Numbers, and Deuteronomy). They arrived at that total because there were 613 letters in the Hebrew text of the Ten Commandments (in Numbers). The rabbis divided those laws into 248 positive affirmations and 365 negative prohibitions. They further divided them into heavy laws, which were absolutely binding, and light laws, which were less binding. There was nothing wrong per se with such a distinction; even Jesus made a similar division in His rebuke of the Pharisees recorded in Matthew 23:23: "Woe to you, scribes and Pharisees, hypocrites! For you tithe mint and dill and cummin, and have neglected the weightier provisions of the law: justice and mercy and faithfulness; but these are the things you should have done without neglecting the others." The rabbis, however, were never able to arrive at a consensus as to which laws were heavy and which were light.

Here is the dilemma that all legalists face. Knowing that they could not possibly keep all 613 laws, the rabbis focused on keeping the heavy or more important ones (as they saw them). They hoped vainly that doing so would satisfy God. But even that was a crushing, unbearable burden (Acts 15:5, 10), so they constantly sought to reduce their list of heavy laws to a few key ones. Unable to keep even those few laws, they focused instead on keeping their man-made traditions (cf. Mark 7:5–13), which were less difficult to observe. In their effort to trap Jesus, the Sanhedrin carried that reductionism still further. The scribe therefore asked Jesus what single commandment was the most important to God. Perhaps, like another frustrated legalist whom Jesus had encountered (Mark 10:17–22), he was seeking that elusive one good deed he could do to obtain eternal life (Matt. 19:16).

THE RESPONSE

Jesus answered, "The foremost is, 'Hear, O Israel! The Lord our God is one Lord; and you shall love the Lord your God with all your heart, and with all your soul, and with all your mind, and with all your strength.' The second is this, 'You shall love your neighbor as yourself.' There is no other commandment greater than these." (12:29–31)

The Lord's response, as always, was perfect and absolutely accurate. When He quoted passages from Deuteronomy and Leviticus that were familiar to all Jews, He affirmed His complete solidarity with Moses and with the truth of the Word of God as recorded by him.

The command Jesus named as the **foremost, Hear, O Israel! The Lord our God is one Lord; and you shall love the Lord your God with all your heart, and with all your soul, and with all your mind, and with all your strength,** is the most basic, foundational Old Testament truth. Known as the Shema (from the Hebrew verb translated "hear" that begins Deut. 6:4), it is still recited daily by religious Jews and as part of the Sabbath synagogue worship.

When the Shema was revealed, Moses was about 120 years old. He was nearing the end of his life and was again delivering God's law to the Jewish people. For the previous forty years the people of Israel, because of God's judgment on their disobedience and unbelief, had wandered in the wilderness between Egypt and Canaan. During that time the entire generation of disobedient, unbelieving, idolatrous people that came out of Egypt in the exodus had died. A new generation had arisen that would enter and possess the Promised Land. Deuteronomy records a series of messages that Moses gave to the people, reminding them of what God required of them. He later wrote those revelations down (Deut. 31:9) so that succeeding generations would have them.

The theme of Deuteronomy is expressed in chapter 5, verses 32 and 33:

So you shall observe to do just as the Lord your God has commanded you; you shall not turn aside to the right or to the left. You shall walk in all the way which the Lord your God has commanded you, that you may live and that it may be well with you, and that you may prolong your days in the land which you will possess.

Building on that theme, Moses began chapter 6 by reiterating that his purpose was to teach the people obedience to God as they entered the Promised Land:

Now this is the commandment, the statutes and the judgments which the Lord your God has commanded me to teach you, that you might do them in the land where you are going over to possess it, so that you and your son and your grandson might fear the Lord your God, to keep all His statutes and His commandments which I command you, all the days of your life, and that your days may be prolonged. (vv. 1–2)

He then gave the motive for that obedience in verses 4 and 5, which Jesus quoted in His reply to the scribe. Obedience cannot be merely external; it must be internal, from the heart, motivated by faithful love for the one true God. The word **love** translates a form of the verb *agapaō*, which is the love of intelligence, of the will, of purpose, choice, sacrifice, and obedience, not *phileō*, which is the love of attraction. Love is connected to fearing God (Deut. 6:2), who is worthy of all devotion and affection. But that love is based on who He is; it is a response to genuine knowledge of the one true God (cf. Phil. 1:9), who alone is to be worshiped (Ex. 20:3).

The Shema requires that God be loved first **with all** our faculties; that is what is intended generally by these separate elements of human nature. It is more about the totality than the individual features. Still, each can be given a shade of definition. The **heart** in the Hebrew understanding is the core of a person's identity; it is the source of all thoughts, words, and actions. For that reason Proverbs 4:23 commands, "Watch over your heart with all diligence, for from it flow the springs of life." Love for God must flow from the deepest part of a person's being. **Soul** adds the emotions. In Matthew 26:38 Jesus said, "My soul is deeply grieved, to the point of death," speaking of His soul as the seat of emotion. **Mind** embraces the will, the intentions, and purposes. **Strength** refers to physical energy and function. The intellectual, emotional, volitional, and physical elements of personhood are all involved in loving God. Genuine love for God is an intelligent love, an emotional love, a willing love, and an active love. In short, it is a comprehensive, all-consuming love and singular adoration. God's wholehearted love for believers must not be reciprocated with halfhearted devotion.

There are repeated calls throughout Deuteronomy for such genuine love for God (cf. 11:13, 22; 13:1–4; 19:9; 30:6, 16, 20; cf. Josh. 22:5). But the leaders and people of Israel in Jesus' day, as had been the case throughout their history, were far from truly loving God. Well aware of the Shema and the numerous other Old Testament commands to love Him, they were incapable of doing so. Disobedient inwardly, their religion was reduced to ritualistic and legalistic externals. Later that same Wednesday, Jesus would denounce the scribes and Pharisees for that in strong, shocking, even terrifying language:

> Woe to you, scribes and Pharisees, hypocrites! For you clean the outside of the cup and of the dish, but inside they are full of robbery and self-indulgence. You blind Pharisee, first clean the inside of the cup and of the dish, so that the outside of it may become clean also. Woe to you, scribes and Pharisees, hypocrites! For you are like whitewashed tombs which on the outside appear beautiful, but inside they are full of dead men's bones and all uncleanness. So you, too, outwardly appear righteous to men, but inwardly you are full of hypocrisy and lawlessness. (Matt. 23:25–28)

No one can perfectly love God or keep His law as He requires, since "there is no man who does not sin" (1 Kings 8:46); "there is no one who does good" (Ps. 14:1); in God's "sight no man living is righteous" (Ps. 143:2); no one can say, "I have cleansed my heart, I am pure from my sin" (Prov. 20:9); and "there is not a righteous man on earth who continually does good and who never sins" (Eccl. 7:20). Nor was the law given as a means of salvation; it is "our tutor to lead us to Christ, so that we may be justified by faith" (Gal. 3:24). The Shema and the rest of Moses's discourses in Deuteronomy should have convinced the people that they could never keep that command on their own. The entire nation should have, like the tax collector did in Luke 18:13, cried out, "God, be merciful to me, the sinner!"

The issue of loving God, as noted above, divides all people into two categories. In Exodus 20:4–6 God declared to Israel,

> You shall not make for yourself an idol, or any likeness of what is in heaven above or on the earth beneath or in the water under the earth. You shall not worship them or serve them; for I, the Lord your God, am a jealous God, visiting the iniquity of the fathers on the children, on the third and the fourth generations of those who hate Me, but showing lovingkindness to thousands, to those who love Me and keep My commandments.

In Deuteronomy 7:9–10, Moses echoed God's pronouncement:

> Know therefore that the Lord your God, He is God, the faithful God, who keeps His covenant and His lovingkindness to a thousandth generation with those who love Him and keep His commandments; but repays those who hate Him to their faces, to destroy them; He will not delay with him who hates Him, He will repay him to his face.

Believers, forgiven for not giving God the devotion He deserves, do desire to love God (Neh. 1:5; Ps. 97:10; 1 Cor. 2:9; 8:3) and the Lord Jesus Christ (John 8:42) more; unbelievers do not love Him at all (John 15:23–25; 1 Cor. 16:22).

The **second** foundational commandment, inseparable from the first because it is a command of God requiring the obedience of love to Him, **is this, "You shall love your neighbor as yourself"** (cf. Lev. 19:18). The two are linked, since "if someone says, 'I love God,' and hates his brother, he is a liar; for the one who does not love his brother whom he has seen, cannot love God whom he has not seen" (1 John 4:20). The command also includes loving one's enemies, as Jesus taught in the Sermon on the Mount (Matt. 5:43–47). The arrogant, prideful scribes, Pharisees, and Sadducees did neither; they failed to love either God or their neighbor (as illustrated by Jesus in the Good Samaritan parable). This command must not be twisted into a call for self-love, which is natural; such is not its intent. The Lord's point is that we are to have the same love and care for neighbors, strangers, and enemies that we possess for ourselves.

Jesus chose these two commands because **there is no other commandment greater than** them. In Matthew 22:40 He added, "On these two commandments depend the whole Law and the Prophets." Together, they sum up the entire Ten Commandments, the first four of which demand features related to love for God; the last six describe features of love for man.

THE REACTION

The scribe said to Him, "Right, Teacher; You have truly stated that He is One, and there is no one else besides Him; and to love Him with all the heart and with all the understanding and with all the strength, and to love one's neighbor as himself, is much more than all burnt offerings and sacrifices." When Jesus saw that he had answered intelligently, He said to him, "You are not far from the kingdom of God." After that, no one would venture to ask Him any more questions. (12:32–34)

The scribe's affirmation that Jesus' answer was correct signaled the failure of the Sanhedrin's final attempt to trap Him. There, in the temple courtyard, this man knew the Lord's answer was correct and acknowledged Jesus as a teacher of truth. Far from being the apostate enemy of Moses, as the Sanhedrin falsely charged, Jesus was in perfect agreement with him. Because **he had answered intelligently,** Jesus **said to him, "You are not far from the kingdom of God."** One can only hope that, unlike the rich young ruler (Mark 10:22), this scribe did not turn his back on the truth and walk away.

The Sanhedrin's attempt to discredit and destroy the Son of God ended in complete failure, and **after** this incident, **no one would venture to ask Him any more questions.** But more confrontation was yet to come. In the next section of Mark's gospel, Jesus would take the offensive and ask the religious leaders a question they could not answer.

Son of David, Lord of All
(Mark 12:35–37)

20

And Jesus began to say, as He taught in the temple, "How is it that the scribes say that the Christ is the son of David? David himself said in the Holy Spirit, 'The Lord said to my Lord, "Sit at my right hand, until I put your enemies beneath your feet."' David himself calls Him 'Lord'; so in what sense is He his son?" And the large crowd enjoyed listening to Him. (12:35–37)

This brief but highly impactful conversation also took place as Christ was teaching in the temple on Wednesday of Passion Week. It addressed His identity and involved the most momentous question that could ever be asked:"Who do you say that I am?" (Matt. 16:15).The answer each person gives to that question determines his or her eternal destiny.

Historically, the Jewish people viewed the messiah as nothing more than a man.They expected him to be an earthly ruler of unparalleled power and influence.He would conquer Israel's enemies and fulfill all the promises that were given to Abraham, repeated to his children, and reiterated and expanded in the promises given to David of a coming king and kingdom.The messiah would be a son (descendant) of David and, like him, defeat Israel's foes and usher in the glorious kingdom. The Jewish people viewed the messiah as the savior of the nation as a whole, but not of individual souls. They did not (and still do not) believe the messiah would be God in human flesh.

Earlier that Wednesday morning, the leaders of Judaism demanded from Jesus to know, "By what authority are You doing these things, or who gave You this authority to do these things?" (Mark 11:28). That was a further indication that they did not believe that He was the Messiah, despite His words (John 7:46) and works (John 5:36; 10:25, 32–33; 14:11). Instead, they hated Jesus because of His assault on their theology, His rebuke of their hypocrisy, His disruption of their business operations in the temple, His widespread influence, all of which diminished them in the eyes of the people, His publicly denouncing them, His exposing their corruption and hypocrisy, and His presenting the divine view of true religion that was in opposition to theirs. Most significantly, however, they hated Jesus and sought to kill Him as a blasphemer because He claimed to be God incarnate (cf. John 5:18; 8:40, 58–59; 10:31–33).

Desperate to eliminate Him, the Sanhedrin had made three attempts to trap and destroy or discredit Jesus (Mark 12:13–33). He had defeated those attempts, in the process humiliating them to the point that they dared not humiliate themselves further by asking Him any more questions (Mark 12:34). In this passage, the Lord turned the tables and posed to them a question, which they proved unable to answer. Fittingly, this final conversation with Israel's religious leaders focused on His identity as the Messiah. The epic conversation consisted of three aspects: the final invitation, the final misconception, and the final exposition.

THE FINAL INVITATION

And Jesus began to say, as He taught in the temple, "How is it that the scribes say that the Christ is the son of David? (12:35)

Jesus began the discussion with the Jewish religious leaders **as He taught in the temple** by asking them a question, most likely prompted by the Lord's statement to the scribe in Mark 12:34, "You are not far from the kingdom of God." It was also a final invitation to that man and the rest of the scribes, Pharisees, and Sadducees to embrace Him as Messiah, Son of God, and Savior.

Despite all the rancor and hatred directed at Him by those leaders, and the superficial, vacillating, indecisiveness of the crowds, Jesus remained a compassionate evangelist. The Son of God took no pleasure in the death of the wicked (Ezek. 18:23; 33:11), whose destruction moved Him to weeping (Luke 19:41–44).

Not all of the members of the Sanhedrin, the scribes, Pharisees, and priests were equally evil, nor had all permanently rejected Christ. In fact, at least two members of the Sanhedrin, Joseph of Arimathea (Mark 15:43) and Nicodemus (John 3:1), became followers of Jesus (albeit in secret; cf. John 19:38), as their willingness to bury His body indicates (John 19:38–39; Joseph is explicitly called a disciple of Jesus in Matt. 27:57). Acts 6:7 records that after Christ's resurrection, "a great many of the priests were becoming obedient to the faith." The Lord's question directed one final evangelistic appeal to those who might have been open to the gospel. His question was not like the ones asked Him by the emissaries from the Sanhedrin. Theirs came from evil motives and were intended to trap and destroy; Jesus' question was an offering of salvation.

According to Matthew's parallel account, Jesus began by asking the religious leaders, "What do you think about the Christ, whose son is He?" They replied, "The son of David." As Mark picks up the conversation, Jesus turned to His disciples and the crowd in the temple courtyard and asked, **"How is it that the scribes say that the Christ is the son of David?"** The implication of the Lord's question is, how can they say that the Messiah is nothing more than the human descendant of David? It exposed their erroneous view that the messiah would be nothing more than a powerful military and political leader, who would deliver Israel from her enemies and establish the promised kingdom.

THE FINAL MISCONCEPTION

The answer given by the religious elites to Jesus' question concerning the Messiah's identity, "The son of David," (Matt. 22:42) was correct. The

Old Testament clearly taught that that would be the case. In 2 Samuel 7:12–14 God promised David,

> When your days are complete and you lie down with your fathers, I will raise up your descendant after you, who will come forth from you, and I will establish his kingdom. He shall build a house for My name, and I will establish the throne of his kingdom forever. I will be a father to him and he will be a son to Me; when he commits iniquity, I will correct him with the rod of men and the strokes of the sons of men.

In Psalm 89 God declared,

> I have made a covenant with My chosen; I have sworn to David My servant, I will establish your seed forever and build up your throne to all generations.... Once I have sworn by My holiness; I will not lie to David. His descendants shall endure forever and his throne as the sun before Me. It shall be established forever like the moon, and the witness in the sky is faithful. (vv. 3–4, 35–37; cf. Amos 9:11; Mic. 5:2)

That was the Jewish popular belief in Jesus' day as well. Matthew 9:27 records that "two blind men followed Him, crying out, 'Have mercy on us, Son of David!'" (cf. 20:30–31). After the Lord healed a blind and mute man, "all the crowds were amazed, and were saying, 'This man cannot be the Son of David, can he?'" (Matt. 12:23). Matthew 15:22 notes that even "a Canaanite woman from that region [Tyre and Sidon] came out and began to cry out, saying, 'Have mercy on me, Lord, Son of David; my daughter is cruelly demon-possessed.'" The frenzied crowds at Christ's triumphal entry "were shouting, 'Hosanna to the Son of David; blessed is He who comes in the name of the Lord; Hosanna in the highest!'" (Matt. 21:9).

The genealogies of Jesus offer irrefutable proof that He was a descendant of David. Both His earthly father, Joseph (Matt. 1:1–17), and His mother, Mary (Luke 3:23–38), were direct descendants of David, thus Jesus was also. His Davidic descent claim could be easily verified or falsified. The genealogical records were carefully preserved in the temple and were no doubt examined by the Sanhedrin. If the Lord had not been descended from David, His claim would have been proven false. That none of His opponents ever challenged Christ's Davidic ancestry offers convincing proof of its validity.

THE FINAL EXPOSITION

David himself said in the Holy Spirit, 'The Lord said to my Lord, "Sit at my right hand, until I put your enemies beneath your feet."' David himself calls Him 'Lord'; so in what sense is He his son?" And the large crowd enjoyed listening to Him. (12:36–37)

The scribes' belief that the messiah would be the son of David was correct, but incomplete. As previously noted, they taught that the messiah would be merely a powerful, triumphant human ruler who would bring Israel's promised prominence. Jesus' exposition of Psalm 110:1, however, reveals the inadequacy of that belief. Psalm 110 is a messianic psalm, quoted several times in the New Testament. Peter used it in Acts 2:34–35, as did the writer of Hebrews (Heb. 1:13; 10:13), while the apostle Paul alluded to it in 1 Corinthians 15:25. Verse 1 proves that the messiah could not be merely a man, since David referred to him as his Lord.

Jesus' simple argument was so powerful and convincing that when it became widely known after the New Testament was written, many Jews, to avoid that obvious reality, denied the historical view that Psalm 110 was messianic. Instead, it was argued that it referred to Abraham, or Melchizedek, or the intertestamental Jewish leader Judas Maccabeus. Modern liberal scholars, who deny Christ's deity and the infallibility of Scripture, have argued that David was simply mistaken in viewing the messiah as his Lord. However, all of those arguments require rejecting the revealed truth that **David himself** called the messiah his Lord because of revelation from **the Holy Spirit.**

Further, God declared to David's Lord, **"Sit at my right hand, until I put your enemies beneath your feet."** Elevating the Messiah to His **right hand,** a reference to the divine position of power (cf. Ex. 15:6; Pss. 20:6; 44:3; 60:5; 89:13), symbolizes His being coequal with the Father in rank and authority, and essentially affirms His deity. Messiah's rule will be absolute, as God will **put** His **enemies beneath** His **feet** or, as Luke writes, "make [his] enemies a footstool for [his] feet" (Luke 20:43). The reference is to the execution of the Messiah's enemies, as illustrated by an incident in Joshua 10:24–26:

> When they brought these kings out to Joshua,... Joshua called for all the men of Israel, and said to the chiefs of the men of war who had gone with him, "Come near, put your feet on the necks of these kings." So they came near and put their feet on their necks. Joshua then said to them, "Do not fear or be dismayed! Be strong and courageous, for thus the Lord will do to all your enemies with whom you fight." So afterward Joshua struck them and put them to death, and he hanged them on five trees; and they hung on the trees until evening.

The Old Testament, then, reveals not only the Messiah Jesus' humanity as David's son but also His deity as David's Lord, exalted at the right hand of the Father. Here is the incomprehensible, infinite truth that Jesus Christ is both fully God and man.

Christ's humanity is clearly revealed in Scripture. He "was born of a descendant of David according to the flesh" (Rom. 1:3), and "kept increasing in wisdom and stature, and in favor with God and men" (Luke 2:52). "Since the children share in flesh and blood, He Himself likewise also partook of the same" (Heb. 2:14). The writer of Hebrews also notes that Jesus "had to be made like His brethren in all things, so that He might become a merciful and faithful high priest in things pertaining to God, to make propitiation for the sins of the people" (Heb. 2:17). Jesus endured the physical limitations of being human. He became hungry (Matt. 4:1–2), thirsty (John 4:7), and tired (John 4:5–6; cf. Matt. 8:23–24). He also experienced the full range of human emotions, including joy (Luke 10:21), grief (Matt. 26:37), love (John 11:5, 36; 15:9), compassion (Matt. 9:36), amazement (Luke 7:9), and anger (Mark 3:5).

But Jesus' deity is also made unmistakably clear in Scripture:

> John 1:1 states that "the Word [Jesus; cf. v. 14] was God." He took for Himself the sacred name of God (YHWH; Ex. 3:14) when He said to His opponents "Truly, truly, I say to you, before Abraham was born, I am" (John 8:58). That the Jewish leaders (unlike modern cultists) understood clearly what He meant is evident from their reaction: they attempted to stone Him for blasphemy (v. 59; cf. Lev. 24:16). In John 10:30, Jesus claimed to be the same essence as God the Father. Once again the Jews attempted to stone Him for blasphemy, because "being a man [He made Himself] out to be God" (v. 33). When Thomas addressed Him as God (John 20:28), Jesus accepted that affirmation of His deity and praised his faith (v. 29). Philippians 2:6 says that Jesus "existed in the form of God" (i.e., that He is God by nature), and Colossians 2:9 adds that "in Him all the fullness of Deity dwells in bodily

form." Titus 2:13 calls Him, "our great God and Savior," and 2 Peter 1:1 calls Him "our God and Savior." In Hebrews 1:8 God the Father said to Jesus, "Your throne, O God, is forever and ever."

Many names or titles used in the Old Testament to refer to God are used in the New Testament to refer to Christ:

YHWH (cf. Isa. 6:5, 10 with John 12:39–41; Jer.23:5–6)
Shepherd (cf. Ps. 23:1 with John 10:14)
Judge (cf. Gen. 18:25 with 2 Tim. 4:1, 8)
Holy One (cf. Isa. 10:20 with Acts 3:14; cf. Ps. 16:10 with Acts 2:27)
First and Last (cf. Isa. 44:6; 48:12 with Rev. 1:17; 22:13)
Light (cf. Ps. 27:1 with John 8:12)
Lord of the Sabbath (cf. Ex. 16:23, 29; Lev. 19:3 with Matt. 12:8)
Savior (cf. Isa. 43:11 with Acts 4:12; Titus 2:13)
I AM (cf. Ex. 3:14 with John 8:58)
Pierced One (cf. Zech. 12:10 with John 19:37)
Mighty God (cf. Isa. 10:21 with Isa. 9:6)
Lord of Lords (cf. Deut. 10:17 with Rev. 17:14)
Alpha and Omega (cf. Rev. 1:8 with Rev. 22:13)
Lord of Glory (cf. Ps. 24:10 with 1 Cor. 2:8)
Redeemer (cf. Isa. 41:14; 48:17; 63:16 with Eph. 1:7; Heb. 9:12)

Jesus Christ possesses the incommunicable attributes of God (those that are unique to God and have no analogy in man):

Eternity (Mic. 5:2; Isa. 9:6)
Omnipresence (Matt. 18:20; 28:20)
Omniscience (Matt. 11:23; John 16:30; 21:17)
Omnipotence (Phil. 3:21)
Immutability (Heb. 13:8)
Absolute sovereignty (Matt. 28:18)
Glory (John 17:5; 1 Cor. 2:8; cf. Isa. 42:8; 48:11)

Jesus Christ also did the works that only God can do:

Creation (John 1:3; Col. 1:16)
Providence (sustaining the creation) (Col. 1:17; Heb. 1:3)
Giving life (John 5:21)
Forgiving sin (Mark 2:7, 10)
Having His Word stand forever (Matt. 24:35; cf. Isa. 40:8)

Finally, Jesus Christ accepted worship, even though He taught that God alone is to be worshiped (Matt. 4:10), and Scripture records that both men (Acts 10:25–26) and angels (Rev. 22:8–9) refused worship:

Matthew 14:33
Matthew 28:9
John 5:23
John 9:38
(see also Phil. 2:10 [cf. Isa. 45:23]; Heb. 1:6)

Another way of demonstrating Christ's deity is to ask the question, "If God became a man, what would we expect Him to be like?"

First, if God became a man, we would expect Him to be sinless, because God is absolutely holy (Isa. 6:3). So is Jesus. Even His bitter enemies could make no reply to His challenge, "Which one of you convicts Me of sin?" (John 8:46). He is "holy, innocent, undefiled, separated from sinners and exalted above the heavens" (Heb. 7:26).

Second, if God became a man, we would expect His words to be the greatest words ever spoken, because God is omniscient, perfectly wise, and has infinite command of the truth and the ability to perfectly express it. Jesus' words demonstrated all that. The officers sent to arrest Him reported back to their superiors, "Never has a man spoken the way this man speaks" (John 7:46; cf. Matt. 7:28–29).

Third, if God became a man, we would expect Him to display supernatural power, because God is all-powerful. Jesus controlled nature, walked on water, healed the sick, raised the dead, dominated the kingdom of Satan and the demons, supernaturally avoided those who tried to kill Him, and performed miracles too numerous to be counted (John 21:25).

Fourth, if God became a man, we would expect Him to exert a profound influence over humanity. Jesus did. He changed the world like no one else in history.

Fifth, if God became a man, we would expect Him to manifest God's love, grace, kindness, compassion, justice, judgment, and wrath. Jesus did.

Jesus Christ was in every way the exact representation of God's nature (Heb. 1:3). (John Macarthur, *Luke 18–24,* The MacArthur New Testament Commentary [Chicago: Moody, 2014], 155–58)

The conclusion to this passage is anticlimactic and tragic. From the majestic heights of Jesus' profound wisdom and masterful exposition of Psalm 110 proving His deity, the reader is plunged into the depths of the hate-driven rejection by the nation's hardened leaders, as well as the amused apathy of **the large crowd,** who merely **enjoyed listening to**

Him, but two days would later cry for His execution. Some hated Him, others were entertained by Him. None, apparently, fell on their faces in the presence of almighty God incarnate to repent and confess Him as Lord and Savior.

In fact, the responses would become far worse two days later. Judas, who was undoubtedly present, would betray Him to His enemies for the price of a slave, knowing all the while that they intended to kill their Messiah. Those enemies, the standard bearers of Judaism, would conduct a series of mock trials and manipulations, leaving the Romans convinced Jesus had to be executed. Christ's gracious final invitation to them, and attempt to overturn their final misconception with a final exposition of a pertinent Old Testament text, only increased their guilt. They were so resolute in their hatred and so blinded by the darkness of their sin, that they could not see the Light of the World when He was standing before them.

Religion and Its Victims (Mark 12:38–44)

21

In His teaching He was saying: "Beware of the scribes who like to walk around in long robes, and like respectful greetings in the market places, and chief seats in the synagogues and places of honor at banquets, who devour widows' houses, and for appearance's sake offer long prayers; these will receive greater condemnation." And He sat down opposite the treasury, and began observing how the people were putting money into the treasury; and many rich people were putting in large sums. A poor widow came and put in two small copper coins, which amount to a cent. Calling His disciples to Him, He said to them, "Truly I say to you, this poor widow put in more than all the contributors to the treasury; for they all put in out of their surplus, but she, out of her poverty, put in all she owned, all she had to live on." (12:38–44)

Unlike many in today's church who promote tolerance of false teachers in the name of love and unity, the Bible writers strongly denounced them and warned of the extreme danger they pose. Scripture does not advocate tolerance for these ever present emissaries from Satan, the father of lies (John 8:44), who disguise themselves as servants of righteousness (2 Cor. 11:13–15). Instead, it denounces false teachers, using striking and graphic expressions. They are described as blind men who know nothing, mute dogs unable to bark, dreamers lying down who love to slumber (Isa. 56:10), demented fools (Hos. 9:7), reckless, treacherous men (Zeph. 3:4), ravenous wolves (Matt. 7:15), blind guides of the blind (Matt. 15:14; cf. 23:16), hypocrites (Matt. 23:13), fools (v. 17), whitewashed tombs full of bones (v. 27), serpents, a brood of vipers (v. 33), thieves and robbers (John 10:8), savage wolves (Acts 20:29), slaves of their own appetites (Rom. 16:18), hucksters peddling the Word of God (2 Cor. 2:17), false apostles, deceitful workers (2 Cor. 11:13), servants of Satan (v. 15), purveyors of a different gospel (Gal. 1:6–8), dogs, evil workers (Phil. 3:2), enemies of the cross of Christ (Phil. 3:18), those who are conceited and understand nothing (1 Tim. 6:4), men of depraved minds deprived of the truth (v. 5), men who have gone astray from the truth (2 Tim. 2:18), captives of the devil (v. 26), deceivers (2 John 7), ungodly persons (Jude 4), and unreasoning animals (v. 10). The Bible also pronounces severe judgment on them (Deut. 13:5; 18:20; Jer. 14:15; Gal. 1:8–9; Rev. 2:20–23).

In sharp contrast to those advocates of tolerance who teach that God accepts people of any religion, the Bible teaches the opposite. For example, in the book of Proverbs alone, the following condemnations of wicked unbelievers appear: "The perverse in heart are an abomination to the Lord" (Prov. 11:20). "The sacrifice of the wicked is an abomination to the Lord" (Prov. 15:8). "The way of the wicked is an abomination to the Lord" (Prov. 15:9). "He who turns away his ear from listening to the law, even his prayer is an abomination" (Prov. 28:9).

The reason for the Bible's strong, emphatic warnings against false teachers is the extreme disaster they bring to people's eternal souls. They lead many astray from the truth of God's Word (Isa. 3:12; 9:16; Jer. 14:13; 23:26–27, 32; 50:6; Matt. 23:13, 15; 24:4–5, 24; Luke 11:46, 52; Rom. 16:17–18; Col. 2:4, 8, 18; 1 Thess. 2:14–16; 2 Tim. 3:13; Titus 1:10; 2 John 7)—especially concerning the need for repentance from sin (Jer. 6:14; 8:11; 23:21–22; Lam. 2:14; Ezek. 13:10, 16, 22). They lure people away from the narrow way of gospel salvation that leads to eternal life in heaven and direct them onto the broad path that leads to eternal damnation in hell (Matt. 7:13–15; cf. 2 Peter 2:1–3; Jude 4–16).

In Israel in the time of Christ, the promoters of satanic falsehoods were the very ones charged with protecting God's truth and teaching it to the people—the scribes, Pharisees, Sadducees, priests, and other religious leaders. Though the people perceived them as devout, respected, responsible shepherds of God's people, they actually were seeking popularity, power, prestige, and above all, money (Mic. 3:5; Luke 16:14; 2 Peter 2:1–3, 14). They claimed to worship and honor God, yet they were intent on murdering the Son of God. That goal united these diverse groups, who frequently differed with each other. Truly their father was the devil (John 8:44).

All day long on that Wednesday of Passion Week, Jesus had taught the people in the temple grounds. During that time the Sanhedrin, as noted in previous chapters, the ruling council of Israel, had made three desperate, last ditch assaults, seeking to bring about His execution (see chapters 17–19 of this volume). The Lord thwarted all three attempts, then confronted them with a question that led to proving His deity from Psalm 110 (see chapter 20 of this volume). No doubt many of the people gathered there in the temple precincts applauded Jesus' clearing the corrupt businesses out of the temple complex on Tuesday. They were surely impressed with the answers He gave to those who had tried to trap Him and His counterquestion to them.

The teaching in this passage Jesus addressed to His disciples (Luke 20:45). After His last confrontation with the religious leaders (12:35–37), the Lord would say nothing more to them until His trial. And while the crowd was also listening to Him, Christ's focus in this text was on His disciples.

The passage may be comprehended in four headings: the caution, the characterization, the condemnation, and the case.

THE CAUTION

In His teaching He was saying: "Beware of the scribes (12:38*a*)

In this **His** final time of public **teaching**, Jesus **was saying** to His disciples, **"Beware of the scribes."** Fittingly, in keeping with what had been a major theme throughout His ministry (cf. Matt. 7:15–20; 15:14; 16:6), all that remained for this final message was a condemnation of the hypocritical apostates, particularly the **scribes,** who were the self-proclaimed experts in the law and rabbinic writings (Matt. 22:35; Luke 7:30; 10:25; 11:45–46, 52; 14:3; cf. 5:17). Since most scribes were Pharisees, they are included in this denunciation and warning.

The Lord's message is a forceful condemnation of all who hold a corrupt view of Scripture, Christ, and the gospel. Unlike many in today's church, Jesus had zero tolerance for false teachers. (For a further discussion of this issue, see my books *The Truth War* [Nashville: Thomas Nelson, 2007] and *The Jesus You Can't Ignore* [Nashville: Thomas Nelson, 2008].)

To hear Jesus denounce the scribes must have shocked those listening to Him, since they were held in such high esteem. According to Jewish tradition, Moses received the law and gave it to Joshua, who gave it to the elders, who gave it to the prophets, who gave it to the scribes. The Mishnah, the codification of the oral laws, declares, "It is more culpable to transgress the words of the Scribes than those of the Torah [the five books of Moses]" (cited in Alfred Edersheim, *The Life and Times of Jesus the Messiah* [Grand Rapids: Eerdmans, 1974], 1:625 n. 1). The scribes were revered as the gatekeepers of the law and the protectors of the people. In theory, they defined the law for all and held all to its standards, obedience to which, they promised, brought blessing. In reality they were hypocrites, sons of hell who made their disciples twice as much sons of hell as they were (Matt. 23:15).

THE CHARACTERIZATION

who like to walk around in long robes, and like respectful greetings in the market places, and chief seats in the synagogues and places of honor at banquets, who devour widows' houses, and for appearance's sake offer long prayers; (12:38b–40a)

After warning the disciples and the crowd, Jesus gave five illustrations of their hypocrisy.

First, they made certain **to walk around in long robes.** These were full length, expensive, ornate outer garments. On their fringes were the required tassels (Num. 15:38–40; cf. Matt. 9:20), which the scribes enlarged in a grandiose display of their supposed piety (Matt. 23:5).

Second, they expected **respectful greetings in the market places.** Their flamboyant robes marked them as scribes, so everyone knew who they were. To fail to deferentially greet them with honor was considered a very serious affront. They affected dignified titles by which they expected to be addressed, such as "Rabbi," signifying that they were the expositors and interpreters of God's law (Matt. 23:7), "Father" (Matt. 23:9); that is, the source of spiritual life and truth, and "Leader" (Matt. 23:10), as befitted those who determined direction and even destiny.

Third, in their overweening pride and craving for attention and adulation, they eagerly sought the **chief seats** (i.e., the most prominent and important) **in the synagogues** (those on the elevated platform at the front) **and places of honor at banquets** (those closest to the host), which prideful practice the Lord referred to in Luke 14:7–11.

While the first three examples revealed the scribes' obsessive pride, the next one was far more sinister. Their insatiable greed led them, in flagrant disregard of the repeated teaching of the Old Testament (e.g., Ex. 22:22; Deut. 10:18; 14:29; 24:17–21; 27:19; Pss. 68:5; 146:9; Prov. 15:25; Isa. 1:17; Jer. 22:3; Zech. 7:10), to prey on the most helpless members of society and **devour widows' houses.** The scribes consumed the limited resources of those who had the least. They abused their hospitality, defrauded them of their estates, mismanaged their property, and took their houses as pledges for debts that they could never repay (cf. Darrell L. Bock, *Luke 9:51–24:53,* The Baker Exegetical Commentary on the New Testament [Grand Rapids: Baker, 1996], 1643). Like they did with everyone caught up in their false religious system, they also demanded that widows give money to purchase God's blessings.

Finally, **for appearance's sake** they offered **long,** public **prayers** to showcase their imagined holiness and devotion to God. "When you pray," Jesus commanded, "you are not to be like the hypocrites; for they love to stand and pray in the synagogues and on the street corners so that they may be seen by men. Truly I say to you, they have their reward in full" (Matt. 6:5). He told a parable in which a "Pharisee stood and was praying this to himself: 'God, I thank You that I am not like other people: swindlers, unjust, adulterers, or even like this tax collector'" (Luke 18:11). Yet it was not the arrogant, self-righteous Pharisee but the broken, humbled, repentant tax collector who was justified (v. 14). The scribes' prayers, like the rest of their religion, was nothing but a pretense; a sham; an outward show; "meaningless repetition" (Matt. 6:7) designed not to honor God but to exalt themselves.

THE CONDEMNATION

these will receive greater condemnation." (12:40*b*)

Instead of being rewarded by God for their self-righteous, self-promoting religion as they expected, the scribes would **receive** the opposite—**greater condemnation.** It is a sobering reality that those who know the truth and reject it will receive more severe punishment than those who never heard it. "How much severer punishment do you think he will deserve," asked the writer of Hebrews, "who has trampled under foot the Son of God, and has regarded as unclean the blood of the covenant by which he was sanctified, and has insulted the Spirit of grace?" (Heb. 10:29). The judgment on Israel's religious leaders would be intensified because not only did they knowingly reject the truth but also led others astray. For that and their many other sins, Jesus pronounced judgment on them in Matthew 23:

> Woe to you, scribes and Pharisees, hypocrites, because you shut off the kingdom of heaven from people; for you do not enter in yourselves, nor do you allow those who are entering to go in. (v. 13)

> Woe to you, scribes and Pharisees, hypocrites, because you travel around on sea and land to make one proselyte; and when he becomes one, you make him twice as much a son of hell as yourselves. (v. 15)

> Woe to you, blind guides, who say, "Whoever swears by the temple, that is nothing; but whoever swears by the gold of the temple is obligated." (v. 16)

Woe to you, scribes and Pharisees, hypocrites! For you tithe mint and dill and cummin, and have neglected the weightier provisions of the law: justice and mercy and faithfulness; but these are the things you should have done without neglecting the others. (v. 23)

Woe to you, scribes and Pharisees, hypocrites! For you are like white-washed tombs which on the outside appear beautiful, but inside they are full of dead men's bones and all uncleanness. (v. 27)

Woe to you, scribes and Pharisees, hypocrites! For you build the tombs of the prophets and adorn the monuments of the righteous, and say, "If we had been living in the days of our fathers, we would not have been partners with them in shedding the blood of the prophets." (vv. 29–30)

Then, summing it all up, the Lord declared to them, "You serpents, you brood of vipers, how will you escape the sentence of hell?" (v. 33).

THE CASE

And He sat down opposite the treasury, and began observing how the people were putting money into the treasury; and many rich people were putting in large sums. A poor widow came and put in two small copper coins, which amount to a cent. Calling His disciples to Him, He said to them, "Truly I say to you, this poor widow put in more than all the contributors to the treasury; for they all put in out of their surplus, but she, out of her poverty, put in all she owned, all she had to live on." (12:41–44)

The story takes a seemingly strange turn as Jesus, after a weary-ing day, **sat down opposite the treasury, and began observing how the people were putting money into the treasury.** At first glance, the inclusion of this story about a widow and her offering is puzzling. The previous section ended with a warning of judgment (v. 40) and the next section resumes that theme (13:1ff.). Universally, this woman is presented as a model of dutiful, faithful giving over against the ugly backdrop of the corrupt pretense of Israel's religious leaders.

Not only is such a perspective foreign to the context, but also if the widow is teaching a lesson on giving, what is it? On that crucial point there is no agreement among commentators. Several options are presented. Some argue that the story teaches that giving is not to be measured by the amount that was given but by what the giver kept back. Others insist that giving must be measured by the level of the giver's self-denial, as reflected by the percentage of the person's resources that was given. Another view is that a gift's value is directly related to the attitude with which it is given. Was it given in selfless humility as an expression of love and devotion to God? The widow, having given everything she possessed, had the least amount possible left after her gift. Therefore, she must have had the attitude most pleasing to God. According to that view, it would seem that the gift that most pleases God is everything one possess.

All of those ideas are imposed on the narrative, however. Jesus drew no principle regarding giving from her behavior. The text does not record that He condemned the rich for their giving, or commended the widow for hers. He offered no comment regarding the true nature of her act, her attitude, or the spirit in which her gift was given. Nor were the disciples instructed to follow her example; in fact, it is not clear from the narrative that she truly knew God or believed in Christ. Since Jesus made no point about giving from her action, this story cannot properly be interpreted as any kind of lesson on stewardship.

What is clear from the passage is that the widow is not the hero of the story but the victim, duped into giving all she had by the false promise of Jewish legalism that doing so would bring blessing. She is a tragic example of how the corrupt religious system mistreated widows, and that is what connects this passage with the judgment passages that precede and follow it.

At the end of a long, wearying day of ministry, Jesus **sat down opposite the treasury.** The **treasury** was located in the Court of the Women, which was open to all Jewish people. It consisted of thirteen trumpet-shaped receptacles into which people placed their offerings. As He sat there looking, the Lord **began observing how the people were putting money into the treasury.** It must have deeply grieved and angered Him to see people sacrificing their money to this wretched, apostate, corrupt system of false religion, under the misguided assumption that doing so would please God and produce divine blessing.

Jesus observed that **many rich** (the Greek word refers to those who are fully supplied and have enough) **people were putting in large sums** of money. They had much and were able to give large amounts, and were therefore mistakenly thought to have the inside track to God's kingdom (see the exposition of 10:25 in chapter 8 of this volume). His attention was especially focused on a **poor widow** who **came and put in two small copper coins** (the smallest denomination of Jewish currency), **which amount to a cent** (one sixty-fourth of a denarius; a denarius was a day's wage for a common laborer).

Seizing the opportunity to use her plight as an illustration, Jesus called **His disciples to Him and said to them, "Truly I say to you, this poor widow put in more than all the contributors to the treasury; for they all put in out of their surplus, but she, out of her poverty, put in all she owned, all she had to live on."** Proportionally, **she put in more than all the contributors to the treasury.** The rich gave **out of their surplus;** she, on the other hand, **put in all she owned, all she had to live on.** Here was a woman who had been devoured by the false religious system and was left totally destitute, without anything left **to live on.**

Far from viewing her giving as a model for that of believers, Jesus was angry with the religious system that had literally taken her last cent. In the next section (13:1ff.), Mark records His response—He pronounced judgment on that apostate system.

The Grim Reality of the Last Days (Mark 13:1–13)

22

As He was going out of the temple, one of His disciples said to Him, "Teacher, behold what wonderful stones and what wonderful buildings!" And Jesus said to him, "Do you see these great buildings? Not one stone will be left upon another which will not be torn down." As He was sitting on the Mount of Olives opposite the temple, Peter and James and John and Andrew were questioning Him privately, "Tell us, when will these things be, and what will be the sign when all these things are going to be fulfilled?" And Jesus began to say to them, "See to it that no one misleads you. Many will come in My name, saying, 'I am He!' and will mislead many. When you hear of wars and rumors of wars, do not be frightened; those things must take place; but that is not yet the end. For nation will rise up against nation, and kingdom against kingdom; there will be earthquakes in various places; there will also be famines. These things are merely the beginning of birth pangs. But be on your guard; for they will deliver you to the courts, and you will be flogged in the synagogues, and you will

stand before governors and kings for My sake, as a testimony to them. The gospel must first be preached to all the nations. When they arrest you and hand you over, do not worry beforehand about what you are to say, but say whatever is given you in that hour; for it is not you who speak, but it is the Holy Spirit. Brother will betray brother to death, and a father his child; and children will rise up against parents and have them put to death. You will be hated by all because of My name, but the one who endures to the end, he will be saved." (13:1–13)

Though the Lord Jesus was sent "to the lost sheep of the house of Israel" (Matt. 15:24), His chosen people willfully rejected Him. As the apostle John explained, "He came to His own, and those who were His own did not receive Him" (John 1:11). Jesus responded to Israel's unbelief by pronouncing divine judgment on the apostate nation (Matt. 12:41–42; cf. 11:20–24). On one hand, their stubborn rebellion moved Him to weep (cf. Luke 13:34–35; 19:41–44), yet it also provoked Him to righteous indignation (cf. Mark 3:5). He repeatedly rebuked the religious leaders for their hypocrisy and hardheartedness, doing so openly and severely (cf. Matt. 15:3–9; 22:18; 23:13–29; Mark 7:1–8; Luke 12:1), and warned His disciples to avoid their influence (Mark 8:15; cf. Matt. 16:6, 11). Twice in His ministry, at both the beginning (John 2:13–22) and the end (Mark 11:15–17), Jesus struck at the heart of corrupt Judaism by attacking the moneymaking operations of the temple, accusing those involved of turning God's house into a robbers' den. But rather than repenting, the religious leaders maliciously arranged to kill their own Messiah (Mark 11:18).

The second of those temple attacks occurred on Tuesday of Passion Week (Mark 11:15–19). The events recorded in this passage (13:1–37) took place the following evening, after a full day of preaching in the temporarily purged temple on Wednesday (cf. 11:20–12:44). On Thursday, Jesus would celebrate the Passover with His disciples and establish the new ordinance of Communion; on Friday, He would be crucified; and on Sunday, He would rise from the dead.

As Jesus left the temple courtyards on Wednesday, He delivered a final pronouncement of judgment on apostate Judaism (13:2). Then, while sitting on the Mount of Olives looking back at the monumental edifice that had become the symbol of that apostasy, He explained to His disciples what must take place before the end of the age and the establishment of His earthly kingdom (vv. 5ff.). The lengthy instruction Jesus gave in Mark 13:5–37 (and in the parallel passages of Matt. 24:4–25:46 and Luke 21:8–36) is known as the Olivet Discourse, so named because it was there on that hill east of the temple that the Lord gave His disciples a sweeping picture of future events.

The Jewish people of Jesus' day expected the Messiah's arrival to immediately usher in His kingdom, shattering the yoke of Roman imperialism and subjugating Israel's enemies. When John the Baptist appeared in the wilderness declaring that the kingdom of heaven was at hand (Matt. 3:2), the people eagerly flocked to hear him preach. Their interest further intensified when Jesus, the one whom John identified as Messiah, launched His public ministry by teaching with authority (cf. Mark 1:21–22), casting out demons (1:23–27), and curing every kind of sickness and disease (cf. 1:34; 3:10). Several years later, when Jesus entered Jerusalem riding on the colt of a donkey, the crowds could not contain their exuberance (Mark 11:1–10). With shouts of exultation, they proclaimed Him to be the promised messianic Son of David (Matt. 21:9) who would restore the glories of the Davidic kingdom (Mark 11:10).

Those enthusiastic expectations were shared by Jesus' disciples, who similarly "supposed that the kingdom of God was going to appear immediately" (Luke 19:11). Because they knew Jesus was the Messiah (cf. Mark 8:29) and the Son of God (cf. Matt. 14:33; 16:16), their hearts undoubtedly raced with anticipation when they heard the cheers of the people during Jesus' triumphal entry into Jerusalem. Everything appeared to be on schedule to usher in the messianic kingdom. But the disciples overlooked the essential necessity of His death and resurrection, though Jesus had repeatedly told them. Because they had no tolerance for such a reality, they failed to understand what He was saying (cf. Mark 9:32; Luke 9:45; 18:34; John 12:16). The disciples must have been stunned to hear Jesus explain that He was also leaving and an extensive period of time would elapse before He would return to establish His kingdom in Jerusalem and rule over the world (Luke 19:11–27; cf. Acts 1:6–7).

In this passage (Mark 13:1–13), the Lord Jesus prophetically described features that would occur during that intervening time between His first coming and His return. In surveying that future history, He depicted five coming realities: the destruction of the temple, the deception of many, the devastation of the earth, the distress of persecution, and finally, the deliverance of true believers.

THE DESTRUCTION OF THE TEMPLE

As He was going out of the temple, one of His disciples said to Him, "Teacher, behold what wonderful stones and what wonderful buildings!" And Jesus said to him, "Do you see these great buildings? Not one stone will be left upon another which will not be torn down." (13:1–2)

Having engaged in a full day of teaching in the temple, delivering His final instruction to the people (cf. 12:1–37) and issuing a stinging denunciation to the religious leaders (12:38–40; cf. Matt. 23:13–38), Jesus left the temple and headed east, exiting Jerusalem through the eastern gate (cf. 11:19). **As He** and His disciples were **going out of the temple, one of His disciples** looked back and **said to Him, "Teacher behold what wonderful stones and what wonderful buildings!"** Situated atop the plateau above the Kidron Valley east of the city, the temple and its surrounding buildings stood as one of the architectural marvels of the ancient world. Built of polished white stone, with its eastern wall covered in gold, the temple's main structure gleamed in the evening light as if it were a massive jewel. The impressive temple complex contained numerous porticos, colonnades, patios, and courtyards—enabling tens of thousands of worshipers to congregate and present their offerings and sacrifices. Its construction had begun nearly five decades earlier, under the direction of Herod the Great, and would still be ongoing forty years later when it was utterly demolished by the Romans.

The sheer enormity of Herod's stone temple, combined with its magnificence and splendor, made it difficult to imagine that such an edifice would be destroyed. But **Jesus said to him, "Do you see these**

great buildings? Not one stone will be left upon another which will not be torn down." In reality, the temple's external beauty was a monument to apostate religion, not unlike a whitewashed tomb (cf. Matt. 23:27). On the outside its polished marble glistened, but on the inside it was characterized by fetidness rising from the corruption, hypocrisy, and hard-hearted unbelief of Judaism's religious leaders and those who followed them. Consequently, the cup of God's fury would be poured out, the temple destroyed, and the house of Israel left desolate (cf. Matt. 23:38).

In A.D. 70, Jesus' words were literally and precisely fulfilled when God brought to Jerusalem the Roman army under Titus Vespasian to destroy the city and the entire temple complex. As the human instruments of divine wrath, the Romans lit massive fires that caused the stones to crumble in the intense heat. By the time they were finished dismantling the temple, having taken all of the gold and thrown the remaining rubble into the Kidron Valley, all that was left were massive foundation stones that formed footings for the retaining wall under the temple mount, elements that were not part of the temple structure itself. As the Lord predicted with perfect accuracy, the temple and its surrounding buildings were completely demolished under the judgment of God.

THE DECEPTION OF MANY

As He was sitting on the Mount of Olives opposite the temple, Peter and James and John and Andrew were questioning Him privately, "Tell us, when will these things be, and what will be the sign when all these things are going to be fulfilled?" And Jesus began to say to them, "See to it that no one misleads you. Many will come in My name, saying, 'I am He!' and will mislead many. (13:4–6)

Having crossed the Kidron Valley and ascended the Mount of Olives, Jesus and the disciples looked back at the temple complex. **As** Jesus **was sitting on the Mount of Olives opposite the temple, Peter and James and John and Andrew were questioning Him**

privately. These two sets of brothers comprised the innermost circle of Jesus' disciples. Having heard prophecy of the temple's destruction, they were eager to learn more about what the future held. Hence, they asked Him, **"Tell us, when will these things be, and what will be the sign when all these things are going to be fulfilled?"** According to the parallel passage in Matthew 24:3, their full question was, "Tell us, when will these things happen, and what will be the sign of Your coming, and of the end of the age?" As Matthew's account indicates, their question was bigger than just an inquiry into the coming ruination and carnage at the temple. They wanted to know about the end of the present age.

As noted above, the disciples (like other first-century Jews) envisioned only a single coming of the Messiah. But God intended the Messiah to come twice—once as the Suffering Servant (cf. Isa. 53:1–12) and again as the conquering King (cf. Rev. 19:11–19)—with an extended period of time elapsing between His two advents. In order to help them understand that reality, Jesus gave His disciples a detailed reply to their question. In fact, the response found in Mark 13 (and the parallel passages in Matt. 24–25 and Luke 21) constitutes the longest recorded answer given by Jesus to any question He was asked. Clearly, the Lord intended it as vitally important truth for His followers to grasp.

Verse 5 marks the actual beginning of the Olivet Discourse, in which Jesus explained what would take place throughout the world, with a particular emphasis on those events that will immediately precede His return to earth. Having already predicted the imminent demolition of the temple and its operations (v. 2), Jesus shifted His focus to the distant future in verses 5–37. Some interpreters (who deny that there will be a future earthly kingdom) insist that everything Jesus foretold in the Olivet Discourse was fulfilled in A.D. 70, around the time of the temple's destruction. But such a concept is untenable for a number of reasons. First, the fact that Jesus used the figure of birth pangs (13:8; cf. 1 Thess. 5:3) indicates that He was speaking about the end of the church age, not the beginning. After all, labor pains do not occur throughout the entire pregnancy but only at the end. Since the destruction of the temple occurred early in church history, the figure of birth pangs could not apply to that event. Second, the Lord indicated that "the gospel must first be preached to all the nations" (v. 10), something that clearly had not occurred by A.D.

70. Third, Jesus spoke about the "Abomination of Desolation" (v. 14), the ultimate desecration of the Antichrist in the temple during a period just before the second coming (cf. Dan. 9:27; 11:31; 2 Thess. 2:4; for further details see, John MacArthur, *The Second Coming* [Wheaton: Crossway, 2006]). That event did not take place in A.D. 70, and in fact has not yet occurred. Fourth, the Lord also spoke of "a time of tribulation such as has not occurred since the beginning of the creation which God created until now, and never will" (v. 19). Those words cannot refer to the destruction in A.D. 70, since they speak of a time when the calamity on earth will be worse than it has ever been in all of human history, even during the time of the flood (cf. v. 20; cf. Matt. 24:38). Finally, Jesus identified heavenly signs that would accompany the end of the age, including the darkening of the sun and moon, and the falling of the stars from heaven (vv. 24–25). Obviously, such cosmic catastrophes have not yet taken place. When they do, Jesus warned that those alive at that time should recognize that He is about to return (v. 29). As He explained, the generation that experiences those end-time events will be the same generation that is alive at the second coming (v. 30), meaning that all of the final cataclysms on earth will occur within the span of a single generation. Since nothing remotely like a global and cosmic upheaval of the magnitude described in the Olivet Discourse occurred in A.D. 70 nor yet in earth's history, the specific fulfillment of these universal judgments must still be future.

In answer to the disciples' question, the Lord delineated some specific birth pangs, or warning signs, that would precede His return. First, as **Jesus began to** explain **to them,** the world will be subjected to relentless deception by spiritual frauds. He **told them, "See to it that no one misleads you. Many will come in My name, saying, 'I am He!' and will mislead many."** The imperative **see** translates a form of the Greek word *blepō.* In this context, it means more than merely "to see" but carries the sense of "beware" or "take heed." In verses 22–23, Jesus repeated the same warning: "For false Christs and false prophets will arise, and will show signs and wonders, in order to lead astray, if possible, the elect. But take heed; behold, I have told you everything in advance." Jesus' followers were to watch out for false teachers (cf. 2 Tim. 3:13; 2 Peter 2:1–3; 1 John 4:1–3), so that they would not be misled. Though there have been many counterfeit messiahs and false prophets throughout history, both before and after the time of Christ, their numbers will vastly increase at the end of the age. Their work of deception foreshadows that of the ultimate false teacher who will be revealed during the time of the tribulation—the Antichrist (cf. Dan. 8:23; 11:36; 2 Thess. 2:3; Rev. 11:7; 13:1–10). Though he will mislead many (cf. 2 Thess. 2:3–4), even the Antichrist will be unable to deceive the elect (cf. John 10:3–5).

THE DEVASTATION OF THE WORLD

When you hear of wars and rumors of wars, do not be frightened; those things must take place; but that is not yet the end. For nation will rise up against nation, and kingdom against kingdom; there will be earthquakes in various places; there will also be famines. These things are merely the beginning of birth pangs. (13:7–8)

As Jesus continued to articulate the birth pangs that will precede His return, He described global devastation resulting from both human conflicts and natural disasters. **Wars and rumors of wars** between nations and kingdoms have been a reality through every generation, including the present. But, in keeping with Christ's analogy of increased pains, these catastrophes will increase in magnitude and intensity near the end of this age. As bad as those painful realities are, believers **do not** need to **be frightened,** because **those things must take place** according to God's sovereign plan for the world, and even **that is not the end.** There is more yet to come. As Jesus explained, **nation will rise up against nation, and kingdom against kingdom.** Yet, those conflagrations, no matter how frequent or intense, only foreshadow the final, climactic conflict when the nations of the world will converge on Israel, and Christ will return to deliver His people and establish His kingdom (cf. Dan. 7:24; 9:27; 11:40–45; Zech. 14:2–3). That final battle, called Armageddon (so named because much of the fighting will take place on the plain of Megiddo, about sixty miles north of Jerusalem), is described in Revelation 16 and 19. When the Lord Jesus returns in victory, He will destroy His enemies (cf. 2 Thess. 1:7–10; Rev. 19:17–21) and cast the Antichrist into the lake of fire (Rev. 19:20).

In addition to the pains of war, **there will be earthquakes in various places.** In his parallel account, Luke records that these will be "great earthquakes" (Luke 21:11). Throughout human history, many powerful tremors have been recorded. But they will be dwarfed by the massive earthquakes that occur during the tribulation. The book of Revelation records one such quake:

> I looked when He broke the sixth seal, and there was a great earthquake; and the sun became black as sackcloth made of hair, and the whole moon became like blood; and the stars of the sky fell to the earth, as a fig tree casts its unripe figs when shaken by a great wind. The sky was split apart like a scroll when it is rolled up, and every mountain and island were moved out of their places. (Rev. 6:12–14)

A later earthquake, recorded in Revelation 11:13, will destroy one-tenth of Jerusalem, killing seven thousand people. But the most devastating earthquake in all of world history is foretold a few chapters later:

> There was a great earthquake, such as there had not been since man came to be upon the earth, so great an earthquake was it, and so mighty. The great city was split into three parts, and the cities of the nations fell. Babylon the great was remembered before God, to give her the cup of the wine of His fierce wrath. And every island fled away, and the mountains were not found. (Rev. 16:18–20)

That global upheaval will dramatically alter both earth's topography and its geopolitical organization. But it is a necessary part of God's judgment on the world at the end of the age.

In addition to wars and earthquakes, **there will also be famines** throughout history, a reality that again prefigures the ultimate devastation of the very end. During the tribulation, famine will contribute to billions of deaths as one-fourth of the world's population perishes (cf. Rev. 6:5–6, 8). The various natural disasters that are part of God's judgment during that tumultuous time, including the poisoning of a third of the world's freshwater supply (Rev. 8:11), will severely affect the vegetation and ecosystems of the earth. The result will be a massive loss of human life.

As the Lord delineated the reality of future wars, earthquakes, and famines, which foreshadow the disasters of the final tribulation, He added that **these things are merely the beginning of birth pangs.** The metaphor of birth pangs, a reference to the contractions experienced by a woman in childbirth, was often employed by ancient Jewish writers to refer to the end times (cf. 1 Thess. 5:1–3). Initially, an expectant mother's contractions are separated and somewhat mild. But as the moment of childbirth grows closer, they intensify both in frequency and severity. The disasters that currently mark human history are merely previews of far more horrible things to come. They are mild compared to the utter devastation that will result from God's judgment at the end of the age.

THE DISTRESS OF PERSECUTION

But be on your guard; for they will deliver you to the courts, and you will be flogged in the synagogues, and you will stand before governors and kings for My sake, as a testimony to them. The gospel must first be preached to all the nations. When they arrest you and hand you over, do not worry beforehand about what you are to say, but say whatever is given you in that hour; for it is not you who speak, but it is the Holy Spirit. Brother will betray brother to death, and a father his child; and children will rise up against parents and have them put to death. You will be hated by all because of My name. (13:9–12)

Jesus had already warned His disciples about the distress they would face for being faithful to Him. In Matthew 10:16–17, He told them, "Behold, I send you out as sheep in the midst of wolves; so be shrewd as serpents and innocent as doves. But beware of men, for they will hand you over to the courts and scourge you in their synagogues." The next evening (on Thursday of Passover Week), when they would gather in the upper room, the Lord would reiterate that same warning. Speaking of those who would persecute them, He told His disciples, "They will make you outcasts from the synagogue, but an hour is coming for everyone who kills you to think that he is offering service to God. These things they will do because they have not known the Father or Me" (John 16:2–3).

On this occasion, the Lord explained that His followers would be mistreated and attacked by both Jewish and Gentile antagonists. Referring to Jewish persecution, He warned, **"But be on your guard; for they will deliver you to the courts, and you will be flogged in the synagogues."** The courts of Israel met in synagogues, where cases were tried by local judges and punishments often took the form of scourging (cf. Acts 5:40; 2 Cor. 11:24) and imprisonment (Acts 5:18; 8:3). The verb **will deliver** translates a form of the Greek word *paradidōmi*, used here in a technical sense meaning "to be arrested" and taken into custody. The book of Acts records many instances in which believers in the early church faced persecution from Jewish opponents (cf. 3:12–26; 4:1–3; 5:18; 6:8–11; 7:57–60; 8:1–3; 9:23–24, 29; 12:1–3; 13:6–8, 45; 14:2, 19; 17:5, 13; 18:6, 12–16; 19:8–9; 20:3, 19; 21:27–32; 23:12–22; 25:2–3; 28:23–28; cf. 2 Cor. 11:24, 26). But Jesus' followers would not only endure opposition from unbelieving Jews. The Lord expanded His explanation to include Gentile authorities: **And you will stand before governors and kings for My sake, as a testimony to them.** No New Testament figure illustrates that reality more dramatically than the apostle Paul, who was imprisoned by the Romans on multiple occasions (cf. Acts 16:23–24; 22:24–29; 23:10, 18, 35; 24:27; 28:16–31; 2 Tim. 1:8; cf. 2 Cor. 11:25; 1 Thess. 2:2) and repeatedly put on trial before Gentile rulers (Acts 16:19–22; 18:12–16; 21:31–33; 22:24–29; 24:1–22; 25:1–12, 21; 26:1–32; 2 Tim. 4:16–17).

Throughout church history, even until the present hour, countless believers follow in the footsteps of Paul and the other apostles by faithfully enduring suffering and mistreatment for the sake of the Lord Jesus Christ. As Paul told Timothy, "All who desire to live godly in Christ Jesus will be persecuted" (2 Tim. 3:12). The book of Revelation reveals that the worst persecution in history will occur just before the Lord returns, as animosity toward God and the gospel intensifies under the leadership of the final and most influential Antichrist. In those days, many will die for the sake of Christ. The apostle John recounted a vision of those martyred believers in Revelation 6:9–11:

> I saw underneath the altar the souls of those who had been slain because of the word of God, and because of the testimony which they had maintained; and they cried out with a loud voice, saying, "How long, O Lord, holy and true, will You refrain from judging and avenging our blood on those who dwell on the earth?" And there was given to each of them a white robe; and they were told that they should rest for

a little while longer, until the number of their fellow servants and their brethren who were to be killed even as they had been, would be completed also. (Rev. 6:9–11; cf. 7:9–10, 14)

In spite of the satanic opposition and persecution believers have endured in the past and will face into the future, the Lord promised that the message of salvation by grace through faith in the Lord Jesus Christ would continue to spread throughout the whole world. As He explained, **The gospel must first be preached to all the nations** before the end comes (cf. Matt. 24:14). Two thousand years into church history, in spite of severe assaults, the gospel has spread to the ends of the earth; and it continues, on a scale never before imagined, to reach into the most remote regions of the globe. Even in the tribulation period, when the church has been raptured and the Antichrist is wreaking havoc, the Lord will raise up His witnesses in the world, including 144,000 believing Jews (Rev. 7:4–8; 14:1–5), the two resurrected witnesses (Rev. 11:1–13), an angel from heaven who continually proclaims the good news of salvation (Rev. 14:6–7), as well as the regenerated believers from every nation (Rev. 7:9–10).

In light of the coming persecution, Jesus gave His followers a personal promise: **When they arrest you and hand you over, do not worry beforehand about what you are to say, but say whatever is given you in that hour; for it is not you who speak, but it is the Holy Spirit.** The halls of church history are filled with examples of people for whom that promise has been fulfilled, as the Spirit of God enabled believers to face their adversaries with extraordinary poise, constancy, and fidelity. Such faithfulness started with Peter and John who, after being arrested for preaching in the temple, addressed the Sanhedrin with supernatural courage and confidence (Acts 4:13). Stephen similarly stood fearlessly before the Jewish council, on the very edge of certain death by a violent mob (Acts 7:1–53). And Paul delivered many eloquent defenses for the gospel as he appeared before governors and kings. Their ability to stand boldly for Christ and the gospel in those moments was made possible by divine power. As Paul explained to Timothy, after appearing on trial before Roman emperor Nero, "The Lord stood with me and strengthened me, so that through me the proclamation might be fully accomplished, and that all the Gentiles might hear; and I was rescued out of the lion's mouth" (2 Tim. 4:17).

In verse 12, Jesus added that the persecution His followers would face, both throughout church history and in the final tribulation, would frequently originate from members of their own families. He told His disciples, **Brother will betray brother to death, and a father his child; and children will rise up against parents and have them put to death.** Those who follow Christ must be willing to endure persecution from even their most intimate friends and family members. As the Lord noted, that persecution may be so intense that it results in death. But not even death can stop the spread of the gospel. Throughout history, the Lord has used the wrongful execution of Christians as a powerful testimony to the watching world. He will do so again in the tribulation (cf. Rev. 11:7–13). Appropriately, the English word "martyr" comes from the Greek word *marturion*, meaning "witness" or "testimony." All who have sacrificed their lives for the sake of Christ, through the Spirit's enabling power, have died as witnesses to the preciousness of the glorious truth of the gospel to those who have come under its power.

The Deliverance of Believers

You will be hated by all because of My name, but the one who endures to the end, he will be saved. (13:13b)

The reason the world hates believers is because it hates the Lord Jesus. As He Himself explained, **You will be hated by all because of My name.** In John 7:7, Jesus said of the world, "It hates Me because I testify of it, that its deeds are evil." Motivated by their enmity toward His message of condemnation on their sins, unbelievers attack those who belong to Him. Jesus expanded on this reality in the upper room,

> "If the world hates you, you know that it has hated Me before it hated you. If you were of the world, the world would love its own; but because you are not of the world, but I chose you out of the world, because of this the world hates you. Remember the word that I said to you, 'A slave is not greater than his master.' If they persecuted Me, they will also persecute you; if they kept My word, they will keep yours also." (John 15:18–20)

The Lord's warning was tethered to a promise: **but the one who endures to the end, he will be saved.** Some have improperly interpreted this phrase as teaching that salvation can be earned through perseverance. But that would make salvation contingent on good works, a point the New Testament repeatedly denies (cf. Acts 15:1–11; Rom. 3:19–28; 11:6; Gal. 2:16; Eph. 2:8–9; Phil. 3:7–11; Titus 3:5). Others argue that this verse implies that true believers can lose their salvation, but that notion is also clearly negated in Scripture (cf. John 6:37, 40; 10:27–29; 17:11; 1 Cor. 1:8; 1 Thess. 5:23–24; Rom. 8:30–39). In reality, Jesus was simply reiterating the fact that those who endure suffering for His sake demonstrate by that very endurance that they are genuine believers (cf. John 8:31; 1 Cor. 15:1–2; Col. 1:21–23; Heb. 2:1–3; 3:14; 4:14; 6:11–12; 10:39; 12:14; James 1:2–4), and as such they **will be saved.** Conversely, those who fall away when persecution comes reveal that they never truly possessed saving faith in the first place (cf. Mark 4:16–17; 1 John 2:19).

Motivated by their love for Christ, true disciples willingly suffer for His sake, considering it a joy to do so (cf. Acts 5:41), knowing that their suffering will one day be rewarded in heaven by the One who first loved them (cf. 2 Cor. 4:16–18). As noted earlier, believers' ability to endure comes not from their own resolve but from the indwelling power of the Holy Spirit, who enables them to stand firm in the midst of adversity. Thus, they can face hardship with unwavering resolve armed with a divinely granted faith (Eph. 2:8–9) that holds firmly to the promise that God will preserve and protect those who are His (cf. Rom. 5:8–10; Phil. 1:6; 2 Tim. 1:12; Heb. 7:25; 1 Peter 1:3–8; Jude 24).

Only those who possess such genuine saving faith, which by its nature endures to the end, **will be saved** to enjoy the eternal glories of heaven. Salvation, in this context, stretches beyond the moment of conversion to the completion of God's saving work in the life of believers— as He delivers them from the present evil system and ushers them into His eternal kingdom. The hope-filled perspective of every Christian is reflected in the words of the apostle Paul, who exclaimed near the end of his life, "The Lord will rescue me from every evil deed, and will bring me safely to His heavenly kingdom; to Him be the glory forever and ever. Amen" (2 Tim. 4:18).

Even during the tribulation period, when deadly persecution

against believers reaches its apex, those who truly belong to Christ will persevere, even though many will become martyrs. In a glorious picture of their faithfulness and subsequent reward, the book of Revelation describes those tribulation saints with these words:

> These are the ones who come out of the great tribulation, and they have washed their robes and made them white in the blood of the Lamb. For this reason, they are before the throne of God; and they serve Him day and night in His temple; and He who sits on the throne will spread His tabernacle over them. They will hunger no longer, nor thirst anymore; nor will the sun beat down on them, nor any heat; for the Lamb in the center of the throne will be their shepherd, and will guide them to springs of the water of life; and God will wipe every tear from their eyes. (Rev. 7:14 –17)

In spite of the coming deception, disasters, and distress, the Lord's words assured His disciples that not everyone would defect. The gospel would prevail. Throughout the remainder of history, and even in the final period of tribulation, God would be at work in the hearts of His elect: saving them from sin, empowering them for service, and preserving them for glory (cf. Mark 13:20). No matter how tumultuous the world becomes, the redemptive chain of Romans 8 can never be broken:

> These whom He predestined, He also called; and these whom He called, He also justified; and these whom He justified, He also glorified. ... For I am convinced that neither death, nor life, nor angels, nor principalities, nor things present, nor things to come, nor powers, nor height, nor depth, nor any other created thing, will be able to separate [believers] from the love of God, which is in Christ Jesus our Lord. (Rom. 8:30, 38–39)

The Future Tribulation (Mark 13:14–23)

23

But when you see the abomination of desolation standing where it should not be (let the reader understand), then those who are in Judea must flee to the mountains. The one who is on the housetop must not go down, or go in to get anything out of his house; and the one who is in the field must not turn back to get his coat. But woe to those who are pregnant and to those who are nursing babies in those days! But pray that it may not happen in the winter. For those days will be a time of tribulation such as has not occurred since the beginning of the creation which God created until now, and never will. Unless the Lord had shortened those days, no life would have been saved; but for the sake of the elect, whom He chose, He shortened the days. And then if anyone says to you, "Behold, here is the Christ"; or, "Behold, He is there"; do not believe him; for false Christs and false prophets will arise, and will show signs and wonders, in order to lead astray, if possible, the elect. But take heed; behold, I have told you everything in advance. (13:14–23)

The second coming of Jesus Christ is one of the Bible's most intriguing and provocative themes, and both believers and unbelievers must carefully consider its eternal implications. For believers, the Lord's return is the realization of God's promise and their hope. Those who love the Lord Jesus are constantly "looking for the blessed hope and the appearing of the glory of [their] great God and Savior, Christ Jesus" (Titus 2:13), knowing that they will be rewarded by Him (cf. 1 Peter 5:4) and will remain forever in His presence (1 Thess. 4:17). Thus, the thought of His return should fill them with joy and anticipation. Conversely, for unbelievers the second coming stands as a terrifying promise of the divine judgment that awaits all who reject the Lord Jesus (2 Thess. 1:9–10). When He returns, not only will He gather His own and welcome them into His eternal kingdom, He will also destroy His enemies and cast them into eternal hell (cf. Matt. 25:31–46). That reality should compel unbelievers to recognize that "the world is passing away, and also its lusts" (1 John 2:17), and that only those who call on the name of the Lord, placing their faith in Him, will be saved from everlasting punishment (cf. Rom. 10:9–13).

In Mark 13:14–23, the Lord Jesus continues His description of the catastrophic circumstances that will precede His return and the establishment of His millennial monarchy. Jesus taught these truths while He was with His disciples on the Mount of Olives. It was evening on Wednesday of Passion Week. The following day He would celebrate the Passover meal with them. On Friday He would die on the cross, and on Sunday He would rise from the grave.

The Lord's activities on Wednesday started with a full day of teaching in the temple courtyard. After pronouncing judgment on the edifice itself and the people engaged in the apostate form of religion it housed (v. 2), Jesus exited Jerusalem with His disciples. They passed out the Eastern Gate, across the Kidron Valley, and up the slope of the Mount of Olives. From there, they could look back and see the marble stones still gleaming in the fading glow of evening. The Lord's earlier declaration of judgment on that massive wonder prompted a question in the minds of Peter, Andrew, James, and John. They asked Him privately, "When will these things be?" (v. 4). Jesus' disciples wanted to know not only about the coming demolition of the temple but also about the signs of the end of the age (cf. Matt. 24:3). In response to their question, the Lord delivered a sermon regarding His return. Known as the Olivet Discourse, it is the longest recorded reply to any question asked Him in the Gospels (cf. Matt. 24:4–25:46; Luke 21:8–36). Jesus' answer foretold the events that would happen in the world before His return, though He did not specify the exact time when those catastrophes would occur (cf. Acts 1:7).

As seen in the exposition of 13:5–13 in the previous chapter of this volume, Jesus first surveyed the cataclysms that will mark the beginning of the final tribulation period, a specific seven years of horrible divine retribution, prophesied in Daniel 9:27 and detailed in Revelation 6–16. (For more on the tribulation as described in the book of Revelation, see John MacArthur, _Because the Time Is Near_ [Chicago: Moody, 2007].) Using the metaphor of birth pangs, the Lord explained that the end of the age will be characterized by false teachers, false messiahs, wars, rumors of wars, earthquakes, famines, and violent persecution against believers. Although similar devastating realities have always been part of earth's troubled history, their frequency and severity will rapidly and dramatically increase at the very end as the final judgment is birthed. The afflictions this world has experienced up to the present time are merely previews of the unparalleled destruction that will occur in the months prior to the return of the Son of God.

The Bible describes the tribulation as a time of universal devastation, in which the full wrath of God will be unleashed all over the earth (cf. Dan. 9:27; Rev. 6–16). It will also be a time of unmitigated evil, as the normal restraining power of the Holy Spirit against evil is withdrawn (2 Thess. 2:7) and demonic activity is permitted to increase (Rev. 9:1–6). Though the church will have already been raptured to heaven (cf. John 14:1–3; 1 Cor. 15:51–52; 1 Thess. 4:15–18; Rev. 3:10), the good news of salvation will still be preached to unbelievers through the testimony of 144,000 redeemed Jews (Rev. 7), two powerful witnesses (Rev. 11), an angel flying in midheaven (Rev. 14:6), and countless numbers of Gentiles who embrace the gospel during that time (Rev. 7:9–10). (For an explanation and defense of the pretribulation rapture of the church, see _1 & 2 Thessalonians_, The MacArthur New Testament Commentary [Chicago: Moody, 2002,] chap. 11.)

In this section (13:14–23), the Lord continued to discuss the future tribulation, specifically focusing on the second half of that era. As

He described these events, He identified the perversion of the Antichrist, the panic of the people, and the protection of the elect.

The Perversion of the Antichrist

But when you see the abomination of desolation standing where it should not be (let the reader understand) (13:14a)

After describing the initial birth pangs, Jesus shifted His focus to a major event that will notify everyone that they are in the final time of tribulation: they will **see the abomination of desolation standing where it should not be.** In Matthew's parallel account, Jesus noted that **the abomination of desolation** was that "which was spoken of through Daniel the prophet, standing in the holy place" (Matt. 24:15). Marking the midpoint of the tribulation (cf. Dan. 9:27), that detestable event will activate the most intense calamities of divine judgment, triggering a time that Jesus described as the "great tribulation" (Matt. 24:21).

The word translated **abomination** (from the Greek term *bdelugma*; along with its Hebrew equivalents *shiqquwts* and *tow`ebah*) refers to that which is detestable, foul, immoral, blasphemous, and abhorrent to God (e.g., Lev. 18:22–29; Deut. 22:5; 25:13–16; 1 Kings 11:5–7; 14:24; 2 Kings 16:3; Prov. 11:1; 12:22; 15:8–9; 20:23; Jer. 16:18). It was often used in reference to idolatry and pagan worship practices (e.g., Deut. 7:25; 27:15; 32:16; Isa. 44:19; Ezek. 5:11; 7:20; 18:12). In the book of Revelation, it describes the wickedness of the city of Babylon (17:4–5). Revelation 21:27 promises that "no one who practices abomination" will be permitted entrance into heaven.

The book of Daniel mentions the **abomination of desolation** three times (9:27; 11:31; 12:11). In Daniel 11:31, the term is used to describe the historical perversion of Antiochus IV, the Seleucid king who controlled Israel from 175–165 B.C. Calling himself "Theos Epiphanes," which means "manifest god," Antiochus desecrated the temple in Jerusalem by sacrificing a pig on the altar, forcing the priests to eat its meat and erecting an idol of Zeus within its walls. With ruthless abandon, Antiochus oppressed the Jewish people, slaughtering thousands and selling many more into slavery. The intertestamental apocryphal books of 1 and 2 Maccabees detail both the atrocities committed by Antiochus and the Jewish people's ability to overthrow him and purify the temple.

But the desecration of the temple by Antiochus IV was only a foreshadowing of the Antichrist's future perversion. Daniel 9:27 and 12:11 describe that end-time event, situated at the midpoint of Daniel's seventieth week, when the Antichrist will set up his throne in a rebuilt temple in Jerusalem and declare himself to be God. After pretending to be a peacemaker by making an alliance with Israel, the Antichrist will turn against the Jewish people, massacring them and desecrating the temple for a period of three and a half years (cf. Rev. 11:2; 12:1). He will also make war with believers (Rev. 13:7), whether Jew or Gentile, killing many for their unwavering faith in the Lord Jesus Christ (cf. Rev. 6:9–11).

During that time, the Antichrist will openly blaspheme God, elevating "himself above every so-called god or object of worship, so that he takes his seat in the temple of God, displaying himself as being God" (2 Thess. 2:4; cf. Rev. 13:15). His "coming is in accord with the activity of Satan, with all power and signs and false wonders, and with all the deception of wickedness for those who perish, because they did not receive the love of the truth so as to be saved" (2 Thess. 2:9–10). Whereas Antiochus IV erected an idol of Zeus in the temple, the final Antichrist will exalt himself as God and demand the worship of all people on earth (cf. Rev. 13:7–8). His blasphemous religion will be promoted by the ultimate false prophet, who will perform great miracles through Satan's power in order to deceive the world (Rev. 13:11–15; cf. 2 Thess. 2:9–10).

As noted in the previous chapter of this volume, the warnings given by Christ in the Olivet Discourse were not intended for the Twelve specifically but for believers who will be alive at the end of the age when these things occur. That interpretation is reinforced by the exhortation to **let the reader understand.** This is not for the listening disciples but for future readers of Scripture. In the years immediately prior to the second coming, people will read Jesus' words and, realizing they are in the midst of the final tribulation, be equipped to understand and endure the trials of that unparalleled trouble.

THE PANIC OF THE PEOPLE

then those who are in Judea must flee to the mountains. The one who is on the housetop must not go down, or go in to get anything out of his house; and the one who is in the field must not turn back to get his coat. But woe to those who are pregnant and to those who are nursing babies in those days! But pray that it may not happen in the winter. (13:14b–18)

During the final tribulation, the Jewish people will particularly be assaulted. Jesus' instruction to those who will one day experience the events that directly target Israel is simple and clear: Get out immediately! When the desecration of Jerusalem's future temple by the Antichrist takes place, **then those who are in Judea must flee to the mountains.** The only safe reaction to the abomination of desolation is to escape from Jerusalem with urgency, because the impending massacre will be so severe. As those closest to the temple, the people living in Jerusalem and Judea at that time will find themselves in the greatest danger from the Antichrist. Though he will assert his deadly dominance over the entire world, his wrath will be aimed especially at the Jewish people, along with believers everywhere. The word **flee** (a form of the Greek verb *phuegō*) is related to the English term "fugitive." In light of the imminent threat, the only hope for Jerusalem's residents will be to abandon the city and hide in the mountains.

In describing these end-time events, the prophet Zechariah declared that only one-third of the Jewish population living in Judea at that time will survive (Zech. 13:8–9). Those who successfully escape will come to saving faith, having been refined by God through the persecution inflicted on them by the Antichrist. As God Himself has promised, at that time "they will call on My name, and I will answer them; I will say, 'They are My people,' and they will say, 'The Lord is my God'" (v. 9b).

The Antichrist's fury against Israel will produce a holocaust far more severe than the Roman assault on Jerusalem in A.D. 70. Though it is true that many of Jerusalem's inhabitants fled to the mountains when Rome's armies attacked, their escape only foreshadowed the future flight that will take place at the very end. Important details from both the Olivet

Discourse and other biblical prophecies were not fulfilled in A.D. 70, such as the destruction of the nations that attack Jerusalem (Zech. 12:8–9), the visible return of Christ (Zech. 14:1–11; Mark 13:24–27; Acts 1:9–11), the judgment of the nations by the Lord Jesus (cf. Matt. 25:31–46), and the establishment of His earthly reign in Jerusalem for a thousand years (Rev. 20:4–6). Those unfulfilled prophecies indicate that the horrors described by Jesus in these verses are future and cannot refer to that first-century event.

Again stressing the urgency of that future situation, Jesus added, **The one who is on the housetop must not go down, or go in to get anything out of his house.** The escalating danger will be so great that there can be no time to waste, not even to go inside one's house to collect personal belongings. In ancient Israel, most houses were built with a flat roof that acted as an outdoor terrace, with stairs leading down on the outside of the house. In the evening hours, people often gathered on their rooftops to unwind from the day and enjoy the cooler weather. Jesus warned that anyone who happens to be on his rooftop when he hears about the abomination of desolation should flee the city immediately. He should not even take a few minutes to retrieve items from inside his home, since the danger will exponentially increase with each passing moment. For that same reason, **the one who is in the field must not turn back to get his coat.** He should leave it behind and flee. Those who cannot make a quick escape, like **those who are pregnant** and **those who are nursing babies,** will find themselves in an extremely precarious position **in those days.** Their inability to move rapidly will increase the risk of capture and death. Yet, those who are part of God's elect remnant will be protected by Him as they go into hiding.

Compared to other places in the world, the winters in Israel are generally mild though it does occasionally snow in Jerusalem. (On average, the city experiences a major snowstorm every few years.) However, when Jesus urged, **Pray that it may not happen in the winter,** His point was simply that any hindrance, including inclement weather, would slow the escape of those attempting to flee. Because the threat will be so great, any obstacle—including cold, rain, or snow—will elevate the danger.

The Protection of God

For those days will be a time of tribulation such as has not occurred since the beginning of the creation which God created until now, and never will. Unless the Lord had shortened those days, no life would have been saved; but for the sake of the elect, whom He chose, He shortened the days. And then if anyone says to you, "Behold, here is the Christ"; or, "Behold, He is there"; do not believe him; for false Christs and false prophets will arise, and will show signs and wonders, in order to lead astray, if possible, the elect. But take heed; behold, I have told you everything in advance. (13:19–23)

As noted above, the abomination of desolation will mark the midpoint of the final seven-year tribulation. The second half of that tribulation period (called the "great tribulation" by Jesus in Matt. 24:21) will be even more severe than the first three and a half years. In fact, **those days will be a time of tribulation such as has not occurred since the beginning of the creation which God created until now, and never will.** At no point in earth's history, even during the global upheaval of the flood, has there been a more catastrophic time than will occur at the very end. Obviously, as noted above, Jesus' description could not be applied to the destruction of Jerusalem in A.D. 70, as some suppose. In Revelation chapters 6–16, the apostle John denotes the unparalleled horrors that will characterize the very end, as God's wrath is poured out on the whole earth. The judgments that mark the latter half of the tribulation period include the following: a great earthquake will devastate the earth (Rev. 6:12–17); hail and fire will consume a third of earth's vegetation (8:6–7); a third of the ocean will be turned to blood (8:8–9); a third of freshwater will be poisoned (8:10–11); a third of the sun, moon, and stars will be darkened (8:12); countless demons will be released from bondage to terrorize mankind (9:1–12); a third of earth's population will be killed (9:13–21); another great earthquake will kill seven thousand people (11:13); incurable sores will cause people great pain (16:2); the entire sea will turn to blood and all sea creatures will die (16:3); the rivers will turn to blood (16:4); the earth will experience extreme heat (16:8–9); darkness will engulf the world (16:10–11); the Euphrates River will dry up (16:12); and a final, global earthquake will cause massive changes to earth's appearance (16:17–21). Clearly, cataclysmic events of that magnitude and succession have never yet occurred in human history. They await fulfillment in the final days, just prior to Christ's return and the establishment of His millennial kingdom.

As Jesus went on to explain, **Unless the Lord had shortened those days, no life would have been saved; but for the sake of the elect, whom He chose, He shortened the days.** The judgment of God on earth, including His allowing the fury of Antichrist against the Jews and the saints, will make the great tribulation an unparalleled time of terror. In fact, it will be so unbearable that God Himself will cut it short. The verb **shortened** (a form of the Greek word *koloboō*) means "to end abruptly" or "to stop instantly." Rather than subjecting the earth to a prolonged period of either divine judgment or satanic tyranny, God has predetermined to put a halt to the devastation before the entire human race is destroyed. Consequently, He will limit the great tribulation to a period of three and a half years (Dan. 7:25; 12:7; Rev. 11:2; 12:14; 13:5).

The elect may refer to believers in general (cf. Rev. 17:14) or to the nation of Israel specifically (cf. Isa. 45:4), since God will preserve a remnant of both redeemed Jews and Gentiles. If He did not put a sudden end to the Antichrist's savage assault on believers, none of the elect would survive. Yet, God has promised to protect His own. Though some will be martyred, many will be preserved as an earthly remnant. When Christ returns, they will be those who populate His earthly kingdom. (For more on the Bible's teaching regarding the millennial kingdom, see John MacArthur and Richard Mayhue, eds., *Christ's Prophetic Plans* [Chicago: Moody, 2012].)

Jesus continued warning that future generation that, during those shortened days, **if anyone says to you, "Behold, here is the Christ"; or, "Behold, He is there"; do not believe him; for false Christs and false prophets will arise.** Due to the chaos and catastrophes that will characterize the great tribulation, religious liars and deceivers will take advantage of people's terror and desperation. Their message of satanic deceit will convince many to believe them, because they **will show signs and wonders.** But though they will try **to lead**

astray, if possible, the elect, they will be unable to do so. God's elect are always personally secured by Him, so that it is impossible to take them out of His hand or the Son's hand (John 10:28–29).

Jesus' words highlight the relationship between human responsibility and divine sovereignty. On the one hand, believers are commanded not to be deceived by false prophets but to endure to the end (Mark 13:13). After all, they have been duly warned. As Jesus said, **Take heed; behold, I have told you everything in advance.** On the other hand, they are also assured that, because they are elect, it is impossible for them to be led astray and lose the gift of salvation (cf. John 6:37,40; 17:11; 1 Cor. 1:8; 1 Thess. 5:23–24; Rom. 8:30–39). True believers know the voice of their Master (John 10:27–29), and they will reject all others (John 10:5). Having been called to place their trust in Him, they can be confident that He will hold them safely until the eternal glories of heaven become theirs (cf. 2 Tim. 4:18).

The terror of those final days, as horrific as it will be, will not last indefinitely. As the next passage reveals (Mark 13:24–27), the Lord Jesus continued by explaining that He will return to earth to defeat the Antichrist and rescue the elect (cf. Rev. 19:11–21). Such is the substance of the Christian hope (Phil. 3:20; 1 Thess. 4:13–18; Titus 2:11–14). Though the great tribulation will occur, human history will not ultimately end in turmoil and calamity but in triumph and victory. When the Lord Jesus Christ returns, He will establish His glorious millennial reign on the earth, where the saints will be exalted with Him. As the book of Revelation declares:

> Then I saw thrones, and they sat on them, and judgment was given to them. And I saw the souls of those who had been beheaded because of their testimony of Jesus and because of the word of God, and those who had not worshiped the beast or his image, and had not received the mark on their forehead and on their hand; and they came to life and reigned with Christ for a thousand years. . . . Blessed and holy is the one who has a part in the first resurrection; over these the second death has no power, but they will be priests of God and of Christ and will reign with Him for a thousand years. (Rev. 20:4, 6)

The Return of Christ
(Mark 13:24–37)

24

"But in those days, after that tribulation, the sun will be darkened and the moon will not give its light, and the stars will be falling from heaven, and the powers that are in the heavens will be shaken. Then they will see the Son of Man coming in clouds with great power and glory. And then He will send forth the angels, and will gather together His elect from the four winds, from the farthest end of the earth to the farthest end of heaven. Now learn the parable from the fig tree: when its branch has already become tender and puts forth its leaves, you know that summer is near. Even so, you too, when you see these things happening, recognize that He is near, right at the door. Truly I say to you, this generation will not pass away until all these things take place. Heaven and earth will pass away, but My words will not pass away. But of that day or hour no one knows, not even the angels in heaven, nor the Son, but the Father alone. Take heed, keep on the alert; for you do not know when the appointed time will come. It is like a man away on a journey, who upon leaving his

house and putting his slaves in charge, assigning to each one his task, also commanded the doorkeeper to stay on the alert. Therefore, be on the alert—for you do not know when the master of the house is coming, whether in the evening, at midnight, or when the rooster crows, or in the morning—in case he should come suddenly and find you asleep. What I say to you I say to all, 'Be on the alert!'" (13:24–37)

The return of the Lord Jesus Christ represents the apogee of human history. It is the blessed hope (Titus 2:12–13), sincere longing (2 Tim. 4:8), and eager expectation (1 Cor. 1:7; 1 Thess. 1:10) of every believer. Though death immediately ushers the redeemed into the presence of their Savior (2 Cor. 5:8); the glorious resurrection of the body awaits the future day when the Lord Jesus will come to take His bride to heaven (1 Cor. 15:51–54; cf. 1 Thess. 4:13–18; 1 John 3:2). Then, the seven-year tribulation will follow on earth. After that time of epic judgments and salvation, the Lord will return to this earth with His raptured and glorified saints, along with the angels, to destroy His enemies and establish His promised kingdom.

Just as Jesus' first coming was a historical event, His second coming will take place at a divinely appointed time in real history. Unlike His first advent, however, the Lord will not arrive as a human baby in a stall. Rather, He will appear suddenly in blazing divine glory in the sky for all the world to see. Jesus explained these prophecies to His disciples in the Olivet Discourse (Matt. 24:4–25:46; Mark 13:5–37; Luke 21:8–36), in which He delineated the signs (or birth pangs) that would precede His future coming and the end of the age, as discussed in the previous chapters of this volume.

It was Wednesday evening of Passion Week. For most of the day, Jesus had been teaching in the temple (Mark 11:27–12:44). As He left the expansive temple grounds and traversed the Kidron Valley to the Mount of Olives, Jesus explained to His disciples that the magnificent buildings they so admired would be destroyed as an act of God's judgment on apostate Israel (cf. 13:2). Hearing Him say that, four of the disciples— namely, Peter, James, John, and Andrew—asked Him privately, "Tell us, when will these things be, and what will be the sign when all these things are going to be fulfilled?" (v. 4). Their question extended beyond the destruction of the temple to encompass the Lord's second coming and the end of the age (cf. Matt. 24:3). Because they knew He was the Messiah (cf. Mark 8:29), they naturally wondered when His messianic kingdom would be established. Our Lord answered their question by explaining that an intervening period of time would elapse before the earthly kingdom began (cf. Luke 19:11–27). As Jesus explained, using the analogy of increasing labor pains, devastating events will intensify throughout earth's history, reaching their apex during the final tribulation period, just prior to the second coming (cf. 13:14–23; cf. Dan. 9:27).

In this passage (13:24–37), having surveyed the events leading up to it, the Lord focused directly on His return in glory. In so doing, He first told His disciples about His spectacular appearance. Second, He gave them a simple analogy to illustrate His point. Third, He underscored the sovereign authority of His Word in predicting the future. Finally, He issued a somber admonition to those who will be alive on the earth at the time of His return.

CHRIST'S SPECTACULAR APPEARANCE

But in those days, after that tribulation, the sun will be darkened and the moon will not give its light, and the stars will be falling from heaven, and the powers that are in the heavens will be shaken. Then they will see the Son of Man coming in clouds with great power and glory. And then He will send forth the angels, and will gather together His elect from the four winds, from the farthest end of the earth to the farthest end of heaven. (13:24–27)

As the Lord described His second advent, He paid particular attention to four aspects of His return: the sequence, the staging, the sign, and the saints.

The Sequence. After warning His disciples about the abomination of desolation in the temple (v. 14), and the terrible holocaust that will follow it (vv. 15–23), Jesus explained that **in those days, after** the **tribulation** period ends, He will return. In light of the context, **those**

days can only refer to the three and a half years of great tribulation that will follow the Antichrist's desecration of the temple in Jerusalem (13:14–19; cf. Matt. 24:21; Rev. 6–19). Earth's final days will be characterized by unrestrained immorality, unparalleled devastation, and unrelenting violence (toward all believers and also toward the Jewish people) under the satanically inspired influence of the Antichrist and his forces. Only as the tribulation ends and its judgments are exhausted will the Lord return to conquer His enemies and establish His earthly reign and rule.

The Staging. The cosmic backdrop for history's most climactic moment will be total darkness, after God extinguishes the sun, moon, and stars (cf. Zech. 14:6–7), which will later be relit during the millennial kingdom (cf. Isa. 30:26). As Jesus explained, at the end of the tribulation period **the sun will be darkened and the moon will not give its light, and the stars will be falling from heaven.** When the One who "upholds all things by the word of His power" (Heb. 1:3) withdraws that sustaining energy, **the powers that are in the heavens will be shaken,** indicating that the orbits of stars and planets will careen off course, and cosmic bodies will begin to rip apart. Yet, God will not allow the universe to disintegrate entirely; He will preserve it for the establishment of Christ's domination.

In predicting these traumatic events, Jesus echoed the words of Old Testament prophecy. The book of Isaiah exclaimed:

> Behold, the day of the Lord is coming ...
> For the stars of heaven and their constellations
> Will not flash forth their light;
> The sun will be dark when it rises
> And the moon will not shed its light.
> Thus I will punish the world for its evil
> And the wicked for their iniquity ...
> Therefore I will make the heavens tremble,
> And the earth will be shaken from its place
> At the fury of the Lord of hosts
> In the day of His burning anger. (Isa. 13:9–13; cf. 24:1–6, 23; 34:1–6)

About a hundred years before Isaiah, the prophet Joel similarly declared:

> Before them the earth quakes,
> The heavens tremble,
> The sun and the moon grow dark
> And the stars lose their brightness.
> The Lord utters His voice before His army;
> Surely His camp is very great,
> For strong is he who carries out His word.
> The day of the Lord is indeed great and very awesome,
> And who can endure it? ...
> The sun will be turned into darkness
> And the moon into blood
> Before the great and awesome day of the Lord comes.
> (Joel 2:10–11,31; cf. 3:15)

Other prophets similarly predicted the devastating events that will occur during the great tribulation (cf. Ezek. 38:19–23; Hag. 2:6–7; Zeph. 1:14–18; Zech. 14:6). Jesus' words corresponded exactly to what the Old Testament promised would take place during the eschatological day of the Lord when He will establish His glory before the watching world.

In response to these cosmic events, unbelievers who are alive on the earth will react in terror and confusion. As Luke's parallel account explains, the Lord added that there will be "on the earth dismay among nations, in perplexity at the roaring of the sea and the waves, men fainting from fear and the expectation of the things which are coming upon the world; for the powers of the heavens will be shaken" (Luke 21:25–26). The world's inhabitants will go into severe shock, some undoubtedly traumatized to death from the unbearable dread over what is happening to them.

The Sign. Against the pitch darkness of that time, suddenly and vibrantly "the Lord Jesus will be revealed from heaven with His mighty angels in flaming fire" (2 Thess. 1:7). His presence will be unmistakable, and all the world will witness His appearing (Rev. 1:7). The disciples had asked Jesus, "What will be the sign of Your coming?" (Matt. 24:3). As Jesus explained to them, God's wrath will be released so that the world will be replete with natural disasters and man-made crises, all of which preview the future, global devastation of the final tribulation period that immediately precedes the second coming. But the ultimate sign will be Jesus Himself, when He appears in glorious and undiminished brilliance (cf. Mark 9:3). Just as He ascended two millennia ago, He will one day descend to this earth (cf. Acts 1:9–11). **Then** all the world **will see the Son of Man coming in clouds with great power and glory.** In describing that future event, Jesus borrowed the language of Daniel 7:13–14, where the prophet Daniel declared:

> And behold, with the clouds of heaven
> One like a Son of Man was coming,
> And He came up to the Ancient of Days
> And was presented before Him.
> And to Him was given dominion,
> Glory and a kingdom,
> That all the peoples, nations and men of every language
> Might serve Him.
> His dominion is an everlasting dominion
> Which will not pass away;
> And His kingdom is one
> Which will not be destroyed.

Coming in the clouds as if they were a divine chariot (cf. Ps. 104:3; Isa. 19:1), the Son of Man will appear with **great power and glory,** returning to establish His kingdom and to destroy the ungodly. On that day, heaven will open to reveal the conquering King. Rather than riding the humble foal of a donkey, as He did at His earthly entrance to Jerusalem (Mark 11:7–10), He will be seated as the eternal Sovereign atop a royal white steed.

The apostle John described the majesty and power of Jesus' return with these words:

> And I saw heaven opened, and behold, a white horse, and He who sat on it is called Faithful and True, and in righteousness He judges and wages war. His eyes are a flame of fire, and on His head are many diadems; and He has a name written on Him which no one knows except Himself. He is clothed with a robe dipped in blood, and His name is called The Word of God. And the armies which are in heaven, clothed in fine linen, white and clean, were following Him on white horses. From His mouth comes a sharp sword, so that with it He may strike down the nations, and He will rule them with a rod of iron; and He treads the wine press of the fierce wrath of God, the Almighty. And on His robe and on His thigh He has a name written, "King of kings, and Lord of lords." Then I saw an angel standing in the sun, and he cried out with a loud voice, saying to all the birds which fly in midheaven, "Come,

> assemble for the great supper of God, so that you may eat the flesh of
> kings and the flesh of commanders and the flesh of mighty men and
> the flesh of horses and of those who sit on them and the flesh of all
> men, both free men and slaves, and small and great." And I saw the
> beast and the kings of the earth and their armies assembled to make
> war against Him who sat on the horse and against His army. And the
> beast was seized, and with him the false prophet who performed the
> signs in his presence, by which he deceived those who had received
> the mark of the beast and those who worshiped his image; these two
> were thrown alive into the lake of fire which burns with brimstone. And
> the rest were killed with the sword which came from the mouth of Him
> who sat on the horse, and all the birds were filled with their flesh. (Rev.
> 19:11–21)

With perfect righteousness and absolute authority, the Lord Jesus will
enact judgment on His enemies (2 Thess. 1:7–10; cf. Isa. 11:4; 63:1–4; Rev.
1:16), including the Antichrist whom He will cast into the lake of fire
(Rev. 19:20). Satan will be bound for a period of a thousand years (20:1–
3), and Christ's millennial reign will begin (20:4–6). Seated at last upon
His earthly throne, the Lord Jesus will unilaterally and perfectly rule the
nations as their sole Sovereign and King (cf. Ps. 2:8–9; Rev. 12:5).

The Saints. At the Lord's return, He will be joined by "many thousands of His holy ones" (Jude 14), a heavenly army that will include both
angels (Matt. 24:31; 25:31; Mark 8:38; 2 Thess. 1:7) and glorified saints
(Col. 3:4; 1 Thess. 3:13; Rev. 19:14). The church, having been raptured
before the seven-year tribulation began (cf. John 14:1–3; 1 Cor. 15:51–52;
1 Thess. 4:15–18; Rev. 3:10), will compose the entourage that accompanies Christ in His triumph. (For a discussion on the timing of the rapture
of the church in light of the Olivet Discourse, see John MacArthur, *Luke
18–24*, The MacArthur New Testament Commentary [Chicago: Moody,
2014], chap. 22.)

After the enemies of Christ are vanquished, **then He will send
forth the angels, and will gather together His elect from the four
winds, from the farthest end of the earth to the farthest end of
heaven.** With the blast of "a great trumpet" (Matt. 24:31), those believers
who are alive on the earth, having come to saving faith during the tribulation and survived, will be gathered from all across the world and assembled together. Their number will include the 144,000 Jews who were
supernaturally protected during the tribulation (Rev. 7:4–8; 14:1–5), along

with myriads of other converts, both Jew (Zech. 12:10–11; cf. Isa. 59:20; Rom. 11:25–26) and Gentile (cf. Rev. 7:9). Having never bowed the knee to the Antichrist but remained faithful to the one true Lord, they will be rewarded by their King and welcomed into His glorious kingdom (cf. Luke 21:28). Joined by all the redeemed of all the ages, all the elect will be assembled together with Christ. Gathered from both **the farthest end of the earth to the farthest end of heaven,** they will enter the perpetual joy of the kingdom where they will reign with Christ for a thousand years (Rev. 20:3–6; cf. Matt. 8:11; Luke 13:29; 1 Cor. 6:2–3), after which they will continue to experience the glories of eternal life on the new earth forever (cf. Rev. 21:1–22:5).

CHRIST'S SIMPLE ANALOGY

Now learn the parable from the fig tree: when its branch has already become tender and puts forth its leaves, you know that summer is near. Even so, you too, when you see these things happening, recognize that He is near, right at the door. Truly I say to you, this generation will not pass away until all these things take place. (13:28–30)

Jesus continued by using a simple illustration to emphasize the appropriate response to His words of warning. He told His disciples, **Now learn the parable from the fig tree.** The imperative **learn** translates a form of the Greek verb *manthanō*, conveying the idea of accepting something as true and applying it to one's life. Fig trees, plentiful in Israel, were commonly used as illustrations (cf. Judg. 9:7–15; Jer. 24:1–10; Hos. 9:10; Joel 1:4–7; Matt. 7:16; Luke 13:6–9). Just the day before, the Lord had similarly used a fig tree to elucidate an important spiritual truth for the disciples (Mark 11:12–14). That particular fig tree had leaves but no fruit, making it an apt illustration of the apostate nation of Israel, which was adorned in religious trappings (like leaves) yet remained spiritually barren and fruitless. To illustrate the divine judgment that would fall on unbelieving Israel, the Lord pronounced a curse on that fig tree and it died instantly.

On this occasion Jesus again referenced a fig tree to make a different point. The parallel account in Luke 21:29 notes that Jesus added "and all the trees," indicating that His illustration did not apply exclusively to fig trees but to any deciduous tree. As the Lord explained, **When its branch has already become tender and puts forth its leaves, you know that summer is near.** Since it was springtime, when deciduous trees were sprouting new leaves, the evidence of that truth would have been all around the disciples.

The familiar analogy was explained to illustrate features of the Lord's return: **Even so, you too, when you see these things happening, recognize that He is near, right at the door.** In the same way that one can predict the coming of summer based on the arrival of tree leaves in spring, so believers at the end of the age will be able to anticipate Christ's return when they witness **these things**—namely, the catastrophic events Jesus had just predicted would mark the future tribulation.

The pronoun **you** does not refer to the disciples directly. Like the Old Testament prophets, who commonly spoke in the second person when foretelling distant events (cf. Isa. 33:17–24; 66:10–14; Zech. 9:9), the Lord spoke as if He were directly addressing those who will be alive during the future period of tribulation (cf. Mark 13:14–23). It is specifically to them that the Lord declared, **Truly I say to you, this generation will not pass away until all these things take place.** Though that phrase has been the subject of much speculation and debate, its meaning is actually quite straightforward in light of the context. **This generation** refers to the generation entering the tribulation period, which will be the same generation alive at the return of Christ. To state that truth another way, since the tribulation covers seven years, climaxing with the second coming, obviously a single generation will experience it all.

As explained in the previous chapters, the generation to which Jesus was referring cannot be the Twelve or the generation of Jewish people that lived during the first century. Although that generation of Jews did witness the destruction of the temple in A.D. 70, they cannot be those described in verse 30, because they neither experienced the unparalleled catastrophes of the great tribulation (vv. 19, 24–25) nor did they witness the visible return of Jesus Christ (v. 26). Those events, and the generation that will be alive when they occur, are still in the future.

CHRIST'S SOVEREIGN AUTHORITY

Heaven and earth will pass away, but My words will not pass away.
(13:31)

The Lord underscored the absolute certainty of His prophetic promise by telling His disciples that even though **heaven and earth will pass away,** His words on this matter will not pass away. Jesus' statement highlighted two fundamental theological realities—namely, that this world is temporary and that His Word is infallible.

The Bible is clear that this earth is not a permanent planet. As the apostle Peter reminded his readers:

> But the day of the Lord will come like a thief, in which the heavens will pass away with a roar and the elements will be destroyed with intense heat, and the earth and its works will be burned up. Since all these things are to be destroyed in this way, what sort of people ought you to be in holy conduct and godliness, looking for and hastening the coming of the day of God, because of which the heavens will be destroyed by burning, and the elements will melt with intense heat! But according to His promise we are looking for new heavens and a new earth, in which righteousness dwells. (2 Peter 3:10–13; cf. 1 John 2:17)

The apostle John similarly described the destruction of this present universe with these words: "Then I saw a great white throne and Him who sat upon it, from whose presence earth and heaven fled away, and no place was found for them" (Rev. 20:11; cf. 21:1; Isa. 65:17; 66:22). The current heavens and earth will be replaced with "a new heaven and a new earth" (Rev. 21:1), which will be the eternal home of the redeemed.

In contrast to the temporal nature of this world, the words of Christ will never pass away. The Lord Jesus used this same expression in the Sermon on the Mount, when He told His listeners, "For truly I say to you, until heaven and earth pass away, not the smallest letter or stroke shall pass from the Law until all is accomplished" (Matt. 5:18). In Luke 16:17 He similarly told the Pharisees, "But it is easier for heaven and earth to pass away than for one stroke of a letter of the Law to fail." Heaven and earth will one day pass away, but not before everything stated in Scripture is perfectly accomplished.

As Jesus reminded His disciples, His Word is permanent and cannot fail (cf. Isa. 40:8; Col. 3:16). It cannot be broken (John 10:35) but endures forever (Ps. 19:9) because it is completely true (John 17:17). As the one who declares "the end from the beginning" (Isa. 46:10), God's Word will always accomplish what He desires (Isa. 55:11). His Word is as immutable and unassailable as its divine Author. Nothing can be added to or subtracted from it (cf. Deut. 4:2; Matt. 5:18; Luke 16:17; Rev. 22:18–19). Thus, what the Lord has said about His return and the end of the age is unalterable truth. It will happen exactly as He said it would, because His words cannot falter or fail.

CHRIST'S SOLEMN ADMONITION

But of that day or hour no one knows, not even the angels in heaven, nor the Son, but the Father alone. Take heed, keep on the alert; for you do not know when the appointed time will come. It is like a man away on a journey, who upon leaving his house and putting his slaves in charge, assigning to each one his task, also commanded the doorkeeper to stay on the alert. Therefore, be on the alert—for you do not know when the master of the house is coming, whether in the evening, at midnight, or when the rooster crows, or in the morning—in case he should come suddenly and find you asleep. What I say to you I say to all, 'Be on the alert!'" (13:32–37)

For believers in the present, the revelation in Scripture of the end times is hopeful truth; but for the people alive when these future events occur, this prophecy takes on extreme urgency. As He declared four times in the final verses of Mark 13, people in that generation should stay on the alert (vv. 33, 34, 35, 37). When they see the signs that Jesus described, they should recognize that His return is nearly upon them.

Though it will be preceded by visible signs, the exact moment of the second coming will not be revealed to anyone. As Jesus explained, **But of that day or hour no one knows, not even the angels in heaven, nor the Son, but the Father alone.** Although its timing is fixed in the Father's plan (Acts 1:7), the Lord's categorical statement excluded the possibility that anyone could accurately predict His return. The definitive and exhaustive nature of Jesus' statement indicates that all who would presumptuously set a date for the second coming are either being delusional or intentionally deceptive—especially if the events of the tribulation have not begun.

By including Himself in that statement, as one who did not know the exact timing of His return, the Lord Jesus was not denying His deity (cf. John 1:1,14). Rather, He was acknowledging the self-imposed restraints on His divine nature. In His humiliation, God the Son voluntarily restricted the exercise of His divine attributes and prerogatives (cf. Phil. 2:6), submitting their use to His Father's will (John 4:34; 5:30; 6:38) and the Spirit's direction (cf. John 1:45–49). Though He demonstrated supernatural knowledge and understanding on many occasions throughout His ministry (cf. John 2:25; 13:3), the Lord limited His omniscience to what the Father revealed to Him (John 15:15; cf. Luke 2:52). After His resurrection, Jesus resumed the full knowledge He possessed from eternity past as the second member of the Trinity (cf. Matt. 28:18; John 21:17; Acts 1:7,24; 1 Cor. 4:5; Rev. 22:7,12,20).

Still addressing the future generation that will witness the signs at the end of the age, the Lord issued this admonition: **Take heed, keep on the alert; for you do not know when the appointed time will come** (cf. Luke 12:40). Because no one other than the triune God will know the exact moment of Christ's coming, believers who are alive during the tribulation will need to be on constant watch (cf. Luke 12:39; 2 Peter 3:10; Rev. 16:15). In a similar way, all believers of every generation are instructed to eagerly await the imminent rapture of the church (cf. 1 Thess. 1:10), which will occur before the beginning of the tribulation.

Jesus illustrated the unexpectedness of the second coming by explaining, **It is like a man away on a journey, who upon leaving his house and putting his slaves in charge, assigning to each one his task, also commanded the doorkeeper to stay on the alert.** Jesus' analogy featured the owner of an estate who left his house to travel abroad for an unspecified period of time. Before leaving, he entrusted each of his household servants with specific duties that he instructed them to perform while he was away. They were expected to do so with an attitude of diligence and alertness, knowing that their master's return home could be at any moment.

The implication for believers in the future tribulation is that those who belong to Christ must **therefore, be on the alert—for** they **do not know when the master of the house is coming, whether in the evening, at midnight, or when the rooster crows, or in the morning—in case he should come suddenly and find** them **asleep.** Like dutiful doorkeepers, they must keep constant watch, so that they are prepared in readiness to welcome their Master upon His arrival. The Roman twelve-hour watch from 6:00 P.M. to 6:00 A.M., consisted of four three-hour periods. Those intervals were generally identified by when they ended: **the evening** at 9:00 P.M., **midnight** at 12:00 A.M., the time **when the rooster crows** at 3:00 A.M., and **morning** at 6:00 A.M. Jesus' point was that His return could occur at any time, even in the middle of the night. Consequently, the believers who are alive in those final days must guard against any temptation toward spiritual complacency, distraction, or slumber (cf. Rom. 13:11–13); being characterized by vigilance.

Repeating that charge with urgency, the Lord again warned, **What I say to you I say to all, "Be on the alert!"** In the parallel passage from Luke 21:34–36, Jesus further explained,

> Be on guard, so that your hearts will not be weighted down with dissipation and drunkenness and the worries of life, and that day will not come on you suddenly like a trap; for it will come upon all those who dwell on the face of all the earth. But keep on the alert at all times, praying that you may have strength to escape all these things that are about to take place, and to stand before the Son of Man.

Those words include an invitation to salvation, through faith in the Lord Jesus Christ, to that future generation alive during the great tribulation. Only those who resist the temptations of the world (including dissipation, drunkenness, and the cares of this world), and place their faith in the Savior, will be spared eternal destruction from the judgment of God and welcomed into the glorious presence of Christ forever.

So in response to the disciples' question about the end of the age, the Lord Jesus explained that He would return after a long period of world history, which will culminate in a final, catastrophic period of global tribulation. Jesus carefully forewarned the future generation that will witness those final events, including the rise of the Antichrist and his desecration of the temple, that the end is near.

Though the events predicted in the Olivet Discourse are still future, its truth serves to instruct every generation of believers throughout church history. On the one hand, it serves as a vivid reminder that the things of this world are temporary (cf. 2 Peter 3:11–13; 1 John 2:15–17; 3:2–3), and that the redeemed are citizens of an eternal kingdom that is yet to be revealed on earth when the Lord comes in glory (Phil. 3:20–21; Heb. 11:16). On the other hand, it provides a compelling motivation for believers to proclaim the glorious gospel of Christ to those who are perishing, so that they might be saved from the impending judgment of God (cf. 2 Cor. 5:20–21; 2 Peter 3:14–15).

Players in the Drama of the Cross (Mark 14:1–16)

25

Now the Passover and Unleavened Bread were two days away; and the chief priests and the scribes were seeking how to seize Him by stealth and kill Him; for they were saying, "Not during the festival, otherwise there might be a riot of the people." While He was in Bethany at the home of Simon the leper, and reclining at the table, there came a woman with an alabaster vial of very costly perfume of pure nard; and she broke the vial and poured it over His head. But some were indignantly remarking to one another, "Why has this perfume been wasted? For this perfume might have been sold for over three hundred denarii, and the money given to the poor." And they were scolding her. But Jesus said, "Let her alone; why do you bother her? She has done a good deed to Me. For you always have the poor with you, and whenever you wish you can do good to them; but you do not always have Me. She has done what she could; she has anointed My body beforehand for the burial. Truly I say to you, wherever the gospel is preached in the whole world, what this woman has done will also

be spoken of in memory of her." Then Judas Iscariot, who was one of the twelve, went off to the chief priests in order to betray Him to them. They were glad when they heard this, and promised to give him money. And he began seeking how to betray Him at an opportune time. On the first day of Unleavened Bread, when the Passover lamb was being sacrificed, His disciples said to Him, "Where do You want us to go and prepare for You to eat the Passover?" And He sent two of His disciples and said to them, "Go into the city, and a man will meet you carrying a pitcher of water; follow him; and wherever he enters, say to the owner of the house, 'The Teacher says, "Where is My guest room in which I may eat the Passover with My disciples?"' And he himself will show you a large upper room furnished and ready; prepare for us there." The disciples went out and came to the city, and found it just as He had told them; and they prepared the Passover. (14:1–16)

The death and resurrection of Jesus Christ have always been the focal point of Christianity, the key to salvation, and the heart of the gospel. The cross represents the apex of redemptive history, the ratification of the new covenant, the final atonement for sin, the epitome of divine mercy, the necessary object of saving faith, and the only hope of eternal life. It is there that the perfect justice of God met both His unmerited grace and infinite wisdom. Recognizing its unparalleled importance, the apostle Paul declared that he would not boast "except in the cross of our Lord Jesus Christ" (Gal. 6:14). As he later told the church in Corinth, "We preach Christ crucified" (1 Cor. 1:23), and "I determined to know nothing among you except Jesus Christ, and Him crucified" (2:2; cf. Gal. 6:14).

As the central theme of Scripture, Jesus' substitutionary death is repeatedly foreshadowed throughout the Old Testament: in the promised deliverer of Genesis 3:15; in the animal God killed to provide a covering for Adam and Eve (3:21); in the acceptable sacrifice offered by Abel (4:4); in the ram caught in a thicket that took Isaac's place on Mt. Moriah (22:13); in the Passover lambs that were slain in Egypt (Ex. 12:6); in the entire system of Levitical sacrifices (cf. Heb. 10:1–13); in the bronze serpent lifted up in the wilderness for healing (Num. 21:8–9; cf. John 3:14–15); and in the concept of the kinsman-redeemer (cf. Ruth 4:14). The cross was also foretold by prophets like David (Ps. 22:1–18), Isaiah (Isa. 53:1–12), Daniel (Dan. 9:27), and Zechariah (Zech. 12:10). In keeping with his predecessors, John the Baptist, the last of the old covenant prophets, declared of Jesus, "Behold, the Lamb of God who takes away the sin of the world!" (John 1:29).

The cross remains central in the New Testament, where it is the focus of all four Gospels (Matt. 26:47–27:58; Mark 14:43–15:45; Luke 22:47–23:52; John 18:2–19:38). The book of Acts traces the proclamation of the cross throughout the world, as the gospel sounded forth from Jerusalem and Judea to Samaria and the ends of the earth (Acts 1:8; cf. 2:23; 5:30; 10:39; 13:29). The Epistles are replete with the profound theology of the cross and its practical implications for believers (cf. 1 Cor. 1:17–18; Gal. 6:14; Eph. 2:16; Col. 2:14; Heb. 12:2; 1 Peter 2:24, etc.). In its sweeping, prophetic summary of the future, the book of Revelation likewise looks back to Calvary, portraying the Lord Jesus as the perfect Lamb who was slain to make redemption possible by His blood (5:6,12; cf. 13:8).

The cross is the central theme of the final section of Mark's gospel (chapters 14–16). From the Olivet Discourse (13:5–37), in which Jesus foretold the glories of His second coming, the narrative transitions to focus on the hallowed culmination of His first coming. The central figure in the unfolding drama of the cross is unarguably the Lord Jesus Christ. But as the account unfolds (in 14:1–16), Mark introduces a full cast of additional characters, each of whom played a vital role in that climactic event. They include God the Father, Jesus' bitter foes, His loving friends, His treacherous false disciple, and His faithful followers.

THE FATHER

Now the Passover and Unleavened Bread were two days away (14:1a)

Though not directly named in this passage, God the Father was clearly at work as the divine director behind the scenes, sovereignly orchestrating everything happening to the Son according to His foreordained plan of redemption. The Father's providential involvement is implied in the opening statement, where Mark explains that **the Passover and Unleavened Bread were two days away.** Far from being incidental, that chronological marker demonstrates that the divine timetable was running precisely according to schedule. On that specific Passover, in the very year that the prophet Daniel had predicted (Dan. 9:25–26), on the same day and at the same time when Passover lambs were being killed in the temple, the Father had purposed that the spotless Lamb of God would be slain.

The **Passover** was celebrated each year on the fourteenth day of the Jewish month Nisan (in late March or early April). It commemorated the night in Egypt when the angel of death passed over the houses of the Israelites who had killed a lamb and sprinkled its blood on their doorposts and lintels (Ex. 12:22–23). The Feast of **Unleavened Bread** began the next day and lasted a full week (from the fifteenth to the twenty-first of Nisan). It commemorated Israel's exodus from Egypt, and was named for the flat bread that the Hebrew people took with them when they made their hasty escape (Deut. 16:3). Because the two celebrations were so closely intertwined, the Passover and the Feast of Unleavened Bread eventually came to be interchangeable terms (cf. Matt. 26:17; Luke 22:1). Together, they made up one of Israel's three major feasts, along with Pentecost (known as the Feast of Weeks in the Old Testament; cf. Ex. 34:22; Acts 2:1) and the Feast of Tabernacles or Booths (Lev. 23:33–43; Deut. 16:16; 2 Chron. 8:13).

That the Passover was yet **two days away** indicates that it was still Wednesday. Jesus knew, in keeping with the Father's perfect plan, that the time had come for Him to die (cf. Matt. 26:18, 45; Mark 14:35; John 12:23; 13:1; 17:1). As He told His disciples in Matthew's parallel account, "You know that after two days the Passover is coming, and the Son of Man is to be handed over for crucifixion" (26:2). Jesus had spoken of His death on a number of earlier occasions (Mark 8:31; 9:31; 10:33; 12:7; cf. Matt. 27:63), demonstrating that throughout His entire ministry He was operating according to a supernaturally ordained and controlled timetable, in order to fulfill His ultimate purpose for coming, "to give His life a ransom for many" (Mark 10:45).

Over the previous three and a half years of His ministry, Jesus' adversaries had repeatedly attempted to take His life (Mark 3:6; Luke 4:28–30; 19:47–48; John 5:18; 7:1,25,32,45–46; 10:31). Even when He was an infant, King Herod sought to murder Him in a slaughter of male babies (cf. Matt. 2:13–21). But those attempts did not succeed because they did not fit the Father's design. Because Jesus operated in full submission to His Father (cf. John 4:34; 5:30; 6:38; Phil. 2:8), He would not lay down His life until the appropriate time had come (cf. John 7:6,8,30). As He explained in John 10:17–18, "I lay down My life so that I may take it again. No one has taken it away from Me, but I lay it down on My own initiative. I have authority to lay it down, and I have authority to take it up again." Later, when Pilate claimed to have the authority to kill Jesus, the Lord informed the pagan governor, "You would have no authority over Me, unless it had been given you from above" (John 19:10–11).

The Father's redemptive plan was that the Son would die at a precise time on a specific date. Thus, Jesus could tell His disciples, on the night before His death, "The Son of Man is going as it has been determined" (Luke 22:22). Nearly two months later, Peter echoed those words on the day of Pentecost, telling the crowd that Jesus was "delivered up by the predetermined plan and foreknowledge of God" (Acts 2:23; cf. 1 Peter 1:19–20). The Lord Jesus went to Calvary as the perfect Passover lamb (cf. 1 Cor. 5:7), according to the schedule preordained by His Father (cf. 1 Peter 1:19–20), just as the Old Testament prophets predicted He would (Acts 3:18; cf. 8:32–35). His death was no unplanned accident, as some skeptics claim (see chapter 16 of this volume). Rather, as noted above, it accomplished the very purpose for which He had been sent (cf. John 3:14–16).

From a human standpoint, the crucifixion of Christ represents an unparalleled miscarriage of justice because He was perfectly innocent in every respect. The Lord Jesus was falsely accused and wrongly condemned to a degree infinitely greater than anyone else in all of history. Yet, in that most heinous act of human injustice, the justice of God was at work. The most evil act ever perpetrated by sinful men was simultaneously an infinitely loving act performed by a holy God. The Father punished the Son for sins He did not commit (cf. Isa. 53:10–12), so that sinners might be clothed with a righteousness they could never earn (cf. 2 Cor. 5:21).

Like a dowry paid for a bride, the cross was the means by which the Lord Jesus purchased sinners "from every tribe and tongue and people and nation" (Rev. 5:9), so that He might "purify for Himself a people for His own possession" (Titus 2:14). All of this was in keeping with the Father's perfect, eternal plan of redemption.

THE FOES

and the chief priests and the scribes were seeking how to seize Him by stealth and kill Him; for they were saying, "Not during the festival, otherwise there might be a riot of the people." (14:1b–2)

On the divine level, God the Father was sovereignly working to accomplish His redemptive purposes through the death of His Son. But that reality does not exonerate the wicked actions of those who, on the human level, orchestrated Jesus' crucifixion. Motivated by their own pride, envy, and stubborn unbelief, the fully culpable Jewish religious leaders had willfully rejected their Messiah and actively sought to destroy Him (cf. John 1:11). On Wednesday of Jesus' Passion Week, apparently at the same time He was speaking to His disciples about the glories of His second coming, the Jewish religious leaders met together to plot His murder.

According to the parallel text in Matthew 26:3, this meeting of **the chief priests and the scribes** took place in the courtyard of the house of Caiaphas the high priest. Representing the elder statesmen of Israel's religious elite, **the chief priests and the scribes** are mentioned together in the Gospels on several occasions (cf. 14:43; 15:1; Matt. 27:41; Luke 9:22; 22:66). The **chief priests** were primarily Sadducees. Their numbers included the high priest, the captain of the temple (who assisted the high priest), and other high-ranking priests. The **scribes**, who were mostly Pharisees, were experts in both Old Testament law and rabbinic tradition. Together, the Sadducees and Pharisees comprised the apostate leadership of Israel, and the Lord Jesus warned His disciples to avoid their hypocritical practices (cf. Matt. 16:6).

Their meeting had a single purpose: they **were seeking how to**

seize Jesus **by stealth and kill Him.** A short time earlier, after the resurrection of Lazarus, the religious leaders had organized a similar meeting. John 11:47–52 recounts the details of that event:

> Therefore the chief priests and the Pharisees convened a council, and were saying, "What are we doing? For this man is performing many signs. If we let Him go on like this, all men will believe in Him, and the Romans will come and take away both our place and our nation." But one of them, Caiaphas, who was high priest that year, said to them, "You know nothing at all, nor do you take into account that it is expedient for you that one man die for the people, and that the whole nation not perish." Now he did not say this on his own initiative, but being high priest that year, he prophesied that Jesus was going to die for the nation, and not for the nation only, but in order that He might also gather together into one the children of God who are scattered abroad. So from that day on they planned together to kill Him.

The leaders of both the Sadducees and the Pharisees were afraid that Jesus' popularity with the people might spark a revolt (cf. Mark 11:9–10; John 6:15), provoking a military response from Rome and causing them to lose their privileged positions of authority. (The ruling Jewish council, the Sanhedrin, comprised of both Sadducees and Pharisees, operated under the jurisdiction and tolerance of the Roman government.) As those who controlled the temple operation, the chief priests and Sadducees especially hated Jesus because He had cleared the temple twice, severely disrupting their moneymaking operations on high income occasions (Mark 11:15–18; cf. John 2:13–16). The scribes and Pharisees, on the other hand, detested Jesus because He openly denounced their elaborate system of legalism, hypocrisy, and unbiblical tradition (Mark 3:4; 7:1–13; cf. Matt. 23:1–36). Though the Sadducees and Pharisees represented rival sects with significant differences, they were unified by their opposition to the Lord Jesus.

In their scheming against Him, they sought to arrest Him covertly, so as not to antagonize the crowds with whom He was still very popular (cf. Mark 11:8–10). Apparently, their plan was to seize Jesus secretly and then wait to murder Him until after the feast was over and the hundreds of thousands of Jewish pilgrims visiting Jerusalem to celebrate the Passover had returned home. Thus, **they were saying, "Not during the festival, otherwise there might be a riot of the people."**

From the perspective of the religious leaders, Passover was the worst time to kill Jesus. They desperately wanted to wait until after the festivities had ended. But their evil schemes could not postpone what God the Father had providentially designed. Over the previous three and a half years, there were multiple occasions when they wanted to murder Jesus in a fit of violence but were thwarted. At this point, their cold calculations led them to postpone His death. Again they did not succeed because they were not in control. When they finally achieved their goal of crucifying Jesus, they did so at the exact moment they were hoping to avoid. Clearly, their plans were superseded by the sovereign providences of God (cf. Prov. 19:21).

THE FRIENDS

While He was in Bethany at the home of Simon the leper, and reclining at the table, there came a woman with an alabaster vial of very costly perfume of pure nard; and she broke the vial and poured it over His head. But some were indignantly remarking to one another, "Why has this perfume been wasted? For this perfume might have been sold for over three hundred denarii, and the money given to the poor." And they were scolding her. But Jesus said, "Let her alone; why do you bother her? She has done a good deed to Me. For you always have the poor with you, and whenever you wish you can do good to them; but you do not always have Me. She has done what she could; she has anointed My body beforehand for the burial. Truly I say to you, wherever the gospel is preached in the whole world, what this woman has done will also be spoken of in memory of her." (14:3–9)

Mark interrupts the narrative at this point with a flashback to the previous Saturday, six days before the Friday of Passover (John 12:1), when the Lord arrived **in Bethany** just east of Jerusalem (Mark 11:1; cf. Matt. 21:1). In stark contrast to the religious leaders, who hated Jesus and wanted Him dead, the woman featured in this short vignette exhibited profound and sacrificial love for her Savior. Though this episode is out of chronological order, its theme fits perfectly in the final section of Mark's gospel, where the focus is on preparations for the death of Christ. It is a window of love in a wall of hate.

The setting for this brief account was **the home of Simon the leper,** where Jesus and His disciples were eating supper (cf. John 12:2). Simon obviously had been healed, otherwise he would not have been able to host a dinner party. Lepers were societal outcasts who were not allowed any close interaction with people (cf. Lev. 13:45–46). Since leprosy was incurable in the ancient world, it is almost certain that Simon had been miraculously healed by Jesus (cf. Mark 1:40–45; Luke 17:11–19). This meal was Simon's way of demonstrating his gratitude to the Lord. According to John 12:1–3, Mary, Martha, and Lazarus also attended.

As Jesus and His disciples were **reclining at the table,** a customary posture for eating meals in first-century Israel, **there came a woman,** whom John 12:3 identifies as Mary, the sister of Martha and Lazarus. A short time earlier, Mary had watched Jesus raise her brother Lazarus from the dead (John 11:32–45). She had always been particularly attentive to Jesus' instruction (cf. Luke 10:39), and on this occasion, seemingly recognized the reality of the Lord's imminent death better than any of the Twelve.

With humble reverence, Mary approached Jesus **with an alabaster vial of very costly perfume of pure nard; and she broke the vial and poured it over His head.** Mary's actions, which undoubtedly startled the other dinner guests, were an unmeasured act of love and adoration for her Lord. She had no concern for the cost of the perfume, nor was she worried about how others might respond. Her only aim was to express honor and worship to Christ by anointing His head with very costly perfume. (It might be noted that this episode should not be confused with the events recorded in Luke 7:36–50, when a different woman in Galilee similarly anointed Jesus' feet. (For more on that account, and its distinction from this one, see John MacArthur, *Luke 6–10* The MacArthur New Testament Commentary [Chicago: Moody, 2011], chap. 18.)

A typical **alabaster vial,** carved from a variety of fine Egyptian marbles, had a long neck with a small opening from which small drops of liquid could be poured out. But Mary did not limit her expression of praise to a few drops of precious perfume. Rather, she broke the bottle, adding to the expense of her offering to Christ, and began effusively pouring its aromatic contents over Jesus' head. The parallel passage in John 12:3 indicates that she also poured some of the perfume on Jesus' feet, and then "wiped His feet with her hair." John further notes that the amount of perfume Mary used was one Roman pound, which corresponds to approximately twelve modern ounces. The fragrant oil **nard,** extracted from a plant native to northern India, was imported the long distance to Israel at great expense. That Mary used **pure nard,** meaning it was undiluted, identified it as even more costly. As a result of her lavish offering to Jesus, "the house was filled with the fragrance of the perfume" (John 12:3).

The scene was stunningly dramatic, and the response from the other dinner guests was mixed. **Some were indignantly remarking to one another, "Why has this perfume been wasted? For this perfume might have been sold for over three hundred denarii, and the money given to the poor."** Though neither Mark nor Matthew mention the names of the detractors, John's account explains that the primary instigator was Judas. According to John 12:4–6,

> But Judas Iscariot, one of His disciples, who was intending to betray Him, said, "Why was this perfume not sold for three hundred denarii and given to poor people?" Now he said this, not because he was concerned about the poor, but because he was a thief, and as he had the money box, he used to pilfer what was put into it.

As the scent of Mary's perfume filled the room, Judas, and apparently a few of the other disciples whom he managed to persuade in the moment, began **scolding her.** They became indignant, insisting that the fragrant oil had been wasted. It could have been sold for **three hundred denarii,** a sizable sum of money, and its proceeds given to the poor. (A denarius equaled a day's wages for a common laborer, making this nearly a year's salary for the average worker.) Of course, Judas had no real interest in the poor. He was a thief who had been embezzling money from the other disciples. He wanted the perfume sold, not so that money could be donated to the poor but so that he could pilfer it.

What a contrast Judas was to Mary. Judas was full of bitterness and hatred toward Jesus, wanting only to get all he could and actively searching for an opportune moment to betray Him (see the discussion regarding v. 11 below). But Mary, motivated by gratitude and love toward Jesus, wanted to give all she could and enthusiastically looked for an opportunity to demonstrate her attitude of heartfelt worship. In spite of Judas's protest, Mary's actions symbolized the affection that character-izes all who genuinely love the Lord Jesus Christ. She could not limit her act of lavish devotion.

Jesus corrected the misguided indignation of the disciples by saying to them, **Let her alone; why do you bother her? She has done a good deed to me.** Mary's behavior constituted a beautiful act of kind-ness and worship. It was not at all a waste. Referencing Deuteronomy 15:11, the Lord reminded the disciples that they would **always have the poor with** them, **and whenever** they might **wish** they could **do good to them.** But His remaining time with them was very short. As Jesus reminded His disciples, **You do not always have Me.** His clear point was that the disciples' priority should have been to worship Him like Mary was doing. Worship is always the ultimate priority. While loving one's neighbor by caring for the poor is noble and necessary, loving the Lord is more important (cf. Mark 12:30–31). That was an especially poignant truth in light of events that would transpire over the next six days. Jesus would be crucified less than a week later. In light of that, this was no time for charity but for worship.

Mary had the right priorities. As on a prior occasion, she had "chosen the good part" (Luke 10:42). Unlike the Twelve, who seemed oblivious, Mary apparently had some understanding of Jesus' impending death. Consequently, He said of her, **She has done what she could; she has anointed My body beforehand for the burial.** Though Mary could do nothing to prevent her Savior's death, she was able to demon-strate her love for Him in a lavish and sacrificial way. Knowing her heart, the Lord commended her on account of her expression of worship. As He explained, **Truly I say to you, wherever the gospel is preached in the whole world, what this woman has done will also be spo-ken of in memory of her.** Though two millennia have passed, the testi-mony of Mary's sacrificial worship still stands as a perpetual memorial of her love for Christ. Her heartfelt gesture—looking to the death, burial, and resurrection of Christ—provides a compelling example of the kind of selfless, extravagant praise that honors the Savior.

THE FALSE DISCIPLE

Then Judas Iscariot, who was one of the twelve, went off to the chief priests in order to betray Him to them. They were glad when they heard this, and promised to give him money. And he began seeking how to betray Him at an opportune time. (14:10–11)

No name in all of human history is more infamous than **Judas Iscariot.** Though he **was one of the twelve,** constantly in the presence of Jesus for more than three years, he squandered that unique privileged opportunity and chose instead to betray the Son of God to His killers. Judas was the only member of the twelve disciples from outside Galilee. **Iscariot** means "man of Kerioth," indicating that he came from that village located nearly twenty-five miles south of Jerusalem. Though he followed Jesus for selfish and materialistic reasons, he managed to deceive the other disciples to the extent that none of them suspected him of being a hypocrite and a traitor (cf. John 13:22). But Judas could not deceive the Lord Jesus, who knew the condition of Judas's wicked heart from the outset, even referring to him as a devil (John 6:64, 70–71).

After the Saturday supper at Bethany, Judas **went off to the chief priests in order** to set a plan in motion **to betray** Jesus **to them.** The religious leaders **were glad when they heard this, and promised to give him money.** For thirty pieces of silver (Matt. 26:15), the price of a slave (cf. Ex. 21:32), they bribed an eager Judas to sell out his Master. From that point forward, throughout the entirety of Jesus' Passion Week, the traitor **began seeking how to betray Him at an opportune time.** Judas knew the prime opportunity would be when Jesus was apart from the multitude (Luke 22:6), and could be arrested in private. Though the other disciples were oblivious to Judas's devious plans, the Lord knew exactly what he was plotting. As Jesus told them in the upper room, "I do not speak of all of you. I know the ones I have chosem; but it is that the Scripture may be fulfilled, 'He who eats My bread has lifted up his heel against Me'" (John 13:18).

Because Judas had hardened his heart against Jesus, God gave him over to Satan (cf. 1 Cor. 5:5). Thus, Luke 22:3 says, "Then Satan entered Judas" (cf. John 13:27). The prince of darkness operated through this unregenerate hypocrite who, like the religious leaders, was himself a child of the devil (John 8:44; cf. Luke 22:53). Ironically, by inciting Judas to betray Jesus, Satan brought about his own demise (cf. 1 John 3:8); the devil's apparent victory actually spelled his ultimate defeat (Heb. 2:14; cf. Gen. 3:15). Earlier in Christ's ministry, Satan had influenced Peter to try to convince Jesus to avoid the cross altogether (cf. Mark 8:32–33). Perhaps now, like the religious leaders, he hoped to disrupt God's timetable by delaying the crucifixion until after the Passover. But whatever Satan's motives, his actions could not override the sovereign will of God (Luke 22:31; cf. Job 1:12; 2:6).

It is shattering to know that the Messiah's betrayer could come from among the Twelve. But as unthinkable as it might seem, God was in complete control. The satanically inspired betrayer was actually fulfilling specific biblical prophecy (cf. Pss. 41:9; 55:12–14; Zech. 11:12–13; cf. Matt. 27:3–10). As Jesus declared in His High Priestly Prayer, "I guarded them and not one of them perished but the son of perdition, so that the Scripture would be fulfilled" (John 17:12). Even Judas's betrayal was part of the eternal plan of redemption. (For additional discussion of the wicked actions of Judas in light of God's sovereignty, see chapter 26 in this volume.)

THE FOLLOWERS

On the first day of Unleavened Bread, when the Passover lamb was being sacrificed, His disciples said to Him, "Where do You want us to go and prepare for You to eat the Passover?" And He sent two of His disciples and said to them, "Go into the city, and a man will meet you carrying a pitcher of water; follow him; and wherever he enters, say to the owner of the house, 'The Teacher says, "Where is My guest room in which I may eat the Passover with My disciples?"' And he himself will show you a large upper

room furnished and ready; prepare for us there." The disciples went out and came to the city, and found it just as He had told them; and they prepared the Passover. (14:12–16)

In verse 12, the narrative moves forward to the Thursday of Jesus' Passion Week, **the first day of Unleavened Bread, when the Passover lamb was being sacrificed.** Knowing that the time of His death was near (Matt. 26:18), the Lord set in motion a plan that would enable Him first to celebrate the Passover with His disciples. It was likely early that day when **His disciples said to Him, "Where do You want us to go and prepare for You to eat the Passover?"**

The Lord responded to their question in a way that undoubtedly perplexed them. But His cryptic answer was necessary because of Judas's treachery. If Judas discovered where Jesus and the disciples would be that evening, he would have undoubtedly alerted the religious leaders, enabling them to arrest Jesus during the Passover meal. But that would have been premature. So, to keep Judas in the dark regarding the place, the Lord made arrangements to observe the Passover in a secret location, known only to Him. In keeping with His plan, **He sent two of His disciples,** whom Luke identifies as Peter and John (Luke 22:8), **and said to them, "Go into the city."** Jesus' subsequent instructions were intentionally vague, mentioning no locations or names, so that Judas would have no advance knowledge about where Jesus would be that evening. Only Peter and John would discover the location beforehand, where they apparently stayed to finish the necessary preparations. The remaining disciples did not know where the meal would take place until they arrived at the house later that evening, leaving Judas no opportunity to report the location to Christ's enemies. They did not know until after Jesus exposed and dismissed Judas (cf. John 13:27–30).

As Jesus explained the clandestine plan, Peter and John would arrive in Jerusalem and encounter a man **carrying a pitcher of water.** The man (who was likely a servant) would stand out because he was performing a domestic task that in first-century Israel was normally done by women. The two were to **follow him; and wherever he** entered, they were **to say to the owner of the house, 'The Teacher says, "Where is My guest room in which I may eat the Passover with My disci-**

ples?"' **And he himself will show you a large upper room furnished and ready; prepare for us there."** The owner whom the disciples were to meet was apparently familiar with Jesus, since they were simply to tell him that **"the Teacher"** had sent them.

Clearly, the Lord had prearranged this, either physically or supernaturally. Either way, He knew that a large room was already furnished and ready for Him and His disciples to eat the Passover meal together. After receiving His instructions, **the disciples went out and came to the city, and found it just as He had told them; and they prepared the Passover.** The necessary preparations for the Passover meal included taking the lamb to the temple to be sacrificed, keeping part of the roasted meat to eat later that evening, and obtaining other ingredients required for the feast, including unleavened bread, wine, and bitter herbs.

Jesus knew that it was critical for Him to celebrate the Passover with His disciples that night (Luke 22:15), because during that final meal, He transformed the Passover celebration into the Lord's Supper, which commemorated His death on the cross (Luke 22:20). Instead of representing the lambs that were killed in Egypt, the bread and the cup would now signify the body and blood of the sacrificial Lamb of God (cf. 1 Cor. 11:23–26). In addition to celebrating the Lord's Supper, Jesus also gave the disciples vital words of promise and hope to strengthen them for His death (cf. John 13–17).

Jesus' celebration of the Passover on the night before His death raises an important question: How could He celebrate the Passover on Thursday night when the Passover lambs were killed on Friday? The answer lies in the fact that, in first-century Israel, the Passover meal was regularly eaten on two evenings. Those from Galilee observed it on Thursday evening, while those from Judea celebrated it on Friday. Consequently, Jesus was able to eat the Passover with His disciples on Thursday night and still die as the Passover lamb on Friday afternoon.

As I explained in my commentary on the gospel of John,

> An apparent discrepancy exists at this point between John's chronology and that of the Synoptic Gospels. The latter clearly state that the Last Supper was a Passover meal (Matt. 26:17–19; Mark 14:12–16; Luke 22:7–15). John 18:28, however, records that the Jewish leaders "led Jesus from Caiaphas into the Praetorium, and it was early [Friday morning;

the day of the Crucifixion]; and they themselves did not enter into the Praetorium so that they would not be defiled, but might eat the Passover." Further, according to John 19:14 Jesus' trial and Crucifixion took place on "the day of preparation for the Passover," not the day after the eating of the Passover meal. Thus the Lord was crucified at the same time that the Passover lambs were being killed (cf. 19:36; Ex. 12:46; Num. 9:12). The challenge, then, is to explain how Jesus and the disciples could have eaten the Passover meal on Thursday evening if the Jewish leaders had not yet eaten it on Friday morning.

The answer lies in understanding that the Jews had two different methods of reckoning days. Ancient Jewish sources suggest that Jews from the northern part of Israel (including Galilee, where Jesus and most of the Twelve were from) counted days from sunrise to sunrise. Most of the Pharisees apparently also used that method. On the other hand, the Jews in the southern region of Israel counted days from sunset to sunset. That would include the Sadducees (who of necessity lived in the vicinity of Jerusalem because of their connection with the temple). Though no doubt confusing at times, that dual method of reckoning days would have had practical benefits at Passover, allowing the feast to be celebrated on two consecutive days. That would have eased the crowded conditions in Jerusalem, especially in the temple, where all the lambs would not have had to be killed on the same day.

Thus, there is no contradiction between John and the synoptics. Being Galileans, Jesus and the Twelve would have viewed Passover day as running from sunrise on Thursday to sunrise on Friday. They would have eaten their Passover meal on Thursday evening. The Jewish leaders (the Sadducees), however, would have viewed it as beginning at sunset on Thursday and ending at sunset on Friday. They would have eaten their Passover meal on Friday evening. (For a further discussion of this issue, see Harold W. Hoehner, *Chronological Aspects of the Life of Christ* [Grand Rapids: Zondervan, 1977], 74–90; Robert L. Thomas and Stanley N. Gundry, *A Harmony of the Gospels* [Chicago: Moody, 1979], 321–22; *John 12–21*, The MacArthur New Testament Commentary [Chicago: Moody, 2008], 62–63.)

The unfolding drama of the cross involved a myriad of actors: from antagonistic religious leaders like Caiaphas to devout worshipers like Mary to turncoat disciples like Judas to faithful followers like Peter and John. Yet, a survey of these human figures ultimately points us back to God the Father, whose invisible hand sovereignly orchestrated all of the details according to His perfect plan (cf. Acts 2:23; 3:18; 4:28). In His crucifixion, the Lord Jesus was no victim. Instead, He was the victorious Son of God who submissively and purposefully obeyed His heavenly Father to the point of death, even death on a cross. For this reason also, God highly exalted Him, and bestowed on Him the name which is above every name, so that at the name of Jesus every knee will bow, of those who are in heaven and on earth and under the earth, and that every tongue will confess that Jesus Christ is Lord, to the glory of God the Father. (Phil. 2:8*b*–11)

The New
Passover
(Mark 14:17–26)

26

When it was evening He came with the twelve. As they were reclining at the table and eating, Jesus said, "Truly I say to you that one of you will betray Me—one who is eating with Me." They began to be grieved and to say to Him one by one, "Surely not I?" And He said to them, "It is one of the twelve, one who dips with Me in the bowl. For the Son of Man is to go just as it is written of Him; but woe to that man by whom the Son of Man is betrayed! It would have been good for that man if he had not been born." While they were eating, He took some bread, and after a blessing He broke it, and gave it to them, and said, "Take it; this is My body." And when He had taken a cup and given thanks, He gave it to them, and they all drank from it. And He said to them, "This is My blood of the covenant, which is poured out for many. Truly I say to you, I will never again drink of the fruit of the vine until that day when I drink it new in the kingdom of God." After singing a hymn, they went out to the Mount of Olives. (14:17–26)

Nearly fifteen hundred years after the first Passover was established by God on the night the Hebrew people were liberated from slavery in Egypt, Jesus and His disciples made their way to an upper room in Jerusalem where they celebrated the last divinely authorized Passover meal. In its place, the Lord instituted a new memorial that pointed to Himself and His work on the cross. While the old Passover commemorated Israel's temporal deliverance from bondage in Egypt, the new Passover celebrated an infinitely greater eternal redemption from the power and penalty of sin. In a single Passover meal, on the night before His death, the Lord Jesus concluded the old celebration and instituted the new. He took components of that final Passover feast and redefined them as elements of His Communion table.

Over the centuries of Old Testament history, millions of lambs were slain as part of the annual Passover observance. Each of those sacrificial animals symbolized the reality that deliverance from divine wrath requires the death of an innocent substitute. But none of those sacrifices could actually atone for sin (cf. Heb. 10:4). This Passover would be different, because the final sacrifice would be slain—namely, the Lamb of God (1 Cor. 5:7; cf. John 1:29) to whom all of them pointed. He is the only sacrifice satisfactory to God as the offering for sin.

Earlier on Thursday, Jesus sent Peter and John into Jerusalem to make preparations for the Passover meal (cf. Luke 22:8). That evening, the rest of the Twelve along with Jesus joined them in an upper room to celebrate the final Passover and inaugurate the first Communion.

THE FINAL PASSOVER

When it was evening He came with the twelve. As they were reclining at the table and eating, Jesus said, "Truly I say to you that one of you will betray Me—one who is eating with Me." They began to be grieved and to say to Him one by one, "Surely not I?" And He said to them, "It is one of the twelve, one who dips with Me in the bowl. For the Son of Man is to go just as it is written of Him; but woe to that man by whom the Son of Man is betrayed! It would have been good for that man if he had not been born." (14:17–21)

The Passover celebration began **when it was evening,** starting after sunset and ending sometime before midnight (cf. Ex. 12:8–14). Jesus and His disciples arrived in the evening, at a location known only to Jesus. Secrecy was required in order to prevent Judas from alerting the religious authorities to their location, so that Jesus could accomplish all that was necessary before His arrest and execution. As the Lord explained to the Twelve, "I have earnestly desired to eat this Passover with you before I suffer" (Luke 22:15). Those words express the deep emotion the Lord attached to the final Passover with His disciples. In that one meal, He would bring to a completion an entire system and launch a new one, while also giving His followers the additional instruction they desperately needed to hear in the hours before the cross.

As noted above, Jesus had already sent Peter and John ahead of the rest, in order to prepare everything for the Passover meal. Mark's comment that **He came with the twelve** is surely a general reference to the apostles, meaning simply that Jesus arrived along with the other ten to join Peter and John.

In keeping with first-century Jewish customs, Jesus and the disciples **were reclining at the table and eating,** resting on cushions with their heads toward the table and their feet extended away from it. The first Passover in Egypt was eaten in a hurry. As the Lord God instructed the Israelites, "You shall eat it in this manner: with your loins girded, your sandals on your feet, and your staff in your hand; and you shall eat it in haste—it is the Lord's Passover" (Ex. 12:11). But through the centuries, Passover celebrations had become prolonged events, allowing the participants to linger during the meal as Jesus and the disciples did on this occasion. This final Passover lasted long enough for Jesus to wash the disciples' feet, confront Judas Iscariot, eat the Passover meal, institute the Lord's Table, and give the disciples a significant amount of additional instruction (cf. John 13–16).

The Passover consisted of several features. The feast began with a prayer of thanksgiving for God's deliverance, protection, and goodness. The opening prayer was followed by the first of four cups of diluted red wine. A ceremonial washing of the hands came next, signifying the need for holiness and cleansing from sin. It was probably at this point in the meal, at the very moment they should have been recognizing their sinfulness, that the

Twelve began debating who among them was the greatest (Luke 22:24). Jesus responded by washing their feet and teaching them an unforgettable lesson about humility (cf.John 13:3–20).

The hand-washing ceremony was followed by the eating of bitter herbs that symbolized the harsh bondage and affliction the Hebrew people endured while enslaved in Egypt.Along with the bitter herbs, loaves of flat bread would also be broken, distributed, and dipped into a thick paste made from ground fruit and nuts.The eating of bitter herbs was followed by the singing of the first two psalms of the Hallel, and the drinking of the second cup of wine.The Hallel (Pss. 113–18) consisted of hymns of praise and is the word from which the term "hallelujah" (meaning, "praise the Lord") is derived. At this point, the head of the household would also explain the meaning of the Passover.

Next, the roasted lamb and unleavened bread would be served. After washing his hands again, the head of the household would distribute pieces of the bread to be eaten with the sacrificial lamb.When the main course was completed, a third cup of wine would be received.To complete the traditional ceremony, the participants would sing the rest of the Hallel (Pss. 115–18), and finally, they would drink the fourth cup of wine.

At some point in the celebration, **Jesus said, "Truly I say to you that one of you will betray Me—one who is eating with Me."** The word **betray** (a form of the Greek verb *paradidōmi*) means "to give over" and was often used to describe criminals being arrested or prisoners being delivered to punishment. Though, on several prior occasions, Jesus had predicted His death, He had not previously explained to the disciples that He would be betrayed by one of them.

Jesus' words echoed those of David who, after being betrayed by one he trusted, exclaimed,

> For it is not an enemy who reproaches me, then I could bear it; nor is it one who hates me who has exalted himself against me, then I could hide myself from him. But it is you, a man my equal, my companion and my familiar friend; we who had sweet fellowship together, [and] walked in the house of God in the throng. (Ps. 55:12–14)

In Psalm 41:9, David similarly lamented, "Even my close friend in whom I trusted, who ate my bread, has lifted up his heel against me." David's pain was caused by the betrayal of his advisor Ahithophel, who joined Absalom's rebellion against David (cf. 2 Sam. 16:15–17:3). In a culture where eating together was regarded as a sign of friendship, to betray someone while eating with them compounded the treachery, making it even more contemptible (John 13:18).

Jesus, of course, knew who it was that would betray Him since He knew what was in the hearts of everyone (John 2:24), including the wicked intentions of Judas (John 6:70–71; 13:11). But the other disciples suspected nothing. Judas was so skilled at hiding his hypocrisy that they trusted him as their treasurer, even while he was pilfering money from them (cf. John 12:6). They ignorantly considered him a man of integrity.

When the disciples heard the stunning claim that one of them would betray their Master, **they began to be grieved and to say to Him one by one, "Surely not I?"** The word **grieved** (from the Greek verb *lupeō*) means to be distressed, sorrowful, and profoundly pained. Matthew 26:22 explains that they were "deeply grieved." With the obvious exception of Judas (cf. Matt. 26:25), the disciples genuinely believed in Jesus and were incredulous when informed one of them was a traitor. Their question was genuine—both in the self-doubt and the sincere affection for Christ that it expressed. Perhaps, having just been rebuked by the Lord for their pride (cf. John 13:5–20), they were sensitized to the potential wickedness of their own hearts.

At the point when the disciples were eating the bitter herbs along with flat bread dipped in the paste of fruit and nuts, **He said to them, "It is one of the twelve, one who dips with Me in the bowl."** Several dipping bowls were likely set around the table, with Judas apparently sitting near Jesus and sharing the same bowl with Him. The disciples apparently did not fully understand the Lord's somewhat cryptic response. As the apostle John explains in his parallel account, they continued to be confused as to the identity of Jesus' betrayer.

> So Simon Peter gestured to [John], and said to him, "Tell us who it is of whom He is speaking." He, leaning back thus on Jesus' bosom, said to Him, "Lord, who is it?" Jesus then answered, "That is the one for whom I shall dip the morsel and give it to him." So when He had dipped the morsel, He took and gave it to Judas, the son of Simon Iscariot. After the morsel, Satan then entered into him. Therefore Jesus said to him, "What

you do, do quickly." Now no one of those reclining at the table knew for what purpose He had said this to him. For some were supposing, because Judas had the money box, that Jesus was saying to him, "Buy the things we have need of for the feast"; or else, that he should give something to the poor. So after receiving the morsel he went out immediately; and it was night. (John 13:24–30)

As wretched and foolish as Judas was, motivated by his own carnal desires, he could neither thwart nor alter the plan of God. In fact, the evil designs of Judas were strategically set by God into His redemptive purposes. As Jesus went on to explain, **For the Son of Man is to go just as it is written of Him.** Everything about to happen to Jesus had been foreordained by God and foretold in Scripture (cf. Acts 2:23). Details about His suffering and crucifixion were predicted in Old Testament passages like Psalm 22; Isaiah 53; and Zechariah 12. Thus Paul could tell the Corinthians "that Christ died for our sins according to the Scriptures, and that He was buried, and that He was raised on the third day according to the Scriptures" (1 Cor. 15:3). The plan had been determined in eternity past (cf. Rev. 13:8) and recorded in the Old Testament. Jesus did not go to the cross as a helpless victim but as the obedient Son fulfilling both the word and will of His Father (cf. Matt. 26:54; Luke 24:44; Phil. 2:8).

It is important to note that, although God used Judas to accomplish His purposes, Judas was still personally culpable for his evil actions. As Jesus went on to explain, **Woe to that man by whom the Son of Man is betrayed!** In His sovereign providence, God constantly overrules people's sinful choices, like those of Judas, for His own ends and glory (cf. Gen. 50:20; Rom. 8:28). But that reality does not exonerate them for their wickedness. The word **woe** is more than a warning; it is a pronouncement of divine judgment and condemnation. Through his willful rejection of Christ, choosing to betray Him rather than believe in Him, Judas doomed his soul to eternal hell (cf. John 17:12).

Jesus continued with a sobering declaration: **It would have been good for that man if he had not been born.** Like all who reject Christ, Judas would be damned forever. Having been given the ultimate privilege of being one of Jesus' disciples, Judas would be punished accordingly with extreme measures (cf. Luke 12:47–48). The eternal retribution that awaited him and all unbelievers is so severe that to have never existed would be infinitely better. The author of Hebrews describes the dreadful consequences that await all who exhibit such obstinate unbelief.

> How much severer punishment do you think he will deserve who has trampled under foot the Son of God, and has regarded as unclean the blood of the covenant by which he was sanctified, and has insulted the Spirit of grace? For we know Him who said, "Vengeance is Mine, I will repay." And again, "The Lord will judge His people." It is a terrifying thing to fall into the hands of the living God. (Heb. 10:29–31)

THE FIRST COMMUNION

While they were eating, He took some bread, and after a blessing He broke it, and gave it to them, and said, "Take it; this is My body." And when He had taken a cup and given thanks, He gave it to them, and they all drank from it. And He said to them, "This is My blood of the covenant, which is poured out for many. Truly I say to you, I will never again drink of the fruit of the vine until that day when I drink it new in the kingdom of God." After singing a hymn, they went out to the Mount of Olives. (14:22–26)

After Judas left (John 13:30–31), and only the faithful eleven remained, Jesus transformed the Passover into the Lord's Table (also called the Lord's Supper or Communion) and thereby signaled the transition from the old covenant to the new. Jesus' words recorded in this passage marked the end of all Old Testament ceremonies, sacrifices and rituals (cf. Mark 15:38). All of the symbols of the old covenant pointed to Christ; in His death, they were perfectly fulfilled and replaced.

That Jesus said these things **while they were eating** suggests that this occurred around the time the roasted lamb was served. In the midst of the Passover celebration, the one true Passover Lamb (1 Cor. 5:7) **took some** of the flat, crisp, unleavened **bread, and after a blessing** in which He gave thanks to His Father (cf. Matt. 14:19; 15:36), **He broke it, and gave it to them.** As Jesus handed a piece of bread to each of the eleven, He **said, "Take it; this is My body."** Eating bread without yeast not only symbolized the Israelites' hasty departure from Egypt (Deut.

16:3), it also represented their separation from the corrupting influences of sin, idolatry, and worldliness (which were symbolized by leaven). In the Lord's Table, that same bread was given new meaning. It served as a figure of His body, which He would soon offer as the sacrifice for sin to propitiate the Father. The breaking of the bread did not signify the nature of His death, since none of His bones were broken during His execution (John 19:36; cf. Ex. 12:46; Ps. 34:20). Rather, the fact that the disciples were each given a piece of the same loaf symbolized their unity in Christ (cf. 1 Cor. 12:12–27). According to the parallel passage in Luke 22:19, Jesus added, "given for you; do this in remembrance of Me" (cf. 1 Cor. 11:24). Those words indicate that the Lord intended His table to be observed by His followers as a perpetual memorial of His death.

As with many doctrines, the Roman Catholic Church has perverted the Lord's Table into the bizarre practice of transubstantiation, in which the substance of the bread and the cup are supposedly transformed into the actual body and blood of Jesus Christ. But Jesus was not speaking literally when He said of the bread, **this is My body.** Similar misunderstandings of Jesus' words incited the Jewish leaders to ridicule Him when He described His body as a temple (John 2:19–21), and caused many superficial disciples to abandon Him when He called Himself the Bread of Life (John 6:35, 48–66). In the same way that Jesus referred to Himself as a door (John 10:9) and a vine (John 15:1,5), Jesus' words in the upper room should be understood in a figurative sense.

After distributing the bread, the Lord Jesus instituted the second element of His table. **When He had taken a cup and given thanks, He gave it to them, and they all drank from it.** The verb translated **given thanks** is a form of the Greek word *eucharisteō*, from which the English word "Eucharist" is derived. ("Eucharist" is a historical title for the Lord's Table that has largely been commandeered and corrupted by the Roman Catholic Church.) This would have been the third cup of the Passover meal, following the main course. That **they all drank from it** demonstrates that Jesus intended all believers to participate in both elements of the Lord's Supper (cf. 1 Cor. 10:16,21; 11:28).

After drinking from the cup, **He said to them, "This is My blood of the covenant, which is poured out for many.** Just as the bread symbolized His body, so the cup symbolized His blood. In order for a covenant to be established, there had to be the shedding of blood (a reference to death, cf. Heb. 9:16–20). But unlike the animal sacrifices required for the Noahic (Gen. 8:20), Abrahamic (Gen. 15:10), and Mosaic covenants (Ex. 24:5–8; Lev. 17:11), the new covenant (Luke 22:20) required the precious blood of the spotless Lamb of God to be spilled in death for the eternal benefit of the many whom He would redeem (cf. Isa. 53:12). Matthew 26:28 adds that the reason Christ's blood had to be shed was "for forgiveness of sins" (cf. Heb. 9:22; 1 Peter 1:2).

On the cross, the Lord Jesus died as the perfect substitute, bearing the guilt of all who were chosen to believe in Him (2 Cor. 5:21). He endured the penalty of God's wrath, satisfied divine justice, and ratified the new covenant of forgiveness and salvation (Jer. 31:34). (For a detailed discussion of the new covenant, see *2 Corinthians*, The MacArthur New Testament Commentary [Chicago: Moody, 2003], chaps. 7 and 8.) Jesus' death constituted final payment, so that there is no longer a need for ongoing animal sacrifices (cf. Heb. 10:4–12). That was clearly demonstrated by the tearing of the veil at the entrance of the Holy of Holies (Matt. 27:51), and the promise of the Lord regarding the complete destruction of the temple in A.D. 70 (cf. Mark 13:1–3).

Jesus concluded the inaugural celebration of the Lord's Supper with a promise to His disciples, **Truly I say to you, I will never again drink of the fruit of the vine until that day when I drink it new in the kingdom of God."** The **fruit of the vine** was a Jewish colloquialism that referred to wine; in this context, it specifically referred to the diluted red wine of the Passover meal. Earlier that same evening, Jesus had also told them, "I say to you, I shall never again eat it until it is fulfilled in the kingdom of God" (Luke 22:16). Those words assured the disciples that He would return (cf. John 14:3), and that He would one day celebrate the Passover with them again in His millennial kingdom (cf. Ezek. 45:18–25). Until His return, believers are to continue to celebrate the memorial meal of His table (cf. 1 Cor. 11:23–24). Thus, the regular celebration of Communion not only looks back to Christ's death but also looks forward with eager anticipation to His coming. The previous evening, Jesus had instructed His disciples about His return and the end of the age (cf. Mark 13:24–27). Now, on the night before His death, He reassured them that the cross did not represent the end of the story.

As the Passover celebration concluded, Jesus and the disciples sang a closing song, likely the final psalm of the traditional Hallel (Ps. 118). It is difficult to imagine a more fitting benediction, since the repeated refrain of Psalm 118 is that the loving-kindness of God is everlasting (vv. 1–3, 29). No refrain could have been more fitting in light of the imminence of the cross. Though the Messiah would be rejected and killed by Israel's religious leaders (cf. v. 22), He would rise victorious on the third day.

Mark concludes his discussion of the upper room by noting simply that **after singing** that final **hymn, they went out to the Mount of Olives.** There, Jesus would pray fervently to His Father that the will of God would be accomplished. Soon the Lamb of God would be arrested and unjustly convicted (1 Peter 1:19; 2:21–24). The most significant moment in redemption history was but a few hours away.

The Agony of the Cup (Mark 14:27–42)

27

And Jesus said to them, "You will all fall away, because it is written, 'I will strike down the shepherd, and the sheep shall be scattered.' But after I have been raised, I will go ahead of you to Galilee." But Peter said to Him, "Even though all may fall away, yet I will not." And Jesus said to him, "Truly I say to you, that this very night, before a rooster crows twice, you yourself will deny Me three times." But Peter kept saying insistently, "Even if I have to die with You, I will not deny You!" And they all were saying the same thing also. They came to a place named Gethsemane; and He said to His disciples, "Sit here until I have prayed." And He took with Him Peter and James and John, and began to be very distressed and troubled. And He said to them, "My soul is deeply grieved to the point of death; remain here and keep watch." And He went a little beyond them, and fell to the ground and began to pray that if it were possible, the hour might pass Him by. And He was saying, "Abba! Father! All things are possible for You; remove this cup from Me; yet not what I will, but what You will."

And He came and found them sleeping, and said to Peter, "Simon, are you asleep? Could you not keep watch for one hour? Keep watching and praying that you may not come into temptation; the spirit is willing, but the flesh is weak." Again He went away and prayed, saying the same words. And again He came and found them sleeping, for their eyes were very heavy; and they did not know what to answer Him. And He came the third time, and said to them, "Are you still sleeping and resting? It is enough; the hour has come; behold, the Son of Man is being betrayed into the hands of sinners. Get up, let us be going; behold, the one who betrays Me is at hand!" (14:27–42)

During His thirty-three years on earth, the Lord Jesus was repeatedly exposed to the trials and temptations of this life (cf. Heb. 4:15). As Isaiah 53:3 predicted of the Messiah, He was "a man of sorrows and acquainted with grief." The New Testament never records a time when Jesus laughed, but it recounts occasions on which He experienced sadness and tears. He lamented the spiritual blindness of the people and their leaders (Mark 8:12, 18), grieved over the physical suffering of the sick and disabled (Mark 7:34; cf. Matt. 14:14; 20:34), and wept at the grave of a beloved friend (John 11:35). With divine perception (cf. John 2:25), the Lord Jesus witnessed the sorrow inherent in a world corrupted by sin, sickness, and death. His understanding of the suffering of others caused Him to be moved with compassion (cf. Mark 1:41; 6:34; 8:2). In John 11:33, His strong emotion is described, "When Jesus therefore saw [Mary] weeping, and the Jews who came with her also weeping, He was deeply moved in spirit and was troubled." This intense feeling was the result of the death of Lazarus, the grief of Mary and Martha, the reality of unbelieving Israel, and the understanding of the impact of sin and death on the history of mankind.

That intense pain over sin was akin to the pain, heartache, and severe anguish He experienced in the garden of Gethsemane. The depths of His agony, in those early morning hours before the cross, were infinitely greater than anything anyone else in human history has ever experienced. The spotless Lamb of God (1 Peter 1:19) would soon be alienated from His heavenly Father (Mark 15:34) and crushed under divine wrath

(Isa. 53:10) in order to bear the sins of others (2 Cor. 5:21). No agony could be greater than knowing He would soon drink the cup of God's judgment against sin (cf. Matt. 20:22; John 18:11).

On Thursday evening, Jesus and His disciples celebrated both the last Passover and the first Communion in an upper room in Jerusalem (Mark 14:12–26). The Passover meal likely lasted five to six hours, from after sunset (around 6:00 P.M.) to not long before midnight. When it was finished, Jesus and the eleven left the city and headed across the Kidron Valley to the Mount of Olives (v. 26). This was the place where, just over twenty-four hours earlier, Jesus had instructed His disciples about the glories of His second coming. Now, around midnight on Friday morning, He would face the excruciating agony of His imminent crucifixion.

Five aspects of the Lord's suffering are highlighted in this passage (Mark 14:27–42). These can be seen in His traumatic prediction, transcendent affliction, tearful petition, tender exhortation, and triumphant submission.

THE LORD'S TRAUMATIC PREDICTION

And Jesus said to them, "You will all fall away, because it is written, 'I will strike down the shepherd, and the sheep shall be scattered.' But after I have been raised, I will go ahead of you to Galilee." But Peter said to Him, "Even though all may fall away, yet I will not." And Jesus said to him, "Truly I say to you, that this very night, before a rooster crows twice, you yourself will deny Me three times." But Peter kept saying insistently, "Even if I have to die with You, I will not deny You!" And they all were saying the same thing also. (14:27–31)

According to Mark 14:26, Jesus and the eleven left the upper room after finishing the Passover and walked toward the Mount of Olives. Leaving Jerusalem through the eastern gate, they would have traversed the Kidron Valley, crossing the brook that was still flowing with water from the late winter rains. During the Passover, the water in the brook was mingled with blood from the lambs slain at the temple—a vivid reminder of the ultimate sacrifice that the Son of God Himself would soon make. As they began to ascend the Mount of Olives, Jesus and His disciples basically followed the same route David had taken a millennium earlier as he fled, barefoot and weeping, from his treacherous son Absalom (2 Sam. 15:30).

Before reaching their destination at the garden of Gethsemane, the Lord issued a traumatic prediction to His disciples, explaining to them that their courage would fail and they would abandon Him. The disciples vehemently protested any such notion, but their words ultimately proved to be far more courageous than their subsequent actions. In just a few hours, everything Jesus predicted about them would occur.

Though the weakness of the disciples is clearly exposed in these verses (vv. 27–31), the text also reveals several wondrous truths about the Lord Jesus. His faithful endurance in the face of suffering shines brightly against the backdrop of their frailty and failure. Their ignorance, cowardice, weakness, and pride serves to highlight His majestic character, putting His knowledge, courage, power, and humility in vivid contrast.

His Knowledge. Over against the ignorance and doubt of the disciples, the Lord Jesus exhibited supernatural knowledge and unwavering certainty in the face of suffering. Because He possessed divine knowledge of the future, He had foreseen both His betrayal by Judas (Mark 14:18–21) and the subsequent scattering of the other disciples (cf. Matt. 26:56). Consequently, **Jesus said to them, "You will all fall away.** The Greek verb translated **fall away** (a form of *skandalizō,* from which the English word *scandalize* is derived) indicated that the eleven would soon abandon Him. Unlike Judas Iscariot, however, their defection would only be temporary. The Lord's perfect knowledge not only included an understanding of what would happen in the future but also a full understanding of His Father's will. Thus, even though He knew He would be arrested and deserted by His followers, Jesus did not shrink back from what His Father called Him to accomplish.

His Courage. The Lord underscored His traumatic prediction by citing words of biblical prophecy. **It is written** was a common formula for introducing content from the Old Testament (cf. Mark 1:2; 7:6; 9:13; 14:21, 27). Quoting from Zechariah 13:7, Jesus continued, **"I will strike**

down the shepherd, and the sheep shall be scattered." Applying those words to Himself as the shepherd and to His disciples as the sheep, Jesus assured His followers that even their failings would not overturn the purposes of God. Their desertion had been foretold by the prophet Zechariah hundreds of years earlier. Jesus knew that He would be struck down while they scattered in fear, yet His resolve did not waver even in the face of abandonment and death. His undaunted courage stands in stark contrast to their disoriented cowardice.

His Power. Looking beyond the cross to His resurrection, the Lord encouraged His disciples by assuring them that their scattering would not be permanent. Though they would all abandon Him, He would gather them again. As He told them, **But after I have been raised, I will go ahead of you to Galilee.** Throughout His ministry, Jesus repeatedly claimed resurrection power (John 2:19–21; 5:28–29; 6:40; 11:25–27), promising the disciples that after His death He would rise again (cf. Matt. 16:21; 17:9, 23; 20:18–19). That divine power contrasted sharply with their obvious weakness.

The Lord's promise, that He would **go ahead of** them **to Galilee,** was precisely fulfilled after the resurrection (cf. Matt. 28:7, 10, 16–17). It was in Galilee that the risen Christ again emphasized His divine power when He commissioned the apostles with these words,

> All authority has been given to Me in heaven and on earth. Go therefore and make disciples of all the nations, baptizing them in the name of the Father and the Son and the Holy Spirit, teaching them to observe all that I commanded you; and lo, I am with you always, even to the end of the age. (Matt. 28:18–20)

His Humility. In spite of the Lord's clear prediction, **Peter** proudly **said to Him, "Even though all may fall away, yet I will not."** In his overconfidence, the strident disciple brashly declared that his courage would never fail. Just a short time earlier, while still in the upper room during the Passover meal, the Lord issued Peter a similar warning. Luke records that prior conversation, beginning with the words of Jesus:

> "Simon, Simon, behold, Satan has demanded permission to sift you like wheat; but I have prayed for you, that your faith may not fail; and you,

when once you have turned again, strengthen your brothers." But [Peter] said to Him,"Lord, with You I am ready to go both to prison and to death!" And He said, "I say to you, Peter, the rooster will not crow today until you have denied three times that you know Me." (Luke 22:31–34)

That same night, as they walked toward the garden of Gethsemane, Peter's stubborn pride again refused to acknowledge the possibility of any weakness.

In response to His disciple's brazen overconfidence, **Jesus** again **said to him, "Truly I say to you, that this very night, before a rooster crows twice, you yourself will deny Me three times."** Of the four gospel writers, Mark alone explains that the rooster would crow twice, an added detail that in no way conflicts with the other gospel accounts. (For a harmony of the gospel accounts regarding the denials of Peter, see John MacArthur, *One Perfect Life* [Nashville: Thomas Nelson, 2012], 437–44.) The "cock crow" represented the third watch of the night, ending at 3:00 A.M., around the time when roosters typically begin to crow in the hours before dawn. It was likely around midnight when Jesus said these words to Peter, as they walked toward the garden of Gethsemane. In a matter of hours, before the sun rose on Friday morning, Peter would deny the Lord three times, exactly as Jesus foretold (cf. Mark 14:66–72).

Refusing to receive the Lord's warning, **Peter kept saying insistently, "Even if I have to die with You, I will not deny You!"** Though Peter's emphatic declaration of loyalty to Christ was noble, his unwillingness to listen to Jesus' admonition was not. The self-assured disciple was blinded by pride and overconfidence. He would soon exemplify the words of Proverbs 16:18, "Pride goes before destruction, and a haughty spirit before stumbling" (cf. Prov. 11:2; 29:23). Though undoubtedly the most outspoken member of the disciples, Peter was not alone in his boastful protests. In overconfidence, as Mark recounts, **they all were saying the same thing also.**

The pride of the eleven was set sharply against the meekness of the Lord Jesus, as He entered the moment of His greatest humiliation (cf. Phil. 2:5–11). Later that day, He would die on a cross to bear their sins, including the foolish pride they exhibited in that moment, along with the sins of all who would believe in Him. After His resurrection, He would graciously restore Peter and the others to Himself, commissioning them for full-time ministry and missionary work (cf. John 21:15–17; Acts 1:8).

THE LORD'S TRANSCENDENT AFFLICTION

They came to a place named Gethsemane; and He said to His disciples, "Sit here until I have prayed." And He took with Him Peter and James and John, and began to be very distressed and troubled. And He said to them, "My soul is deeply grieved to the point of death; remain here and keep watch." (14:32–34)

Finally reaching their destination on the western slope of the Mount of Olives, Jesus and the disciples **came to a place named Gethsemane,** meaning "olive press." The private garden (John 18:1) was probably owned by a wealthy follower of Jesus who gladly made it available to Him. Because of its proximity to Jerusalem, the secluded retreat was regularly used by the Lord and His disciples as a place of rest and escape from the bustling city (cf. John 18:2).

The garden itself was likely surrounded by a fence or wall with a gated entrance. When they arrived at the place, Jesus **said to His disciples, "Sit here until I have prayed."** Leaving eight of the eleven near the entrance to keep watch and to pray (cf. Luke 22:40), **He** went deeper into the garden, taking **with Him Peter and James and John.** These three, who along with Andrew comprised the innermost circle of the Twelve, were the privileged witnesses of Jesus' heavenly glory at the transfiguration (Mark 9:2). Now they would witness the agonies of His earthly suffering in the garden of Gethsemane. This occasion would teach Peter, James, and John an important lesson about their own frailty and the vital necessity of prayer in the face of temptation. As the leaders of the apostles, they would pass what they learned along to the others.

As He anticipated what would soon take place, Jesus **began to be very distressed and troubled.** The word **distressed** (a form of the Greek verb *ekthambeō*) means to be alarmed or amazed. **Troubled** (from the Greek word *adēmoneō*) is a strong term indicating severe distress and anguish. This was the deepest sorrow Jesus had ever experienced (cf. John 11:33). The intensity of the pain was so great that He was astonished by it.

The primary cause of His anguish was not Israel's rejection, Judas's defection, or the disciples' desertion. Nor was it the injustice of the religious leaders, the mockery of the Roman soldiers, or even the impending reality of physical death. All of those considerations, as hurtful or horrifying as they must have been, were secondary. The agony and astonishment that overcame Jesus in the garden went infinitely beyond any of those things. His grief was fueled, first and foremost, by the horrifying recognition that He would soon become the bearer of sin and the object of divine wrath (2 Cor. 5:21). For the first time in all of eternity, He would experience alienation from His Father (Mark 15:34; cf. Hab. 1:13), being crushed by Him as a guilt offering for sinners (Isa. 53:10). The reality of it was nearly too much for even Jesus to survive. As **He said to** His disciples, **"My soul is deeply grieved to the point of death; remain here and keep watch."** The Greek adjective *perilupos* (**deeply grieved**) conveys the notion of being surrounded by sorrow and overwhelmed with sadness. The wave of anguish that flooded Jesus' mind was so intense it nearly killed Him, causing His subcutaneous capillaries to dilate and burst so that His sweat was like drops of blood (Luke 22:44).

The Lord's Tearful Petition

And He went a little beyond them, and fell to the ground and began to pray that if it were possible, the hour might pass Him by. And He was saying, "Abba! Father! All things are possible for You; remove this cup from Me; yet not what I will, but what You will." (14:35–36)

As noted above, the sorrow and grief that Jesus experienced in the garden defies comprehension, because it was a supernatural struggle. Outside of the cross itself, this was the apex of His suffering. It was in Gethsemane that Jesus experienced His greatest moment of temptation, as He contemplated the cup of divine wrath that would soon be poured out on Him. The battle He faced there was far more intense than His earlier encounter with the devil in the wilderness (Matt. 4:1–11; Mark 1:12–13; Luke 4:1–13). It similarly exceeded the temptation He faced in Mark 8:32–33, when Peter became a spokesman for Satan in trying to persuade Jesus to avoid the cross.

Around midnight, just hours before His death, the Son of God endured Satan's final attempt to dissuade Him from the cross (cf. Luke 22:53), being tempted to put His own human will above that of His heavenly Father. If the devil had succeeded, Jesus would not have accomplished God's redemptive purposes. His messianic mission would have ended in failure; God's Word would be untrue; the gospel would be meaningless; heaven would be empty; and Satan would have claimed the victory. Knowing what was at stake, Jesus earnestly petitioned His heavenly Father. **He went a little beyond** Peter, James, and John (cf. Luke 22:41) and **fell to the ground and began to pray.** Unlike the disciples, who kept falling asleep rather than staying vigilant, Jesus responded to each wave of temptation with intense periods of prolonged prayer (cf. vv. 35, 39; cf. Matt. 26:39, 42, 44). As the author of Hebrews explains, "He offered up both prayers and supplications with loud crying and tears" (Heb. 5:7).

The content of Jesus' tearful petition was **that if it were possible, the hour** of His suffering and death **might pass Him by.** As He anticipated His suffering, Jesus asked the Father if the cross might be avoidable within the framework of God's redemptive purposes. (The words of Jesus' petition are recorded in the following verse.) **And He was saying, "Abba! Father!** As He consistently did when He prayed, Jesus addressed God as His heavenly Father (cf. Matt. 6:9; 11:25; Luke 23:34, 46; John 5:18; 17:1, 5, 11, 21, 24, 25). **Abba** is an Aramaic term of endearment and intimacy, and is basically equivalent to the English words "Papa" or "Daddy" (cf. Rom. 8:15; Gal. 4:6). Jesus' use of the term reflected the earnestness and sincerity of His heartfelt plea.

In His prayer, Jesus began by acknowledging His Father's omnipotence, saying, **All things are possible for You.** As the Lord articulated, nothing is outside of the power, privilege, and prerogative of God to do. Yet, Jesus also knew that God never acts contrary to His character, purpose, or Word. Clearly, He was not asking the Father to violate His redemptive plan or go back on His promises. Instead, Christ's petition was an inquiry into whether or not redemption might be accomplished through some other means. Jesus' request was not a sign of weakness, but the utterly expected response of one whose pure, sinless character necessarily and severely recoiled at the thought of bearing man's sin and guilt, and suffering God's wrathful judgment. If He had not reacted that way, it would raise questions about His absolute holiness, so Jesus beseeched the Father to **remove this cup from** Him. In the Old Testament, the **cup** was often used as a metaphor for the wrath of God (cf. Pss. 11:6; 75:8; Isa. 51:17, 22; Jer. 25:15–17; 49:12; Lam. 4:21; Ezek. 23:31–33; Hab. 2:16; Zech. 12:2). On the cross, Jesus would drink the cup of divine wrath against sin (John 18:11).

Though His horror made Him cry out to avoid the cross, the Lord was wholly submissive to the will of His Father (cf. Matt. 6:10). Thus, He articulated His triumphant resolution with these words, **yet not what I will, but what You will.** Submission to the Father's will had characterized Jesus' entire life and ministry (cf. John 4:34; 5:30; 6:38–40; 12:49; 14:31; 17:8); it would also characterize Him in death. Ultimately knowing that the cross was essential to the redemptive purposes of God (cf. Mark 8:31; 9:31–34; Luke 9:22, 44; John 12:32), Jesus surrendered Himself entirely to the Father, willingly "becoming obedient to the point of death, even death on a cross" (Phil. 2:8).

THE LORD'S TENDER EXHORTATION

And He came and found them sleeping, and said to Peter, "Simon, are you asleep? Could you not keep watch for one hour? Keep watching and praying that you may not come into temptation; the spirit is willing, but the flesh is weak." Again He went away and prayed, saying the same words. And again He came and found them sleeping, for their eyes were very heavy; and they did not know what to answer Him. And He came the third time, and said to them, "Are you still sleeping and resting? (14:37–41*a*)

In the midst of His agonizing struggle, Jesus compassionately returned to Peter, James, and John. **And He came and found them**

sleeping, and said to Peter, "Simon, are you asleep? Could you not keep watch for one hour?" Luke explains that the reason for their weariness was not only fatigue (due to the lateness of the hour) but compounded by sorrow and despair (Luke 22:45). Realizing their Lord was about to die, and having been forewarned that they would abandon Him, the disciples were overcome by the weariness of grief. Still, their sadness was no excuse. On such a critical night, they should have done whatever was necessary to stay alert, as Jesus had earlier instructed them to do (v. 34).

By addressing him as **Simon,** rather than by his new name Peter (cf. Matt. 16:18), Jesus may have been highlighting Peter's frailty in the moment. Yet, the Lord's rebuke, in light of all that was happening, was particularly mild and gracious. Even in the midst of His profound agony, the Lord was genuinely concerned about His men. That they could not remain vigilant **for one hour** suggests that Jesus had been praying for about that duration of time. He came and woke them, not to shame them but to tenderly exhort them to **keep watching and praying** so **that** they would **not come into temptation** (cf. Matt. 6:13). Jesus' command to **keep watching** meant to stay alert, not only physically but spiritually (cf. Rom. 13:11–13), remaining vigilant in the face of spiritual attack. As Peter himself said, many years after he learned this lesson in Gethsemane, "Be of sober spirit, be on the alert. Your adversary, the devil, prowls around like a roaring lion, seeking someone to devour" (1 Peter 5:8).

The Lord's instruction to watch and pray was necessary because, as He explained, **the spirit is willing, but the flesh is weak.** If they were to overcome the weakness of their unredeemed flesh, they desperately needed to rely on divine power. The disciples undoubtedly wanted to stay alert. They likewise desired to remain loyal to Christ, insisting that they would never abandon Him (cf. vv. 27–31). Yet, even though they had good intentions, in both cases they succumbed to the flesh (cf. Rom. 7:15–23).

Leaving them, **again He went away and prayed, saying the same words** recorded in verse 36. As the parallel passage in Matthew 26:42 explains, "He went away again a second time and prayed, saying, 'My Father, if this cannot pass away unless I drink it, Your will be done.'" After a second period of intense petition with His heavenly Father, Jesus again came to check on His disciples. **And again He came and found them sleeping, for their eyes were very heavy.** For the second time, Jesus awakened them, likely repeating the questions He had asked them earlier (v. 37). Recognizing they could offer no valid excuse, **they did not know what to answer Him.**

Jesus then returned to pray a third time (cf. Matt. 26:44). Like the apostle Paul in 2 Corinthians 12:8, who prayed three times for the thorn in the flesh to be removed, the Lord Jesus besought His Father three times to remove the cup of suffering. After the third wave of temptation ended, the submissive Son of God emerged triumphant from the battle, fully settled in His resolve to trust Himself to the Father's will. The tempter had been vanquished, and Jesus remained in perfect step with His heavenly Father. When the Lord defeated Satan in the wilderness, God sent angels to minister to Him (Matt. 4:11); an angel from heaven was similarly dispatched on this occasion (Luke 22:43). Now that His final temptation was over, Jesus was ready to endure the cross.

Meanwhile, the disciples had again fallen asleep. **And He came the third time, and said to them, "Are you still sleeping and resting?"** In the weakness of their flesh, Peter, James, and John proved unable to stay alert, even after being awakened and exhorted twice by Jesus. When they should have been prayerfully readying themselves for the coming confrontation, they were sleeping. Now, the moment had arrived and they were woefully unprepared.

THE LORD'S TRIUMPHANT SUBMISSION

It is enough; the hour has come; behold, the Son of Man is being betrayed into the hands of sinners. Get up, let us be going; behold, the one who betrays Me is at hand!" (14:41b–42)

Having yielded fully and unreservedly to His heavenly Father during those hours of prayer, Jesus left Gethsemane triumphant in His commitment to do all that the Father asked Him to do. Thus, He could tell the disciples, **It is enough; the hour has come.** Any temptation to avoid the cross was now past; the time had arrived for the Messiah to fulfill His earthly mission as the Lamb of God who would take away the sins of the world (John 1:29; cf. Isa. 53:10–12).

Much to the shock of His sleepy disciples, the Lord announced, **behold, the Son of Man is being betrayed into the hands of sinners.** A hostile mob—led by Judas Iscariot (John 18:3) and comprising a cohort of Roman soldiers (numbering up to six hundred men), the temple police, and antagonistic members of the Sanhedrin following— was on its way to take Jesus into custody. Whether He physically saw them approaching, or simply knew about them through divine omniscience, Jesus recognized that His enemies had nearly arrived at the garden.

Rather than shrinking back in fear or trying to hide, Jesus boldly went out to meet His attackers. Looking at Peter, James, and John—who were finally awake by this point—Jesus said, **Get up, let us be going; behold, the one who betrays Me is at hand!"** Having entrusted Himself to "the One able to save Him from death" (Heb. 5:7) and raise Him from the grave (Rom. 1:3–4; 6:4), the Lord exhibited no fear in the face of death. The cup of divine wrath was in His hand, but He was no longer trembling. Drops of blood, sweat, and tears were still visible on His brow when He issued the triumphant command to go out and meet the enemy. Instead of running away from the cross, Jesus moved toward it with settled confidence. His death at Calvary constituted His ultimate act of submission to the will of His Father (cf. Phil. 2:8; Heb. 12:2).

Commenting on the Lord's triumphant submission in Gethsemane, the nineteenth-century British preacher Charles Spurgeon declared:

> No clarion blast, nor firing of cannon, nor waving of flags, nor acclamation of the multitudes ever announced such a victory as our Lord achieved in Gethsemane. He there won the victory over all the griefs that were upon him, and all the griefs that were soon to roll over him, like huge Atlantic billows. He there won the victory over death, and over even the wrath of God which he was about to endure to the utmost for his people's sake. There is true courage, there is the highest heroism, there is the declaration of the invincible Conqueror in that cry, "Not as I will, but as thou wilt." With Christ's perfect resignation, there was also his strong resolve. He had undertaken the work of his people's redemption, and he would go through with it until he could triumphantly say from the cross, "It is finished." (Charles Spurgeon, "Christ in Gethsemane," *The Metropolitan Tabernacle Pulpit* [Pasadena, TX: Pilgrim Publications, 1979], 56:152)

The Ultimate Betrayal
(Mark 14:43–52)

28

Immediately while He was still speaking, Judas, one of the twelve, came up accompanied by a crowd with swords and clubs, who were from the chief priests and the scribes and the elders. Now he who was betraying Him had given them a signal, saying, "Whomever I kiss, He is the one; seize Him and lead Him away under guard." After coming, Judas immediately went to Him, saying, "Rabbi!" and kissed Him. They laid hands on Him and seized Him. But one of those who stood by drew his sword, and struck the slave of the high priest and cut off his ear. And Jesus said to them, "Have you come out with swords and clubs to arrest Me, as you would against a robber? Every day I was with you in the temple teaching, and you did not seize Me; but this has taken place to fulfill the Scriptures." And they all left Him and fled. A young man was following Him, wearing nothing but a linen sheet over his naked body; and they seized him. But he pulled free of the linen sheet and escaped naked. (14:43–52)

It was in the garden of Gethsemane, shortly after midnight on Friday morning, that the Lord Jesus endured the ultimate temptation (14:32–42). It was also there that He experienced the ultimate betrayal. Unmoved in His obedient submission to the Father's will (v. 36), the faithful Son of God resolutely set His face toward the cross. He did not hide or attempt to escape when the soldiers arrived to arrest Him. Instead, He boldly went out to confront them (v. 42), knowing they had been guided there by the betrayer.

The arrest of the Lord Jesus set into motion a rapid-fire series of events that culminated in His crucifixion later that same day. In a matter of mere hours, Jesus would stand trial before multiple magistrates, including the Jewish Sanhedrin (Mark 14:53–65; cf. Luke 22:66–71; John 18:13–27), the Roman governor Pilate (Mark 15:1–15; cf. John 18:29–19:16), and Herod Antipas, the tetrarch of Galilee (Luke 23:6–12). After being sentenced to death, He would be tortured by Roman soldiers (Mark 15:16–19), paraded through the streets to Golgotha (15:20–23), then executed by being nailed to a wooden cross (15:24–37). By about 3:00 that afternoon, the Man of Sorrows would be dead, having completed His atoning work as the one true and sufficient Passover Lamb (Isa. 53:10–12; Mark 15:37; Luke 23:44–46; John 19:30).

The events of Jesus' Passion Week climaxed at His crucifixion. On Monday, He had entered the city of Jerusalem in triumph, as crowds lined the streets to hail Him as the messianic Son of David (Mark 11:1–11). Tuesday, He came to the temple and denounced its corruption by expelling the proliferating merchants and money changers who had turned His Father's house into a den of robbers (11:15–18). Wednesday, He returned to the temple, teaching the people and preaching against the spiritual treachery of the religious leaders (11:27–12:44; cf. Matt. 23:1–39). That evening, He answered His disciples' questions about His second coming and the end of the age (13:5–37).

Meanwhile, the religious leaders, fearful of His popularity and incensed by His actions against them, plotted His destruction (14:1–2; cf. 11:18). Recognizing they needed to capture Him away from the crowds, they were elated when one of the Twelve appeared unexpectedly and offered to lead them to Him in a private place (14:10–11). In exchange for betraying Jesus, those elite religionists paid Judas thirty pieces of silver, the traditional price of a slave (Ex. 21:32).

On Thursday evening, Jesus celebrated the final Passover with His disciples, having earlier sent Peter and John to prepare the meal at a secret location so that Judas would not know where it was. It was there, in an upper room, that Jesus instituted the Lord's Supper and gave His apostles final words of instruction and encouragement before His death (cf. John 13–17). In the midst of their Passover celebration, Jesus unmasked the traitor (Mark 14:18), Judas, who being possessed by Satan, immediately left to carry out his wicked schemes (John 13:27; cf. Luke 22:3).

Late Thursday night or very early Friday morning, Jesus and the eleven remaining disciples left Jerusalem and walked to the garden of Gethsemane, located on the Mount of Olives (Mark 14:26, 32). It was there, while His disciples slept, that Jesus entered into three prolonged periods of intense communion with His heavenly Father (14:35–40). As the Lord finished praying the third time, Judas and the hostile forces accompanying him arrived to arrest Jesus (vv. 41–42).

Having left the upper room after dark (John 13:30), Judas found the chiefs of Judaism with whom he had already agreed to betray Jesus (Matt. 26:3–16). A sizable force of temple police and Roman soldiers was hastily assembled, which Judas subsequently led to the place where he knew Jesus would be (Luke 22:39; John 18:2). A secluded private garden at night, outside the city and isolated from the crowds, provided the opportune situation for them to apprehend their target while avoiding commotion or the risk of a riot.

The unfolding drama surrounding the Lord's arrest included several key characters: the hostile crowd, the duplicitous traitor, the impulsive disciple, and the cowardly apostles. But on that historic night, against the backdrop of mayhem and darkness, the undaunted majesty and triumphant tranquility of Christ shone as brightly as ever.

THE HOSTILE CROWD

Immediately while He was still speaking, Judas, one of the twelve, came up accompanied by a crowd with swords and clubs, who were from the chief priests and the scribes and the elders. (14:43)

For the Lord, the hours spent in the garden of Gethsemane (from late Thursday night to early Friday morning) had been filled with agonizing prayer and spiritual preparation. They were also hours of irresponsible slumber for the disciples. When the Lord awakened them the third time, He said to them, "Are you still sleeping and resting? It is enough; the hour has come; behold, the Son of Man is being betrayed into the hands of sinners. Get up, let us be going; behold, the one who betrays Me is at hand!" (14:41–42). The moment of His betrayal and arrest had arrived. As Mark explains, **immediately while He was still speaking, Judas** and his arresting entourage reached the garden. The placid isolation of the night was abruptly shattered by the sudden appearance of the menacing mob.

The notion that the Messiah's betrayer would come from the circle of His apostles was so shocking that all four gospel writers explicitly state with a measure of incredulity that Judas was **one of the twelve** (Matt. 26:14, 47; Mark 14:10, 20, 43; Luke 22:47; John 6:71; cf. 18:1–11); as if, otherwise, it would be impossible to believe. As part of that intimate group who accompanied Jesus throughout His ministry, Judas's privilege was unparalleled, making the tragedy of his life also unparalleled. For several years, he had been exposed daily to the miracles and teaching of Christ but turned his back on all of it, instead choosing to sell out the Son of God for money.

When the traitor **came up** to the garden, he was **accompanied by a crowd with swords and clubs.** Unlike the throngs of people who had hailed Jesus as the Messiah just a few days earlier at His triumphal entry (Mark 11:8–10), this crowd was comprised of armed men who had come to arrest Him. The hostile multitude included antagonistic religious leaders (Luke 22:52), officers of the temple (members of the Jewish temple police, cf. John 7:32, 44–46), and a detachment of Roman soldiers from the cohort stationed at Fort Antonia in Jerusalem (John 18:3, 12). Because they feared the crowds, and because they needed Rome's permission and assistance to execute Jesus, the Jewish rulers enlisted the help of Roman troops. Having been convinced by the Jews that Jesus was a dangerous revolutionary like Barabbas (Mark 15:7), the Romans came with an overwhelming show of force. At full strength, a cohort consisted of six hundred to one thousand soldiers, though a smaller group of two hundred soldiers (known as a maniple) may have been dispatched on this occasion. The short, double-edged **swords** of the Romans, along with the wooden **clubs** of the temple police, meant that this crowd was well-trained and well-armed. According to John 18:3, they also carried torches and lanterns.

Mark identifies the organizers of this military force as **the chief priests and the scribes and the elders.** These representative parties of the Sanhedrin (the Jewish Supreme Court, comprised of seventy-one members) were often at odds with one another (cf. Acts 23:6–10). Yet, their interests converged in their desire to eliminate Jesus and the threat He posed to them. Along with the high priest, **the chief priests**

> included former holders of the high priestly office, . . . the commander of the Temple Guard, the steward of the Temple, and the three Temple treasurers. The "elders" represented the most influential lay families in Jerusalem, and seem to have been primarily wealthy landowners. The chief priests and the elders constituted the old ruling class in Jerusalem, with Saducean leanings, who still held the balance of power in the Sanhedrin. The third group, the representatives of the scribes, consisted primarily of lawyers drawn from the middle classes who tended to be Pharisaic in their convictions. (William L. Lane, *The Gospel According to Mark*, New International Commentary on the New Testament [Grand Rapids: Zondervan, 1974], 531–32)

The representative leaders from both the Sadducees and the Pharisees were motivated by several factors. First, they feared that Jesus' unprecedented popularity would ignite a revolution (cf. Mark 11:9–10; John 6:15), causing Rome to retaliate and thereby placing their delegated positions of authority in jeopardy (cf. John 11:47–53). Second, because they controlled the temple, the chief priests and Sadducees were especially offended when Jesus forcibly expelled the merchants and money changers during the busy Passover week, a feat He performed at both the beginning (John 2:13–16) and end (Mark 11:15–18) of His ministry. Third, the religious leaders also deeply resented Jesus' public defiance of their unbiblical system of rabbinic tradition (Mark 3:6; 7:1–13; cf. Matt. 23:1–36). Jealous of His miraculous power, fearful of His influence with the people, and incensed by His authoritative teachings and actions, the Sadducees and Pharisees found themselves united by a common enemy.

The Duplicitous Traitor

Now he who was betraying Him had given them a signal, saying, "Whomever I kiss, He is the one; seize Him and lead Him away under guard." After coming, Judas immediately went to Him, saying, "Rabbi!" and kissed Him. They laid hands on Him and seized Him. (14:44–46)

In the humiliation of His incarnation, Jesus looked and dressed like any other first-century Jewish man. Nothing about His physical appearance distinguished Him as divine (cf. Isa. 53:2). Consequently, in the middle of the night, it would have been difficult for the soldiers to differentiate Jesus from His disciples. To identify which person to arrest, **he who was betraying Him had given them a signal, saying, "Whomever I kiss, He is the one; seize Him and lead Him away under guard."** In ancient Middle Eastern culture, the kiss was a sign of respect, affection, and homage. Of the various ways in which a kiss might be delivered (such as on the feet, the hand, or the hem of the garment), Judas chose to kiss Jesus on the cheek—an act that symbolized close friendship and mutual affection. The fact that Judas betrayed the Lord through an action that normally expressed devotion and love reveals the despicable depths of his hypocrisy and treachery.

After coming to the garden, inspired by Satan and motivated by greed, **Judas immediately went to** Jesus, **saying, "Rabbi!" and kissed Him.** According to the parallel passage in Luke 22:47–48, as Judas was about to kiss Him, Jesus asked the sobering question, "Judas, are you betraying the Son of Man with a kiss?" (Luke 22:48). The Greek word *kataphileō* (**kissed**) is an intensified verb meaning to show continual affection or to kiss fervently (cf. Luke 7:38, 45; 15:20; Acts 20:37). The implication is that Judas prolonged his dramatic show of false affection for Jesus, making it last long enough for the soldiers to identify their target.

Jesus, of course, was not surprised by Judas's act of treachery. The Lord had predicted it beforehand, declaring that it fulfilled biblical prophecy (Mark 14:20–21). After allowing Judas to kiss Him, Jesus simply told the duplicitous traitor, "Do what you have come for" (Matt. 26:50). At that point, **they laid hands on Him and seized Him,** tying Him up

(John 18:12) to escort Him back to Jerusalem. Jesus offered no resistance and displayed no anger or anxiety (cf. 1 Peter 2:23). Instead, He continued to place His unwavering trust in the providential care of His heavenly Father.

Mark gives no further record of what happened to Judas Iscariot after that moment in Gethsemane. Matthew recounts his tragic demise:

> Then when Judas, who had betrayed Him, saw that He had been condemned, he felt remorse and returned the thirty pieces of silver to the chief priests and elders, saying, "I have sinned by betraying innocent blood." But they said, "What is that to us? See to that yourself!" And he threw the pieces of silver into the temple sanctuary and departed; and he went away and hanged himself. (Matt. 27:3–5)

The book of Acts further indicates that when Judas hanged himself, the rope broke and his body fell and smashed on the rocks below (Acts 1:18–19). Though he died in a gruesome fashion, Judas's suicide was only the beginning of his torments—since he entered into eternity as an unrepentant enemy of the Son of God (cf. Mark 14:21). As the disciple who betrayed the Messiah, Judas is the epitome of wasted opportunity and squandered privilege in all of human history. His deplorable betrayal, botched suicide, and horrifying entrance into eternal punishment stand as a sober warning to all who would trample underfoot the Son of God (Heb. 10:29).

The Impulsive Disciple

But one of those who stood by drew his sword, and struck the slave of the high priest and cut off his ear. (14:47)

Seeing Jesus being arrested, the disciples asked, "Lord, shall we strike with the sword?" (Luke 22:49). **But** instead of waiting for an answer, **one of those who stood by** impulsively **drew his sword, and struck the slave of the high priest and cut off his ear.** John 18:10 identifies that disciple as Peter, and the high priest's slave as Malchus. Peter used one of the two swords the disciples had in their possession for emergency defense and self-protection (Luke 22:38). Undoubtedly aiming for the head, the fisherman missed his mark and only severed an ear when Malchus ducked (cf. Luke 22:50).

Peter's reckless actions were probably motivated by a desire on his part to prove his unfaltering courage and loyalty to Jesus (cf. Mark 14:29; Luke 22:33). He was also emboldened by the dramatic display of Christ's power, just moments earlier, when the entire multitude fell to the ground in response to Jesus' divine declaration, "I am He" (John 18:4–6). But the Lord put an abrupt end to Peter's brash heroics. Knowing that the kingdom of salvation does not advance by force (John 18:36), Jesus issued a direct command to Peter and the other disciples, "Stop! No more of this" (Luke 22:51). Then, in an act of unrequited mercy and divine power, the Lord touched the ear of Malchus and miraculously re-created it.

Jesus proceeded to give Peter three reasons not to use his sword that way. First, the impulsive disciple needed to learn that "all those who take up the sword shall perish by the sword" (Matt. 26:52). The Lord's point was that those who participate in unlawful killing are guilty of murder, and murder is a capital offense that warrants the death penalty (cf. Gen. 9:6). As murderers, those who slay with the sword will one day face the sword of the executioner (Rom. 13:4). Had Peter successfully killed Malchus or anyone else in the crowd that night, he would have been justly arrested and tried for capital murder.

Second, Peter needed to recognize that if Jesus wanted military assistance, He could instantly summon legions of superpowerful angels. He did not need His sleepy disciples (and their small weapons) to defend Him. As the Lord asked Peter, "Do you think that I cannot appeal to My Father, and He will at once put at My disposal more than twelve legions of angels?" (Matt. 26:53). A Roman legion was made up of 6,000 soldiers. If a single angel killed 185,000 soldiers in a single night (2 Kings 19:35), twelve legions of angels (72,000 angels) represented unimaginable power.

Third, the brazen apostle needed to understand that any defense by Jesus and His followers at that moment actually ran contrary to what Old Testament prophecy had declared must happen. Thus, the Lord asked Peter, "How then will the Scriptures be fulfilled, which say that it must happen this way?" (Matt. 26:54). Jesus' point was that His suffering had been foretold centuries before by the prophets. Peter's actions may have been well-intentioned, but in reality he was fighting against the very Word of God.

THE GLORIOUS CHRIST

And Jesus said to them, "Have you come out with swords and clubs to arrest Me, as you would against a robber? Every day I was with you in the temple teaching, and you did not seize Me; but this has taken place to fulfill the Scriptures." (14:48–49)

Seeing the formidable, well-armed, and highly trained force that had assembled to arrest Him, **Jesus said to** the Jewish leaders who stood before Him (Luke 22:52), **"Have you come out with swords and clubs to arrest Me, as you would against a robber?"** In the midst of the chaos, Jesus stood with majestic tranquility, posing a reasonable question to His captors. Since He was not a violent criminal, why was it necessary to bring an excessive military force to apprehend Him? A **robber** (from the Greek noun *lēstēs*) normally referred to an armed bandit or brigand who would violently resist arrest and try to escape. But Jesus had not been hiding from them. As He went on to state, **"Every day I was with you in the temple teaching, and you did not seize Me."** No place in Jerusalem was more public than the **temple.** His statement exposed their hypocrisy and cowardice. If He truly was the dangerous threat to Rome they accused Him of being (John 19:12), why had they not arrested Him in the temple earlier that week? His question exposed their fear that the people, enamored with Jesus, would turn against them (Luke 22:2). To avoid the possibility of a public reaction, they waited to arrest Him, doing so outside of the city, under the cover of darkness, and accompanied by military force.

Though it did not reduce the guilt of their wicked actions, the Lord acknowledged that the events surrounding His arrest were taking **place to fulfill the Scriptures.** Everything was running according to the Father's perfect schedule. Even in their hostility toward Christ, the apostate leaders of Israel were fulfilling the redemptive plan of God, as predicted by the Old Testament prophets (cf. Pss. 41:9; 55:12–14; Isa. 53:3,

7–8,12; Zech. 11:12; 13:7) and by Jesus Himself (cf. Mark 8:31; 9:31; 10:32–34). God sovereignly used their wicked schemes to accomplish His eternal purposes (cf. Gen. 50:20).

No matter how many soldiers accompanied them, the Jewish leaders could not have taken Jesus unless He surrendered Himself into their custody. Throughout His ministry, Jesus' enemies had repeatedly tried to take His life (cf. Mark 3:6; Luke 4:28–30; 19:47–48; John 5:18; 7:1, 25, 32, 45–46; 10:31), but without success because those attempts were not in keeping with the Father's timetable. The Lord Jesus would lay down His life, but not until His hour had come (cf. John 7:6, 8, 30; 19:10–11). As He declared in John 10:17–18, "I lay down My life so that I may take it again. No one has taken it away from Me, but I lay it down on My own initiative. I have authority to lay it down, and I have authority to take it up again." Even in His death, everything Jesus did was under His control and in perfect accord with the Father's will (cf. John 4:34; 5:30; 6:38; Phil. 2:8).

The Cowardly Apostles

And they all left Him and fled. A young man was following Him, wearing nothing but a linen sheet over his naked body; and they seized him. But he pulled free of the linen sheet and escaped naked. (14:50–52)

After an initial display of bravado, in which Peter flashed his sword, **all** eleven disciples **left** Jesus **and fled.** The Lord had earlier instructed them to keep watch and pray (14:38; cf. Luke 22:40), but instead they had fallen asleep. When the moment of temptation arrived, they were woefully unprepared. Thus, all reacted with fear. Just as the Lord had predicted they would (cf. 14:27), the disciples quickly fled the scene, realizing that Christ was unwilling to resist His attackers, and that if they stayed, they too would be arrested (cf. John 18:8).

Mark closes his account of Jesus' arrest in the garden with a striking illustration of one man's cowardice. As Mark reports, **A young man was following Him, wearing nothing but a linen sheet over his**

naked body; and they seized him. But he pulled free of the linen sheet and escaped naked. Because this detail is unique to Mark's gospel, some interpreters have suggested that perhaps the young man was Mark himself. But nothing in the text indicates who the man was, making attempts to identify him entirely speculative. Clearly, the man's identity is irrelevant to Mark's purpose for including this shocking detail in his historical record.

Mark's point was likely to emphasize the complete isolation Christ experienced in that moment. The huge crowds who had heard hear Him teach in the temple were nowhere to be found. The only crowd that gathered around Him that night was there to take Him captive. His apostles, each of whom promised they would never desert Him, had all abandoned Him. Even an unidentified bystander—a **young man** who may have been awakened by the ruckus caused by the soldiers and, after getting out of bed and donning a sheet, went out to investigate—fled naked into the night, leaving his bedsheet behind. When everyone else ran away, the Lord Jesus made no attempt to escape. The Man of Sorrows was left alone, surrounded by no one but His adversaries. From Gethsemane, He would be escorted back into Jerusalem, to the house of the high priest, where a mock trial against Him would commence shortly (14:53).

Even in His capture, Jesus moved toward the cross with triumphant confidence. He knew the redemptive purposes of God would be accomplished. Old Testament prophecies about His betrayal and abandonment had already come to pass (cf. Pss. 41:9; 55:12–14; Zech. 11:12; 13:7). Additional prophecies would be fulfilled later that day, as He offered Himself as the final sacrifice for sin (cf. Heb. 7:27). Though He had been placed under arrest and bound by the soldiers (John 18:12), the Lord Jesus nonetheless went willingly, compelled by a submissive love for His Father, saving love for His redeemed, and steadfast pursuit of His own glory (Heb. 12:2).

The Ultimate Miscarriage of Justice
(Mark 14:53–65)

29

They led Jesus away to the high priest; and all the chief priests and the elders and the scribes gathered together. Peter had followed Him at a distance, right into the courtyard of the high priest; and he was sitting with the officers and warming himself at the fire. Now the chief priests and the whole Council kept trying to obtain testimony against Jesus to put Him to death, and they were not finding any. For many were giving false testimony against Him, but their testimony was not consistent. Some stood up and began to give false testimony against Him, saying, "We heard Him say, 'I will destroy this temple made with hands, and in three days I will build another made without hands.'" Not even in this respect was their testimony consistent. The high priest stood up and came forward and questioned Jesus, saying, "Do You not answer? What is it that these men are testifying against You?" But He kept silent and did not answer. Again the high priest was questioning Him, and saying to Him, "Are You the Christ, the Son of the Blessed One?" And Jesus said, "I am; and

you shall see the Son of Man sitting at the right hand of Power, and coming with the clouds of heaven." Tearing his clothes, the high priest said, "What further need do we have of witnesses? You have heard the blasphemy; how does it seem to you?" And they all condemned Him to be deserving of death. Some began to spit at Him, and to blindfold Him, and to beat Him with their fists, and to say to Him, "Prophesy!" And the officers received Him with slaps in the face. (14:53–65)

The book of Deuteronomy contains Moses's final instruction to the Israelites as they prepared to enter the Promised Land. Its main theme is unmistakably clear: if the people responded to the Lord God in love and obedience, they would experience His blessing; but if they did not, they would receive His judgment. As they conquered Canaan and established their new nation, they needed to remember that only by following God's statutes could they cultivate a society that would prosper and flourish.

Part of that instruction emphasized the responsibility of the people to govern themselves in a way that was righteous and just. In Deuteronomy 16:18–20, Moses explained,

> You shall appoint for yourself judges and officers in all your towns which the Lord your God is giving you, according to your tribes, and they shall judge the people with righteous judgment. You shall not distort justice; you shall not be partial, and you shall not take a bribe, for a bribe blinds the eyes of the wise and perverts the words of the righteous. Justice, and only justice, you shall pursue, that you may live and possess the land which the Lord your God is giving you.

Throughout Israel's history, a concerted effort was made to uphold that divine imperative. By the time of Jesus' ministry in the first century, the Jewish people had developed a sophisticated system of jurisprudence based on the principles outlined in the Mosaic law. They prided themselves on maintaining a just and equitable society, enforced by a system of courts and judges.

A local council, or court, could be established in any town with at least 120 men who were heads of their household. Each council, known as a sanhedrin (from the Greek word *sunedrion*, meaning "sitting together"), provided legal governance to its community. These local councils were composed of twenty-three men, often drawn from the leadership of the synagogue. An odd number of council members ensured that, whenever they voted on an issue or determined a verdict at a trial, there would always be a majority decision.

The supreme court of Israel was located in Jerusalem and met daily in the temple, except on the Sabbath and other holy days. Known as the Great Sanhedrin, it consisted of seventy-one members, including the high priest (who presided over the council) and representatives from the chief priests, elders, and scribes. Alternatively called "the Council of the elders" (Luke 22:66; cf. Acts 22:5) or "the Senate of the sons of Israel" (Acts 5:21), the Great Sanhedrin was the most powerful Jewish legislative and judicial body. Though it had been founded on the principles established in the Mosaic law, the Great Sanhedrin had become significantly corrupted, both religiously and politically, by the time of Christ. Nepotism, social prominence, and political considerations (including the self-serving interests of Herod and the Romans) heavily influenced who was appointed to the council, including who filled the role of high priest.

Based on the stipulations articulated in the Old Testament, the Jewish legal system provided those accused of a crime with several protections: a public trial held during daylight hours, an adequate opportunity to make a defense, and the rejection of any charge unless it was supported by the testimony of at least two witnesses. Perjury (bearing false witness) was taken very seriously (cf. Ex. 20:16). If a person falsely accused another of a crime, the penalty for that crime was to be enacted against the perjurer. As Deuteronomy 19:16–19 explains:

> If a malicious witness rises up against a man to accuse him of wrongdoing, then both the men who have the dispute shall stand before the Lord, before the priests and the judges who will be in office in those days. The judges shall investigate thoroughly, and if the witness is a false witness and he has accused his brother falsely, then you shall do to him just as he had intended to do to his brother. Thus you shall purge the evil from among you.

Additionally, in cases where the death penalty was enacted, the people who testified against the accused had to inflict the first blows of execution (Deut. 17:7). Since the Jewish form of capital punishment was stoning, this meant the witnesses had to cast the first stones. Doing so ensured that they had a clear conscience in standing behind their testimony and would back up their words with action.

In capital cases, Jewish law mandated that a full day must pass between the announcement of the guilty verdict and the carrying out of the death sentence. During that intervening time period, the members of the court were required to fast, taking time to reflect soberly on the verdict they had delivered. The delay also allowed for further testimony or evidence to be found. Consequently, trials were not conducted on the day before a feast, when fasting was not permitted. When it operated according to its rules and regulations, the Jewish system of jurisprudence was merciful and fair. But at the trial of Jesus, the Great Sanhedrin disregarded nearly every one of its own statutes.

Jesus's trial included two major phases, the Jewish phase and the Gentile phase, each of which consisted of three parts. When tried by the religious authorities (the Jewish trial), Jesus appeared before Annas (John 18:13–24), then Caiaphas and the Sanhedrin (Mark 14:53–65; cf. Matt. 26:57–68; Luke 22:54), and then the Sanhedrin a second time after dawn (Luke 22:66–71). From there, He was sent to the secular authorities (the Roman trial), where He stood before Pilate (Mark 15:1–5; cf. Matt. 27:11–14; Luke 23:1–5; John 18:28–38), then Herod Antipas (Luke 23:6–12), and then Pilate again (Mark 15:6–15; cf. Matt. 27:15–26; Luke 23:13–25; John 18:33–19:16).

Mark, in this section, focuses on the second part of the Jewish trial, when Jesus was unjustly convicted by Caiaphas and the Sanhedrin. Everything that happened that night was a miscarriage of justice. That wicked men would falsely condemn the perfect Son of God made it the ultimate injustice. In clear violation of Mosaic law, Jesus' trial took place in private, at night, away from the temple, and just hours before the Passover began. His enemies brought charges without credible witnesses, gave no opportunity for a proper defense, pronounced an illegitimate verdict, and sought immediate execution the same day. From the arraignment to the interrogation to the testimonies to the sentencing, nothing about the proceedings was legal or just.

The Illegal Arraignment

They led Jesus away to the high priest; and all the chief priests and the elders and the scribes gathered together. Peter had followed Him at a distance, right into the courtyard of the high priest; and he was sitting with the officers and warming himself at the fire. (14:53–54)

Having been arrested in the garden of Gethsemane long before dawn, Jesus was **led away** in the darkness **to** be tried at the house of **the high priest.** A guilty verdict had already been determined before the trial began (cf. John 11:50), making the procedure a mere formality, in which **all the chief priests and the elders and the scribes gathered together** in order to condemn Him.

Though not recorded in the Synoptic Gospels, John indicates that Jesus was first taken to Annas, a former high priest, before being brought to Caiaphas and the Sanhedrin. As John explains, "So the Roman cohort and the commander and the officers of the Jews, arrested Jesus and bound Him, and led Him to Annas first; for he was father-in-law of Caiaphas, who was high priest that year" (John 18:12–13). Although Annas had served as high priest earlier (from A.D. 6–15), having been removed by Rome for unknown reasons, he continued to wield significant influence at this time through his son-in-law, Caiaphas, who served as the high priest from A.D. 18 to 36. At one time or another, five of Annas's sons held the office of high priest, in addition to his son-in-law. Like a first-century mafia family, Annas and his sons controlled the lucrative temple operation, including money changing and the sale of sacrificial animals, which was so closely associated with him that it became notoriously nicknamed the Bazaar of Annas. Jesus disrupted the corrupt enterprise when He singlehandedly evacuated the temple earlier that week (Mark 11:15–18).

While the members of the Sanhedrin gathered at the house of Caiaphas, likely located across the courtyard from the residence of Annas, Jesus appeared before the former high priest to be questioned and arraigned. John 18:19–24 describes that scene with these words:

> The [former] high priest then questioned Jesus about His disciples, and about His teaching. Jesus answered him, "I have spoken openly to the world; I always taught in synagogues and in the temple, where all the Jews come together; and I spoke nothing in secret. Why do you question Me? Question those who have heard what I spoke to them; they know what I said." When He had said this, one of the officers standing nearby struck Jesus, saying, "Is that the way You answer the high priest?" Jesus answered him, "If I have spoken wrongly, testify of the wrong; but if rightly, why do you strike Me?" So Annas sent Him bound to Caiaphas the high priest.

Clearly, Annas's only interest in Jesus was to create false evidence with which he could manufacture a case against Him. The questions directed at Jesus were not intended to uncover the truth but to trap Him so that He would incriminate Himself. As the Lord noted in His reply, if Annas actually wanted to know the truth, he could easily discover it by asking any of the countless thousands of people who had heard Jesus teach. His ministry had been a matter of public record. Moreover, Jesus' words reminded Annas that, legally, he was required to call witnesses if he wanted to bring charges against Him. The Lord's response was neither inappropriate nor inaccurate. But it exposed Annas's corrupt intentions, prompting one of the officers standing nearby to retaliate with violence for the insult.

Though Annas had many reasons to hate Jesus, especially since He had disrupted the temple twice (John 2:13–17; Mark 11:15–18), he could find nothing for which to charge Him of a capital offense. With no official charges made, Jesus should have been released. Instead, Annas sent Him to Caiaphas and the Sanhedrin for the next attempt to fabricate a crime worthy of death. By that time, the entire council had gathered together at Caiaphas's house.

Mark interrupts the narrative at this point with a parenthetical comment about **Peter.** Torn by mixed feelings of fear and loyalty, the former fisherman **had followed** Jesus **at a distance,** and come **right into the courtyard of the high priest** (cf. John 18:15–16). Hoping to remain incognito while **sitting with the officers and warming himself at the fire,** Peter placed himself in a precarious position. He would soon be recognized as one of Jesus' disciples, and as the questions began to mount Peter's courage eroded into denial (cf. 14:66–72).

THE ILLEGAL TESTIMONIES

Now the chief priests and the whole Council kept trying to obtain testimony against Jesus to put Him to death, and they were not finding any. For many were giving false testimony against Him, but their testimony was not consistent. Some stood up and began to give false testimony against Him, saying, "We heard Him say, 'I will destroy this temple made with hands, and in three days I will build another made without hands.'" Not even in this respect was their testimony consistent. (14:55–59)

Having failed to incriminate Jesus, Annas sent Him to Caiaphas's house where the entire Sanhedrin was assembled. No official indictment had yet been made against Jesus, nor had any credible evidence of a violation been produced. Knowing they needed to charge Him before they could convict Him, **the chief priests and the whole Council kept trying to obtain testimony against Jesus to put Him to death.** Mark likely singled out **the chief priests** because they were the primary instigators in the case against Jesus, leading **the whole Council** in their quest to condemn and murder Him.

According to Jewish law, the Sanhedrin was not permitted to initiate charges. They could only investigate and adjudicate the cases that were presented to them. Yet, at the trial of Jesus, the members of the council illegally acted as prosecutors searching for grounds on which to indict Him. But **they were not finding any** charge against Jesus. Though **many were giving false testimony against Him,** being willing to lie in order to manufacture a capital crime (Matt. 26:59), **their testimony was not consistent.** Instead of proving His guilt, their contradictory stories only highlighted the stark contrast between His innocence and the blatant corruption of all who spoke.

Eventually they found two willing liars (Matt. 26:60) who **stood up and began to give false testimony against Him, saying, "We heard Him say, 'I will destroy this temple made with hands, and in three days I will build another made without hands.'"** Twisting words the Lord had spoken three years earlier (in John 2:19), these false witnesses claimed that Jesus threatened to destroy the actual temple (cf.

v. 20). Jesus, of course, had been referring to His body and the fact that He would be raised after three days (cf. vv. 21–22). Again, the allegations brought against Him were garbled. As Mark explains, **not even in this respect was their testimony consistent.**

That night at the house of Caiaphas, in clear violation of Deuteronomy 19, the Sanhedrin tried to construct a case against Jesus based entirely on lies. Because Jesus was sinless, no true testimony could have ever been produced that would have justly incriminated Him. Yet, even when resorting to the malicious testimony of perjurers, His enemies still could not coordinate a case against Him.

The Illegal Interrogation

The high priest stood up and came forward and questioned Jesus, saying, "Do You not answer? What is it that these men are testifying against You?" But He kept silent and did not answer. (14:60–61*a*)

Repeated efforts to concoct a case against Jesus had failed until two witnesses agreed in claiming that Jesus threatened to destroy the temple. Hearing their testimony, Caiaphas pounced. **The high priest stood up and came forward and questioned Jesus, saying, "Do You not answer? What is it that these men are testifying against You?"** Because He was innocent, Jesus knew no reply was necessary. Thus **He kept silent and did not answer.** The Lord's silence was that of integrity, innocence, and majestic tranquility. He refused to give these mock proceedings any appearance of legitimacy. Moreover, the Lord knew the words of Isaiah 53:7, which prophesied of the Messiah, "He was oppressed and He was afflicted, yet He did not open His mouth; like a lamb that is led to slaughter, and like a sheep that is silent before its shearers, so He did not open His mouth." The silence of Jesus was in stark contrast to the lies that reverberated throughout the court.

Though motivated by pure evil and hatred, and though using illegal and unjust means to condemn the Son of God, the Jewish leaders were nonetheless fulfilling the redemptive purposes of His Father. Their abject wickedness would be used to magnify God's perfect righteousness (cf. Gen. 50:20; Rom. 8:28). A short time earlier, when the Sanherdrin had plotted to murder Him, Caiaphas had told the council,

> "You know nothing at all, nor do you take into account that it is expedient for you that one man die for the people, and that the whole nation not perish." Now he did not say this on his own initiative, but being high priest that year, he prophesied that Jesus was going to die for the nation, and not for the nation only, but in order that He might also gather together into one the children of God who are scattered abroad. (John 11:49–52)

God turned the malicious words of Caiaphas into a prophecy regarding the substitutionary nature of the death of His Son. As that example demonstrates, everything Jesus' enemies did to cause His suffering was actually used by God to accomplish His eternal plan of salvation (cf. Acts 2:22–24; 4:27–28; 5:30–31; 13:26–33).

THE ILLEGAL SENTENCE

Again the high priest was questioning Him, and saying to Him, "Are You the Christ, the Son of the Blessed One?" And Jesus said, "I am; and you shall see the Son of Man sitting at the right hand of Power, and coming with the clouds of heaven." Tearing his clothes, the high priest said, "What further need do we have of witnesses? You have heard the blasphemy; how does it seem to you?" And they all condemned Him to be deserving of death. Some began to spit at Him, and to blindfold Him, and to beat Him with their fists, and to say to Him, "Prophesy!" And the officers received Him with slaps in the face. (14:61b–65)

Enraged by Jesus' silence, the high priest continued to barrage Jesus with accusatory questions. **Again the high priest was questioning Him, and saying to Him, "Are You the Christ, the Son of the Blessed One?"** The **Blessed One** was a reference to God the Father. According to the parallel passage in Matthew 26:63, Caiaphas accented his question by invoking God Himself: "I adjure You by the living God, that You tell us whether You are the Christ, the Son of God." In his presumption and arrogance, the high priest hypocritically demanded truth from Jesus while perpetuating lies against Him.

Nonetheless, this was the first legitimate question posed to Jesus throughout the entire trial. It was a straightforward inquiry that called for a truthful response. The Lord understood, of course, that Caiaphas was hoping to trap Him in a statement the council would regard as blasphemous. The high priest knew that Jesus had repeatedly claimed to be the Messiah (cf. Luke 4:18–21; John 4:25–26; 5:17–18; 8:58) and to be the Son of God, making Himself equal with God (John 5:18; 8:16–19; 10:29–39). He hoped to coax Jesus to repeat that claim before the Sanhedrin.

The Lord Jesus knew exactly what was happening. But rather than sidestepping the issue or remaining silent, He responded with a bold and unambiguous declaration of both His messiahship and deity. Referencing Psalm 110:1 and Daniel 7:13–14, **Jesus said, "I am; and you shall see the Son of Man sitting at the right hand of Power, and coming with the clouds of heaven."** The title **Son of Man** was a well-known designation for the Messiah (Dan. 7:13–14), and **Power** was a figurative title for God (cf. Acts 2:33; 7:55). With undaunted majesty, Jesus faced His accusers and announced to them that He was their Messiah and their divine Judge. Though they might kill Him that day, He would rise again and ascend to the right hand of His Father. And though they might judge Him unjustly, He would judge them eternally with perfect justice (cf. John 5:22).

Jesus knew that His statement would seal His death. But He was ready. Having endured the agony of temptation in the garden of Gethsemane, He had already determined to submit to the Father's will all the way to the cross (cf. Mark 14:36). With feigned outrage, Caiaphas responded to Jesus' words by **tearing his clothes,** a symbol of righteous indignation. The Jews typically tore their garments as an expression of immense grief (cf. Gen. 37:29; Lev. 10:6; Job 1:20; Acts 14:14). According to Leviticus 21:10, the high priest was forbidden to tear his clothes, though the Talmud allowed it in cases when God was blasphemed. On the outside, Caiaphas pretended to honor God by rending his garments in supposed horror and shock over blasphemy by Jesus. But inwardly, the hypocritical high priest cared nothing about honoring God. He was elated to have finally found a means by which to condemn the incarnate God.

Exultant in his apparent victory, **the high priest said, "What further need do we have of witnesses?"** His rhetorical question indicated that the case was closed and the verdict set. The members of the Sanhedrin finally had what they needed to support before the people the sentence they had predetermined to pass. Witnesses who could agree on an accusation against Jesus were no longer needed. Caiaphas's second question called for an immediate verdict, **"You have heard the blasphemy; how does it seem to you?"** The Old Testament identified **blasphemy** as defiant irreverence of God (cf. Lev. 24:10–23), and taught that "the one who blasphemes the name of the Lord shall surely be put to death" (v. 16). For a mere man to claim equality with God was rightly regarded as blasphemy (cf. John 5:18). But the sentence Caiaphas called for was illegal because Jesus was not guilty of **blasphemy.** The Lord's words were absolutely true. He was the Messiah, the Son of God, the One who had come from heaven. In reality, the high priest and the other members of the council were the blasphemers (cf. Luke 22:65).

Normally, a decision in the Sanhedrin followed an orderly process, in which members cast their votes one at a time, starting with the younger members so that they would not be unduly influenced by the older members. The votes were carefully tabulated by a scribe. But on this night, the council was characterized by a mob mentality in which **they all condemned Him to be deserving of death.** (It might be noted that Joseph of Arimathea, whom Luke 23:50–51 indicates was a member of the Sanhedrin who did not approve of Jesus' condemnation, was apparently not present for this part of the proceedings.)

The Sanhedrin knew they would need to elicit Rome's help to execute Jesus. Because a claim of equality with God was not a crime the Romans deemed worthy of death, the Jewish leaders had invented new charges about which Rome would be concerned. When they later brought Jesus to Pilate, they alleged that He was guilty of fomenting an insurrection against the empire. They told the governor, "We found this man misleading our nation and forbidding to pay taxes to Caesar, and saying that He Himself is Christ, a King" (Luke 23:2). Once again, they invented a bald-faced lie in order to see Jesus condemned and executed.

The members of the Sanhedrin responded to Jesus' alleged blasphemy by raucously declaring Him worthy of death. In their anger and hatred, **some began to spit at Him, and to blindfold Him, and to beat Him with their fists, and to say to Him, "Prophesy!"** Revealing their true decadence, the supreme court of Israel descended into chaos and resorted to shameful physical abuse. For the Jews, the act of spitting constituted the most detestable form of personal insult (cf. Num. 12:14; Deut. 25:9). Taking matters one step further, they blindfolded Jesus in order to strike Him with their fists. Their jeering taunt, **"Prophesy!"** expressed their irreverent mockery of His divine omniscience. The parallel passage in Matthew 26:68 provides a fuller statement of their scornful derision, "Prophesy to us, You Christ; who is the one who hit You?" Jesus, of course, knew exactly who was hitting Him. Yet He said nothing. Then, after they grew tired of the taunts and abuse, they turned Jesus back over to the temple police. **The officers received Him,** and following the pattern continued the abuse **with slaps in the face.**

The maltreatment Jesus suffered at their hands fulfilled exactly what He had earlier told His disciples,

> The Son of Man will be delivered to the chief priests and the scribes; and they will condemn Him to death and will hand Him over to the Gentiles. They will mock Him and spit on Him, and scourge Him and kill Him, and three days later He will rise again. (Mark 10:33–34)

As noted above, the Lord understood that the wicked actions of these men would be used by God to accomplish His redemptive purposes.

Caiaphas and his fellow council members may have sat in judgment over Jesus that one night, but they would stand before His glorious throne to face eternal judgment (Heb. 9:27). Like them, every sinner who rejects Christ will one day face punishment for their unbelief (cf. Matt. 23:15). Yet, it was for the sake of sinners that Jesus endured those very hostilities, so that all who would embrace Him in saving faith might escape that judgment and receive eternal life (cf. John 3:15–18; 11:25–26). As the apostle Peter explained in his first epistle,

> While being reviled, He did not revile in return; while suffering, He uttered no threats, but kept entrusting Himself to Him who judges righteously; and He Himself bore our sins in His body on the cross, so that we might die to sin and live to righteousness; for by His wounds you were healed. (1 Peter 2:23–24)

Peter's Denial: A Warning about Self-Confidence (Mark 14:66–72)

30

As Peter was below in the courtyard, one of the servant-girls of the high priest came, and seeing Peter warming himself, she looked at him and said, "You also were with Jesus the Nazarene." But he denied it, saying, "I neither know nor understand what you are talking about." And he went out onto the porch. The servant-girl saw him, and began once more to say to the bystanders, "This is one of them!" But again he denied it. And after a little while the bystanders were again saying to Peter, "Surely you are one of them, for you are a Galilean too." But he began to curse and swear, "I do not know this man you are talking about!" Immediately a rooster crowed a second time. And Peter remembered how Jesus had made the remark to him, "Before a rooster crows twice, you will deny Me three times." And he began to weep. (14:66–72)

Although they are new creatures in Christ (2 Cor. 5:17), believers understand that their flesh (body and mind) is still fallen (Rom. 7:18; Gal.

5:17–21). They have experienced the redemption of their souls, but not yet their bodies (Rom. 8:23). Thus, the old self and its remaining corruption must be continually put to death (Rom. 8:13; Col. 3:5–10). Though the regenerated spirit desires to pursue righteousness, the flesh is prone to weakness and sin (cf. Mark 14:38). As the apostle Paul expressed, "Wretched man that I am! Who will set me free from the body of this death?" (Rom. 7:24).

The Bible teaches that all men and women, as members of the fallen human race, are weak, sinful, and corrupt (cf. Rom. 3:23). At conversion, believers are regenerated through the power of the Holy Spirit (Titus 3:3–7; cf. John 3:3–8), so that their desires, aspirations, and longings change to reflect the new creation (2 Cor. 5:17). Yet, they still have to fight against the fallenness of remaining sin, arming themselves for the incessant spiritual battle (Eph. 6:12–17; cf. Rom. 13:12; 2 Cor. 10:3–4).

Failure to recognize the enemy within places believers in danger. Paul explained that precarious reality to the Corinthians, "Therefore let him who thinks he stands take heed that he does not fall" (1 Cor. 10:12). Like vigilant soldiers, Christians must be on constant guard, not only against Satan and the world but also against the resident lusts of the flesh (cf. 1 John 2:15–17). Those who become prideful and overconfident make themselves easy targets for the enemy (cf. 1 Peter 5:5–8). In this passage (Mark 14:66–72), Peter serves as an example of one who fell when he presumptuously thought he could stand.

The gospel records portray Peter as a genuine believer who deeply loved the Lord Jesus. After leaving everything behind (Mark 10:28), he followed the Savior, heeded His preaching, witnessed His miracles, and embraced Him in saving faith. It was Peter who said, "Lord, to whom shall we go? You have words of eternal life. We have believed and have come to know that You are the Holy One of God" (John 6:68–69). Later, he exuberantly declared to Jesus, "You are the Christ, the Son of the living God" (Matt. 16:16). In the upper room, when Jesus told Peter that if He did not wash his feet, he had no part in Him, Peter quickly replied, "Lord, then wash not only my feet, but also my hands and my head" (John 13:9). Among the disciples, no one was more vocal about loving Christ than Peter (cf. Mark 14:29).

Yet, on the same night that Judas betrayed Jesus, Peter denied

Him. It was a repeated denial that kept occurring over a two-hour period of time—likely from about 1:00 A.M. to 3:00 A.M. While Jesus stood trial before both Annas and Caiaphas, Peter lingered outside in the courtyard where he insisted that he had never even met Jesus. The Lord stayed silent before His accusers, opening His mouth only to speak the truth even though He knew it would cost Him His life (14:62). What a contrast to Peter, who fearfully kept speaking lies to protect himself.

On the one hand, the story of Peter's failure serves as a sobering reminder of the weakness of the flesh and the grievous consequences of sin in spite of the best intentions. On the other hand, it is also an encouragement to believers regarding the forgiveness of God. Though Peter's iniquity was grievous and blatant, it did not take him beyond the reaches of divine mercy, grace, and restoration. The account of Peter's denials highlights his foolish confidence, his failing cowardice, and his fervent contrition.

FOOLISH CONFIDENCE

The seeds of Peter's failure were sown hours before he entered the courtyard of the high priest and began to deny his Lord. While in the upper room and then in the garden, Peter exhibited signs of overconfidence and pride that further set him up for a fall (cf. Prov. 16:18). He boasted too much, listened too poorly, prayed too little, acted too fast, and followed too far.

Peter boasted too much. As Jesus and the disciples ate the Passover meal, the Lord said to Peter, "Simon, Simon, behold, Satan has demanded permission to sift you like wheat; but I have prayed for you, that your faith may not fail; and you, when once you have turned again, strengthen your brothers" (Luke 22:31–32). Peter responded to that somber admonition not with honest, self-doubting humility and prayerful introspection but by boasting about his courage: "Lord, with You I am ready to go both to prison and death!" (v. 33). On the way to the garden of Gethsemane, when Jesus repeated a similar warning, Peter again replied with smug confidence, "'Even though all may fall away, yet I will not'" (Mark 14:29); and once more, "Even if I have to die with You, I will not deny You!" (14:31). Clouded by his own self-reliance, Peter thought he was spiritually invincible and incapable of disloyalty to Christ.

Peter listened too poorly. Peter's pride not only blinded his mind but also deafened his ears. Instead of truly hearing Jesus, he ignored the Lord's repeated warnings. Peter understood that Jesus was the Son of God (Matt. 16:16), and that He knew all things (cf. John 21:17), yet he refused to heed His words on this occasion. When Jesus told the eleven, "You will all fall away" (Mark 14:27), and then said to Peter individually, "Truly I say to you, that this very night, before a rooster crows twice, you yourself will deny Me three times" (14:30), the stubborn disciple closed his ears and even began to argue with Jesus, blatantly contradicting what the Lord Himself had just said (14:31).

Peter prayed too little. When Jesus and the disciples arrived at the garden, the Lord specifically instructed them, "Pray that you may not enter into temptation" (Luke 22:40; cf. Matt. 6:13). This was the time for Peter and the other apostles to arm themselves for the traumatic events that were about to take place. But, when he should have been calling out for heaven's help, Peter was napping. As Mark records,

> And He came and found them sleeping, and said to Peter, "Simon, are you asleep? Could you not keep watch for one hour? Keep watching and praying that you may not come into temptation; the spirit is willing, but the flesh is weak." Again He went away and prayed, saying the same words. And again He came and found them sleeping, for their eyes were very heavy; and they did not know what to answer Him. And He came the third time, and said to them, "Are you still sleeping and resting? (14:37–41a)

Peter lost the personal struggle in the dark garden when, instead of drawing on divine power, he confidently slept. Consequently, when temptation arose in the heat of the battle, he was woefully unprepared.

Peter acted too fast. The slumbering disciples awoke to the sound of soldiers approaching, and watched in horror as one they thought a true disciple betrayed Jesus with a kiss! In a moment of overzealous courage, Peter impetuously drew his sword against the surrounding multitude (Mark 14:47; cf. John 18:10). Still operating in the strength of his flesh, and wanting to prove his earlier professions of loyalty to Christ, he did not wait for instructions from Jesus. Instead, he attacked, managing to cut off the ear of the high priest's servant. On one level, Peter's attempt to defend Jesus with a sword may seem noble. But, as Jesus explained to him in Matthew 26:52–54, Peter's impulsive actions in that moment were reckless (v. 52), unnecessary (v. 53), and actually ran contrary to the Word of God, which foretold that the Messiah must suffer (v. 54). And such an act could result in Peter's death sentence (vv. 51–52). Sadly, rash behavior would continue to characterize Peter over the subsequent hours.

Peter followed too far. Luke 22:54 explains that as the soldiers led Jesus back to the house of the high priest, "Peter was following at a distance." Peter found himself caught between faith and fear, loyalty and terror, courage and cowardice. He was curious to see what would happen to Jesus; yet not brave enough to stand with Him. Thus, he entered the high priest's residence to watch the trial but hoped to blend in so that no one would notice who he was. His desire to remain incognito would lead to his undoing. Remaining at a distance, Peter exposed himself to a spiritually precarious situation for which he was wholly unprepared.

FAILING COWARDICE

As Peter was below in the courtyard, one of the servant-girls of the high priest came, and seeing Peter warming himself, she looked at him and said, "You also were with Jesus the Nazarene." But he denied it, saying, "I neither know nor understand what you are talking about." And he went out onto the porch. The servant-girl saw him, and began once more to say to the bystanders, "This is one of them!" But again he denied it. And after a little while the bystanders were again saying to Peter, "Surely you are one of them, for you are a Galilean too." But he began to curse and swear, "I do not know this man you are talking about!" Immediately a rooster crowed a second time. (14:66–72a)

As Zechariah 13:7 predicted they would, the eleven disciples responded to Jesus' arrest by scattering into the night (Mark 14:50). The Lord was taken first to the house of Annas, a former high priest and the patriarch of the priestly family (John 18:13–24). Though he had been removed from office around A.D. 15, Annas was replaced by several of his sons in succession. His son-in-law Caiaphas (who served as high priest from A.D. 18–36) held the position at the time of Jesus' arrest, allowing Annas to wield ongoing influence as high priest emeritus. The high priesthood was originally designed as a lifetime position (cf. Num. 35:28), but by the time of the New Testament, there were constant changes. From Herod the Great to the destruction of Jerusalem in A.D. 70, there were nearly thirty men in that office, reflecting its corruption and control by the Romans.

The gospel accounts imply that Annas and Caiaphas both lived at the same large estate. In first-century Israel, multiple generations of a family often lived together, and the high priestly mansion was large enough to accommodate Annas and members of his extended family, including Caiaphas. Large homes in ancient Israel were laid out like great, multistoried rectangles surrounding a sizable inner courtyard. Within the mansion, Annas and Caiaphas would have had separate living areas, or "houses," while sharing the same inner courtyard. Hence, the courtyard of Caiaphas (Matt. 26:57–58) and the courtyard of Annas (John 18:15–16) refer to the same location. To go from the residence of Annas to that of Caiaphas, Jesus traversed the common courtyard between the different wings of the estate (cf. John 18: 24). It was here, at the house of the high priest, that all of Peter's denials occurred.

Peter's failings in those nighttime hours are recorded in all four gospels, a comparison of which reveals that they occurred in three separate episodes, with each incident involving multiple rapid-fire accusations from bystanders and repeated renunciations from the cowardly apostle. The fact that the gospel writers highlight different aspects of Peter's denials in no way calls their historical reliability into question. Rather, the details from each account harmonize perfectly to paint a single, harrowing picture of Peter's experience on that dramatic night. (For a harmony of the denials of Peter, see John MacArthur, *One Perfect Life* [Nashville: Thomas Nelson, 2012], sections 182, 184.)

The house of the high priest, surrounded by a wall, would have been entered from the street via a gate, which opened to a corridor leading into the inner courtyard. Because Peter was unknown to the high priest's family, he would not have been allowed to enter if it had not been for another "disciple, who was known to the high priest, [who] went out and spoke to the doorkeeper, and brought Peter in" (John 18:16; cf. v. 15). Traditionally, the other disciple has been identified as John, the beloved disciple (John 13:23–24) who authored the fourth gospel. The New Testament gives no indication what happened to John that night, after he helped Peter gain entry. The focus of the narrative remains on **Peter,** who having come through the gate, **was below in the courtyard.**

At first, Peter was covertly warming himself by the fire, trying to blend in with officers of the temple guard and members of the household staff, when he was suddenly recognized. **One of the servant-girls of the high priest,** the same household slave who had opened the gate for Peter (cf. John 18:15–17), **came, and seeing Peter warming himself, she looked at him** intently (Luke 22:56). That whole week, Jesus and His disciples had frequented the temple. Perhaps it was there that this servant girl had seen Peter. Or her suspicions may have been aroused when she initially opened the gate so that Peter could come in (cf. John 18:17). Recognizing him as a disciple of Jesus, she **said, "You also were with Jesus the Nazarene."** Because her words are slightly varied in the various gospel accounts, it is likely that she stated her same basic accusation several times, repeating it loudly enough that the entire group huddled around the fire heard her (cf. Matt. 26:70).

The girl's accusations came as a shock to Peter, whose immediate response exposed his vulnerability. Caught completely by surprise, Peter panicked and **denied it, saying "I neither know nor understand what you are talking about."** The other gospel writers note that Peter also said, "Woman, I do not know Him" (Luke 22:57); and when accused of being Jesus' disciple, he added, "I am not" (John 18:17). In a moment of weakness, the overconfident apostle was laid low by the simple questions of a lowly servant girl. Embarrassed and eager to escape, Peter left the fire and **went out onto the porch,** the corridor that led back to the street. There, in the entryway, he hoped to regain his composure and maintain his anonymity.

At this point in the narrative, some English translations (such as the New King James Version) add the phrase, "and a rooster crowed." However, that addition was likely not part of Mark's original gospel, since it is not found in the earliest manuscripts. It was probably inserted by a later scribe trying to account for Mark's subsequent comment that a rooster crowed a second time (v. 72). If a rooster did crow at this time, Peter was apparently unaware of it, since it seemingly had no effect on his actions.

Peter's escape to the entryway was short-lived. A little while later (Luke 22:58), he was again recognized as he stood in the corridor. **The servant-girl saw him, and began once more to say to the by-standers, "This is one of them!"** This time, she was joined in her allegations by at least two other servants, one female (Matt. 26:71) and another male (Luke 22:58). Assaulted by the chorus of accusations, and feeling the gaze of additional bystanders, **again he denied it.** Unlike Peter's first repudiation, this act of cowardice was premeditated, since he was not caught off guard as he had been earlier. Rather than acknowledging the truth, Peter became even more intense, adamantly disavowing any association with Jesus "with an oath" and saying, "I do not know the man" (Matt. 26:72).

In spite of the allegations and questions being directed his way, Peter decided to stay at the house of the high priest, probably curious to find out what would happen to Jesus. **After a little while** had passed (Luke 22:59 reports that it was about an hour later), he was confronted a third time by a group of **bystanders** who **were again saying to Peter, "Surely you are one of them, for you are a Galilean too."** Peter's Galilean accent had given him away (Matt. 26:73). Moreover, a man in the group recognized him from the garden of Gethsemane. As John reports, "One of the slaves of the high priest, being a relative of the one whose ear Peter cut off, said, 'Did I not see you in the garden with Him?'" (John 18:26). Once again, the reluctant disciple found himself hemmed in on all sides.

Peter's final disavowal of Christ was the most vehement and demonstrative of all. **He began to curse and swear, "I do not know this man you are talking about!"** The verb **to curse** (from the Greek word *anathematizō*, from which the English word "anathematize" is derived) indicates that Peter pronounced a curse of divine judgment on his own head if he were lying. The verb to **swear** (a form of *omnuō*) refers to a solemn pledge of truthfulness. What began as a knee-jerk reaction to the inquiry of a servant girl had escalated into a premeditated tirade of dogmatic deceit and disloyalty, punctuated with cursing and swearing, that echoed throughout the courtyard.

Just as Jesus had predicted (Mark 14:30), as soon as this third episode ended, **immediately a rooster crowed a second time.** (Mark is the only gospel writer who notes that the rooster crowed twice, an added detail that in no way contradicts the other gospel accounts.) By this time, Jesus' trial at Caiaphas's house had come to its conclusion. The Lord had been falsely accused, convicted of blasphemy, and mocked and beaten by the Sanhedrin and the temple police (14:56–65). At that very moment, He was likely being led back across the courtyard. According to Luke 22:61, just after the rooster crowed, "The Lord turned and looked at Peter." The penetrating gaze of Christ caught Peter's eye, pierced his soul, and burned deep into his conscience. Instantly, Peter's heart and mind flooded with feelings of guilt, remorse, and shame. It was a look he certainly never forgot.

FERVENT CONTRITION

And Peter remembered how Jesus had made the remark to him, "Before a rooster crows twice, you will deny Me three times." And he began to weep. (14:72*b*)

Under the gaze of his Lord, **Peter** felt the full weight of his sin and **remembered how Jesus had made the remark to him, "Before a rooster crows twice, you will deny Me three times."** He had done exactly what Jesus said he would do. His arrogant boasts from a few hours earlier (cf. Mark 14:31) had proven hollow. He had been disloyal, disobedient, and dishonest. But although his courage had failed, his faith would not (Luke 22:32). Unlike Judas, who felt remorse and committed suicide (Matt. 27:3–10), Peter felt remorse and repented (cf. 2 Cor. 7:10). Deeply convicted and broken over his actions, he fled the scene (Luke 22:62) **and he began to weep** bitterly (Matt. 26:75). He sobbed with tears of fervent contrition in the aftermath of severe weakness and failure.

Though Peter sinned greatly, his true character is not seen in his denials but in his repentance, beginning with heartfelt sorrow. He had discovered the corruption of his own flesh even in the face of his best intentions. But Peter's failures are not the end of his story. Evidence of the genuineness of Peter's faith can be seen almost immediately. It was Peter and John who raced to the empty tomb (John 20:2–10). Peter was one of the first to see the risen Christ (cf. 1 Cor. 15:5). He was with the disciples when they gathered in the upper room (John 20:19–20). He went to Galilee to wait for the Lord as instructed (Matt. 28:10; cf. John 21:1–11). And it was there, in Galilee, that Peter was fully restored to ministry by the Lord Jesus. As John 21:15–17 recounts,

> So when they had finished breakfast, Jesus said to Simon Peter, "Simon, son of John, do you love Me more than these?" He said to Him, "Yes, Lord; You know that I love You." He said to him, "Tend My lambs." He said to him again a second time, "Simon, son of John, do you love Me?" He said to Him, "Yes, Lord; You know that I love You." He said to him, "Shepherd My sheep." He said to him the third time, "Simon, son of John, do you love Me?" Peter was grieved because He said to him the third time, "Do you love Me?" And he said to Him, "Lord, You know all things; You know that I love You." Jesus said to him, "Tend My sheep."

Peter had repeatedly and adamantly denied the Lord Jesus on three separate occasions. Jesus therefore questioned Peter three times about his love for Him. For each episode of denial, Peter was given an opportunity to affirm his devotion to Christ.

Incredibly, the man who fearfully disavowed the Lord Jesus would become the fervent preacher of the book of Acts—boldly proclaiming the gospel on the day of Pentecost (Acts 2:14–40) less than two months after the devastating collapse of courage recorded in this passage. Jesus had predicted that Peter, after he was restored, would strengthen his fellow believers (cf. Luke 22:32). That promise was fulfilled, not only in Acts (cf. Acts 4:14–31) but also years later when Peter explained to persecuted Christians in Asia Minor that true faith cannot fail, even when severely tested (cf. 1 Peter 1:6–7).

In his failings, Peter learned that pride and overconfidence make believers spiritually vulnerable. But God grants the victory to those who are humble, dependent on Him, and on guard in the face of temptation (cf. 2 Peter 3:17–18). As the forgiven apostle explained in 1 Peter 5:5–8,

All of you, clothe yourselves with humility toward one another, for God is opposed to the proud, but gives grace to the humble. Therefore humble yourselves under the mighty hand of God, that He may exalt you at the proper time, casting all your anxiety on Him, because He cares for you. Be of sober spirit, be on the alert. Your adversary, the devil, prowls around like a roaring lion, seeking someone to devour.

Pilate before Jesus
(Mark 15:1–15)

31

Early in the morning the chief priests with the elders and scribes and the whole Council, immediately held a consultation; and binding Jesus, they led Him away and delivered Him to Pilate. Pilate questioned Him, "Are You the King of the Jews?" And He answered him, "It is as you say." The chief priests began to accuse Him harshly. Then Pilate questioned Him again, saying, "Do You not answer? See how many charges they bring against You!" But Jesus made no further answer; so Pilate was amazed. Now at the feast he used to release for them any one prisoner whom they requested. The man named Barabbas had been imprisoned with the insurrectionists who had committed murder in the insurrection. The crowd went up and began asking him to do as he had been accustomed to do for them. Pilate answered them, saying, "Do you want me to release for you the King of the Jews?" For he was aware that the chief priests had handed Him over because of envy. But the chief priests stirred up the crowd to ask him to release Barabbas for them instead. Answering again, Pilate said

to them, "Then what shall I do with Him whom you call the King of the Jews?" They shouted back, "Crucify Him!" But Pilate said to them, "Why, what evil has He done?" But they shouted all the more, "Crucify Him!" Wishing to satisfy the crowd, Pilate released Barabbas for them, and after having Jesus scourged, he handed Him over to be crucified. (15:1–15)

The gallery of rogues in the unfolding drama of Jesus' murder includes a greedy traitor named Judas, high priestly hypocrites Annas and Caiaphas, and a petty tyrant, Herod Antipas. To that list, the name of a vacillating pagan politician, Pontius Pilate, must be added. These men comprise the notorious lineup of coconspirators who, on a human level, effected the unjust execution of the Son of God.

From the divine perspective, however, God was the true power at work in bringing His Son to the cross (cf. Acts 4:27–28). When Pilate asked Jesus, "'Do You not know that I have authority to release You, and I have authority to crucify You?' Jesus answered, 'You would have no authority over Me, unless it had been given you from above'" (John 19:10–11a). As Jesus' words indicate, God the Father was sovereignly working to accomplish His saving purposes in spite of the wicked schemes of evil men (cf. Gen. 50:20). Peter echoed that truth on the day of Pentecost, explaining that Christ was "delivered over by the predetermined plan and foreknowledge of God" (Acts 2:23a; cf. Luke 22:22; Acts 3:18; 1 Peter 1:20). In keeping with the divine plan of salvation, the Son of God would be crushed as the Father's chosen atoning substitute, bearing the Father's wrath and, thereby, reconciling sinners to God (Isa. 53:5, 11; 2 Cor. 5:19–21).

Having taking Jesus prisoner about 1:00 a.m. on Friday morning, the Jewish religious heads brought Him to the house of the high priest where He was first questioned by Annas (John 18:19–24) and then tried before Caiaphas and the Sanhedrin (Mark 14:55–65). When the council failed to produce consistent testimony against Jesus, they resorted to accusations of blasphemy and subsequently condemned Him to death. The trial before Caiaphas likely ended about 3:00 A.M., at the time when Peter's denials also ended (cf. 14:66–72). For the next couple hours, Jesus would have been held prisoner by the temple police, who continued to mock and mistreat Him (cf. v. 65).

At daybreak, near 5:00 A.M., the Sanhedrin reconvened. As Mark explains, **early in the morning the chief priests with the elders and scribes and the whole Council, immediately held a consultation.** Knowing that Jewish law required all trials to be held in the daytime, and wanting to maintain a veneer of legality, the council created a quick mock trial to condemn Jesus officially (Luke 22:66–71). Jewish law required that a full day pass between sentencing and execution to allow for new evidence or testimony to surface. But in their venal haste to expedite Jesus' death, the members of the Sanhedrin deliberately ignored the due process of their own legal system.

The council's brief **consultation** constituted the third and final phase of the Jewish portion of Jesus' trial and set the stage for the Romans to get involved. The Roman sham trial likewise consisted of three phases. First, Jesus was questioned by the governor of Judea, Pontius Pilate. Then, He was sent briefly to Herod Antipas, the Roman-client tetrarch of Galilee and murderer of John the Baptist. After being mocked and abused by Herod, Jesus was sent back to Pilate where He faced the final sentencing.

THE FIRST ROMAN PHASE: BEFORE PILATE

and binding Jesus, they led Him away and delivered Him to Pilate. Pilate questioned Him, "Are You the King of the Jews?" And He answered him, "It is as you say." The chief priests began to accuse Him harshly. Then Pilate questioned Him again, saying, "Do You not answer? See how many charges they bring against You!" But Jesus made no further answer; so Pilate was amazed. (15:1*b*–5)

The Sanhedrin knew they needed Rome's permission to legally enact a sentence of execution. Thus, **binding Jesus, they led Him away and delivered Him to** Pontius **Pilate,** the Roman prefect (or governor) of Judea. Having been appointed by Emperor Tiberius in A.D. 26, Pilate was responsible to command the Roman military, collect taxes, and adjudicate certain legal matters. Though he was often brutal and impulsive, Pilate also exhibited, at times, weakness and indecision. Nothing certain is known about Pilate's life before becoming governor. However, his tenure in Judea is attested by several extrabiblical sources, including Tacitus, Josephus, Philo, and the Pilate Stone (discovered in 1961 in Caesarea) on which the names of Tiberius and Pilate are both inscribed.

Sometime shortly after daybreak, Jesus was delivered to Pilate's judgment hall, the Praetorium, likely located in Fort Antonia just north of the temple. His official residence was at Caesarea Maritima, on the Mediterranean coast, but he was in Jerusalem for the Passover. John 18:28 notes the hypocritical duplicity of the religious leaders as they arrived at Pilate's quarters: "Then they led Jesus from Caiaphas into the Praetorium, and it was early; and they themselves did not enter into the Praetorium so that they would not be defiled, but might eat the Passover." Incredibly, the chief priests and scribes sanctimoniously refused to enter a Gentile residence for fear of becoming ceremonially unclean, yet they had no compunction about lying in order to murder the Son of God (cf. Ex. 20:13, 16). (Being from Galilee, Jesus and His disciples had already celebrated the Passover the previous evening. For an explanation of the different times when Galilean and Judean Jews observed the Passover, see chapter 26 of this volume.)

The fourth gospel continues to set the scene:

> Therefore Pilate went out to them and said, "What accusation do you bring against this Man?" They answered and said to him, "If this Man were not an evildoer, we would not have delivered Him to you." So Pilate said to them, "Take Him yourselves, and judge Him according to your law." The Jews said to him, "We are not permitted to put anyone to death," to fulfill the word of Jesus which He spoke, signifying by what kind of death He was about to die. (John 18:29–32)

Clearly, the members of the Sanhedrin did not want Pilate to act as judge but merely as executioner. They had already declared Jesus guilty; they only needed the Roman governor to approve and exact his power of capital punishment. Though the Sanhedrin occasionally executed people without obtaining official permission (Acts 6:12–15; 7:54–60; cf. 23:12–15), Jesus' public profile was too high for the Jewish council to take that risk. The chief priests and scribes hoped to avoid appearing responsible for His death, pinning the blame on Rome in case there were reprisals from the people (cf. Matt. 21:46; Mark 12:12; Luke 20:19).

It should be noted that God required Rome's involvement to fulfill biblical prophecy. The cross was foreshadowed in the Old Testament (Deut. 21:22–23; Num. 21:5–9; Ps. 22:1, 12–18; Isa. 53:5; Zech. 12:10) and explicitly predicted by Jesus in the Gospels (cf. Matt. 20:18–19; John 12:32). The Jewish people did not use crucifixion as a form of execution (traditionally carrying out capital punishment by stoning, cf. Josh. 7:25; Acts 7:58), as the Romans did.

To make Jesus appear to be a revolutionary (and thus a threat to Rome), the Jewish leaders accused Him of deceiving the nation, forbidding people to pay taxes and claiming to be a king who threatened Caesar (Luke 23:2). Those charges, if true, would have constituted serious crimes against the Roman government. But Jesus was no insurrectionist. He never advocated rebellion or even civil disobedience against Rome (cf. Matt. 5:21). Rather, He instructed His listeners to pay their taxes (Luke 20:21–25) and avoided those who tried to make Him king by force (cf. John 6:15). Though Jesus is the King of kings and will establish His earthly kingdom in the future (Rev. 19:15), He had no intention of fighting against the imperial Roman government or inciting His servants to do so (John 18:36; cf. Matt. 26:52–54).

As the governor of Judea, staying in Jerusalem during the Passover to maintain order and keep the peace, Pilate must have been made aware of who Jesus was and all He had done in the city that week, from His triumphal entry to His clearing of the temple. The Roman cohort that arrested Jesus after midnight on Friday morning would not have been dispatched without Pilate's knowledge or permission. Even so, the Roman governor never believed that Jesus posed a serious political threat, as the Sanhedrin alleged.

Standing before the governor, His face battered and bloody and His garments stained with dirt, sweat, and blood, the Man of Sorrows did not appear to be a king (cf. Isa. 53:3). Incredulous, **Pilate questioned Him, "Are You the King of the Jews?"** Though Pilate's words dripped with mocking sarcasm, Jesus responded directly and truthfully. **And He answered him, "It is as you say."** Mark's brief summation of the interchange between Jesus and Pilate is supplemented by details from the gospel of John:

Therefore Pilate entered again into the Praetorium, and summoned Jesus and said to Him, "Are You the King of the Jews?" Jesus answered, "Are you saying this on your own initiative, or did others tell you about Me?" Pilate answered, "I am not a Jew, am I? Your own nation and the chief priests delivered You to me; what have You done?" Jesus answered, "My kingdom is not of this world. If My kingdom were of this world, then My servants would be fighting so that I would not be handed over to the Jews; but as it is, My kingdom is not of this realm." Therefore Pilate said to Him, "So You are a king?" Jesus answered, "You say correctly that I am a king. For this I have been born, and for this I have come into the world, to testify to the truth. Everyone who is of the truth hears My voice." Pilate said to Him, "What is truth?" And when he had said this, he went out again to the Jews and said to them, "I find no guilt in Him." (John 18:33–39)

The pagan governor was an agnostic who questioned the very essence of reality. Yet, in spite of his doubt and derision, Pilate clearly did not believe Jesus was guilty of any capital crime (cf. Matt. 27:19, 24; Mark 15:14; Luke 23:14–15; John 18:38; 19:4, 6). The official findings of the Roman magistrate exonerated Christ of any guilt, and he repeatedly said that he found no fault in Him.

Upon hearing Pilate's findings, **the chief priests began to accuse Him harshly,** saying insistently, "He stirs up the people, teaching all over Judea, starting from Galilee even as far as this place" (Luke 23:5). But Jesus refused to respond to their false accusations (Matt. 27:12–14). **Then Pilate questioned Him again, saying, "Do You not answer? See how many charges they bring against You!"** The unrestrained anger and deceit of the Jews stood in stark contrast to the majestic silence of the Lord Jesus. Though they relentlessly and vehemently hurled lies at Him, **Jesus made no further answer; so Pilate was amazed.** The word **amazed** (from the Greek verb *thaumazō*) means "to marvel" or "to be in wonder." To Pilate's shock, though Jesus was falsely accused of serious crimes, He offered no testimony in self-defense. Christ's innocence had already been declared by the Roman governor (Luke 23:4; John 18:38), making any additional defense unnecessary. Moreover, His silence fulfilled the words of Old Testament prophecy (Isa. 42:1–2; 53:7).

THE SECOND ROMAN PHASE: BEFORE HEROD ANTIPAS

When the religious leaders mentioned Galilee in the midst of their vicious tirade against Jesus (Luke 23:5), Pilate "asked whether the man was a Galilean. And when he learned that He belonged to Herod's jurisdiction, he sent Him to Herod, who himself also was in Jerusalem at that time" (vv. 6–7). Hoping for help in deciding what to do with Jesus, Pilate reached out to the tetrarch of Galilee who similarly had arrived in Jerusalem for the Passover.

Herod Antipas, a son of Herod the Great (cf. Matt. 2:1, 19), was a regional monarch who ruled over Galilee and Perea, under the jurisdiction of Rome. When Herod the Great died (in 4 B.C.), his territory was divided among several of his sons, including Antipas. His brother Archelaus (cf. Matt. 2:22) was given the southern territories of Judea, Samaria, and Idumea. But due to cruelty and incompetence, Archelaus was deposed by Rome in A.D. 6 and replaced with a series of governors, one of whom was Pontius Pilate. The northern regions of Trachonitis and Ituraea went to Philip the Tetrarch (Luke 3:1), the half brother of Antipas.

That Herod Antipas was wicked and debauched is illustrated in Mark 6:14–29. Having illegally divorced his first wife, Antipas seduced and took the wife of his half brother Herod II (also known as Herod Philip I, not to be confused with Philip the Tetrarch) and married her. Because she was also his niece, his marriage to Herodias was both adulterous and incestuous. When John the Baptist boldly confronted the illicit union, Antipas had the faithful prophet imprisoned and later, during a drunken party, called for him to be beheaded.

When Herod Antipas heard about Jesus, he became superstitiously fearful that He might actually be John the Baptist, having risen from the dead to seek revenge. His initial interest in Jesus, then, was motivated by a desire to kill Him in case that was true (Luke 13:31–33). But the Lord had deliberately evaded Herod's clutches, meaning that this was the first time Herod saw Jesus face-to-face. Luke records the encounter in his gospel:

> Now Herod was very glad when he saw Jesus; for he had wanted to see
> Him for a long time, because he had been hearing about Him and was

hoping to see some sign performed by Him. And he questioned Him at some length; but He answered him nothing. And the chief priests and the scribes were standing there, accusing Him vehemently. And Herod with his soldiers, after treating Him with contempt and mocking Him, dressed Him in a gorgeous robe and sent Him back to Pilate. Now Herod and Pilate became friends with one another that very day; for before they had been enemies with each other. (Luke 23:8–12)

When Herod finally faced Jesus, he was unimpressed. Realizing He was not John in resurrected form, the regional despot quickly slid from fear to curiosity to ridicule. He instructed his soldiers to dress Jesus in a dazzling royal robe, treating the Son of God as a mock king and turning the whole affair into a bizarre joke for his own depraved amusement. Herod then returned Jesus to Pilate without adding any charges, thereby affirming the Lord's innocence despite the incessant accusations of the chief priests and scribes. Just as the Sadducees and Pharisees united in their hatred for Jesus, former enemies Herod and Pilate became friends that day, finding common ground in their scornful disdain for the Man of Sorrows.

THE THIRD ROMAN PHASE: BEFORE PILATE AGAIN

Now at the feast he used to release for them any one prisoner whom they requested. The man named Barabbas had been imprisoned with the insurrectionists who had committed murder in the insurrection. The crowd went up and began asking him to do as he had been accustomed to do for them. Pilate answered them, saying, "Do you want me to release for you the King of the Jews?" For he was aware that the chief priests had handed Him over because of envy. But the chief priests stirred up the crowd to ask him to release Barabbas for them instead. Answering again, Pilate said to them, "Then what shall I do with Him whom you call the King of the Jews?" They shouted back, "Crucify Him!" But Pilate said to them, "Why, what evil has He done?" But they shouted all the more, "Crucify Him!" Wishing to satisfy the crowd, Pilate released Barabbas for them, and after having Jesus scourged, he handed Him over to be crucified. (15:6–15)

When Herod sent Jesus back to Pilate, the Roman governor found himself in a difficult political position. Though he knew Jesus was innocent and wanted to preserve justice, he was concerned about offending the Jewish leaders. Pilate's tenure as governor had been fraught with brash missteps that angered his subjects. Any further incidents would likely result in his removal by Rome, thereby ending his political career.

Pilate's folly began when he allowed his soldiers to enter Jerusalem, carrying banners and standards bearing the image of Caesar. The Jews regarded such depictions as idolatrous. The people, incensed by Pilate's irreverent actions, traveled to his headquarters in Caesarea to complain. After five days of protests, Pilate finally agreed to meet them in the amphitheater. Rather than listening to their complaint, he surrounded them with his soldiers and threatened to have them slain on the spot if they would not stop demonstrating. The Jews refused to back down, defiantly baring their necks as a sign of their willingness to die. Pilate realized that he could not carry out his bluff, since such a massacre would have sparked a larger revolt. Humiliated, he reluctantly acquiesced and removed the images.

On a subsequent occasion, Pilate seized sacred funds from the temple treasury to build an aqueduct in Jerusalem. When the people rioted in response, the governor disguised his soldiers as civilians, sent them into the crowd, and commanded them to attack the protesters with swords and clubs. Luke 13:1 refers to a similar occasion in which Pilate's soldiers slaughtered a group of Galilean Jews while they were offering sacrifices in the temple. That kind of brutality only fueled the people's resentment toward Pilate.

Another conflict erupted when Pilate insisted on placing gold-covered shields honoring Tiberius Caesar in Herod's palace in Jerusalem. Again, the Jews were deeply offended, seeing the shields as idolatrous, and asked Pilate to remove them. He stubbornly refused. Finally, a Jewish delegation traveled to Rome and appealed directly to Caesar who, angered by Pilate's insensitive provocations of the people, ordered him to take the shields down.

By the time of Jesus' trial, Pilate had already put himself in a precarious political position. If another bad report about him reached Caesar, it would likely spell his removal from power. When the Jewish leaders told Pilate, "If you release this Man, you are no friend of Caesar" (John 19:12), he understood exactly what they were threatening. Years later, around A.D. 36, Pilate blundered again when he unwisely ordered his troops to ambush a group of Samaritan worshipers. When the people of Samaria complained to his immediate superior, the Roman legate of Syria, Pilate was summoned back to Rome. After that, little is known about him. According to tradition, he was banished in disgrace to Gaul where he eventually committed suicide.

In the trial of Jesus, Pilate attempted to retain some shred of justice by making a final appeal to the Jewish council, explaining that he had found no guilt at all in Jesus and neither had Herod (cf. Luke 23:14–15). Pilate knew there were no grounds on which to execute the Galilean. Accordingly, he still offered to punish Jesus unjustly in the hope that a little bloodshed would appease the vindictive prosecutors (v. 16). But they would not relent until He was crucified.

Hoping for a way out, Pilate appealed to an annual Passover tradition. As Mark explains, **Now at the feast he used to release for them any one prisoner whom they requested.** Each year, the governor would grant amnesty to one sentenced criminal of the people's choice as a way to cultivate goodwill and to demonstrate Rome's mercy. Pilate thought the crowd would select Jesus, thereby solving his dilemma. The other option was a violent **man named Barabbas,** a robber (John 18:40) and insurrectionist **who had been imprisoned with the insurrectionists** and who **had committed murder in the insurrection** (cf. Luke 23:18–19). It is likely that the wood that held Jesus, situated between the two thieves, was initially intended for Barabbas. Ironically, the name **Barabbas** means "son of the father." Here the lawbreaking son of a human father was being offered to the people in the place of the sinless Son of the divine Father.

Pilate was glad to oblige when **the crowd went up and began asking him to do as he had been accustomed to do for them.** Aware of Jesus' popularity from just a few days earlier (Mark 11:8–10), the governor was confident the crowd would never choose Barabbas. Pilate's plan was simple: when the multitude selected Jesus, there would be nothing the Jewish council could do. He could preserve justice and at the same time garner favor with the people. Thus, **Pilate answered them, saying, "Do you want me to release for you the King of the Jews?"** By calling Jesus the King of the Jews, Pilate intentionally sought to snub the religious leaders (cf. John 19:21), **for he was aware that the chief priests had handed Him over because of envy.** The governor recognized their motivation for executing Jesus had nothing to do with loyalty to Rome, and everything to do with safeguarding their influence and prestige with the people. Unmoved by any option and driven by jealousy and pride, they rejected their own Messiah, the Son of God, because He exposed their hypocrisy, challenged their authority, and threatened their religion and power. Put simply, He performed miracles, they could not; He proclaimed truth, they did not; He was from God, and they were not.

In the middle of the unfolding drama, Pilate received an unexpected message from his wife. Matthew 27:19 records the peculiar incident: "While he was sitting on the judgment seat, his wife sent him a message, saying, 'Have nothing to do with that righteous Man; for last night I suffered greatly in a dream because of Him.'" Her fear, having manifested itself in a vivid nightmare, prompted Pilate's wife to issue an urgent warning to her husband. (Perhaps she had been awake the night before when her husband's soldiers were dispatched to arrest Christ, causing her to be anxious while she slept.) Though Pilate ultimately disregarded the words of his wife, her frightened warning was another testimony to the innocence of the Lord Jesus.

While Pilate was considering his wife's intense concern, **the chief priests** were moving throughout the multitude, stirring **up the crowd to ask him to release Barabbas for them instead** of Jesus. Consequently, when Pilate posed his question to them, they exclaimed of Jesus, "Away with this man, and release for us Barabbas!" (Luke 23:18). **Answering again, Pilate said to them, "Then what shall I do with Him whom you call the King of the Jews?"** The governor was undoubtedly surprised by their ruthless response. Though the crowds on Monday exclaimed enthusiastic support for Jesus, this crowd on Friday **shouted back, "Crucify Him!"** Incredulous, **Pilate said to them, "Why, what evil has He done?"** The crowd's reply was loud, incessant, and relentless. **They shouted all the more, "Crucify Him!"**

As the mob began to riot (cf. Matt. 27:24), the mounting pressure on Pilate became overwhelming. Another uprising would end his political career, and the only means of quieting the demands of this angry mob was to sentence Jesus to death. Using a Jewish custom (Deut. 21:1–9) to symbolize his reluctance to grant their request, Pilate "took water and washed his hands in front of the crowd, saying, 'I am innocent of this Man's blood; see to that yourselves'" (Matt. 27:24). He had repeatedly declared the innocence of Christ, and now Pilate tried to maintain his own. In reality, he was blackmailed and fell guilty of deliberately perverting justice for the sake of political expediency. Unlike Pilate, those in the angry crowd gladly acknowledged their culpability in the death of Christ. "And all the people said, 'His blood shall be on us and our children!'" (Matt. 27:25; cf. Acts 2:22–23). Incredibly, at the very time when the nation was preparing to remember God's mercy and goodness through the Passover, the people were violently screaming for the death of His Son, and wanting to be held fully responsible for the crime.

The final phase of Jesus' Roman trial ended with a wavering politician caving to the violent demands of a raucous mob. **Wishing to satisfy the crowd, Pilate released Barabbas for them, and after having Jesus scourged, he handed Him over to be crucified** (15:15). To be **scourged** was to be whipped with a device known as a flagellum, consisting of a wooden handle with long leather thongs attached. The thongs, which were embedded with sharp pieces of bone and metal, were designed to rip the flesh to the bone. The victim would be tied to a post, his hands extended high over his head and his feet suspended off the ground so that his body was taught. As the scourge tore into his back, muscles would be lacerated, veins cut, and internal organs exposed. Intended to hasten death on the cross, scourging itself was sometimes fatal. After enduring such a debilitating form of torture, the Lord Jesus was handed **over to be crucified.**

With a final sentence, Pilate condemned Jesus to a cruel form of execution. Though it seemed as if Christ were on trial before Pilate, in reality, the Roman governor was on trial before the Son of God (cf. John 5:22–30; Acts 10:42; Rom. 2:16; 2 Tim. 4:1, 8). Though he lacked spiritual awareness, Pilate articulated the ultimate question that every human being must answer, "What shall I do with Him whom you call the King of the Jews?" (Mark 15:12). The destiny of every person is determined by what he or she does with Jesus Christ, the King of kings. Those who reject Him will face everlasting judgment (Heb. 6:2), but all who embrace Him as Lord and Savior will be rescued from divine wrath and receive salvation (Rom. 10:9). Tragically for Pilate and his coconspirators, their calloused antagonism and unbelief sealed their eternal destruction.

The Shameful Scorn of Jesus Christ
(Mark 15:16–32)

32

The soldiers took Him away into the palace (that is, the Praetorium), and they called together the whole Roman cohort. They dressed Him up in purple, and after twisting a crown of thorns, they put it on Him; and they began to acclaim Him, "Hail, King of the Jews!" They kept beating His head with a reed, and spitting on Him, and kneeling and bowing before Him. After they had mocked Him, they took the purple robe off Him and put His own garments on Him. And they led Him out to crucify Him. They pressed into service a passer-by coming from the country, Simon of Cyrene (the father of Alexander and Rufus), to bear His cross. Then they brought Him to the place Golgotha, which is translated, Place of a Skull. They tried to give Him wine mixed with myrrh; but He did not take it. And they crucified Him, and divided up His garments among themselves, casting lots for them to decide what each man should take. It was the third hour when they crucified Him. The inscription of the charge against Him read, "The King of the

Jews." They crucified two robbers with Him, one on His right and one on His left. [And the Scripture was fulfilled which says, "And He was numbered with transgressors."] Those passing by were hurling abuse at Him, wagging their heads, and saying, "Ha! You who are going to destroy the temple and rebuild it in three days, save Yourself, and come down from the cross!" In the same way the chief priests also, along with the scribes, were mocking Him among themselves and saying, "He saved others; He cannot save Himself. Let this Christ, the King of Israel, now come down from the cross, so that we may see and believe!" Those who were crucified with Him were also insulting Him. (15:16–32)

Although excruciating, the physical suffering experienced by Jesus was not what made His death unique. Tens of thousands died by crucifixion at the hands of the Persians, Greeks, and Romans, from the fourth century B.C. until the death of Jesus. The crown of thorns, the shard-laden whips, the iron nails, and the wooden cross all inflicted indescribable pain. Even on the night before His death, it was not the thought of bodily torture that traumatized Him in the garden. Instead, it was the anticipation of knowing that soon He would drink the full cup of divine wrath for the sins of all whom God has chosen for salvation (cf. Mark 14:33–37).

The four gospels are markedly restrained in their description of the physical torments Christ endured. In a day when crucifixion was a common form of capital punishment, detailed descriptions of its horrors were unnecessary since the sight of that torture was burned into the memories of everyone. What is emphasized by the New Testament writers, instead, is the irreverent mockery hurled at Jesus throughout His trial and execution. From the courtyard of Caiaphas to the judgment hall of Pilate to the cross itself, the Son of God was repeatedly treated with unrestrained scorn and derision. The blasphemous cruelty of Jesus' enemies stands in stunning contrast to the infinite mercy and grace of God, who allowed His Son to suffer unspeakable humiliation and death in order to save sinners, including blasphemers and murderers (1 Tim. 1:12–15; cf. Acts 2:36–38; 3:14–16; 4:10–12).

As noted in the previous chapters, Jesus' trial consisted of two segments, one Jewish and one Roman, each of which involved three phases.

During the Jewish portion of His trial, the Lord was interrogated by Annas (John 18:19–24), put on trial by Caiaphas (Mark 14:55–65), and then officially condemned by the Sanhedrin after daybreak on Friday morning (Mark 15:1; Luke 22:66–71). The Roman trial began with Pilate (Mark 15:1–5), who repeatedly declared Jesus to be innocent (cf. Matt. 27:19, 24; Mark 15:14; Luke 23:14–15; John 18:38; 19:4, 6). Upon learning that He was from Galilee, Pilate sent Jesus to Herod, who had jurisdiction there. The petty ruler dressed Him in a royal robe to mock Him before sending Him back to Pilate (Luke 23:8–12). In an attempt to release Him, Pilate invoked his annual goodwill custom during the Passover of granting pardon to a condemned criminal of the people's choice (Mark 15:6–10). The crowd, agitated by the scribes and Pharisees, demanded that Jesus be crucified and a murderous insurrectionist named Barabbas be set free (vv. 11–13). The governor, unable to pacify the angry mob, capitulated and sent Jesus to be scourged in preparation for His execution (v. 15).

In describing the crucifixion of Christ in this section (15:16–32), Mark focuses on the blasphemous scoffers who derided the Lord Jesus as He was taken from Pilate's judgment hall to the cross. Against the backdrop of the soldiers' comedic parody and the sneering participants, the suffering Savior is seen ingloriously enduring the punishment for sin in obedience to His Father's will (cf. Phil. 2:8).

The Soldiers' Parody

The soldiers took Him away into the palace (that is, the Praetorium), and they called together the whole Roman cohort. They dressed Him up in purple, and after twisting a crown of thorns, they put it on Him; and they began to acclaim Him, "Hail, King of the Jews!" They kept beating His head with a reed, and spitting on Him, and kneeling and bowing before Him. After they had mocked Him, they took the purple robe off Him and put His own garments on Him. And they led Him out to crucify Him. (15:16–20)

Pilate reluctantly acquiesced to the crowd's bloodthirsty demands even though he knew Jesus was innocent. After the unjust and illegal order was given for Him to be scourged (v. 15), **the soldiers took Him away into the palace (that is, the Praetorium).** The **palace** (from the Greek *aulē*, meaning "courtyard" or "walled space"), which Mark equates with **the Praetorium,** likely referred to the headquarters of the commanding officer of the Roman military (in this case Pilate), located in the Fortress Antonia. Pilate's headquarters were normally located in Caesarea but shifted to Jerusalem when he was staying there.

After scourging Jesus, the soldiers continued to torture Him with mockery, insults, and abuse. (For a description of Roman scourging, see the previous chapter in this volume.) The Lord's face was already battered and swollen from being repeatedly hit (Mark 14:64–65). His lacerated back was also bleeding profusely from the wounds inflicted by scourging (15:15). Yet the calloused soldiers turned His suffering into a parody, likely borrowing the idea from Herod's men (Luke 23:11). **They called together the whole Roman cohort** (a full cohort consisted of six hundred soldiers), inviting their comrades to join in the sadistic charade. In order to give Him the appearance of royalty, **they dressed Him up in purple,** a reference to the scarlet colored mantle that comprised part of a Roman soldier's uniform. The soldiers undoubtedly draped an old, sun-faded robe across the bloodied back of Jesus. Though it once was scarlet (Matt. 27:28), its color had faded over time to produce a purplish hue (cf. John 19:2).

After twisting a crown of sharp **thorns,** intended to imitate the golden laurel wreath worn by Caesar, **they put it** on His head with crushing force, lacerating His skull and causing blood to flow down His brow and into His face. Matthew adds that in dressing Him up like a king in their little comedy, they put a reed in His hand to imitate a scepter. Then "they knelt down before Him and mocked Him" (Matt. 27:29). To complete their sadistic joke, the solders **began to acclaim Him, "Hail, King of the Jews!"** The Sanhedrin had scorned Him as a prophet just a few hours earlier (Matt. 26:68); now, Roman soldiers taunted Him as a joker-king. Mercilessly, **they kept beating His head with a reed** (the Greek word *kalamos* refers to a stick), **and spitting on Him, and kneeling and bowing before Him.** In Mark 10:34, Jesus had predicted that the Messiah would be treated this way: "They will mock Him and spit on Him, and scourge Him and kill Him, and three days later He will rise again." That prediction was in accordance with Old Testament prophecy. Speaking of the Suffering Servant, Isaiah records, "I gave My back to those who strike Me, and My cheeks to those who pluck out the beard; I did not cover My face from humiliation and spitting" (Isa. 50:6).

John's gospel provides additional details regarding the mistreatment Jesus endured at the hands of Pilate's soldiers. After they scourged Him, crowned Him, mocked Him, and repeatedly slapped Him in the face, the soldiers brought Jesus back to Pilate who paraded Him once more before the Sanhedrin (John 19:4–5). Still wanting to release Jesus, the governor hoped that displaying Him in His weakened and bloodied condition would invoke pity from the chief priests and scribes (cf. Luke 23:16). But they would not relent in screaming for His death. Pilate responded indignantly, "Take Him yourselves and crucify Him, for I find no guilt in Him" (John 19:6). But the Jewish leaders insisted that Rome carry out the execution. Their response repeated their primary charge of blasphemy to indict and convict Jesus and, by implication, put the onus back on Pilate to execute: "We have a law, and by that law He ought to die because He made Himself out to be the Son of God" (v. 7).

Hearing that Jesus claimed to be the Son of God, the pagan governor became increasingly afraid (v. 8; cf. Matt. 27:19). He returned to Jesus and asked Him,

> "Where are You from?" But Jesus gave him no answer. So Pilate said to Him, "You do not speak to me? Do You not know that I have authority to release You, and I have authority to crucify You?" Jesus answered, "You would have no authority over Me, unless it had been given you from above; for this reason he who delivered Me to you has the greater sin." As a result of this Pilate made efforts to release Him. (vv. 9b–12a)

Though Pilate recognized Jesus was innocent of any crime or threat, the chief priests and scribes intensified their manipulative tactics, threatening to report Pilate to Caesar if he let Jesus go free: "If you release this Man, you are no friend of Caesar; everyone who makes himself out to be a king opposes Caesar" (v. 12). Based on his dismal record as governor (for details on how Pilate had previously offended the Jewish people, see the previous chapter in this volume), Pilate knew that one more scandal would likely result in his removal by Rome, thus ending his political career. Crumbling under the pressure, he capitulated.

When Pilate heard these words, he brought Jesus out, and sat down on the judgment seat at a place called The Pavement, but in Hebrew, Gabbatha. Now it was the day of preparation for the Passover; it was about the sixth hour. And he said to the Jews, "Behold, your King!" So they cried out, "Away with Him, away with Him, crucify Him!" Pilate said to them, "Shall I crucify your King?" The chief priests answered, "We have no king but Caesar." (vv. 13–15)

The spiritual leaders of Israel and self-proclaimed representatives of God, in a tragic twist, declared their loyalty to a pagan emperor and son of the devil while simultaneously clamoring for the murder of the Messiah and Son of God.

Mark picks the account back up at this point, explaining that **after they had mocked Him, they took the purple robe off Him and put His own garments on Him. And they led Him out to crucify Him.** The Mosaic law required executions to be performed outside the city (Num. 15:35), which is why Jesus was taken outside the gates of Jerusalem.

THE SAVIOR'S PUNISHMENT

They pressed into service a passer-by coming from the country, Simon of Cyrene (the father of Alexander and Rufus), to bear His cross. Then they brought Him to the place Golgotha, which is translated, Place of a Skull. They tried to give Him wine mixed with myrrh; but He did not take it. And they crucified Him, and divided up His garments among themselves, casting lots for them to decide what each man should take. It was the third hour when they crucified Him. (15:21–25)

As a prisoner condemned to death, Jesus was required to carry His cross (i.e., the heavy horizontal crossbeam) to the place of execution. He carried it for a distance (John 19:17), perhaps as far as the city gate, but was eventually unable to continue, having been weakened by sleeplessness, blood loss, and the severe injuries inflicted on Him during His scourging.

To keep the procession moving, the Roman soldiers **pressed into service a passer-by coming from the country.** Spontaneously selecting **Simon of Cyrene** out of the crowd, the soldiers conscripted him **to bear** Jesus' **cross.** The port city of **Cyrene** was located on the North African coast in modern-day Libya. A vibrant trade center, the city was also home to a large Jewish population (cf. Acts 2:10; 6:9). Simon, like so many others, was a Jewish pilgrim who had traveled to Jerusalem to observe the Passover.

The soldiers' choice of Simon may seem random, but in reality it was anything but. God's invisible hand was sovereignly at work, providentially using the witless actions of Roman soldiers to draw this hapless bystander to saving faith (cf. John 6:44). Mark identifies Simon as **the father of Alexander and Rufus,** an unexplained reference that indicates Mark's readers were familiar with Simon's sons. Since Mark wrote for Gentile believers in Rome, Alexander and Rufus were almost certainly active in the church there. That conclusion is supported by Paul's mention of Rufus and his mother (Simon's wife) in Romans 16:13. Wondrously, the man who carried Jesus' cross came to embrace Him in saving faith, as did his wife and sons.

As the Lord was being escorted to the crucifixion site, He gave a final public message. As Luke explains,

> And following Him was a large crowd of the people, and of women who were mourning and lamenting Him. But Jesus turning to them said, "Daughters of Jerusalem, stop weeping for Me, but weep for your-selves and for your children. For behold, the days are coming when they will say, 'Blessed are the barren, and the wombs that never bore, and the breasts that never nursed.' Then they will begin to say to the mountains, 'Fall on us,' and to the hills, 'Cover us.' For if they do these things when the tree is green, what will happen when it is dry?" (Luke 23:27–31)

Christ's somber response to these weeping women (who were likely professional mourners, cf. Mark 5:38–40) served as a prophetic warning of the destruction that would fall on Jerusalem in A.D. 70. Beyond that, His words also previewed the coming devastation of the great tribulation that will occur at the end of the age (cf. Mark 13:6–37).

The procession finally reached its destination, as the soldiers

brought Him to the place Golgotha, which is translated, Place of a Skull. Located outside the city gates (cf. Heb. 13:12), along a major highway (so that the crucified victims would be visible by passersby), and possibly on a hill, **Golgotha** was likely a site where crucifixions were regularly performed. The Aramaic name literally means **Skull**; and is equivalent to the Latin term calvaria, from which the word "Calvary" is derived. Some scholars believe the place was so named because it was situated atop a hill that looked like a skull. Others have suggested that the skulls of crucified victims were left lying on the ground, though it seems unlikely the Jewish people would have tolerated such a practice (cf. Num. 19:11). Whatever the actual origin of the name, Golgotha was a place intrinsically linked with horrific and very public death.

Before nailing Jesus to the cross and setting it upright, the soldiers **tried to give Him wine mixed with myrrh; but He did not take it.** Matthew's parallel account explains that "after tasting it he was unwilling to drink it" (Matt. 27:34). **Myrrh** was a narcotic that was also used as an anointing oil (Ex. 30:23) and a perfume (Ps. 45:8; Prov. 7:17; Matt. 2:11; John 19:39). Based on Proverbs 31:6, the Jews had a custom of offering crucifixion victims a type of pain-deadening medication (cf. Ps. 69:21). But Jesus, wanting to maintain full awareness as He completed His atoning work, refused to drink it.

Mark articulates what happened next with one very simple phrase: **and they crucified Him.** A well-known form of execution in the ancient world, crucifixion needed no additional description for Mark's original audience to understand its horrors. The Roman writer Cicero described it as "the cruelest and most hideous punishment possible." Apparently originating in Persia, crucifixion was later used by the Romans as a brutal means of inflicting death on its victims while also deterring other would-be criminals. It is estimated that, by the time of Christ, Rome had crucified some 30,000 people in Israel alone. After the fall of Jerusalem in A.D. 70, so many Jewish rebels were killed by crucifixion that the Romans ran short of lumber to make crosses.

Crucifixion victims were first scourged (cf. Mark 15:15), resulting in severe injuries and massive blood loss that hastened death on the cross. Even so, crucifixion was a prolonged form of dying designed to induce maximum suffering and pain. When the condemned criminal arrived at the place of execution, he was forced onto his back and nailed to the cross as it lay on the ground. The nails, measuring five to seven inches long and resembling modern railroad spikes, were driven through the wrists (rather than the palms of the hand) in order to support the full weight of the victim's slumping body. The victim's feet were then secured with a single spike, with the knees bent so that he could push himself up in order to breathe. The nails would tear through the nerves in the wrists and feet, causing severe bolts of pain throughout the victim's impaled arms and legs.

The cross was then slowly raised until it was vertical. The foot of the cross was subsequently dropped into place in a deep posthole, landing with a reverberating thud that sent excruciating pain jolting through the victim's body. Though the wounds from the nails caused severe agony, they were not intended to be fatal. The normal cause of death was slow suffocation. The hanging position of the body constricted the diaphragm, which made it impossible to breathe. In order to get air, the victim had to push himself up, placing his weight on the nail wounds in his feet and wrists, and rubbing his lacerated back against the rough wood of the cross. As the victim grew tired, experienced muscle spasms, and became overwhelmed by the pain, his ability to breathe was increasingly hindered. As a result, carbon dioxide would build up in his bloodstream and he would eventually suffocate to death. If needed, soldiers could hasten asphyxiation by breaking the victim's legs (cf. John 19:31–32). (For more detail on the agonies of crucifixion, see John MacArthur, *The Murder of Jesus* [Nashville: Thomas Nelson, 2004], chap. 10.)

After securing Jesus on the cross, the soldiers **divided up His garments among themselves, casting lots for them to decide what each man should take.** Traditional Jewish apparel included an inner garment, an outer garment (or tunic), a belt, sandals, and a headpiece. Though Mark does not specify how Jesus' clothing was divided, the gospel of John provides some additional details:

> Then the soldiers, when they had crucified Jesus, took His outer garments and made four parts, a part to every soldier and also the tunic; now the tunic was seamless, woven in one piece. So they said to one another, "Let us not tear it, but cast lots for it, to decide whose it shall be"; this was to fulfill the Scripture: "They divided My outer garments

among them, and for My clothing they cast lots." Therefore the soldiers did these things. (John 19:23–25)

Having distributed His clothing among themselves as prophesied (cf. Ps. 22:18), the soldiers posted a watch around the cross. The squad, known as a *quaternion* because it consisted of four guards, was required to stay until the crucified victim was dead, keeping anyone away who might try to rescue or ease the suffering of the condemned criminal.

Mark notes that **it was the third hour** (or 9:00 A.M.; the Jewish method of reckoning the hours of the day began about 6:00 A.M.) **when they crucified Him.** The statement in John 19:14, that it was "about the sixth hour" when Pilate sentenced Jesus earlier that morning, does not contradict what Mark says here. John was using the Roman method of reckoning time, which began counting hours at midnight. Consequently, the sixth hour in John's gospel referred to 6:00 A.M, three hours before Jesus was nailed to the cross.

Just the night before, Jesus had been celebrating the Passover meal with His disciples in the upper room. The events of Jesus' crucifixion transpired very quickly; but they did so according to God's predetermined timetable, in which the Lamb of God would celebrate a final meal with His disciples on Thursday night, and then die at the same time the Passover lambs were being slaughtered on Friday afternoon.

THE SNEERING PARTICIPANTS

The inscription of the charge against Him read, "The King of the Jews." They crucified two robbers with Him, one on His right and one on His left. [And the Scripture was fulfilled which says, "And He was numbered with transgressors."] Those passing by were hurling abuse at Him, wagging their heads, and saying, "Ha! You who are going to destroy the temple and rebuild it in three days, save Yourself, and come down from the cross!" In the same way the chief priests also, along with the scribes, were mocking Him among themselves and saying, "He saved others; He cannot save Himself. Let this Christ, the King of Israel, now come down

from the cross, so that we may see and believe!" Those who were crucified with Him were also insulting Him. (15:26–32)

Above the head of the crucified victim, a wooden board would be fastened to the cross that delineated his crimes. In the case of Jesus, **the inscription of the charge against Him read, "The King of the Jews."** A comparison of the four gospels reveals that the full inscription was, "This is Jesus of Nazareth, the King of the Jews." It was written in Aramaic, Hebrew, and Greek (John 19:20). That was not the charge the Jewish leaders wanted Pilate to write (v. 21), but he refused to change it (v. 22), seeing it as a means of vengeance aimed at the chief priests and scribes who had blackmailed him into condemning an innocent man (cf. Luke 23:4, 14, 15, 22).

During the course of Jesus' trial, the Jewish leaders had leveled at least seven indictments against Him (cf. Mark 15:4). They alleged, first, that He was a threat to destroy the temple (Mark 14:58); second, that He was an evildoer (John 18:30); third, that He was misleading the nation (Luke 23:2); fourth, that He was forbidding people to pay taxes (Luke 23:2); fifth, that He was claiming to be a king who threatened Caesar (Luke 23:2); sixth, that He was stirring up the people and fomenting an insurrection (Luke 23:5); and finally, that He made Himself out to be the Son of God (John 19:7). Of those accusations, only the final one was based in fact. Jesus indeed claimed to be the Son of God because He was (cf. Mark 1:1). But in the twisted perception of the Sanhedrin, that claim constituted blasphemy, a capital offense (Lev. 24:16; Mark 14:63–64). Yet, of the charges Pilate could have listed, he intentionally selected the one he knew would be most offensive.

Perhaps wanting to goad them even further, Pilate had the "King of the Jews" **crucified** like a common criminal alongside **two** low-life **robbers;** they were executed **with Him, one on His right and one on His left.** The term translated **robbers** (from the Greek word *lēstēs*) indicates that these men were not petty thieves but fierce bandits who plundered and stole, leaving a trail of abuse and desolation in their wake. They may have been involved in the murderous rebellion led by Barabbas (cf. Luke 23:19), for which they had been sentenced to death. The statement in verse 28 (that **the Scripture was fulfilled which says,**

"And He was numbered with transgressors") is not in the earliest manuscripts, so was likely not part of Mark's original gospel, causing modern translations to place it in brackets. Nonetheless, it is true that the prediction made in Isaiah 53:12 regarding the Suffering Servant finds its fulfillment here. Whatever his motives, Pilate's decision to execute Jesus with criminals accorded perfectly with Old Testament prophecy (cf. Acts 4:27–28).

Adding to the agonizing pain of the cross was the shame and disgrace of being publicly executed in such a degrading fashion (cf. Heb. 12:2). Everything about crucifixion was designed to humiliate and debase its victims, sending a clear message about the repercussions of being an enemy of Rome. Moreover, the Jews regarded anyone hanging on a tree or a cross to be cursed by God (Deut. 21:23; Isa. 53:4, 10; Gal. 3:10–13), which heightened their disdain for those who were crucified (cf. 1 Cor. 1:23).

Those in the crowd who had screamed hours earlier for Jesus' death (15:13–14) joined the religious leaders in trailing Him to the site of His execution. As they were **passing by,** they **were hurling abuse at Him** and **wagging their heads,** a gesture of hatred and scorn (cf. 2 Kings 19:21; Pss. 22:7; 44:14; 109:25; Jer. 18:16; Lam. 2:15). Repeating the false charges raised against Jesus before the Sanhedrin (Mark 14:58; cf. John 2:19), the people, many of whom had praised Him when He arrived in Jerusalem on Monday (Mark 11:8–10), taunted Him on Friday by **saying, "Ha! You who are going to destroy the temple and rebuild it in three days, save Yourself, and come down from the cross!"** Their screams of contempt evidenced the astonishing and wicked fickleness of unbelieving hearts (cf. John 2:24–25; 6:66).

Having instigated the crucifixion as the Lord predicted they would (Mark 8:31; 14:43), the Jewish authorities continued to fan the flames of hate and abuse. As Mark explains, **In the same way the chief priests also, along with the scribes,** representing the leadership of the Sanhedrin, **were mocking Him among themselves.** According to the parallel passage in Luke 23:35, "The rulers were sneering at Him." The word "sneering" literally means to lift up one's nose in disdain (cf. Matt. 27:41). Their harassment of Jesus had begun at the house of the high priest (Mark 14:55, 65) and continued even after He was nailed to the cross. Their mistreatment of the Messiah was foretold by David in Psalm 22:7–8:"All who see me sneer at me; they separate with the lip, they wag the head, saying, 'Commit yourself to the Lord; let Him deliver him; let Him rescue him, because He delights in him.'" With a gloating tone of derision, they were **saying, "He saved others; He cannot save Himself."** Their scornful taunt was not an admission of Christ's ability to save but rather a sarcastic denial of His divine power. How could He claim to save others, they jeered, when He could not even rescue Himself? They knew about His miracles, which they could not deny (John 11:47). Yet in spite of His astonishing works, they willfully refused to believe in Him (cf. John 5:36; 10:38). Though the mockers intended their words as an insult, they unintentionally hit on a profound gospel truth: it is because the Lord Jesus submissively refused to rescue Himself from the cross that He is able to save others from sin and death (cf. Mark 10:45; Rom. 5:19; Phil. 2:8; Heb. 2:9–10; 5:7–8).

Continuing their tirade of verbal abuse, they cried out, **"Let this Christ, the King of Israel, now come down from the cross, so that we may see and believe!"** They purposely ignored the countless miracles Jesus had performed throughout His ministry and claimed they would believe if He performed but one more (cf. Mark 8:11–12). But their declaration was nothing more than a hypocritical and sarcastic taunt. After He died, Jesus' body was taken down from the cross and laid in a tomb. When He rose from the dead on the third day, just as He had predicted He would, the chief priests and scribes still did not believe (cf. Luke 16:30–31). Instead, they bribed the Roman soldiers to spread lies about what happened, claiming the disciples stole Jesus' body (Matt. 28:11–15). No miracle would have persuaded them to believe. They loved their sin far too much.

Incredibly, **those who were crucified with Him were also insulting Him.** The two thieves on either side of Jesus joined the hostile crowd in mocking the Son of God, even though they were being justly executed in the same way. As the parallel passage in Matthew 27:44 explains,"the robbers who had been crucified with Him were also insulting Him with the same words"as they heard from the leaders and the surrounding crowd. The hardened criminals were no doubt accustomed to berating and abusing others. In spite of their imminent deaths, they joined in the blasphemous ridicule of the Son of God.

THE SINNER'S PLEA

As noted at the beginning of this chapter, it was against that dark backdrop of venomous hate that the grace and mercy of God was displayed. The Father could have destroyed the blasphemers on the spot and rescued His Son from the cross. Instead, He was pleased to crush Him and put Him to death (Isa. 53:10), so that He might rescue many of those very blasphemers, along with countless others, from sin and eternal destruction.

Of the thieves who mocked Him, one became a trophy of God's grace that very day. Luke recounts the dramatic account:

> One of the criminals who were hanged there was hurling abuse at Him, saying, "Are You not the Christ? Save Yourself and us!" But the other answered, and rebuking him said, "Do you not even fear God, since you are under the same sentence of condemnation? And we indeed are suffering justly, for we are receiving what we deserve for our deeds; but this man has done nothing wrong." And he was saying, "Jesus, remember me when You come in Your kingdom!" And He said to him, "Truly I say to you, today you shall be with Me in Paradise." (Luke 23:39–43)

Of the soldiers who mistreated Him, a centurion would soon realize, "Truly this man was the Son of God!" (Mark 15:39). Of the people in the crowd who scorned Him, many would believe on the day of Pentecost and in the subsequent weeks and months (cf. Acts 2:37–38, 41; 4:4; 6:1). Even many of the priests of Israel, Acts 6:7 reports, "were becoming obedient to the faith."

The apostle Paul was a former Pharisee who violently persecuted the church out of antagonism toward the Lord Jesus. Yet, by His grace, God transformed that murderous blasphemer into a courageous missionary. As Paul explained to Timothy:

> I thank Christ Jesus our Lord, who has strengthened me, because He considered me faithful, putting me into service, even though I was

formerly a blasphemer and a persecutor and a violent aggressor....It is a trustworthy statement, deserving full acceptance, that Christ Jesus came into the world to save sinners, among whom I am foremost of all. (1 Tim. 1:12–13, 15)

The salvation of the blasphemer Paul, like every sinner, is only possible because the Lord Jesus "bore our sins in His body on the cross" (1 Peter 2:24). In keeping with His eternal purpose of redemption, God the Father "made Him who knew no sin to be sin on our behalf, so that we might become the righteousness of God in Him" (2 Cor. 5:21). Because of His substitutionary sacrifice, all who savingly place their faith in Him will be saved from divine wrath and receive eternal life (cf. John 20:31; Rom. 10:9–10; Acts 16:31).

God Visits Calvary
(Mark 15:33–41)

33

When the sixth hour came, darkness fell over the whole land until the ninth hour. At the ninth hour Jesus cried out with a loud voice, "Eloi, Eloi, lama sabachthani?" which is translated, "My God, My God, why have You forsaken Me?" When some of the bystanders heard it, they began saying, "Behold, He is calling for Elijah." Someone ran and filled a sponge with sour wine, put it on a reed, and gave Him a drink, saying, "Let us see whether Elijah will come to take Him down." And Jesus uttered a loud cry, and breathed His last. And the veil of the temple was torn in two from top to bottom. When the centurion, who was standing right in front of Him, saw the way He breathed His last, he said, "Truly this man was the Son of God!" There were also some women looking on from a distance, among whom were Mary Magdalene, and Mary the mother of James the Less and Joses, and Salome. When He was in Galilee, they used to follow Him and minister to Him; and there were many other women who came up with Him to Jerusalem. (15:33–41)

In all of human history, the murder of Jesus constitutes the most blasphemous act of evil ever committed, as wicked men subjected God the Son to humiliation, torture, and death (cf. Acts 3:14–15). The second-century church father Melito of Sardis expressed that shocking reality with these poignant words:

> He that hung up the earth in space was Himself hanged up; He that fixed the heavens was fixed with nails; He that bore up the earth was born up on a tree; the Lord of all was subjected to ignominy in a naked body—God put to death! … [I]n order that He might not be seen, the luminaries turned away, and the day became darkened—because they slew God, who hung naked on the tree. . . . This is He who made the heaven and the earth, and in the beginning, together with the Father, fashioned man; who was announced by means of the law and the prophets; who put on a bodily form in the Virgin; who was hanged upon the tree. (Melito, 5. Translation from Alexander Roberts and James Donaldson, *Ante-Nicene Fathers* [repr., Peabody, MA: Hendrickson Publishers, 2012], VIII:757)

Incredibly, despite their outrageous crimes, the perpetrators were not instantly consumed by divine wrath. Unbeknownst to them, the murder of Jesus was necessary in God's eternal plan of redemption (cf. Phil. 2:6–8). The Father sovereignly superseded the evil deeds of sinful men to accomplish His saving purposes (Acts 4:27–28; cf. Gen. 50:20).

Thus, when God came to Calvary, it was not to protect His Son from evildoers but to punish His Son on their behalf. As Isaiah prophesied of the Messiah, "The Lord was pleased to crush Him, putting Him to grief" in order that "as a result of the anguish of His soul," He might justify many by bearing their iniquities (Isa. 53:10–11; cf. Zech. 12:10). The righteous One was put to death as a substitute for the unrighteous (1 Peter 3:18), becoming a curse for sinners so that He might redeem them from the penalty for violators of the law, which is eternal death (Gal. 3:13).

The Father's presence at Calvary was particularly evident during the final three hours of Jesus' crucifixion, the period of time depicted in these verses (Mark 15:33–41). In this section, Mark describes the consummation of the Savior's suffering, the confession of an awestruck soldier, and the confusion of Christ's loyal sympathizers.

THE CONSUMMATION OF THE SAVIOR'S SUFFERING

When the sixth hour came, darkness fell over the whole land until the ninth hour. At the ninth hour Jesus cried out with a loud voice, "Eloi, Eloi, lama sabachthani?" which is translated, "My God, My God, why have You forsaken Me?" When some of the bystanders heard it, they began saying, "Behold, He is calling for Elijah." Someone ran and filled a sponge with sour wine, put it on a reed, and gave Him a drink, saying, "Let us see whether Elijah will come to take Him down." And Jesus uttered a loud cry, and breathed His last. And the veil of the temple was torn in two from top to bottom. (15:33–38)

Verses 33–38 depict the highpoint of salvation history, the atoning death of the Lord Jesus Christ. His sacrificial work of redemption was planned by God in eternity past (Titus 1:2; 1 Peter 1:18–21; cf. Eph. 1:4; 2 Tim. 1:9) and will be celebrated in heaven through eternity future (Rev. 5:6–12; cf. 22:3). It was there, at Calvary, that the long-awaited and acceptable Lamb of God died to satisfy divine righteousness by paying sin's penalty in full for all who would believe in Him (cf. Col. 2:14).

According to the Jewish reckoning of time (which began counting hours from sunrise, about 6:00 A.M.), **when the sixth hour came,** it was noon and Jesus had already been on the cross for three hours (cf. Mark 15:25). The Gospels record three statements Jesus made during that three-hour period. First, evidencing His infinite compassion and mercy, He prayed for His persecutors, saying, "Father, forgive them; for they do not know what they are doing" (Luke 23:34). One of the two crucified thieves who had been mocking Jesus, undoubtedly hearing Christ's words about forgiveness, became convicted and sought the divine pardon Jesus offered. Second, the Son of God responded to the sinner's faith with the promise of eternal life, saying, "Truly I say to you, today you shall be with Me in Paradise" (23:43). Third, the Lord also took a moment to care for His widowed mother. Looking down from the cross, "Jesus then saw His mother, and the disciple whom He loved standing nearby, He said to His mother, 'Woman, behold, your son!' Then He said to the disciple, 'Behold, your mother!' From that hour the disciple took her into his own household" (John 19:26–27).

As the noonday sun reached its zenith, a supernatural **darkness** suddenly **fell over the whole land until the ninth hour** (i.e., 3:00 P.M.). The geographical extent of the three hours of **darkness** is not described in the Gospels, though the Greek word *gē* (**land**) can refer to the entire earth. Reports from several of the early church fathers (including Tertullian and Origen) suggest that the darkness extended beyond the borders of Israel and throughout the Roman Empire.

The cause of the darkness was not Satan (since God alone possesses such cosmic power, cf. Job 9:7–8; Isa. 45:6–7; Ezek. 32:7–8). Nor was it a naturally occurring eclipse (since solar eclipses only occur during a new moon and Passover was always celebrated at full moon). Rather, the darkness was caused by God the Father Himself. The Old Testament often depicts God's glorious presence in terms of blazing light (cf. Pss. 18:12, 28; 27:1; 104:2; Isa. 60:20; Ezek. 8:2; 10:4; 43:2; Dan. 7:9; Hab. 3:4; Mic. 7:8). Yet it also describes the manifestation of His presence in terms of darkness (cf. Gen. 15:12; Ex. 10:21–22; 19:16–18; 20:18–21; Ps. 18:11; Isa. 5:30; 13:10–11), especially in association with His judgment (cf. Joel 1:15; 2:1–2, 10–11, 30; Amos 5:20; 8:9; Zeph. 1:14–15). Hell, for example, is characterized by eternal darkness because it is a place of divine wrath and everlasting punishment for sin (cf. Matt. 8:12; 22:13; 25:30; cf. 2 Peter 2:4; Jude 6).

The darkness at Calvary did not represent the absence of God but His holy, terrifying presence. The Father descended in judgment on Golgotha in thick gloom as the divine executioner to unleash His fury not against sinners but against the sin bearer (cf. 1 Peter 2:24). The full weight of God's wrath was poured out on the Son of God (cf. Isa. 53:5), as the spotless Lamb of God was sacrificed for sin so that sinners might be justified through Him (2 Cor. 5:21; Heb. 9:28; cf. Rom. 4:25; 1 Cor. 15:3; 1 John 4:10). Moved by His perfect justice, God's infinite wrath released an eternity of punishment on the incarnate Son who, as an infinite and eternal person, absorbed the tortures of hell in a finite span of time. This was the dreadful cup of divine judgment that Jesus anticipated while sweating blood in the garden of Gethsemane (Mark 14:36; Luke 22:44).

At the ninth hour (3:00 P.M.), the judgment ended and the darkness began to lift. As it did, the Lord **Jesus** for a fourth time spoke from the cross.This time, He **cried out with a loud voice** as if calling heaven to hear His painful shout. He addressed His Father, saying, **"Eloi, Eloi, lama sabachthani?" which is translated, "My God, My God, why have You forsaken Me?"** Those words are from the Aramaic version of Psalm 22:1 (the parallel text in Matt. 27:46 gives the same phrase in Hebrew).With intense agony, the Son of God experienced that which He had never known before, the abandonment of His Father.That separation was not one of nature or essence; the Lord Jesus never ceased to be the second member of the Trinity. Rather, it was a separation of the loving communion He had eternally known with the Father (cf.John 17:21–24).

This is the only place in the gospel record where Jesus referred to God by any other title than "Father."The repeated name, **My God, My God,** expressed the Son's profound affection and longing for the Father, mingled with the agony and pain of His separation from Him. Unmistakably, the Father visited Calvary in massive judgment, but He was absent in comfort. Unlike the temptations Jesus endured in the wilderness and the garden of Gethsemane, after which the Father sent angels to minister to His Son (Mark 1:13; Luke 22:43), no relief was given to Jesus on the cross. Such is a picture of hell, in which the full fury of God's wrath is ever present, but the comfort of His love and compassion is utterly absent. On the cross, the Lord Jesus endured the full reality of hell's torments, including being forsaken by His Father.

The pain of the Father's absence was made more acute by the hostile presence of the religious leaders and the crowd who continued to harass Jesus until He died. **When some of the bystanders heard it, they began saying, "Behold, He is calling for Elijah."** It was not that they misunderstood what Jesus said, since Psalm 22:1 was a well-known portion of Scripture. Rather, they were responding to His anguished cry with more mockery. Malachi 4:5–6 predicted that Elijah, or a prophet like him, would come as the forerunner to the Messiah (cf. Matt. 11:13–14). By accusing Jesus of calling for Elijah, the derisive bystanders were scornfully taunting Him, asserting that if He really were the Messiah, perhaps Elijah would appear to rescue Him.

When Jesus cried out, "I am thirsty" (John 19:28; cf. Ps. 69:21), **someone ran and filled a sponge with sour wine, put it on a reed, and gave Him a drink.** Yet, what might first seem like an act of mercy was actually motivated by ridicule and derision. The one who offered Him the drink of cheap wine simultaneously mocked Jesus, **saying, "Let us see whether Elijah will come to take Him down."** The ungrateful derision of these sinners formed an ugly backdrop for the sin-bearing work of the Savior. As the prophet Isaiah had written seven centuries earlier:

> He was despised and forsaken of men,
> A man of sorrows and acquainted with grief;
> And like one from whom men hide their face
> He was despised, and we did not esteem Him.
> Surely our griefs He Himself bore,
> And our sorrows He carried;
> Yet we ourselves esteemed Him stricken,
> Smitten of God, and afflicted.
> But He was pierced through for our transgressions,
> He was crushed for our iniquities;
> The chastening for our well-being fell upon Him,
> And by His scourging we are healed. (Isa. 53:3–5)

Even after enduring the physical torture of the cross and the infinite torments of divine judgment, Jesus demonstrated that He was still mentally alert and physically strong when He **uttered a loud cry.** His life did not gradually slip away due to exhaustion; rather, He willingly laid it down (John 10:17–18). John 19:30 reports that, after being offered the drink of sour wine, the Lord Jesus shouted, "It is finished!" The work of redemption had been accomplished and His suffering was complete. Then, He uttered a final prayer, "Father, into Your hands I commit My spirit" (Luke 23:46), **and He breathed His last.**

Jesus' death, as the perfect sacrifice for sin, marked the end of the Old Testament sacrificial system and all of the trappings that went with it (Heb. 10:4–10; cf. Rom. 14:1–6; Col. 2:16–17). God signaled that termination with a dramatic sign: **the veil of the temple,** the massive woven curtain that permanently separated the Holy of Holies from the outer sanctuary (cf. Ex. 26:31–33; 40:20–21; Lev. 16:2; Heb. 9:3), **was** miraculously **torn in two from top to bottom.** For nearly fifteen hundred years, only the high priest had been allowed to enter the Holy of Holies, and only for a brief time once a year on the Day of Atonement. At that time, he sprinkled blood on the mercy seat, atop the ark of the covenant, to signify that the required sacrifice had to be made to atone for their sins.

The curtain that blocked the Holy of Holies served as a continual reminder of the sinner's separation from God's holy presence. No animal sacrifice ever tore that curtain open. But on that Friday afternoon, at the very time the priests in the temple were sacrificing lambs for Passover, God demonstrated that the work of atonement symbolized by animal deaths had been finished by the sacrifice of the Lamb of God. The barrier to God had been permanently removed. Access to God's presence was now open through the completed work of Christ (cf. Heb. 4:16). At that moment, the old covenant passed away, and the new covenant was ratified. Although the temple edifice would survive another forty years (being destroyed in A.D. 70, cf. Mark 13:2), Christ's death immediately rendered its sacrifices, rituals, ceremonies, and worship practices obsolete (cf. John 4:21–24; Heb. 9:11–14; 10:19).

The exact time of the death of the Lord Jesus was accompanied by two additional miracles: a powerful earthquake followed by a preview of the resurrection. Both are recorded in the gospel of Matthew. After the veil in the temple was ripped from top to bottom, "the earth shook and the rocks were split. The tombs were opened, and many bodies of the saints who had fallen asleep were raised; and coming out of the tombs after His resurrection they entered the holy city and appeared to many" (Matt. 27:51–53). Earthquakes, like darkness, are often associated in Scripture with the presence of God (cf. Ex. 19:18; 1 Kings 19:11–12; Pss. 18:7; 68:8; Isa. 29:6; Nah. 1:5; Zech. 14:5; Rev. 16:18). The power to raise the dead, similarly, belongs only to Him (cf. John 5:21; Acts 2:24; 3:15; 5:30; Rom. 8:11; 1 Cor. 6:14; 2 Cor. 4:14; Gal. 1:1). Both of these miraculous signs prefigured the resurrection of Jesus (which was likewise accompanied by a severe earthquake, Matt. 28:2) and demonstrated the truth that life after death is only possible because of Christ's victory over sin at the cross (cf. 1 Cor. 15:26; 2 Tim. 1:10; Heb. 2:14).

So, the presence of God the Father at Golgotha was powerfully displayed through four remarkable miracles: an ominous darkness that covered the land, the veil of the temple being torn in two, an earthquake powerful enough to split rocks, and the resurrection of many Old Testament saints. At Mt. Sinai, God's presence was similarly accompanied by stormy darkness and a great earthquake (cf. Ex. 19:18). But unlike Sinai, where the law and its penalties were given, at Calvary the law and its penalties were forgiven by the divine lawgiver Himself, for all who believe in the person and work of His Son (cf. Rom. 8:3–4).

THE CONFESSION OF THE AWESTRUCK SOLDIER

When the centurion, who was standing right in front of Him, saw the way He breathed His last, he said, "Truly this man was the Son of God!" (15:39)

As an officer in the Roman military, **the centurion** had been placed in charge of Jesus' crucifixion. He and his men (centurions commanded one hundred soldiers) may have been involved in Jesus' arrest, as part of the Roman cohort that accompanied Judas and the religious leaders (John 18:3). It is possible that they were also witnesses to His trial before Pilate. Perhaps the centurion was listening when the Lord explained to the governor that He indeed was a king, but that His kingdom was not of this world (18:36–37). Or, perhaps, he heard the religious leaders complain that Jesus claimed to be the Son of God (19:7). The elite and hardened soldier would certainly have noticed that Pilate repeatedly pronounced Jesus to be innocent and yet sentenced Him to death anyway.

Because he was the leader of the execution squad, the centurion undoubtedly participated in Jesus' brutal scourging. Afterward, he and his men joined in the mockery of their prisoner as a crown of thorns was pressed on His head, a scratchy robe draped on His lacerated shoulders, and a mock scepter placed in His hand. At the execution site, it was the centurion's squad that nailed Jesus' hands and feet to the cross, cast lots for His clothing, and repeated the jeers and taunts of the hostile crowd. The Roman soldiers stationed at Golgotha could not have fully understood why the Jewish leaders hated Jesus so much, but they joined in the brutal ridicule nonetheless.

For the previous six hours, the execution squad had dutifully kept watch over Jesus and the two thieves. Because he **was standing right in front of Him,** the centurion must have heard the words spoken by the Lord Jesus from the cross. He watched as Jesus responded to the scorn and derision of His enemies by asking the Father to forgive them. He listened as the Lord extended the hope of heaven to a penitent thief who had previously mocked Him. From noon to 3:00 P.M., the centurion stood guard in the midst of inexplicable and menacing darkness. When the darkness finally lifted, he heard Jesus' triumphant shout, "It is finished" and **saw the way He breathed His last.** Though he had likely participated in countless executions, he had never before encountered anyone like this victim—who suffered with such dignity and died with such triumphant authority. Then, the violent earthquake ensued. As the centurion felt the earth tremble, he could contain his astonishment no longer. Speaking for himself and the other soldiers (cf. Matt. 27:54), **he said, "Truly this man was the Son of God!"** Significantly, this is the first time in Mark's gospel that a human being made that confession (cf. Mark 1:1). The Father articulated it at Jesus' baptism (1:11) and transfiguration (9:7). The demons acknowledged it on several occasions (3:11; 5:7). But Mark does not record that confession from the lips of a human being until here at the end of his gospel. Because Mark wrote to a Roman audience, he purposefully emphasized the salvation of Gentiles (cf. Mark 7:24–36), including the climactic acknowledgment of Jesus' deity from a pagan Roman soldier. The parallel account in Luke 23:47 adds that "when the centurion saw what had happened, he began praising God, saying, 'Certainly this man was innocent.'" His worshipful exclamation was both an affirmation of Jesus' blamelessness and a declaration of His divine righteousness.

From the crucified thief to this pagan commander, trophies of divine grace were on display even in the midst of Jesus' suffering and death. One was a scoundrel, the other a soldier; and both were blasphemers who mocked and persecuted the Son of God. Yet, in His infinite mercy, God reached down and rescued them eternally, granting them salvation through the very One whose crucifixion they witnessed. Their sudden conversions demonstrate that even the worst sinners and blasphemers are not beyond the reach of God's sovereign love and unmerited favor (cf. 1 Tim. 1:12–15).

The Confusion of the Loyal Sympathizers

There were also some women looking on from a distance, among whom were Mary Magdalene, and Mary the mother of James the Less and Joses, and Salome. When He was in Galilee, they used to follow Him and minister to Him; and there were many other women who came up with Him to Jerusalem. (15:40–41)

In contrast to the centurion, who was moved from confusion to belief, the faith of Jesus' followers was mingled with sorrow and confusion. The gospel of John indicates that **some** of the **women,** along with the apostle John, initially gathered at the foot of the cross (John 19:25–27). Perhaps unable to bear the sight of Jesus' suffering up close, they withdrew and continued **looking on from a distance.** They loved Jesus deeply and believed in Him sincerely, yet they were baffled, discouraged, and devastated by the scene of His death.

Mark identifies three of these women, starting with **Mary Magdalene,** from whom Jesus had cast out seven demons (Luke 8:2). She was from the village of Magdala, near Capernaum on the western shore of the Sea of Galilee. The fact that Mary was known by her place of origin, rather than by the name of her husband or children, may indicate she was unmarried. A second woman named **Mary** was distinguished as **the mother of James the Less and Joses.** (The name "Mary," a derivative of the Hebrew name Miriam, was very popular in first-century Israel. At least six women in the New Testament share that name, including Mary, the mother of Jesus; Mary Magdalene; Mary of Bethany, the sister of Martha and Lazarus; Mary, the mother of James and Joses; Mary, the mother of John Mark; and Mary of Rome, mentioned in Rom. 16:6.) **James the Less** was one of the Twelve and is also called James, the son of Alphaeus (cf. Matt. 10:3; Acts 1:13). In John 19:25, Mary is alternately identified as "Mary the wife of Clopas," an apparent variant of Alphaeus. **Salome** was the wife of Zebedee (cf. Matt. 27:56), the mother of James and John (Mark 10:35), both of whom were also apostles of Jesus. According to John 19:25, Salome was the sister of Jesus' mother, Mary.

Though the women are denoted in all four gospels (Matt. 27:55–56; Mark 15:40–41; Luke 23:49; John 19:25–26), the apostles are not mentioned as being present at Calvary, except for John (John 19:26–27). The obvious implication is that while ten of the eleven disciples scattered and hid, these women came boldly to display their courageous and sympathetic loyalty to Christ. They had followed Jesus **when He was in Galilee,** throughout the second year of His public ministry of preaching and miracles. From that time on, **they used to follow Him and minister to Him.** The imperfect tense of the verbs **to follow** and to **minister** indicates continual action over a prolonged period of time. These faithful followers of Jesus continually sought to learn from Him while also seeking to serve and support Him (cf. Luke 8:2–3). It is from the Greek verb *diakoneō* (**minister**) that the English words "deacon" and "deaconess" are derived. In the gospel of Mark, only two groups of people are ever said to have ministered to Christ: the angels (1:13), and these women from Galilee who were joined by **many other women who came up with Him to Jerusalem.**

Though they were not empowered to do miracles or preach like the apostles, the women were representative of the precious faithful who did not forsake their Lord even at His death. Their loyalty would be rewarded three days later. On Sunday morning, they would be the first to learn of His glorious resurrection (cf. Mark 16:1–8; John 20:11–18; Matt. 28:8–10). But on Friday afternoon as they gazed at the cross, they found themselves in the throes of shock, heartbreak, and bewilderment. This was not the ending they had anticipated. While the rest of the people in the gawking crowd returned to Jerusalem "beating their breasts" in superficial remorse over the death of the miracle-worker (Luke 23:48), the faithful few watched from a distance in stunned sorrow (v. 49).

But the depths of their disappointment and mourning on Friday would not last long. Jesus would rise again on Sunday morning, just as He had repeatedly promised (Mark 8:31; 9:31; 10:34). As the angel reminded the women when they came to the empty tomb, "He is not here, for He has risen, just as He said" (Matt. 28:6). In His death, the Lord Jesus bore sin's penalty. In His resurrection, He conquered death's power. Both are essential to the gospel (1 Cor. 15:3–4), and both must be believed in order to be saved (Rom. 10:9).

Speaking of the wonder of Christ's substitutionary atonement, which was accomplished by God at Calvary, an anonymous Christian author from the second century wrote this:

> [God] gave His own Son as a ransom for us, the holy One for transgressors, the blameless One for the wicked, the righteous One for the unrighteous, the incorruptible One for the corruptible, the immortal One for them that are mortal. For what other thing was capable of covering our sins than His righteousness? By what other one was it possible that we, the wicked and ungodly, could be justified, than by the only Son of God? O sweet exchange! O unsearchable operation! O benefits surpassing all expectation! that the wickedness of many should be hid in a single righteous One, and that the righteousness of One should justify many transgressors! (*Epistle to Diognetus*, 9.2–5. Translation from Alexander Roberts and James Donaldson, *Ante-Nicene Fathers* [repr., Peabody, MA: Hendrickson Publishers, 2012], 1:28)

How God Buried His Son (Mark 15:42–47)

34

When evening had already come, because it was the preparation day, that is, the day before the Sabbath, Joseph of Arimathea came, a prominent member of the Council, who himself was waiting for the kingdom of God; and he gathered up courage and went in before Pilate, and asked for the body of Jesus. Pilate wondered if He was dead by this time, and summoning the centurion, he questioned him as to whether He was already dead. And ascertaining this from the centurion, he granted the body to Joseph. Joseph bought a linen cloth, took Him down, wrapped Him in the linen cloth and laid Him in a tomb which had been hewn out in the rock; and he rolled a stone against the entrance of the tomb. Mary Magdalene and Mary the mother of Joses were looking on to see where He was laid. (15:42–47)

In his first epistle to the Corinthians, the apostle Paul identified three historical facts that comprise the essence of the gospel: "that Christ died for our sins according to the Scriptures, and that He was buried, and that He was raised on the third day according to the Scriptures" (1 Cor. 15:3–4). As those verses demonstrate, an event of fundamental importance lies between the Lord's crucifixion and resurrection. The burial of Jesus is recorded in all four gospels (cf. Matt. 27:57–66; Mark 15:42–47; Luke 23:50–56; John 19:38–42), underscoring its significance as that which affirmed both the deity of Christ and the veracity of Scripture. Though it did not involve miracles like those that accompanied the crucifixion and resurrection (cf. Matt. 27:45, 51–53; 28:2–6), Jesus' burial put the handiwork of God on stunning display by showcasing the wonder of divine providence.

The Scriptures repeatedly assert the absolute sovereignty of God over every person and event in the universe, explaining that He ordains all things and brings them to pass (cf. 1 Chron. 29:11–12; Job 23:13; Pss. 115:3; 135:6; Prov. 21:30; Isa. 46:9–10; Dan. 4:34–35; Eph. 1:11). Though God has rarely intervened in history through miracles (like the twelve plagues in Egypt or the parting of the Red Sea), He always works by providentially orchestrating natural processes and ordinary events to accomplish His purposes. Miracles are rare and involve a temporary suspension of the laws of nature, but providence is constant (cf. John 5:17) and incalculably more complex. Because He is all-powerful, all-knowing, and all-wise, God has predetermined everything and is able to direct every part of His creation (including seemingly random events, cf. Ps. 103:19; Prov. 16:33) to accomplish exactly and completely all that He has planned and promised to do. He sovereignly coordinates a near infinite number of contingencies and superintends the behaviors of all His creatures, so that all things, including people's choices and actions, ultimately align with His perfect purposes (cf. Rom. 8:28). Still, He is not the source of any sin (James 1:13), nor is human responsibility lessened or removed.

Many places in Scripture illustrate divine providence in action, emphasizing God's control and power over the desires and determinations of people (cf. 1 Sam. 2:6–9; Job 5:12; Pss. 33:10; 76:10; Prov. 16:9; 19:21; 20:24; Isa. 8:9–10; Jer. 10:23; Phil. 2:13). Time after time, God providentially moved in the hearts of men, including unrighteous kings, to accomplish His purposes (Prov. 21:1; cf. Deut. 2:30; Josh. 11:18–20; 2 Sam. 17:14; 1 Kings 12:15; 1 Chron. 5:26). It was His providential hand that superintended the evil schemes of Joseph's brothers so that Joseph would be elevated to a position of leadership in Egypt (Gen. 39:2–3, 23; 45:7–8; 50:20). Divine providence motivated Pharaoh to harden his heart so that the glory of God would be displayed in Israel's deliverance from slavery (cf. Ex. 14:4; Rom. 9:17–18). The providential working of God moved the pagan ruler Cyrus to allow the Jews to return home after seventy years of captivity (Ezra 1:1–4; cf. Isa. 44:28–45:5). And providence placed Esther in a position of influence in Persia so that her people would not suffer genocide (Est. 4:14).

Divine providence is similarly seen throughout the life and ministry of the Lord Jesus, as evidenced by numerous fulfilled prophecies (cf. Matt. 1:21–23; 2:15, 17, 23; 26:56; 27:9–10; Mark 14:49; Luke 22:37; 24:44; John 13:18–19; Acts 1:16; 3:18). Even before Jesus was born, God providentially prompted Caesar Augustus to decree that a census be taken (Luke 2:1), requiring Joseph and Mary to travel to Bethlehem so that Old Testament prophecy might be fulfilled (Matt. 2:5–6; cf. Mic. 5:2). And after Jesus died, the providence of God similarly orchestrated the events so that His burial took place exactly according to plan. God's will was being precisely fulfilled at the burial of His Son.

From the indifferent soldiers to the loving saints to the spiteful religious leaders, the human figures surrounding the burial of Jesus were all motivated by personal desires, emotions, and responsibilities. But even though their words and deeds were their own, God controlled every detail so that the choices they made worked together to fulfill biblical prophecy and accomplish precisely His purposes.

The Indifferent Soldiers

God's superintending hand in the burial of Jesus is manifest first by the actions of Pilate's soldiers, who had no particular interest in Christ other than to carry out their orders. Though Jesus died at about 3:00 P.M. (cf. Matt. 27:45), having laid down His life by His own authority (cf. John 10:17–18), the two thieves who were crucified with Him were still alive as the afternoon transitioned into evening. The Jewish leaders, in keeping with Old Testament law (cf. Deut. 21:22–23) and especially because it was Passover, wanted all three bodies removed from the cross before the

Sabbath day began (which, according to the Jewish reckoning of time, started at sundown, or approximately 6:00 P.M.). Ironically, though the hypocritical religious leaders had just participated in the murder of the Messiah, they nevertheless remained fastidious in their self-righteous efforts to avoid religious defilement.

Knowing the Romans would not remove the victims until they were dead, the religious leaders asked Pilate to accelerate the execution. As John 19:31 explains,

> Then the Jews, because it was the day of preparation, so that the bodies would not remain on the cross on the Sabbath (for that Sabbath was a high day), asked Pilate that their legs might be broken, and that they might be taken away.

In order to breathe, the crucified victim had to push up with his legs, thereby elongating his diaphragm and allowing his lungs to fill with air. Soldiers could therefore hasten death by using a massive iron mallet to crush the femurs of both legs (a process known as *crurifragium*). Unable to push up for air, the victim would die of asphyxiation shortly thereafter.

Acquiescing to the religious leaders (as he had been doing all day), Pilate gave his soldiers the order. As John explains, "So the soldiers came, and broke the legs of the first man and of the other who was crucified with Him; but coming to Jesus, when they saw that He was already dead, they did not break His legs" (John 19:32–33). As professional executioners, the Roman soldiers knew when a crucified victim was truly dead. In order to be sure, "one of the soldiers pierced His side with a spear, and immediately blood and water came out" (v. 34). The flow of blood and water (serous pleural and pericardial fluid) demonstrated beyond any doubt that Jesus was no longer alive.

What probably seemed like an insignificant decision to the soldiers, that they chose not to break Jesus' legs but instead to pierce His side with a spear, exactly fulfilled messianic prophecy (cf. John 19:36–37). Psalm 34:20 prophesied of the Messiah that "He keeps all his bones, not one of them is broken." In order to be acceptable to God, Passover lambs could not have any broken bones (cf. Ex. 12:46; Num. 9:12). Thus, it was imperative that the perfect Lamb of God not have His legs broken. The prophet Zechariah further predicted that the Messiah would be pierced (Zech. 12:10), a detail fulfilled at Calvary by a Roman spear. The pagan soldiers would have been utterly unaware of those Old Testament passages. Even if they had been, they had no motivation for trying to bring them to pass. Yet, their behavior was guided by the invisible hand of almighty God. The unwitting actions of the indifferent soldiers stemmed from their own motives, impulses, and will; yet they were also under the absolute governing control of God so that Scripture would be fulfilled and the Messiah affirmed.

THE LOVING SAINTS

When evening had already come, because it was the preparation day, that is, the day before the Sabbath, Joseph of Arimathea came, a prominent member of the Council, who himself was waiting for the kingdom of God; and he gathered up courage and went in before Pilate, and asked for the body of Jesus. Pilate wondered if He was dead by this time, and summoning the centurion, he questioned him as to whether He was already dead. And ascertaining this from the centurion, he granted the body to Joseph. Joseph bought a linen cloth, took Him down, wrapped Him in the linen cloth and laid Him in a tomb which had been hewn out in the rock; and he rolled a stone against the entrance of the tomb. Mary Magdalene and Mary the mother of Joses were looking on to see where He was laid. (15:42–47)

During the final few hours before sunset on Friday, the providence of God was again put on display through the actions of Jesus' followers, and of one man in particular. As Mark explains, **When evening** (lasting from about 3:00 to 6:00 P.M.) **had already come, because it was the preparation day, that is, the day before Sabbath, Joseph of Arimathea came** to take charge of Jesus' body for burial. Not much is known about **Joseph of Arimathea,** since he is only mentioned in Scripture in connection to this event. The exact location of **Arimathea** is unknown, though some scholars associate it with the birthplace of Samuel (1 Sam. 1:1, 19; 2:11). Luke explains that it was "a city of the Jews"

(Luke 23:51), indicating that it was in Judea.

Incredibly, Joseph was **a prominent member of the** very **Council** (namely, the Sanhedrin) that had falsely accused, wrongly convicted, and illegally sentenced Jesus to death earlier that morning. Yet, unlike most of his fellow councilmen, Joseph was "a good and righteous man" (Luke 23:50), who had been brought to saving faith in the Lord Jesus. Though he was a member of the Sanhedrin, Luke 23:51 clarifies that "he had not consented" to the religious leaders' malevolent treatment of Jesus, likely indicating that he was not present when Jesus' trial occurred (cf. Mark 14:64–65).

Both Matthew and John describe Joseph as "a disciple of Jesus" (Matt. 27:57; John 19:38), indicating that he was a true believer **who himself was waiting for the kingdom of God.** Joseph understood the Old Testament promises of salvation and had come to the conviction that the Lord Jesus was indeed the messianic king. Yet, he kept his opinions about Jesus secret "for fear of the Jews" (John 19:38). Joseph must have been elated earlier that week when Jesus entered the city to shouts of messianic expectation from the people (Mark 11:8–10). The following day, when the Lord attacked the corruption of the temple (11:15–18), the secret disciple would have endorsed that as a righteous act of cleansing. He eagerly hoped Jesus would usher in the Old Testament promises regarding the messianic kingdom. But when Jesus was crucified, those expectations turned to heartbreak.

After being declared dead, the body of a crucified victim would be taken down from the cross and disposed of in one of two ways—either by giving it to members of the victim's family, if they requested it, or by tossing it into a hastily made common grave or even the garbage dump. With the women still lingering at the cross (cf. Mark 15:40, 47), and the apostles having fled (except for John, who was caring for Jesus' mother, cf. John 19:26–27), the request to claim Jesus' body came from an unexpected place. Joseph of Arimathea, motivated by love and sympathy for his Lord, **gathered up courage and went in before Pilate, and asked for the body of Jesus.** The verb *tolmaō* (**gathered up courage**) means "to dare" or "to be bold." Joseph realized his actions would raise the ire of the other council members because his loyalty to Jesus would be exposed.

Having been asked by the religious leaders to make sure the crucified victims were off the cross before the Sabbath began (John 19:31), and having ordered his soldiers to hasten the execution (v. 32), the Roman governor was still waiting for confirmation when Joseph arrived. Thus, **Pilate wondered if** Jesus **was dead by this time, and summoning the centurion, he questioned him as to whether He was already dead. And ascertaining** that Jesus was dead **from the centurion, he granted the body to Joseph.** With permission received, Joseph returned to the crucifixion site to dispose of Jesus' lifeless body.

On the human level, Joseph (whom Matt. 27:57 notes was wealthy) was clearly motivated by a desire to honor Jesus. He wanted to see Him buried properly and not dumped in a mass grave. But on the divine level, God was orchestrating Joseph's actions to fulfill biblical prophecy. In Isaiah 53:9, the prophet predicted of the Suffering Servant, "His grave was assigned with wicked men, yet He was with a rich man in His death." It would not have been possible to fully comprehend the implications of that prophecy until after Jesus died. Only then did it become clear that, although the Romans planned to discard His body as if He were a common criminal, the Messiah would actually be buried in the tomb of a prominent and wealthy man.

God was also at the burial, working to ensure everything happened according to the divine schedule. The timing was crucial, so that Jesus' body would be in the grave for at least part of three different days, just as He had predicted (cf. Matt. 12:40; 16:21; 17:23; 20:19). To assure that, God moved the religious leaders to demand that the bodies be taken down on Friday and prompted Pilate to grant their request. Then, He compelled Joseph to be courageous and ask for Jesus' body, and again moved the governor to give permission. Now, God enabled Joseph to secure, transport, prepare, and bury Jesus' body, and do it all before the Sabbath began so that He was in the tomb on Friday.

The Jews did not embalm, which explains why **Joseph bought a linen cloth, took Him down,** "took Him away" (John 19:38), and **wrapped Him in the linen cloth.** The body was wrapped using cloth strips that were packed with aromatic spices to combat the odors caused by decomposition. In preparing Jesus' body for burial, Joseph was not alone. As the apostle John reports,

> Nicodemus, who had first come to Him by night, also came, bringing a mixture of myrrh and aloes, about a hundred pounds weight. So they took the body of Jesus and bound it in linen wrappings with the spices, as is the burial custom of the Jews. (John 19:39–40)

Nicodemus, the prominent Jewish teacher who met with the Lord at night, early in Jesus' ministry (John 3:1–21), was also a member of the Sanhedrin (John 7:50). Like Joseph, he too had been given the faith to embrace Jesus as Lord. His desire to honor Christ in His burial is indicated by the significant amount of spices he brought.

After the preparations for burial were complete, Joseph **laid Him in a tomb which had been hewn out in the rock.** Matthew explains that it was Joseph's own tomb (Matt. 27:60); and John notes that it was located in a garden near Golgotha (John 19:41–42). In ancient Israel as elsewhere, it was common for tombs to be reused. The body would decompose until only the bones were left; then the bones would be collected in an ossuary and the tomb would become available again. But Joseph placed Jesus in a tomb in which no one had ever been buried (Luke 23:53; John 19:41). In order to keep out any unwanted intruders, whether animals or grave robbers, **he rolled a stone against the entrance of the tomb.** In keeping with God's will, all of this took place before sundown on Friday.

Some of the women who had been watching the crucifixion from a distance (v. 40), including **Mary Magdalene and Mary the mother of Joses** (and possibly others from Galilee, Luke 23:55), were still at the cross when Joseph arrived to claim Jesus' body. The text does not indicate whether or not the women knew Joseph or if they assisted him and Nicodemus in Jesus' burial. In any case, they followed him, **looking on to see where** Jesus **was laid.**

Any skeptical claim that the women went to the wrong tomb on Sunday morning is easily dispelled by the fact that they had seen the tomb on Friday evening. Moreover, both Joseph and Nicodemus knew which tomb was the right one, as did the hostile religious leaders (cf. Matt. 27:66). If Jesus' followers had mistakenly gone to a wrong tomb that was empty, His enemies could have easily pointed them to the right one that He still occupied. That they did not do so demonstrates they knew that the women had gone to the correct location and that Jesus was not there.

The women watched Jesus' body be interred in the tomb before returning to their homes that evening. As the sun began to set on Friday, they were beginning to prepare their own spice mixtures, which they planned to take back to Jesus' tomb after the Sabbath (Luke 23:56; 24:1). But when they arrived at the tomb on Sunday morning, they would be in for a shocking discovery.

THE SPITEFUL LEADERS

Clearly, God was ruling over and controlling the actions of both Pilate's indifferent soldiers and Jesus' loving followers. He was also accomplishing His purposes through His enemies, the hateful religious leaders.

The gospel of Matthew records a meeting between the religious leaders and Pilate that took place the following day, during the Sabbath.

> Now on the next day, the day after the preparation, the chief priests and the Pharisees gathered together with Pilate, and said, "Sir, we remember that when He was still alive that deceiver said, 'After three days I am to rise again.' Therefore, give orders for the grave to be made secure until the third day, otherwise His disciples may come and steal Him away and say to the people, 'He has risen from the dead,' and the last deception will be worse than the first." Pilate said to them, "You have a guard; go, make it as secure as you know how." And they went and made the grave secure, and along with the guard they set a seal on the stone. (Matt. 27:62–66)

Aware of the predictions made by Jesus during His ministry (cf. Matt. 12:38–40), the religious leaders worried that His disciples would steal His body to make it look like He had risen from the dead. To prevent that possibility, they made the tomb secure by stationing a guard and setting a seal (probably given to them by Pilate to signify Roman protection) on the stone. In truth, the disorganized and deserting disciples (cf. Mark 14:50) had no such intentions. That they did not expect Jesus to rise from the dead is seen in the fact that they went into hiding, fearful that the religious authorities would target them next (John 20:19). Moreover, if they had faked the resurrection by stealing Jesus' body, they would never have given their lives as martyrs for what they knew was a fraud (cf. 1 Cor. 15:14–19).

The intent of the religious leaders was to avert a hoax. But in God's providence, their antagonistic actions unwittingly validated the truth of Jesus' resurrection. Because Christ's enemies sealed the tomb and put it under Roman guard, they made it impossible for Jesus' body to be removed, unless He did in fact rise from the dead. Though they later claimed the disciples stole the body (Matt. 28:11–14), their allegations were falsified by their own actions. The security measures they put in place around the tomb ensured that the disciples could not have stolen Jesus' body.

The numerous details and contingencies surrounding the burial of Jesus vividly demonstrate the remarkable nature of divine superintendence. The indifferent soldiers, loving followers, and hostile religious leaders all acted in keeping with their own motives and desires. Yet, whether they were apathetic, sympathetic, or antagonistic toward Jesus, their actions accomplished God's predestined and sovereign will. Consequently, the Messiah's legs were not broken; His side was pierced; He was with a rich man in His burial; His body was in the grave for three days; and His tomb was sealed and guarded by His enemies, making it impossible for His disciples to have stolen His body, thereby affirming the truth of His resurrection. The invisible hand of God left its prints on every detail, perfectly fulfilling biblical prophecy and further affirming the messiahship of the Son, the Lord Jesus (cf. Mark 1:1).

Amazement at the Empty Tomb (Mark 16:1–8)

35

When the Sabbath was over, Mary Magdalene, and Mary the mother of James, and Salome, bought spices, so that they might come and anoint Him. Very early on the first day of the week, they came to the tomb when the sun had risen. They were saying to one another, "Who will roll away the stone for us from the entrance of the tomb?" Looking up, they saw that the stone had been rolled away, although it was extremely large. Entering the tomb, they saw a young man sitting at the right, wearing a white robe; and they were amazed. And he said to them, "Do not be amazed; you are looking for Jesus the Nazarene, who has been crucified. He has risen; He is not here; behold, here is the place where they laid Him. But go, tell His disciples and Peter, 'He is going ahead of you to Galilee; there you will see Him, just as He told you.'" They went out and fled from the tomb, for trembling and astonishment had gripped them; and they said nothing to anyone, for they were afraid. (16:1–8)

The resurrection is not simply a component of the gospel, it is the main event. It is the glorious centerpiece of divine redemption, the cornerstone of gospel promise, and the guarantee of eternal life for those who believe. The resurrection is not the epilogue or postscript to the life of Christ, it is the culminating climax of His atoning work.

The death of the Lord Jesus at Calvary is absolutely central to the gospel (cf. 1 Cor. 15:3). Yet without the resurrection, the cross would be meaningless and there would be no hope of salvation from sin. As Paul told the Corinthians, "If Christ has not been raised, then our preaching is vain, your faith also is vain ... and if Christ has not been raised, your faith is worthless; you are still in your sins" (vv. 14, 17). But because He has risen (v. 20), believers have hope both for this life and the life to come (cf. v. 19). The church meets on Sunday, not Friday, because Easter stands as the validation of Good Friday. By the resurrection, God vindicated the work of His Son on the cross (Acts 17:31), affirming for all time that divine justice had been fully satisfied and God propitiated through Jesus' sacrificial death (cf. Rom. 4:25; 1 Peter 2:24).

The gospel does not merely promise believers that their sins have been forgiven, it also confirms that having been made right with God, they will one day receive a glorified resurrection body in which they will dwell forever in His presence (cf. 1 Cor. 15:35–58; 1 Thess. 4:13–18; 1 John 3:2). That promise is founded on the historic reality of the resurrection of the Lord Jesus (1 Cor. 15:20–23), which demonstrates His power over death (cf. John 11:25–26; Heb. 2:14–15). Accordingly, the "resurrection of life" (John 5:29) made possible by Christ (John 14:19; Rom. 4:25; 1 Peter 1:3; 3:21) has been the hope of God's people in every age (Job 14:14; 19:25–26; Dan. 12:2; Acts 24:15) and the hallmark of New Testament preaching (cf. Acts 2:24; 4:2; 10:38–40; 13:27–30; 17:31; Rom. 6:4; 2 Cor. 4:14; Eph. 1:20; 1 Peter 1:3).

All four gospel writers combine to report on the features surrounding Jesus' resurrection. Though each author reveals unique elements that bear upon the narrative (a fact that contradicts the modern critical notion that the gospel writers copied from a common source), they harmonize perfectly because they share a common divine Author (cf. John 14:26; 2 Tim. 3:16; 2 Peter 1:21). Each of the Fospels explains that Jesus died on the cross on Friday afternoon and was buried that evening (Matt. 27:47–61; Mark 15:33–47; Luke 23:44–56; John 19:28–42). He remained in the tomb all day Saturday. But early Sunday morning, when the women arrived to anoint the body with burial spices, the tomb was empty. Their confusion turned to wonder when an angel appeared and explained to them that Jesus was alive. After that, the Lord Himself began to appear to His followers. (For a harmony of the gospel accounts of Jesus' postresurrection appearances, see John MacArthur, *One Perfect Life* [Nashville: Thomas Nelson, 2012].)

One feature is conspicuously absent from all four accounts: a description of the resurrection itself. The biblical authors give no details of what happened in that critical moment when Jesus' dead body again surged with life. Instead, they focus on the aftermath of the resurrection, using understated language to describe the remarkable scene. As one commentator explains:

> None of [the Gospels] includes an account of the actual rising of Jesus from death, and all assume that this has taken place at some time prior to the discovery of the empty tomb. The setting for the discovery is remarkably down-to-earth. . . . This is not the stuff of a heroic epic, still less a story of magic and wonder, and yet what underlies it is an event beyond human comprehension: the Jesus they had watched dying and being buried some forty hours earlier is no longer dead but risen. . . . It is in this incongruous combination of the everyday with the incomprehensible that many have found one of the most powerful and compelling aspects of the NT accounts not of Jesus' resurrection (for there are none) but of how the first disciples discovered that he had risen. (R. T. France, *The Gospel of Mark*, New International Greek Testament Commentary [Grand Rapids: Eerdmans, 2002], 675)

Of the four gospels, Mark's account is the most succinct, in keeping with the fast-paced style of his history. Though brief, its demonstration of the reality of Jesus' resurrection is more than sufficient. Mark's account yields three points of evidence to make his case: the testimony of the empty tomb, the testimony of the angels, and the testimony of the eyewitnesses.

THE TESTIMONY OF THE EMPTY TOMB

When the Sabbath was over, Mary Magdalene, and Mary the mother of James, and Salome, bought spices, so that they might come and

anoint Him. Very early on the first day of the week, they came to the tomb when the sun had risen. They were saying to one another, "Who will roll away the stone for us from the entrance of the tomb?" Looking up, they saw that the stone had been rolled away, although it was extremely large. Entering the tomb (16:1–5*a*)

The Jews marked their days at sundown rather than midnight, so **the Sabbath** ended on Saturday evening around 6:00 P.M. But Mark's statement, that it **was over,** does much more than simply convey the timing of Jesus' resurrection (cf. Mark 16:2). It also stands as a theological marker indicating that the Sabbath itself was now obsolete because a new era of redemptive history had begun. No Sabbath observance has been divinely authorized or mandated since the resurrection (cf. Col. 2:16–17). Like the Passover, which ended when Jesus instituted the Lord's Supper as the new memorial feast commemorating His death (Mark 14:22–25), the Sabbath was replaced by the Lord's Day to commemorate His resurrection every first day of the week (cf. Acts 20:7; 1 Cor. 16:2; Rev. 1:10).

Once that final Sabbath passed, **Mary Magdalene, and Mary the mother of James, and Salome** went into action to complete what they prepared on Friday evening (Luke 23:56; John 19:39–40). They **bought** additional **spices, so that they might come and anoint Him.** The other gospel writers explain that Joanna and other women were also there (Luke 24:10; cf. 15:41), including Mary the mother of Jesus (John 19:26). These women had followed Jesus in Galilee and were present at the cross (cf. Mark 15:40–41). At least two of them observed Joseph of Arimathea and Nicodemus wrapping Jesus' body with spices for His burial on Friday (John 19:39; cf. Mark 15:46). Yet they wished to prepare their own spices to anoint their Lord. Understandably, they desired one last opportunity to demonstrate their love. Because the Jewish people did not embalm the bodies of their dead, anointing was an act borne of necessity, to mitigate the powerful odors of a decomposing body.

The Israelites did not name the days of the week but simply numbered them, culminating in the seventh day, the Sabbath. On the **first day of the week,** which was Sunday, the women came **very early** in the morning, arriving at **the tomb when the sun had risen.** Matthew explains that they came "as it began to dawn" (Matt. 28:1); and Luke, "at early dawn" (24:1). The various descriptions reflect the different ways in which the gospel writers depicted the same time of day: the transition between night and day just as the sun began to dawn. According to John's account, Mary Magdelene came to the tomb first, evidently walking ahead of her companions and arriving "while it was still dark" (John 20:1). The other women followed, arriving at the tomb a short time later as the sun began to crest the horizon.

When Mary arrived and saw the stone rolled away, she was struck with grief and immediately assumed someone had stolen Jesus' body. In her panic, she fled to tell Peter and John. The possibility that Jesus had risen never crossed her mind, as evidenced by her words to the two apostles: "They have taken away the Lord out of the tomb, and we do not know where they have laid Him" (John 20:2).

Trailing behind Mary, the other women **were saying to one another** as they approached the garden, **"Who will roll away the stone for us from the entrance of the tomb?"** They knew Joseph had secured the gravesite with a large, heavy stone (Mark 15:46) and wondered how they would be able to remove it. Because Friday was the last time any of them had seen the tomb, they were unaware that the religious leaders had sealed it on Saturday and set a detachment of Roman soldiers to guard it (cf. Matt. 27:62–66). They were also unaware of the localized earthquake that occurred earlier that morning, and the arrival of the angel who rolled the stone away and incapacitated the soldiers (Matt. 28:2–4), ultimately causing them to flee (v. 11). By the time the women arrived at the tomb, the soldiers had disappeared and the tomb's entrance was wide-open.

To the women's surprise, as they looked **up, they saw that the stone had been rolled away, although it was extremely large.** It is important to note that the reason the angel removed the stone was not to let Jesus out. In His resurrection body, the Lord could pass through walls without needing a door (cf. Luke 24:31; John 20:19). Rather, it was to let the women inside, since they would have been unable to remove the heavy stone themselves. **Entering the tomb** and seeing it was unoccupied (Luke 24:3), their initial thought, like Mary Magdalene, was surely that someone had stolen Jesus' body. That they were not expecting a resurrection is indicated by the fact that they had come to the tomb with burial spices—an unnecessary act if they thought Jesus was alive. Soon they would learn the glorious truth.

Evidence for the resurrection begins with the simple yet conclusive fact that Jesus' tomb was empty. The Roman soldiers knew it was empty (Matt. 28:11), as did the Jewish religious leaders (v. 13), the women (Luke 24:3; John 20:2), Peter and John (John 20:6–7), and others like Joseph of Arimathea. Significantly, Jesus' enemies never disputed the empty tomb. Instead, they tried to explain it away by bribing the soldiers to lie and say His disciples had stolen the body (Matt. 28:12–15). In reality, the tomb being empty had nothing to do with the disorganized and cowardly disciples (cf. Mark 14:50; John 20:19), and everything to do with Jesus rising triumphantly from the dead, just as He promised He would do (cf. Matt. 12:40; Mark 8:31; 9:31; 10:33–34; Luke 13:32; 18:33; John 2:19).

THE TESTIMONY OF THE ANGELS

they saw a young man sitting at the right, wearing a white robe; and they were amazed. And he said to them, "Do not be amazed; you are looking for Jesus the Nazarene, who has been crucified. He has risen; He is not here; behold, here is the place where they laid Him. (16:5b–6)

In an instant, the women went from being perplexed to being terrified, when the morning gloom was abruptly dispelled by the dazzling brilliance of **a young man** (an angel appearing in human form, Matt. 28:5; John 20:12; cf. Gen. 18:2; 19:1–5; Dan. 10:16). **Sitting at the right, wearing a white robe,** the angel's dazzling appearance (Matt. 28:3; Luke 24:4; cf. Matt. 17:2; Acts 1:10; Rev. 19:14) unmistakably identified him as a messenger from heaven. Luke (24:4) and John (20:12) indicate that there were actually two angels (perhaps to fulfill the biblical requirement of multiple witnesses, cf. Deut. 19:15). Because only one of the angels spoke, Mark and Matthew mention only him. (The gospel writers similarly handle the accounts of two demon-possessed men at Gerasa, where only one spoke [cf. Matt. 8:28–29; Mark 5:2, 7; Luke 8:27–28], and of two blind men near Jericho, where only Bartimaeus spoke [Matt. 20:30; Mark 10:46; Luke 18:38].)

Not surprisingly, when the women saw the angels, **they were amazed.** The Greek verb *ekthambeō* (**were amazed**) indicates that the women were terrified and bewildered, falling with their faces toward the ground (Luke 24:5; cf. Dan. 8:15–18; 10:9; Luke 1:12; 2:9; Acts 10:3–4; Rev. 22:8). However, unlike the Roman soldiers who collapsed like dead men (Matt. 28:2–4), the women received hope and comfort from the heavenly messengers. It was angels who brought tidings of great joy at the birth of Jesus (Luke 2:10–15); and angels who announced the wondrous reality of His resurrection.

Aware of their terror, the angel **said to them, "Do not be amazed; you are looking for Jesus the Nazarene, who has been crucified."** The angel's identification of Jesus left no doubt that the women had come to the correct tomb. As the heavenly messenger went on to explain, **He has risen; He is not here.** The aorist passive form of the Greek verb *egeirō* (**has risen**) is more accurately rendered, "has been raised" (cf. Acts 2:24, 32; 3:15, 26; 4:10; 5:30; 10:40; 13:30, 33, 34, 37; Rom. 4:24–25; 6:9; 7:4; 8:34; 10:9; 1 Cor. 6:14; 15:4, 12–20; 2 Cor. 4:14; Eph. 1:20; Col. 2:12; 1 Thess. 1:10; 1 Peter 1:21). Though Jesus Himself possessed the authority to lay down His life and to take it up again (John 10:18), the New Testament also teaches that He was raised by the power of both the Father (Rom. 6:4; Gal. 1:1; 1 Peter 1:3) and the Holy Spirit (Rom. 8:11). That reality is not contradictory but rather affirms the unity of God within the Trinity, since each member of the Godhead participated in the resurrection (as they did in creation, cf. Gen. 1:1–3; John 1:1–3).

According to Luke 24:5, the angel also asked the women, "Why do you seek the living One among the dead?" That mild rebuke, in the form of a question, reminded the women that they should have anticipated Jesus' resurrection, since He had promised it throughout His ministry (Luke 24:6; cf. Matt. 16:21; 17:22–23; 20:17–19; 26:2; 27:63). However, it was not until after the angel explained what had happened that they "remembered His words" (Luke 24:8).

As they recovered from their initial shock, the women were directed by the angel to examine **the place where they laid Him.** When Peter and John came to the tomb later that morning, they "saw the linen wrappings lying there, and the face-cloth which had been on His head, not lying with the linen wrappings, but rolled up in a place by itself" (John 20:6–7). The women would have seen the same burial cloths lying undisturbed, except for the facecloth, which had been neatly set to one side. As Jesus did not need the stone removed to exit the tomb, so He had no need to be unwrapped. His glorified resurrection body left the grave clothes behind unchanged.

As an emissary of God (cf. Luke 1:19,38; Heb. 1:14; 2:2), the angel's announcement represented the testimony of the Father Himself. This was heaven's authoritative explanation of the reason the tomb was empty. It was also the first postresurrection declaration of the gospel. As one author observes:

> The announcement of the divine emissary establishes an inseparable continuity between the historical Jesus and the resurrected Jesus. The one whom the angel invites them to know is the one whom they have known. The announcement of the angel is literally the gospel, good news, and the place which the gospel is first preached is the empty tomb that both received and gave up the Crucified One. (James R. Edwards, *The Gospel According to Mark,* Pillar New Testament Commentary [Grand Rapids: Eerdmans, 2002], 494)

THE TESTIMONY OF THE EYEWITNESSES

But go, tell His disciples and Peter, 'He is going ahead of you to Galilee; there you will see Him, just as He told you.'" They went out and fled from the tomb, for trembling and astonishment had gripped them; and they said nothing to anyone, for they were afraid. (16:7–8)

A third line of evidence for the resurrection comes from the testimony of the eyewitnesses to whom the risen Christ appeared. It is this line of evidence to which the New Testament primarily appeals (cf. Acts 1:3; 2:32; 3:15; 5:32; 10:39; 13:31; 1 Cor. 15:3–8). Because the apostles (along with many others) had seen the risen Lord, they willingly suffered for the sake of His name (cf. Acts 5:30–32,41; Phil. 3:10). Had the resurrection been a counterfeit, they would have never given their lives as martyrs for what they knew was a lie.

Speaking on God's behalf, the angel instructed the women to **go, tell His disciples and Peter, 'He is going ahead of you to Galilee; there you will see Him, just as He told you.'"** Peter was singled out in this instance not only because he was the leader of the disciples but to reassure him in light of his recent denials (Mark 14:66–72). With these words from the angel, the women's perplexity and panic was transformed into proclamation. The truth had been revealed to them, now they were to declare it to the disciples.

In response, **they went out and fled from the tomb, for trembling and astonishment had gripped them.** The term *tromos* (**trembling**) speaks of physical shaking caused by great fear, and *ekstasis* (**astonishment**) is the Greek word from which the English word "ecstasy" is derived. Awestruck by the news they had just received, they immediately went to find the disciples, saying **nothing to anyone** else along the way. That they **were afraid** (a form of the Greek verb *phobeō*, from which the English word "phobia" is derived) stemmed not from the threat of being harmed but from a sense of bewilderment and wonder. Matthew explains that their fear was mingled with exceeding joy at the realization that Jesus was alive (cf. Matt. 28:8).

After the women had left, Peter and John arrived at the empty tomb (John 20:3–9; cf. Luke 24:12). Mary Magdalene also returned to the tomb, after Peter and John were gone (John 20:10). This time, she too saw the angels (v. 12) and encountered the risen Lord Himself, initially thinking He was merely the gardener (vv. 14–18). Jesus appeared to the rest of the women also, as they were walking on the road to meet the disciples. Matthew records that joyous reunion:

> [The women] left the tomb quickly with fear and great joy and ran to report it to His disciples. And behold, Jesus met them and greeted them. And they came up and took hold of His feet and worshiped Him. Then Jesus said to them, "Do not be afraid; go and take word to My brethren to leave for Galilee, and there they will see Me." (Matt. 28:8–10)

When the women, including Mary Magdalene (cf. John 20:18), found the disciples and reported what had happened, the eleven initially refused to believe their news (Luke 24:10–11). Their lack of faith made them slow to respond to Jesus' command to go to Galilee. It was not until after the risen Christ repeatedly appeared to them in Jerusalem (cf. Luke 24:13–32; John 20:19–31) that they finally were willing to head for Galilee (Matt. 28:7, 16).

When Jesus promised to meet His disciples in Galilee (Matt. 28:10), He was not saying that His first postresurrection appearance would be there but that His supreme appearance (to hundreds of His followers at one time) would take place in Galilee. In Judea, He appeared to Mary Magdalene (John 20:11–18), the other women (Matt. 28:8–10). Peter (Luke 24:34), the two disciples on the road to Emmaus (Luke 24:15), ten of the apostles in the upper room (John 20:19), and all eleven including Thomas eight days later (John 20:26). When the apostles arrived in Galilee, Jesus appeared to seven of them on the shore of the lake (John 21:1–25). He later appeared to more than five hundred disciples (1 Cor. 15:6) on a mountain, where He commissioned the apostles to take the gospel to the ends of the earth (cf. Matt. 28:16–17). At some point, Jesus also appeared to His half brother James (1 Cor. 15:7) and then a final time to the eleven apostles on the Mount of Olives, just before His ascension to heaven (Acts 1:4–11). Additional appearances seem indicated in Acts 1:2–3, where Luke says of the apostles, "To these He also presented Himself alive after His suffering, by many convincing proofs, appearing to them over a period of forty days and speaking of the things concerning the kingdom of God." The Old Testament required the testimony of two or three witnesses to substantiate an event (Deut. 19:15). But God ensured that the resurrection would be verified by hundreds of eyewitnesses on many occasions who had personally seen the risen Christ. The reality of the resurrection—affirmed by collective testimony of the empty tomb, the angels, and the eyewitnesses—proves Jesus is who He claimed to be.

Mark began his historical record by declaring Jesus to be the "Christ, the Son of God" (Mark 1:1). Everything throughout his gospel confirms that fact, but the resurrection proves it beyond any doubt. Jesus is the divine Messiah, the Savior of sinners, the Son of God, and the Lord over all (cf. Phil. 2:10–11).

Intellectual acknowledgment of the historical fact of Jesus' resurrection is necessary to be saved, but in itself not sufficient to save.

Romans 10:9 requires: "If you confess with your mouth Jesus as Lord, and believe in your heart that God raised Him from the dead, you will be saved." Saving faith goes beyond mental affirmation of the facts; it grips the heart with love for Christ and submits the will in obedience to Him as sovereign Lord.

For believers, the fear of death is removed and the hope of glory is assured by Jesus' resurrection. He has conquered the grave and promised the same victory to all who embrace Him in saving faith (cf. 1 Cor. 15:54–57). As D. Martyn Lloyd-Jones explained to his congregation one Easter Sunday:

> This morning as I look over this evil, sinful world it does not depress me, because I expect from it nothing better. Whatever may be going against me, whatever may be happening in my own body, this is what I must expect, because of sin. But though I die, I shall rise again. I shall see Him face to face. I shall see Him as He is, and I shall be like Him, like Him in a body glorified, with every power renewed. And I shall be living in a realm that is incorruptible and undefiled, a realm that can never fade away.
>
> That is the living hope of the Resurrection. That is the message of this Easter morning. And that hope is absolutely safe and secure. The Resurrection itself guarantees it all. Every enemy has been destroyed. Christ has conquered them every one....
>
> Christ is our Forerunner (Heb. 6:20). He has gone to prepare a place for us, and He will come again to receive us unto Himself (John 14:2b–3). We shall "reign with him as kings and priests." We shall "judge the world." We shall even "judge angels." That is Christ's guarantee, and nothing can stop it. Can death? Of course not, for He has already conquered death! Can the devil? No, Christ has vanquished the devil. Can hell? No, no! "O death, where is thy sting? O grave, where is thy victory? ... Thanks be to God, which giveth us the victory through our Lord Jesus Christ"! (1 Cor. 15:55, 57). The resurrection of Christ announces that He has conquered every enemy. He has vanquished every foe. He has risen triumphant from the grave. Neither death nor life, neither hell nor anything else, can prevent or delay the coming of His Kingdom in all its glory. He alone is King of kings and Lord of lords. (D. Martyn Lloyd Jones, "A Living Hope of the Hereafter," in *Classic Sermons on the Resurrection of Christ,* ed. Warren W. Wiersbe [Peabody, MA: Hendrickson Publishers, 1991], 48–49)

The Fitting End to Mark's Gospel (Mark 16:9–20)

36

Now after He had risen early on the first day of the week, He first appeared to Mary Magdalene, from whom He had cast out seven demons. She went and reported to those who had been with Him, while they were mourning and weeping. When they heard that He was alive and had been seen by her, they refused to believe it. After that, He appeared in a different form to two of them while they were walking along on their way to the country. They went away and reported it to the others, but they did not believe them either. Afterward He appeared to the eleven themselves as they were reclining at the table; and He reproached them for their unbelief and hardness of heart, because they had not believed those who had seen Him after He had risen. And He said to them, "Go into all the world and preach the gospel to all creation. He who has believed and has been baptized shall be saved; but he who has disbelieved shall be condemned. These signs will accompany those who have believed: in My name they will cast out demons, they will speak with new tongues; they will pick up serpents, and

if they drink any deadly poison, it will not hurt them; they will lay hands on the sick, and they will recover." So then, when the Lord Jesus had spoken to them, He was received up into heaven and sat down at the right hand of God. And they went out and preached everywhere, while the Lord worked with them, and confirmed the word by the signs that followed. (16:9–20)

This final section of Mark's gospel is missing from the most reliable ancient manuscripts, and that has caused a lot of unnecessary consternation in some circles. Careful students who have made a serious study of the transmission of the biblical text would virtually all agree that verses 9–20 are a gloss—a later uninspired scribal addition appended to the original inspired text. Indeed, those last twelve verses bear the hallmarks of an attempt to cover up a perceived imperfection. That section does not fit the style and structure of the rest of Mark.

And yet, without those closing verses, Mark's gospel seems to end early and hurriedly, with Mark's description of the disciples' fearful flight from the empty tomb. The angel at the tomb is the only one who even mentions the resurrection (v. 6). And the closing words of verse 8 tell us the disciples **said nothing to anyone, for they were afraid.** Without verses 9–20, Mark's ending sounds abrupt and incomplete. We know that is not the end of the story. Why would Mark stop there?

Before discussing the answer to that question, it is necessary to consider the reliability of the biblical text and why the presence of variations in some biblical manuscripts is no threat to the authority, reliability, and inerrancy of Scripture.

No ancient book has been better preserved through the centuries than the Bible. By way of comparison, consider Herodotus's *History*, of which only eight manuscripts have survived, the oldest dating to approximately thirteen hundred years after the original. Of Caesar's *Gallic Wars*, a mere ten manuscript copies have been discovered, the earliest of which is a thousand years removed from its author. There are likewise only eight surviving manuscripts of the *History of the Peloponnesian War* by Thucydides, all of them dating more than thirteen centuries after the original. Many similar examples could be given, from the writings of Aristotle to Tacitus, but the point remains the same: When it comes to the preservation of ancient manuscripts, no other text comes close to the writings of Scripture. In the words of the renowned scholar F. F. Bruce, "There is no body of ancient literature in the world which enjoys such a wealth of good textual attestation as the New Testament" (F. F. Bruce, *The Books and the Parchments* [Old Tappan, NJ: Revell, 1963], 178).

The second most well-attested work of antiquity is Homer's *Iliad*, of which 643 surviving copies have been found. But even the manuscript evidence for the *Iliad* falls far short of that for the Bible. Ancient Greek manuscripts of the New Testament number more than five thousand, ranging from small fragments of papyri to complete codices containing all twenty-seven books. A few of those manuscripts are only twenty-five to fifty years removed from the original autographs. When ancient translations (such as Latin and Ethiopic) are included, the number of manuscripts mushrooms to nearly 25,000. Additional testimony comes from the ante-Nicene church fathers, whose writings contain some 32,000 citations or allusions to the New Testament text. (cf. Josh McDowell, *The New Evidence That Demands a Verdict* [Nashville: Thomas Nelson, 1999], 34–45.) In His sovereign providence, the Spirit of God preserved a myriad of ancient witnesses to the biblical text so that, after two millennia, believers can rest assured in the trustworthiness of their copies of Scripture.

The science of textual criticism analyzes and compares ancient biblical manuscripts to determine the contents of the original autographs. Before the invention of the printing press around 1450, biblical manuscripts were copied entirely by hand, sometimes resulting in scribal errors. But through the careful process of textual analysis, such errors and embellishments can be identified and corrected by comparing the manuscript in question with other, earlier manuscripts. Because so many New Testament manuscripts have survived, biblical scholars are able to determine the original text with an extremely high degree of accuracy (cf. Archibald T. Roberston, *An Introduction to the Textual Criticism of the New Testament* [Nashville: Broadman, 1925], 22). Such textual scholarship gives believers today great confidence in the integrity of their Bibles, because it not only identifies what was original to the text but also exposes any errors or alterations.

All of this has a direct bearing on the final section of the gospel of Mark because it demonstrates that these verses (16:9–20), known as the "longer ending" of Mark, were almost certainly not part of the original divinely revealed text. Like the well-known account in John 7:53–8:11, this passage was inserted into the gospel at a later date. Both external evidence (from the Greek manuscripts, early versions, and church fathers) and internal evidence (from the passage itself) call its authenticity into question, which is why modern English translations place these verses in brackets.

Regarding external evidence, the earliest and most important New Testament manuscripts do not contain this section. For example, the famous fourth-century codices Sinaiticus and Vaticanus both end Mark's gospel at 16:8. Summarizing the external evidence, William Lane explains:

> To the witness of the two earliest parchment codices, Vaticanus (B) and Sinaiticus (א), may be added minuscule 304 and 2386. The absence of Ch. 16:9–20 in the Old Latin MS [manuscript] *k*, the sinaitic Syriac, several MSS [manuscripts] of the Armenian version, the Adysh and Opiza MSS of the Georgian version, and a number of MSS of the Ethiopic version provide a wide range of support for the originality of the abrupt ending. . . . Moreover, a number of MSS which do contain them have scholia [marginal notes] stating that older Greek copies lack them (e.g. 1, 20, 22, 137, 138, 1110, 1215, 1216, 1217, 1221, 1582), while in other witnesses the final section is marked with asterisks or obeli, the conventional signs used by scribes to mark off a spurious addition to a literary text. The evidence allows no other assumption than that from the beginning Mark circulated with the abrupt ending of Ch. 16:8. (William L. Lane, *The Gospel According to Mark,* The New International Commentary on the New Testament [Grand Rapids: Eerdmans, 1974], 601. See also R. T. France, *The Gospel of Mark,* The New International Greek Testament Commentary [Grand Rapids: Eerdmans, 2002], 685–86)

Additionally, some manuscripts contain a different ending, known as the "shorter ending" (cf. the further discussion below). The fact that multiple possible endings to Mark's gospel circulated in the early centuries of church history casts further doubt on the authenticity of the longer ending.

Evidence from the church fathers also weighs against the authenticity of the longer ending. The church historian Eusebius of Caesarea (c. 265–340), along with the Bible translator Jerome (c. 347–420), both explain that almost all of Greek manuscripts available in their day omitted verses 9–20. Though some of the church fathers (like Irenaeus and Tatian) show a familiarity with the longer ending, others (such as Clement of Alexandria, Origen, and Cyprian) seem unaware of its existence.

Regarding internal evidence from the passage itself, several factors cast further doubt on its authenticity as part of Mark's original gospel. First, the transition between verse 8 and verse 9 is awkward and disjointed. The conjunction **now** (from the Greek word *de*) implies continuity with the preceding narrative, but the focus of verse 9 abruptly shifts to Mary Magdalene rather than continuing a discussion of the women referred to in verse 8. Moreover, it would be strange for Mark to wait until the end of his narrative to introduce **Mary Magdalene,** as if for the first time (noting that she was woman **from whom** Jesus **had cast out seven demons**) when she was already mentioned three times in the prior context (Mark 15:40, 47, 16:1). A similar discontinuity regards Peter, who is singled out in verse 7 yet not mentioned again in verses 9–20. The "shorter ending" (which circulated as an alternative to the longer ending, and was sometimes combined with it) attempts to rectify those incongruities by highlighting both Peter and the other women. It states, "And they promptly reported all these instructions to Peter and his companions. And after that, Jesus Himself sent out through them from east to west the sacred and imperishable proclamation of eternal salvation." But this shorter ending has even weaker manuscript evidence to support it than the longer ending. Moreover, as one commentator observes, it "reads like an early attempt to tidy loose ends; the last clause in particular does not sound Marcan in its expression" (R. Alan Cole, *The Gospel According to Mark* [Grand Rapids: Eerdmans, 1989], 334).

Second, the vocabulary, style, and structure of the longer ending is not consistent with the rest of Mark's gospel. There are eighteen words in this section that are not used elsewhere in Mark. For example, the title "Lord Jesus" is used here (v. 19) but is never used anywhere else in Mark's account (cf. James R. Edwards, *The Gospel According to Mark,* Pillar New Testament Commentary [Grand Rapids: Eerdmans, 2002], 498–99). The obvious differences in these verses from the rest of Mark's narrative have led most scholars to agree with the conclusion of C. E. B. Cranfield, who writes, "In style and vocabulary they are obviously non-Markan" (*The Gospel According to Saint Mark* [New York: Cambridge University Press, 1972], 472).

Third, the inclusion of apostolic signs does not fit the way the other three gospels conclude their accounts of the resurrection and ascension of Jesus Christ. Though many of the signs mentioned in this section parallel portions of the book of Acts (cf. Acts 2:4; 9:17; 10:46; 28:8), some are clearly without biblical support, such as being able to **pick up** venomous **serpents** (though perhaps loosely based on Paul's experience in Acts 28:3–5) or **drink any deadly poison** (cf. Walter W. Wessel and Mark L. Strauss, "Mark," in *The Expositor's Bible Commentary*, ed. Tremper Longman III and David E. Garland [Grand Rapids: Zondervan, 2010], IX:988).

The evidence, both external and internal, conclusively demonstrates that verses 9–20 were not originally part of Mark's inspired record. While they generally summarize truths taught elsewhere in the New Testament, they should always be evaluated in light of the rest of Scripture. No doctrines or practices should be established solely on them. The snake-handling preachers of the Appalachians provide a prime example of the errors that can arise from accepting these verses as authoritative.

Nonetheless, knowing that Mark 16:9–20 is not original should give believers more confidence in the accuracy of the New Testament, not less. As noted above, the science of textual analysis makes it possible for biblical scholars to identify the very few passages that were not part of the original. Such places are clearly marked in modern translations, making it easy for students of Scripture to identify them. Consequently, believers can approach the rest of the text with the settled assurance that the Bible they hold in their hands accurately reflects the original.

The reality that these verses were not part of Mark's original gospel raises at least two questions that must be answered. First, since Mark did not write this section, where did it originate? And, second, if Mark's narrative ends at 16:8, why did he conclude his gospel so abruptly?

WHERE DID THIS SECTION ORIGINATE?

Because Mark's narrative ends abruptly in 16:8, and because it does not include the postresurrection history found in the other three gospels, some early Christians apparently felt it was incomplete. Consequently, at some point in the early to mid-second century, the content of verses 9–20 was added to give Mark's account a more fully developed conclusion. In the words of one commentator,

> Nearly all scholars think that verses 9–20 began to be attached some-time in the second century or later by scribes trying to make Mark read more like the other Gospels. In the course of time, these verses became the ending to Mark in the great mass of Greek manuscripts and were popularly regarded as a genuine part of the Gospel. The earliest and best Greek manuscripts do not, however, contain these verses, and the testimony of the earliest "fathers" of the church (in the first four cen-turies) indicates that these verses were known only in a few copies of Mark and were not regarded as original with the book. (Larry W. Hurtado, *Mark*, Understanding the Bible Commentary [Grand Rapids: Baker, 2011], 287–88)

No one knows who the scribe or scribes were who added verses 9–20. But it is obvious where they obtained their material. A survey of the longer ending evidences that most of its content was summarized or bor-rowed from other places in the New Testament, as the following verse-by-verse comparison demonstrates:

(Mark 16:9–10) **Now after He had risen early on the first day of the week, He first appeared to Mary Magdalene, from whom He had cast out seven demons. She went and reported to those who had been with Him, while they were mourning and weeping.**

(John 20:1) Now on the first day of the week Mary Magdalene came early to the tomb, while it was still dark, and saw the stone already taken away from the tomb.

(Luke 8:2) Mary who was called Magdalene, from whom seven demons had gone out

(John 20:17–18) Jesus said to her, "Stop clinging to Me, for I have not yet ascended to the Father; but go to My brethren and say to them, 'I ascend to My Father and your Father, and My God and your God.'" Mary Magdalene came, announcing to the disciples, "I have seen the Lord," and that He had said these things to her.

(Mark 16:11) **When they heard that He was alive and had been seen by her, they refused to believe it.**

(Luke 24:10–11) Now they were Mary Magdalene and Joanna and Mary the mother of James; also the other women with them were telling these things to the apostles. But these words appeared to them as nonsense, and they would not believe them.

(Mark 16:12–13) **After that, He appeared in a different form to two of them while they were walking along on their way to the country. They went away and reported it to the others, but they did not believe them either.**

(Luke 24:13–35) And behold, two of them were going that very day to a village named Emmaus, which was about seven miles from Jerusalem. And they were talking with each other about all these things which had taken place. While they were talking and discussing, Jesus Himself approached and began traveling with them....Then their eyes were opened and they recognized Him; and He vanished from their sight....And they got up that very hour and returned to Jerusalem, and found gathered together the eleven and those who were with them, saying, "The Lord has really risen and has appeared to Simon." They began to relate their experiences on the road and how He was recognized by them in the breaking of the bread.

(Mark 16:14) **Afterward He appeared to the eleven themselves as they were reclining at the table; and He reproached them for their unbelief and hardness of heart, because they had not believed those who had seen Him after He had risen.**

(Luke 24:36–40) While they were telling these things, He Himself stood in their midst and said to them, "Peace be to you." But they were startled and frightened and thought that they were seeing a spirit. And He said to them, "Why are you troubled, and why do doubts arise in your hearts? See My hands and My feet, that it is I Myself; touch Me and see, for a spirit does not have flesh and bones as you see that I have." And when He had said this, He showed them His hands and His feet.

(Mark 16:15) **And He said to them, "Go into all the world and preach the gospel to all creation."**

(Matt. 28:19–20) Go therefore and make disciples of all the nations, baptizing them in the name of the Father and the Son and the Holy Spirit, teaching them to observe all that I commanded you; and lo, I am with you always, even to the end of the age.

(Mark 16:16) **He who has believed and has been baptized shall be saved; but he who has disbelieved shall be condemned.**

(John 3:18) He who believes in Him is not judged; he who does not believe has been judged already, because he has not believed in the name of the only begotten Son of God. (cf. v. 36)

(Mark 16:17) **These signs will accompany those who have believed: in My name they will cast out demons, they will speak with new tongues;**

(Acts 2:43) Everyone kept feeling a sense of awe; and many wonders and signs were taking place through the apostles. (cf. 4:30; 5:12; 2 Cor. 12:12)

(Acts 16:18) Paul was greatly annoyed, and turned and said to the spirit, "I command you in the name of Jesus Christ to come out of her!" And it came out at that very moment.

(Acts 2:4) And they were all filled with the Holy Spirit and began to speak with other tongues, as the Spirit was giving them utterance.

(Mark 16:18) **they will pick up serpents, and if they drink any deadly poison, it will not hurt them; they will lay hands on the sick, and they will recover.**

(Acts 28:3–5) But when Paul had gathered a bundle of sticks and laid them on the fire, a viper came out because of the heat and fastened itself on his hand....However he shook the creature off into the fire and suffered no harm.

(Mark 16:19–20) **So then, when the Lord Jesus had spoken to them, He was received up into heaven and sat down at the right hand of God. And they went out and preached everywhere, while the Lord worked with them, and confirmed the word by the signs that followed.**

(Luke 24:51–53) While He was blessing them, He parted from them and was carried up into heaven. And they, after worshiping Him, returned to Jerusalem with great joy, and were continually in the temple praising God. (cf. Acts 1:9)

(Heb. 1:3) When He had made purification of sins, He sat down at the right hand of the Majesty on high. (cf. Acts 2:33; 5:31; 7:55)

(Heb. 2:3–4) How will we escape if we neglect so great a salvation? After it was at the first spoken through the Lord, it was confirmed to us by those who heard, God also testifying with them, both by signs and wonders and by various miracles and by gifts of the Holy Spirit according to His own will.

The result in Mark 16:9–20 is a concise patchwork drawn from various New Testament texts (especially from the other gospels and

Acts).As demonstrated above, the content of the longer ending generally reflects biblical truths, with the notable exceptions of snake handling and drinking poison (v. 18), which have no scriptural precedent. It should also be noted that verse 16 does not teach the necessity of baptism for salvation, since the second half of the verse clarifies that condemnation is for unbelief, not a lack of being baptized. Beyond those points of clarification, an exposition of these verses is not warranted, since they are not original to Mark's inspired account. Though they reflect traditions from early church history, they are not part of the inerrant and authoritative Word of God.

WHY DOES MARK'S GOSPEL END SO ABRUPTLY?

Though most scholars agree verses 9–20 are not original to Mark's gospel, they differ on whether Mark intended his narrative to end with verse 8. Those who think Mark wrote more beyond verse 8 insist that his original ending was and is still lost. But that claim is entirely speculative, since no historical evidence suggests that any such ending ever existed. A better approach is to see verse 8 as the true ending to Mark's gospel. After all, it is the ending the Holy Spirit chose in His sovereign providence to preserve for subsequent generations of Christians to read. Thus, no matter the intentions of the human author, it was clearly God's plan to end this gospel with verse 8: **They went out and fled from the tomb, for trembling and astonishment had gripped them; and they said nothing to anyone, for they were afraid.**

The dramatic trauma of what the women experienced is captured by Mark with four descriptions. First, they were **trembling** (from the Greek word *tromos*), meaning they were physically shaking in response to the news from the angel (cf. vv. 6–7). Second, they were gripped by **astonishment** (from the Greek word *ekstasis*, from which the English word "ecstasy" is derived). Third, they were stunned into silence, saying **nothing to anyone.** And finally, they **were afraid** (a form of the Greek verb *phobeō*, from which the English word "phobia" is derived). Overwhelmed by the shocking and wondrous reality of the resurrection, the empty tomb left the women shaking and speechless. It had the same effect on Mark. How fitting that the end was so dramatic and powerful that neither the women nor the narrator could speak.

Mark's ending is abrupt but it is not incomplete. The tomb was empty; the angelic announcement explained that Jesus had risen; and multiple eyewitnesses confirmed those events. The purpose of Mark's gospel was to demonstrate that Jesus is the Christ, the Son of God (1:1). Having amply made that point, no further proof was necessary. By the end of Mark's narrative, the declaration of the centurion standing at the cross echoes in the mind of any honest reader: "Truly this man was the Son of God!" (15:39). In fact, Mark's sudden ending is consistent with the abrupt nature of his beginning, in which he skips the birth of Christ and begins directly with the ministry of John the Baptist. It also fits his staccato style and the repeated use of the word "immediately" to push the narra-tive along quickly (cf. 1:10, 12, 18, 20, 21, 28, 29, 30, 42, 43; 2:8, 12; 3:6; 4:5, 15, 16, 17, 29; 5:2, 29, 30, 42; 6:25, 27, 45, 50, 54; 7:25; 8:10; 9:15, 20, 24; 10:52; 11:2, 3; 14:43, 45, 72; 15:1).

Verse 8 ends on a striking note, with the words **for they were afraid.** The women were not in fear for their safety. Rather, they were experiencing bewildered astonishment mixed with profound joy (cf. Matt. 28:8) at the thought of the risen Savior. Mark's gospel, then, ends on a note of wonder, awe, and amazement about the Lord Jesus Christ. That same theme pervades his gospel account (cf. James H. Brooks, *Mark*, New American Commentary [Nashville: Broadman, 1991], 274). In 1:22, the crowds responded to Jesus' instruction by being "amazed at His teach-ing." After He cast out an unclean spirit, "they were all amazed" (1:27). When He healed the paralyzed man, those who witnessed the miracle "were all amazed and were glorifying God, saying, 'We have never seen anything like this'" (2:12). His disciples "became very much afraid" (4:41) of Jesus after He instantly calmed a storm on the Sea of Galilee. When the residents of Gerasa observed the calm demeanor of the man whom the Lord delivered from a legion of demons, "they became frightened" (5:15). The woman who was healed of her twelve-year hemorrhage fell down before Him, "fearing and trembling, aware of what had happened to her" (5:33). Jairus and his wife, upon witnessing the resurrection of their daughter, "were completely astounded" by Jesus (5:42). After He walked on water and calmed the tempest, the disciples in the boat "were utterly astonished" by what He had done (6:51). At His transfiguration, Peter, James, and John "became terrified" (9:6). The crowds "were amazed" by His presence (9:15); His disciples were "afraid to ask Him" about the suffering He predicted (9:32); they "were amazed" when He confronted the rich young ruler (10:24); and as they made their final trek to Jerusalem, "Jesus was walking on ahead of them; and they were amazed, and those who followed were fearful" (10:32). Even His enemies were amazed by Him, including the chief priests and scribes (11:18; 12:17) and the Roman governor, Pilate (15:5). After all those references, it is hardly surprising that the women would be similarly "amazed" and "afraid" when they found the tomb empty (16:5) and heard the astounding news of Jesus' resurrection (16:8).

Throughout his gospel, Mark consistently punctuated key events in the life of the Lord Jesus by emphasizing the wonder He evoked in the hearts and minds of others. Mark simply moves from one point of amazement about Christ to the next. So the narrative ends where it ought to end. It climaxes with amazement and bewilderment at the resurrection of the crucified Savior (cf. John 20:31). In so doing, it leaves the reader in a place of wonder, awe, and worship, centered on its glorious subject: the Lord Jesus Christ, the Son of God.

Bibliography

Brooks, James A. *Mark*. New American Commentary. Nashville: Broadman & Holman, 1991.

Cole, R. Alan. *The Gospel According to St. Mark*. Tyndale New Testament. Grand Rapids: Eerdmans, 1961.

Cranfield, C. E. B. *The Gospel According to Saint Mark*. Cambridge Greek Testament Commentary. New York: Cambridge University Press, 1972.

Edwards, James R., *The Gospel According to Mark*. Pillar New Testament Commentary. Grand Rapids: Eerdmans, 2001.

France, R. T. *The Gospel of Mark*. New International Greek Testament Commentary. Grand Rapids: Eerdmans, 2002.

Garland, David E. *Mark*. NIV Application Commentary. Grand Rapids: Zondervan, 1996.

Grassmick, John D. "Mark," in John F. Walvoord and Roy B. Zuck, eds., *Bible Knowledge Commentary*. Vol. 2. Wheaton: Victor Books, 1985.

Hendricksen, William. *The Gospel of Mark*. Grand Rapids: Baker, 1975.

Hiebert, D. Edmond. *Mark: A Portrait of the Servant*. Chicago: Moody, 1974.

Horne, Mark. *The Victory According to Mark*. Moscow, ID: Canon Press, 2003.

Hughes, R. Kent. *Mark: Jesus, Servant and Savior.* Preaching the Word Commentary. Westchester, IL: Crossway, 1989.

Lane, William L. *The Gospel According to Mark*. New International Commentary on the New Testament. Grand Rapids: Eerdmans, 1974.

Paisley, Harold. *Mark: What the Bible Teaches*. Kilmarnock, Scotland: John Ritchie, 1984.

Stein, Robert H. *Mark*. Baker Exegetical Commentary. Grand Rapids: Baker Academic, 2008.

Swete, Henry B. *Commentary on Mark*. Reprint; Grand Rapids: Kregel, 1977.

Taylor, Vincent. *The Gospel According to St. Mark*. New York: St. Martin's Press, 1966.

Wuest, Kenneth S. *Mark in the Greek New Testament*. Grand Rapids: Eerdmans, 1957.

Indexes

Index of Greek Words

phuegō, 246
planaō, 190

skandalizō, 44,296
sōzō, 117
thaumazō, 348

timaō, 65
toioutōn, 66
tolmaō, 390
toutois, 66
tromos, 403,416

Index of Hebrew/Aramaic Words

Index of Scripture

Apocryphal Works

Ancient Texts

Index of Subjects

God's reasons for hating, 55
and intermarriage with pagan
    women, 52–53, 59
Israel's accommodation of, 54
Donkey's colt, 125, 126
Doubt, 28, 92, 145, 146
Drink the cup, 106
    See also The Cup
Drinking poison, 412, 416
Dual days reckoning method. *See*
    Passover, 279–80

Earthquakes, 233, 248, 249, 389
Edersheim, Alfred, 113
Elders, 156, 311
The elect, 249, 250, 258
Elijah, 6. 7, 17–19, 377
Elimelech, 189
Elisha-Spring, 113
Elliot, Jim, 87
Emmaus, 404
The empty tomb, 400
Enemies, 209, 405
Essenes, 185–86
Esther, 387
Eternal destruction, 355
Eternal life, 77, 81, 86
Ethiopian eunuch, 138
Eucharist, 290. *See also* Communion;
    Lord's Supper
Eusebius of Caesarea, 410
Evangelism, 71, 207
Evil, 100, 243, 326
Eye of a needle, 84–85
Ezekiel, 168, 184
Ezra, 59–60

Faith
    Christ's lessons on, 23
    importance of, 22, 28
    and prayer, 145–46
    saving, 238, 332, 340, 405
    as trust in God, 144
False coronations, 122, 129
False evidence, 324
False religion, 175–76
False teachers, 129, 213–14, 218
Family, persecution by, 237
Famines, 233
Fear, 85, 92, 403, 416–18

Feast of Tabernacles, 7, 268
Feast of Unleavened Bread, 268
Fig tree. *See* Cursing of the fig tree
Final tribulation, 253
    See also Great tribulation
Flat bread, 286, 287
    See also Bread
Flattery, 177, 178
Forgiveness, 148, 149

Galilee, 34, 113, 114, 297, 349, 404
Gallic Wars (Julius Caesar), 408
Garden of Gethsemane, 296, 299–301,
    305
Gehenna, 47-48
    See also Hell
Generation, 259
Gentiles, 138, 139, 140
Gentiles' salvation, 381
Gethsemane. *See* Garden of
    Gethsemane
Gideon, 102
Giving, 221–23
Global devastation, 254, 255
Glory of Christ, 3, 4, 5, 13
God
    compassion of, 27
    curse on mankind, 56–57
    and hatred of divorce, 55
    justice of, 269–70
    and light, 3
    love for, 196, 201, 203, 275
    man's search for, 74–75
    patience limit of, 158–59
    power of, 190, 297, 328
    providence of, 386–87
    trust in, 22, 144, 145
    wrath of, 358
God the Father
    at crucifixion, 375–81
    and Jesus' authority, 153, 262
    at Jesus' transfiguration, 8, 23
    redemptive plan of, 267–70, 280,
        344
    rejection of Jesus by, 96
Golgotha, 364, 379
Gomer, 60
Good works, 71, 77, 238
Gospel
    essence of, 15, 385–86

Stewardship, 122
Stoning, 321–22, 347
Strength, 201
Substitutionary death/atonement, 109,
    383–84
Suffering
    of believers, 235–38
    of Christ, 96–98, 106
    of demon-possessed boy, 25–28
    of Job, 68–69
Supernatural power, 212

Tabernacles, 7
Tacitus, 346, 408
Talmud, 184
Taxation, 178–82
Teacher, 177, 188
Temple
    architecture and construction of,
        228
    Christ's clearing of, 136–39
    Christ's curse on, 132, 135, 136
    Roman destruction of, 169, 229
    tearing of temple curtain, 291,
        378–79
Temple treasury, 351
Temptation
    in Gethsemane, 300–301, 304
    leading others into, 44, 45
Tertullian, 376
Testimony, 326
Textual analysis/criticism, 409–12
Theos Epiphanes, 244
Thieves at cross 369, 370, 381, 387
    See also Robbers
This generation, 259
Thucydides, 408
Tiberius Caesar, 180, 345, 351
Timaeus, 115
Titus Vespasian, 229
Tolerance, 216
The tomb (of Christ's), 392, 400
Topheth, 48
Trajan (Emperor), 107
Transfiguration, 2–8, 13–15

Transubstantiation, 290
Treasury (temple), 222
Trials, 322, 325
Tribulation period, 236, 238
Tribulations, 8, 95
Trust in God, 22, 144, 145
Truth, 175, 177, 178, 261
Twelve legions of angels, 314
The twelve disciples, 92, 277, 284
The two thieves, 387, 388

Unbelief, 200, 226, 270, 330, 355
Unclean spirits, 29
    See also Demon possession
Unleavened bread, 268, 286, 289

Valley of dry bones vision, 184
Valley of Hinnom, 48
Vaticanus (Greek New Teatament
        manuscript), 410
Veil of temple, 291, 378–79
Venomous serpents, 412
Verbal abuse. *See* Mockery
Vigilance, 303
Vineyards, 165–67

Warner, Charles Dudley, 175
Watchfulness, 261–63 *See also* Alertness
Weak faith, 146
Wealth, 77, 81–84, 87, 137, 223
Webb, R.A., 68
White horse, 256
Widows, 220–22
The wife's desire, 56, 57
Wine, 285, 286, 291
Witnesses, 321, 322, 324
Words of Christ, 260, 261
Works-righteousness, 71, 77, 238
Worship, 273, 275
Wrath of God, 302

Zealots, 186
Zebedee, 382
Zechariah, 168, 248, 388–89
Zeus idol. *See* Antichrist, 244, 245